PLATE I

THE ROYAL ARCH AS DEPICTED BY LAURENCE DERMOTT
The illustration is from *The Register of Excellent Masters*;
date about 1783.
By courtesy of United Grand Lodge

FREEMASONS'
BOOK OF THE ROYAL ARCH

First published in Great Britain 1957
by HARRAP BOOKS Ltd
Chelsea House, 26 Market Square,
Bromley, Kent BR1 1NA

Reprinted: 1965
Reprinted with corrections: 1969; 1970
Reprinted: 1972; 1975; 1980; 1986; 1990

Copyright. All rights reserved
No part of this publication may be reproduced
in any form or by any means without the prior
permission of Harrap Books Ltd.

ISBN 0 245 58284 3

Printed and bound in Singapore by
Intellectual Publishing Co.

PREFACE

This book, uniform in style and presentation with my earlier *Freemasons' Guide and Compendium*, which, in the main, dealt with Craft masonry, is an attempt to provide a simple explanation of the origin, rise, and development, and the customs, ritual, and symbolism, of Royal Arch masonry so far as present knowledge and considerations of masonic propriety permit. I use the word 'attempt' advisedly, for great difficulties are in the way of complete achievement in writing historically of this "elusive degree," although, let me say, in the task of coping with them I have been greatly cheered by recollections of the indulgence given me by readers of my earlier book.

The greatest obstacle in the path of the writer seeking to explain the early history of Royal Arch masonry is his comparative ignorance of the formative days of the Order—the mid-eighteenth-century period. The facts on record are not enough to preclude different interpretations and conflicting views. Perhaps it is a slight compensation that the *traditional* history upon which the ceremonial of the Order is founded was clearly anticipated in published writings to an extent considerably greater than in the case of the Craft, for whereas, for example, there is hardly any recorded foreknowledge of the Third Degree Hiramic story, the Legend of the Crypt might well have been inspired by one known to have been in written form in the fourth century of the Christian era, while the sword-and-trowel *motif*, derived from the Old Testament account of the return of the Jews from exile, was the pride and glory of a Crusading Order of the early Middle Ages.

What I have tried to do in writing this book is to make available to Companions who have had little opportunity for specialized study an essentially readable account, as authentic as possible, of the history and lore of the Royal Arch, affording an insight into some matters which in the past have tended to escape the attention of all but the serious student. Not only do I hope that my readers will enjoy reading my book, but that some few of them will be able to use it as a source of material for short, simple addresses designed to arouse and foster the interest of their Companions. And most sincerely, also, do I hope that the serious student will find in it occasion for kindly, constructive criticism; indeed, I am butions to authentic masonic history. I have well profited by them.) Also, I would thank Harry Carr, for his painstaking revision of the section on the Ineffable Name; George S. Draffen (Grand Librarian, Grand Lodge of Scotland), for placing his manuscript *The Triple Tau* at my disposal in advance of publication and for permission to quote from it; Gilbert Y. Johnson, for help in connexion with the history of York Royal Arch masonry and for lending me his writings on the subject; Bruce W. Oliver, for his loan of an old MS. ritual, of which I have been able to make considerable use; Sydney Pope, for arranging for the photographing of an ancient banner preserved in the Canterbury Masonic Museum, of which he is Curator; Norman Rogers, for help in general and for the loan of his MS. on Royal Arch masonry in Lancashire; Fred L. Pick, for arranging for the loan of many photographs, some preserved in the museum of which he is Curator and others belonging to the Manchester Association of Masonic Research; John R. Rylands, for reading two early sections, the loan of his papers on Yorkshire Royal Arch masonry, and permission to use his photographs of the Wakefield jewels; William Waples, for his many notes on North-east Royal Arch masonry and for permission to use two photographs; and Eric Ward, for providing me with copies of minutes of old military chapters.

Also, I wish to thank Ward K. St Clair, Chairman, Library and Museum Committee, Grand Lodge of New York, U.S.A., for his courtesy and for permission to quote from his MS. paper relating to the "Past Master Degree" in United States freemasonry; Norman Hackney, for the use of photograph and description of an ancient Indian metal plate carrying significant symbols; G. S. Shepherd-Jones, for the use I have made of his explanation of the symbolism of the Royal Arch jewel; C. F. Waddington, for his help in connexion with some of the Bristol ceremonies; and the great many lodges and chapters whose records I have quoted and whose treasured possessions I have, in some cases, been able to illustrate, suitably acknowledged where possible.

I take particular pleasure in recording my great debt to members of the staff of the Library and Museum, Freemasons' Hall, London, who over a period of years have freely given me of their knowledge, and have allowed me, times out of number, to bother them in my search for information. To the Librarian and Curator, to whom I have already referred; the Assistant Librarian, Edward Newton (who has suffered much of my importunity); to H. P. Smith and T. Barlow, members of the staff—to all of them I offer my warm thanks for assistance in so many, many matters; to Henry F. D. Chilton, the Assistant Curator, I record my sincere appreciation of his help in choosing from among the Museum exhibits many of the diverse subjects included in the thirty-one photographic plates with which the Publisher has so generously adorned this book. In this connexion I wish to thank the United Grand Lodge, the Supreme Grand Chapter, and also Quatuor Coronati Lodge for their loan of a great many of the illustrations, and the first named for its particular kindness in taking the trouble on my behalf of having photographs made of a number of its Library and Museum treasures.

It will be understood, therefore, that it is with a lively sense of the help I myself have enjoyed that I now address myself to Companions everywhere in the hope that my book, in adding, as I trust, to their knowledge of Royal Arch masonry, will serve also to add to the happiness and satisfaction which they derive from membership of the Order.

B.E.J.

Bolney
   Sussex

PREFACE TO THE REVISED IMPRESSIONS

Twelve years have passed since this monumental work on the Royal Arch was first published, and in preparation for a new impression opportunity has been taken to make a number of important amendments in the light of modern studies in this field. The main changes occur in the sections dealing with the organization of the 'Antients' Royal Arch. Research has shown that there never was an 'Antients' Grand Chapter as such, so frequently mentioned in the earlier impressions; its Royal Arch activities were controlled by the 'Antients' Grand *Lodge*. Similarly, it was something of a misnomer to refer to the 'Moderns' Grand Chapter, which was, throughout its history, the premier and the only Grand Chapter in England. The requisite modifications have now been made, together with necessary corrections in the section dealing with the Ineffable Name and minor corrections of dates, captions, spellings, etc., where needed. The general scheme of the original work, and the pagination, remain unchanged.

In preparing the 1970 impression the opportunity has been taken to amend two further sections, namely those devoted to John Coustos and to the Royal Arch in Scotland.

H.C.
A.R.H.

June 1970
27 Great Queen Street
London, w.c.2

CONTENTS

SECTION	PAGE
1. Whence came the Royal Arch?	19
2. How Craft Conditions prepared the Way for the Royal Arch	31
3. The Early Years of Royal Arch Masonry	36
4. The 'Antient' Masons and the Royal Arch	52
5. The 'Moderns' Masons and the Royal Arch	62
6. The First Grand Chapter in the World	68
7. The So-called 'Antients' Grand Chapter	93
8. York Royal Arch Masonry	100
9. Some Familiar Terms	105
10. The 'union'—Supreme Grand Chapter, 1817	109
11. Traditional History: The Crypt Legend	126
12. Traditional History: The Biblical Background	138
13. The Ineffable Name	148
14. The Ritual and its Development	156
15. The Principals and their Installation	175
16. An Early Qualifying Ceremony: Passing the Chair	181
17. Passing the Veils	195
18. Sequence and Step Degrees	201
19. The Irish Royal Arch	208
20. The Scottish Royal Arch	219
21. Symbols: Introductory Remarks; The Circle	226
22. Symbols: The Tau and the Triple Tau	233

SECTION		PAGE
23.	Symbols: The Triangle and Interlaced Triangles	238
24.	The Altar Stone, Lights, Banners	245
25.	Royal Arch Clothing	252
26.	Royal Arch Jewels	258
	Appendix: The Charter of Compact	272
	Bibliography	277
	Index	279

ILLUSTRATIONS

PLATES IN HALF-TONE

	PAGE
I. The Royal Arch as depicted by Laurence Dermott	*frontispiece*
II. Sword-and-trowel Emblem, from Geoffrey Whitney's "Choice of Emblemes," and Triple Arches from Royal Arch Certificates	32
III. Frontispiece of Samuel Lee's "Orbis Miraculum," or "The Temple of Solomon" (1659) and Frontispiece to "Ahiman Rezon" (1764), including in its Upper Part the Arms of the 'Antient' Masons	33
IV. The Charter of Compact	48
V. Cadwallader, ninth Lord Blayney (1720–75)	49
VI. Two Decorative Aprons of the Late Eighteenth Century	64
VII. The Kirkwall Scroll	65
VIII. The Development of the Royal Arch Emblem and Jewel	80
IX. Ancient Metal Plate and the All-seeing Eye in Wrought-iron Ornament	81
X. The Crypt of York Minster and Two Typical Summonses, Late Eighteenth Century	96
XI. Some Early Variations of the Royal Arch Jewel	97
XII. Tracing-board of Churchill Lodge, No. 478, Oxford, and Ceremonial Sword used in 'Antients' Grand Lodge and now borne in Supreme Grand Chapter	112
XIII. Two Painted Aprons worked in Appliqué	113
XIV. Banner painted in Colours, Late Eighteenth Century	128
XV. Combined P.M. and P.Z. Jewels, Late Eighteenth Century	129

XVI.	Charter of the Cana Chapter, Colne, No. 116 and Banner of an Old Lodge, No. 208, at Wigton, Cumberland	144
XVII.	Two Handsome Chairs, Combined Craft and Royal Arch	145
XVIII.	Aprons of the 1790 Period	160
XIX.	Toddy Rummer, Early 1820's	161
XX.	Plate Jewels and Heavy Cast Jewels, Late Eighteenth Century	176
XXI.	Old Prints Emblematic of Traditional History	177
XXII.	Five Small Jewels, 1780–1825 Period	192
XXIII.	A Set of Principals' Robes, Aprons, and Head-dresses	193
XXIV.	The Unique Jewels of Unanimity Chapter, Wakefield	208
XXV.	Head-dresses, Ancient and Traditional	209
XXVI.	Richly Ornamented Aprons of the 1800 Period	224
XXVII.	Jugs decorated with Masonic Transfers	225
XXVIII.	The Belzoni and Other Rare Jewels all set in Brilliants	240
XXIX.	A Miniature Pedestal and the Newcastle Water-clock	241
XXX.	Four Aprons, Past and Present	256
XXXI.	Five Noteworthy and Contrasting Jewels	257

ILLUSTRATIONS IN THE TEXT

	PAGE
The Catenarian Arch	134
Symbolic Circles	231
Variations of the Cross	233
The T-over-H and the Triple Tau	233
How the Plain Cross developed into Forms of the Swastika or Fylfot	234
Symbolic Figures	234
Symbolic Triangles	238
The Hexalpha (Six-pointed Star) and a Few of its Variations	241

ILLUSTRATIONS

	PAGE
A Variety of Interlaced Triangles found in Masonic Illustration	242
Many Masonic Devices built up with and within Interlaced Triangles	243
The Pentalpha (Five-pointed Star) in Some of its Variations	244
A Pierced Jewel showing Triple Arches and Figure of Sojourner	259
A Jewel of the Three Crowned Stars Lodge, Prague	259
Two Sides of Old Jewel of Uncommon Shape and Crowded with Emblems	261
A Square-and-sector Collar Jewel of Bold and Attractive Design, dated 1812	263
Obverse and Reverse of the English Royal Arch Jewel	264
Obverse and Reverse of the Scottish Royal Arch Jewel	265
Obverse of the Irish Royal Arch Jewel	265
A Design (date 1630) by the French Engraver Callot, a Possible Prefigurement of the Royal Arch Jewel (1766)	266
Two Irish Silver Jewels, Late Eighteenth Century	267
An Early Irish Jewel carrying Emblems of Many Degrees and showing Sojourner with Sword and Trowel	268

Section One

WHENCE CAME THE ROYAL ARCH?

THERE has been long argument on how Royal Arch masonry came into existence. Was it present in some slight form in the earliest fabric of speculative masonry or was it, frankly, just an innovation in the first half of the eighteenth century?

Those accepting the first possibility believe that long before the earliest recorded dates of Craft masonry—the Acception in the London Company of Freemasons in 1621 and the 'making' of Elias Ashmole in 1646—there was a legend or a series of legends from which was developed (*a*) the Hiramic Degree which was working in a few lodges certainly as early as the 1720's; (*b*) the Royal Arch Degree known to be working by the 1740's and 1750's; and (*c*) some additional degrees. All three were thought to have come from one common source and, although developed on very different lines, to have running through them a recognizable thread. Students of the calibre of J. E. S. Tuckett and Count Goblet d'Alviella were prominent in advancing such a possibility. They felt that the legends relating to Hiram and to the Royal Arch were the surviving portions of a Craft lore that originally contained other and similar legends, the Count holding that freemasonry sprang from "a fruitful union between the professional Guild of Medieval Masons and a secret group of philosophical adepts." The Guild furnished the form and the philosophers the spirit.

Many students have thought that the Royal Arch was torn from the Hiramic Degree and that the 1813 Act of Union between the 'Antients' and the 'Moderns'[1] did scant justice in pronouncing "that pure Ancient Masonry consists of Three Degrees and no more, namely those of the Entered Apprentice, the Fellow Craft and the Master Mason including the Supreme Order of the Holy Royal Arch." We know that the Hiramic Degree was developing into a practicable ritual in the years following 1717, in which year the Premier Grand Lodge was founded, and that the Royal Arch Degree was going through a similar experience two or three decades later; this sequence in time is held to favour the idea that from the store of tradition came first the Hiramic story of the First Temple and secondly the Sojourner story of the Second Temple.

[1] For explanation of these terms see the author's *Freemasons' Guide and Compendium*, chapter 12.

Although Count Goblet d'Alviella suggests a union between medieval masons and the philosophers, most students (the present writer among them) cannot see even a slight possibility that the Royal Arch has developed from operative masonry. The Count probably had in mind the association between the slight speculative masonry of the seventeenth century possibly centred in the London Company of Freemasons and the learned mystics practising Rosicrucian and alchemical arts. Many of the learned men who came into masonry in those early days were scholars well acquainted with classical and medieval literature, who brought with them a curious and special knowledge and, so far as can be judged, grafted some of that knowledge upon the short and simple ceremonies which then constituted speculative masonry. There is a good case for assuming that much of the symbolism of masonry was brought in by those mystics, and there can be no doubt whatsoever that some of the best-known symbols of Royal Arch masonry bear a close resemblance to those of alchemy; this point will be developed later; for the moment we must accept the likelihood that Royal Arch masonry borrowed directly from the alchemical store of symbolism. But this or any similar statement does not imply that Craft and Royal Arch masonry came from one common source, for while, on the one hand, there are suggestions in Biblical and medieval literature on which a sort of Hiramic Degree could be based and, on the other hand, traditions which almost certainly supplied the basis of the Royal Arch story, we do not know of any traditions containing fundamentals common to both—an ignorance on our part that is far from proof that such a source never existed! With this slight introduction let us now inquire more closely into the problems that arise.

Did the Royal Arch develop from the Hiramic Degree?

At times it has been strongly and widely held that the original Third Degree of the Craft was 'mutilated' to provide material for the Royal Arch ceremonial. Dr Mackey, the well-known American writer, stated that, "until the year 1740, the essential element of the R.A. constituted a part of the Master's degree and was, of course, its concluding portion." Both the Rev. A. F. A. Woodford and the Rev. Dr Oliver asserted that the Royal Arch was the second part of the Old Master's Degree; Dr Oliver maintained that "the difference between the 'Antient' and the 'Modern' systems consisted solely in the mutilation of the Third Degree," and that "the R.A. was concocted by the 'Antients' to widen the breach and make the line of distinction between them and the Premier Grand Lodge broader and more indelible." It has been said that the 'Moderns,' resenting taunts on their having transposed the words and signs of the First and

Second Degrees, were merely retaliating when they accused the 'Antients' of mutilating the Third Degree.

It so happens that the reverend gentlemen, A. F. A. Woodford and George Oliver, are seldom reliable when dealing with any matter relating to the great division in eighteenth-century masonry (a division which is explained in the author's earlier book[1]). Both of them, forming their opinions somewhat lightly, wrote in a day lacking the new information which research has brought us in this matter. Dr Oliver professed to have a Third Degree ritual of 1740 in which some of the esoteric knowledge now associated with the R.A. is mixed up with similar knowledge now associated with the Third Degree, but it is doubtful if such a document exists. The modern student would require to see the document and give close attention to its provenance—that is, its origin and true date.

W. Redfern Kelly believed that a Mason Word, recognized under the ancient operative system and included in the First and Second Degrees round about 1717, was transferred to the Third Degree in the 1720's (apparently by the Premier Grand Lodge), and that later, perhaps about the year 1739, the Third Degree was seriously mutilated to provide a fourth degree, it being an easy matter, once again, to transfer both the Word and some of the legendary matter to the new creation. But, frankly, few students nowadays accept these beliefs or look kindly upon the term 'mutilation' when used to describe the process by which the Third Degree is assumed to have yielded to the R.A. some of its choice content. To the present writer 'mutilation' seems to be quite beside the mark.

Who is supposed to have been responsible for this process, whatever it was? The 'Moderns' are alleged to have taunted the 'Antients' with being the offenders, but the suggestion is ridiculous—and for the very good reason that the R.A. was being worked as a separate degree before the 'Antients' got into their stride! How could there be any obvious 'mutilation' in view of the fact that the Craft ceremonies as worked by the 'Antients' more or less agreed with those worked by the Irish and Scottish masons? It is certain that the Irish and the Scottish Grand Lodges, which were in the closest association with the 'Antients,' did not mutilate the Third Degree to provide a Royal Arch Degree, nor did they countenance others doing so, for, officially, they were just as hostile to the Royal Arch as the 'Moderns' were, and took a long, long time to modify their attitude. At a particular date, it is known, says Hughan, that there was no essential difference between the first three degrees in the French working and those in the English, proof that no violent alterations had been made in the Third Degree for the sake of an English Royal Arch rite. If the 'Antients' did not 'mutilate' the Craft degrees it is inconceivable that the

[1] *Freemasons' Guide and Compendium* (Harrap, 1950).

'Moderns' did so; it would be quite ridiculous to suggest that officially they 'mutilated' a Craft degree to produce something which they then repudiated or treated with frigid indifference. This point will be returned to.

No; it can be taken for granted that the most enlightened students agree that there was no extraction from or transfer of any *large* part of the Third Degree. There does not seem to be any evidence to support the statement that the Royal Arch was originally a part of any Craft degree.

A point of real importance is that the Hiramic Degree itself had only been more or less generally worked in England from some time late in the 1720's, and that if the argument that it was 'mutilated' has anything in it we should have to believe that a newly worked degree was itself pulled to bits to provide another one. Douglas Knoop, a professional historian of marked ability, stated definitely that there is no evidence that our Third Degree legend and our R.A. legend were ever combined in one ceremony.

But let it be freely admitted that, while, on the available evidence, there were no 'mutilations,' it is likely—indeed, certain—that there were *borrowings*. We know, for example, that mention of any stone-turning in the Craft ritual of the 1730's known to John Coustos (see p. 44) did not remain in the Craft working, but that the *motif*, amplified and drastically developed, does find a place in the R.A. working. Certain French tracing-boards of the 1740's depict ideas which are not now in the Third Degree but are present in the R.A., but tracing-boards are seldom convincing evidence in such a matter as this, because in the early days Craft and Royal Arch ceremonies were worked in the same lodges, and inevitably an artist introduced into a tracing-board emblems from all the degrees known to him. Similarly, early jewels commonly depict both Craft and Royal Arch emblems, but by the time such jewels became popular the lines of the then early Royal Arch ceremony had been fairly well defined. These early jewels often include the emblems not only of the Craft and Royal Arch, but of one or two or more added degrees.

A lodge that would be working Craft degrees on one Wednesday, let us say, and the Royal Arch the next Wednesday, in the same inn room and to a large extent with the same Brethren present, would be likely, given time enough, to arrive at some admixture of detail; all the more likely would this be in the absence of printed rituals and any close control from superior authority. Given time enough, it is not difficult to see that in such conditions a feature could pass from one degree to another without causing much disturbance. This process of borrowing, in a day in which communication was slow, may have led to some of the variation in working occurring between one district and another. Hughan thought that a particular test given in one of the sections of the Third Degree had found its way into a prominent position in the Royal Arch Degree; the "test" he had in mind is apparently the *Word*, and the statement is made that this word is still recognized in some Master Masons' lodges on the Continent. Hughan's allusion is probably to a Craft ritual given in an irregular print of the year 1725: "Yet for all this I want the primitive Word. I answer it was God in six terminations, to wit I am and *Johova* is the answer to it."

A telling argument against the suggestion that the Royal Arch was a ceremony *largely* taken from the Third Degree has already been referred to. It arises from the question: If such 'mutilation' took place, how could the official 'Moderns' have denied the authenticity of the Royal Arch? They would obviously have *known* the treatment to which the Third Degree had been subjected; they would have been aware that a new ceremony had been made by partly unmaking another one, but they could hardly have questioned its *essentials* if originally these had been part of their own rite! Still more obviously, how vastly different the Third Degree of the 'Moderns' would have been from that of the 'Antients'! We know, of course, that there were detail differences between them, but the two ceremonies were recognizably and essentially the same. Until proof is produced that the 'Moderns' practised a Third Degree vastly different from that of the 'Antients'—a degree retaining cardinal features which the other side knew only in the Royal Arch—until then we have no option but to conclude that the Third Degree certainly was not 'mutilated' to provide a separate degree.

A strange version of the 'mutilation' idea put forward by W. Redfern Kelly is that, to assist in bringing about the complete reconciliation of the two rival bodies at the Craft Union of 1813, some section of the Third Degree may have been transferred to the Royal Arch! Surely the idea is quite hopeless! Where, in the rituals of the 1820's, which are reasonably well known to us, should we look for the transposed "section"? Officially, the 'Antients' would not have allowed any serious alteration of a degree which to them was certainly "more august, sublime and important than those [degrees] which precede it and is the summit and perfection of Antient Masonry" (*Laws and Regulations*, 1807). The 'Moderns' would certainly not have robbed a Craft ceremony for the purpose of strengthening a rite whose status as a fourth degree they were trying (officially) to belittle and disparage.

Was the Royal Arch 'devised' or 'invented'?

We cannot hide the fact that there is a considerable body of opinion in favour of the theory that Royal Arch masonry was a creation, a 'fabrication,' of French origin, brought to England round about 1730. The French had taken their freemasonry from England, and in their eyes it must have lacked the qualities of colour and drama, or so we must conclude from the fact that the ceremonies that came back from France had become dramatically effective. The sword had found a place in the Initiation ceremony, as one example. Something different from the original rather colourless English rite had been brought into existence, and in the light of this innovation many students have come to regard the Royal Arch as a degree deliberately contrived by the imaginative Frenchman to appeal to the English Master Mason, to whom it might have been presented quite naturally as a fourth degree.

Chevalier Ramsay (to whom we return on a later page) has often been credited with having brought a number of new degrees from France to England, among them the Royal Arch. The Rev. Dr Oliver, already mentioned, was quite definite in his statements to this effect, but there is not a scrap of real evidence in support of an idea which seems to depend solely upon a few words in an address by Ramsay composed in the year 1737 (see p. 42). But, if not Ramsay, it is possible that some other Continental (almost certainly French) framer of degrees might have evolved the Royal Arch ceremonial with a foreseeing eye on what he thought to be the needs of the English mason. Such an innovation might, in the process of time, have been amplified and embellished and ultimately become moulded into the degree that is now such an important part of the masonic system. W. Redfern Kelly thought that the R.A. was created in or about the year 1738 or 1739, and might have been taken by an English reviser from a newly fabricated Continental degree. Indeed, the general idea among those who believe that the Royal Arch was an innovation is that an English editor in the late 1730's availed himself of a framework provided by one of the new French degrees. Through so many of these ran the idea of the secret vault and the Ineffable Name. These are the selfsame degrees that some students believe to have provided the basis for the Rite of Perfection of twenty-five degrees later absorbed in the Ancient and Accepted Scottish Rite of thirty-three degrees more particularly developed early in the 1800's.

But it is certainly worth noting that Royal Arch masonry has never at any time flourished in France and, further, that the statement that there were Irish Royal Arch chapters in France in 1730, which, if true, would have greatly strengthened the suggestion of a French origin, is simply and finally repudiated by Hughan as a mere typographical error. There were not Royal Arch lodges in France at that early date, and very few at any later date, either.

Students who support the theory that the Royal Arch came from the same stock of lore as the Hiramic Degree argue against the suggestion of a Continental origin by pointing out that the historical setting of the English

R.A. is not to be found in any Continental setting. Against this, however, we must admit the possibility that a clever deviser—assuming for a moment that the R.A. *was* an innovation—might, in drawing his foundation story from ancient classic legends, have done his best to produce his new degree not for Continental consumption, but for export to England, where, let it never be forgotten, speculative masonry had its birth and its richest development. Then, too, as already suggested, the R.A. *idea* might have been French, although the *development* was English.

There are those who hold that, as the Royal Arch is believed to have first gained popularity with the 'Antients,' who must have regarded it as having time-immemorial sanction, it follows that it was much more likely to have grown from an original masonic lore than to be a mere innovation. But what is the argument worth? While the 'Antients' glibly dubbed their opponents 'innovators,' they themselves were more often the real innovators, for by the time their Grand Lodge was established, at about the middle of the eighteenth century, they had been led to introduce or adopt more than one ceremony which certainly had no place in the masonic rite when the first Grand Lodge was formed.

A Compromise Theory probably the Truest

We may fairly be expected to offer a statement of our own belief in these matters. We do not believe that the Royal Arch developed from the same source as the Hiramic Degree, and we have found no trace of any connexion with operative masonry. But neither do we believe that the Royal Arch Degree was an out-and-out fabrication. We feel that some masons and some lodges were early acquainted with elements now associated with the Royal Arch ceremonial, in which respect we have been greatly influenced by the reference to stone-turning and the finding of the Sacred Name made by John Coustos in his evidence when in the hands of the Inquisition (see p. 44). And we cannot disregard Gould's suggestion that the much-talked-of and little-known Scots degrees, worked in the early eighteenth century, were cryptic in character and might well have provided ideas that developed on the Royal Arch pattern. We cannot ignore certain of the early allusions to the Royal Arch idea or *motif* given in the next section of this book, and we are realizing that such words as 'created' and 'fabricated' do not apply in their acknowledged and accepted meanings to the manner in which the Royal Arch was brought into the world of masonic observance. The arranger or editor might well have been French, but could as easily have been English; there is not a scrap of evidence on the point.

In the main the theme of the Royal Arch story is provided by versions of an ancient crypt legend with which many learned men would have been quite familiar. The arranger might first have gone to one or more of these versions (as in our opinion he undoubtedly did) and then incorporated an idea or ideas present in the Craft ceremonials in use by some few lodges. The arranger—with the material of the old crypt legends, the references in the Craft ritual, and the Old Testament story of the Jewish exile—was able to erect what was actually a new degree or rite containing the features of the vault, the discoveries and the reiterated belief in the 'Word.' The restoration of the Christian content and of the 'true secrets,' together with a story attractive and even dramatic in itself, assured the popularity of the new degree. The essential elements known to us to-day were in the early ceremonies—the *essential* elements—but, as the ritual took half a century to develop and was heavily revised and rearranged in the 1830's, it is quite obvious that the early ceremony was little more than the primitive form of to-day's.

With the opinion as above expressed in this difficult and controversial matter J. Heron Lepper, whose knowledge of Royal Arch history, both English and Irish, was unrivalled, might well be held as being in agreement. In an address (1933) to Supreme Grand Chapter (unfortunately not suitable for extensive quotation in this place) he takes certain of Dassigny's statements (see p. 45), relates them to significant references to a tripartite word in an irregular print of the year 1725 (see p. 38), and concludes that "various essential portions of the degree of R.A. were known to our forerunners in England as early as the Craft Degrees themselves. . . . . Definite traces of the stepping-stones from the Craft to the R.A. still exist in our ritual." He feels that such proof of the real antiquity of the degree justifies "the traditions and good-faith of our predecessors of 1813" (the Brethren who, in recognizing the Union, declared that pure Ancient Masonry consisted of three degrees, including the Royal Arch). Well, it is said that the heart makes the theologian. Perhaps it sometimes makes the historian also. Heron Lepper's was a kind heart, and in it a great love for the Royal Arch, and maybe this took him farther along the road leading back through the centuries than many far lesser students, the present author among them, would care to go. But it is good to know that such a scholar as Heron Lepper believed the Royal Arch to be far from the mere innovation that many a critic has lightly dubbed it.

A 'Completion Degree'

The reflection that the Royal Arch provides something that is missing from the Third Degree provokes a few comments. Although there may possibly be those who agree with Alexander Lawrie, who in his *History of Freemasonry* (1859) held that the Craft degrees were complete in themselves and that the "lost word" can only be found "behind the veil of time," the great majority of masons feel that the Third Degree is not complete and may not have been intended to be. Dr W. J. Chetwode Crawley, a learned student, was firmly convinced that the Royal Arch Degree was the completing part of the masonic legend, and that if it fell into desuetude the cope-stone of freemasonry would be removed and the building left obviously incomplete. But the full import of this belief carries with it the implication that both the Hiramic and the Royal Arch Degrees had but one single origin, and were simply the developments of the first and second parts of one and the same legend—all very simple and satisfying to those who can accept it; but few students can. There is small doubt, though, that this is the way in which the 'Antients' regarded the matter. To them the R.A. 'completed' the Hiramic Degree; in it was regained something which in the Third Degree was declared to be lost; to them the two degrees were parts of the same time-immemorial fabric of masonic tradition and legend. And the 'Moderns' also were quick to accept all this *unofficially*, but on the part of their Grand Lodge there was a frigid lack of recognition which continued to the end of the eighteenth century, all the more baffling because quite a large proportion of the 'Moderns' Grand Lodge officers became in the normal course R.A. masons.

The Christian Character of the Early Ritual

It may come as a surprise to many masons to learn that the Royal Arch at its inception and for half a century or more had a decidedly Christian character. There is difficulty in offering any satisfactory explanation of the way in which a dramatized rendering of certain Old Testament incidents came to include distinctly New Testament teaching, a teaching that remained in the ritual until well into the nineteenth century and echoes or reflections of which persist to this day—some of them where least suspected by the uninformed. But it may help if we consider two points: The Old Manuscript Charges known to operative masonry from the fourteenth century bequeathed to symbolic masonry a strongly Christian feeling, which in general prevailed through the eighteenth century in spite of what may be called the official de-Christianizing of the Craft ritual by the first *Constitutions*. In perhaps a majority of the Craft lodges in which the R.A. was nurtured the ritual had Christian characteristics. That must be an important consideration; perhaps a more pertinent one is that the crypt legend so skilfully woven into the Old Testament story of the Jewish return from exile came originally from the writings of the early Church fathers, who tended to interpret everything from an exclusively Christian standpoint. Thus the R.A. story is a blend of two stories, one wholly Jewish and dating back to some centuries *before* Christ, and the other largely Christian and recorded some few centuries *after* Christ.

The Christian content of early symbolic masonry is a subject upon which much has been written. Anderson's *Constitutions* of 1723 and 1738 did in effect de-Christianize the Craft ritual by insisting that masons should "be *good men and true*, or Men of Honour and Honesty, by whatever Denominations or Persuasions they may be distinguish'd; whereby Masonry becomes the *Center of Union* and the Means of conciliating true Friendship among Persons that must have remain'd at a perpetual distance." Whereas, as already explained, the Old Charges had a decidedly Christian character, the new *Constitutions* no longer insisted that freemasons should be loyal to Holy Church or look upon Christ as the Saviour of mankind: "'Tis now thought more expedient only to oblige [Members of the Order] to that Religion in which all men agree, leaving their peculiar opinions to themselves." Not that Anderson, a Presbyterian minister, regarded with favour "the stupid atheist" or the "irreligious libertine" or men of no religion or men to whom one religion is as good as another. It has been suggested that he may have intended to represent the triune of deities having the one Godhead—a distinctly Christian idea—but such an intention, if it existed, could rarely if ever have been recognized in the lodges, and to most masons his words offered a system of teaching in which God the Father had a high place and the Sonship none. And this *official* elimination of the Christian element, even though ignored by many of the lodges, undoubtedly left for many masons a blank of which they were acutely conscious and which the introduction of the Royal Arch as a Christian degree helped to fill and make good.

A Canadian writer, R. E. A. Land, has suggested that Chevalier Ramsay's oration (a famous piece of Royal Arch evidence referred to on later pages) was inspired by the Pope with the object of winning over the English Craft to the new system of masonry (the Royal Arch) and incidentally to the Jacobite cause; masons, he thought, were invited to substitute for their theistic creed an acknowledgment of "a descent from the knightly orders and a specifically Christian teaching," but this attempt to bring masons "back under the wing" of the Catholic Church was at once seen to be a failure, and the wording of the first Charge in Anderson's second *Constitutions* (approved January 1738) was no accident, but the deliberate reply of the Grand Lodge of England; this was resented by the Pope, who therefore promulgated his Bull (April 24, 1738) condemning masonry. This, of course, is just a writer's conjecture, and it is extremely doubtful whether there is anything in it (the closeness of the two dates mentioned does not make for confidence), but it is quoted here to show that the teaching of the early R.A. was reputed to be definitely Christian.

Throughout the eighteenth century the ritual continued to include Christian characteristics, the more obvious of which disappeared in the revision of the early nineteenth century, but there still remain phrases, allusions, and symbols having a Christian origin. Not only in the Royal Arch, but in Craft masonry also, there continued in many parts of England and other countries throughout the eighteenth century, and in spite of the *Constitutions*, a markedly Christian atmosphere, and from one ritual (date 1760) we learn that the prayer over the Craft Initiate contained this invocation: "Let Grace and Peace be multiplied unto him, through the knowledge of our Lord Jesus Christ."

There are *two* passages in the Bible opening with the words "In the beginning"—namely, the first verse of the Book of Genesis and the first verse of St John's Gospel. Even to this day in certain Royal Arch chapters of antiquity it is the opening verse of the Gospel according to St John, and not the three opening verses of Genesis, with which the Candidate is confronted when he opens the scroll. There is good reason to believe that, in general, until the revision of the ritual in the 1830's, the scroll carried the quotation from the New Testament and not that from the Old.

Dr Oliver, who professed to have a genuine manuscript copy of Dunckerley's version of the R.A. ritual (we cannot answer for the accuracy of his claim), quoted from it as follows:

> The foundation-stone was a block of pure white marble, without speck or stain, and it alluded to the chief corner-stone on which the Christian Church is built, and which, though rejected by the builders, afterwards became the head of the corner. And when Jesus Christ, the grand and living representative of this stone, came in the flesh to conquer sin, death and hell, he proved himself the sublime and immaculate corner-stone of man's immortality.

From a Dublin ritual, published later in the same century, we take the following questions and answers:

Q. Why should eleven make a Lodge, Brother?
A. There were eleven Patriarchs, when Joseph was sold in Egypt, and supposed to be lost.
Q. The second reason, Brother?
A. There were but eleven Apostles when Judas betrayed Christ.

Right at the end of the eighteenth century John Browne produced a *Master Key*, in which masonic ceremonies are presented in cipher. The structure of some of these ceremonies is definitely Christian, the Craft lodge, for instance, being dedicated to St John the Baptist, the "Harbinger or Forerunner of the Saviour." While many obvious Christian references were eliminated when the Craft ritual was revised at the time of the Union, there still remains "the bright and morning star," a phrase familiar to every Master Mason, to remind us of the text in Revelation xxii, 16: "I am the root and the offspring of David, and the bright and morning star."

A Craft certificate issued to a Brother in a lodge of the Eighth Garrison Battalion (in the city of Cork, 1809) includes these words: "Now I command you, Brethren, in the Name of our Lord Jesus Christ that you withdraw yourselves from every brother who walketh disorderly and not after the tradition which he receiveth of us." An R.A. ritual of the early nineteenth century (it might belong to a chapter in the Scots Lowlands) invokes "the Grace of the Divine Saviour": "That shining light which the Pilgrims saw when searching the Arches where the Blessed Inspired Books were found under the Key-stone." And in a ritual, roughly of the 1820's, of a decidedly R.A. flavour occurs the phrase "the three peculiar initials of the Redeemer of Mankind."

An irregular print of the 1824–26 period shows that the Craft ritual then contained many Christian allusions. It spoke of the lodge as being of the Holy St John; of free Grace; of our Holy Secret; and said that the twelve lights were the Father, Son, Holy Ghost, Sun, Moon, Master, and so on. Then, too, the Dumfries No. 4 Manuscript of a century earlier contains many references to "our Lord Jesus Christ," the "Doctrine of Christ," "Christ as the door of life," "ye Glory of our High Priest Jesus Christ," "the unity of ye humanitie of Christ," "ye bread signifies Christ," "ye bread of life." And the Bible formerly in use in a now extinct Ballygowan (Ireland) lodge and preserved in the provincial museum of Down affords visual evidence that the Obligation was taken on the first chapter of St John's Gospel, for the book falls open naturally at that place, revealing two pages that have become discoloured with use. The Coustos evidence under the Inquisition (see p. 44) leaves no doubt that one or two London lodges in the 1730's followed the same custom.

Enough has been said to make it clear that many rituals, both Craft and R.A., up to the early nineteenth century were definitely of a Christian character, and it can be asserted with confidence that between the lines of to-day's R.A. ritual may still be discerned traces of the old Trinitarian influence.

Section Two

HOW CRAFT CONDITIONS PREPARED THE WAY FOR THE ROYAL ARCH

WHEN trying to picture the condition of English freemasonry at the introduction of the R.A. it is necessary to remember that speculative masonry—*recorded* speculative masonry—was then about a hundred years old. The present writer's *Freemasons' Guide and Compendium* sets the scene at some length, and all that need now be done is to give the reader enough background for him to understand how the conditions of Craft masonry in the early eighteenth century allowed of the grafting on of such an extremely important addition as the Royal Arch.

English Craft masonry had apparently developed many years prior to 1621, possibly from operative lodges, but if its true origin was in those lodges, then the path to speculative masonry led from them to and through the London Company of Freemasons. In the middle of the seventeenth century there were many operative lodges in Scotland, and some of these in the next century played their part in the founding of the Scottish Grand Lodge, although apparently their speculative masonry had largely, and perhaps almost wholly, reached them from England. Conditions in the two countries were vastly different, but it is safe to say that recorded history does not certainly reveal any story of natural development between any operative lodges whatsoever and speculative freemasonry. In the early seventeenth century there must have been quite a few English speculative Craft lodges, and by the end of that century there were probably many, but we know hardly anything of their ceremonies, although we have reason to assume that these were simple, probably bare, and contained little—but definitely an important *something*—of an esoteric nature; whatever it was, it attracted the attention of a few learned, classically educated men—many of an alchemical turn of mind—who undoubtedly left their impress upon the ritual. So, at any rate, it seems to the writer, who, the more he learns of the symbolism of the old alchemists, realizes increasingly that much of the classical allusion and symbolism which entered freemasonry by the middle of the eighteenth century must have been contributed by men who, in professing to study the method of transmuting base metals into gold, were actually speculatives of a high order—men of fine character and mostly of profound religious conviction.

Before 1717 we have only the sketchy records of lodges at that time in existence, but in that year four time-immemorial lodges came together to form the Premier Grand Lodge, the first Grand Lodge in the world. These four lodges "thought fit to cement under a *Grand Master* as the Center of Union and Harmony," but much more than that may have been in the minds of the founders. This first Grand Lodge created a masonic centre with a Grand Master, Quarterly Communications, Annual Assembly and Feast, and provided *Constitutions* that would replace the Old Charges. The first-known of these Old Charges, going back to about 1380, had been designed for "different days, different men and wholly different conditions."

The first *Constitutions*, 1723, written and compiled by a Scot, Dr James Anderson, were issued "with a certain measure of Grand Lodge authority." The title came probably from the practice of the London Masons Company (a gild), who gave the name to their copies of the Old Charges. It is believed that Anderson had the help of John Theophilus Desaguliers, the third Grand Master, and, possibly because of this, Grand Lodge, which was critical of Anderson's first effort, eventually permitted the publication of the rewritten manuscript, which was in print by January 1723. These *Constitutions*, apart from being the original laws governing the masonic Order, are of particular interest to Royal Arch masons, inasmuch as they include the charge "Concerning God and Religion," already discussed, which was at marked variance with much of the contents of the Old Charges. "The next thing that I shall remember you of is to avoid Politics and Religion," says Anderson. It is highly likely that general experience had already shown the desirability of uniting freemasons on "a platform that would divide them the least." "Our religion," says Anderson, "is the law of Nature and to love God above all things and our Neighbour as ourself; this is the true, primitive, catholic and universal Religion agreed to be so in all Times and Ages."

There is much point in quoting Anderson in this place; he could not know that the Christian element which he, with the approval of Grand Lodge, was trying (far from successfully) to eliminate would surely be restored by a later generation, not to the First and Second Degrees—probably the only masonic ceremonies known to him—not to a Third Degree then developing in a few lodges, but to what the freemasons of the second half of the century would call a "fourth" degree—the Royal Arch—that would arise within a few decades.

The new Grand Lodge, by assuming authority and publishing its *Constitutions*, was not necessarily assuring itself of the allegiance of the whole masonic body. While it is difficult to get at the facts, it has become obvious that many lodges and many freemasons remained outside its

PLATE II

Above:

SWORD-AND-TROWEL EMBLEM, FROM GEOFFREY WHITNEY'S "CHOICE OF EMBLEMES"

This book, first published in 1586, contains reproductions of still older engravings.

By courtesy of Brighton Public Library

Right:

TRIPLE ARCHES FROM ROYAL ARCH CERTIFICATES

The certificates were issued by Phœnix Lodge, Paris, in 1818 and 1821 respectively, but are of English origin.

By courtesy of United Grand Lodge

PLATE III

Left: Frontispiece of Samuel Lee's "Orbis Miraculum," or "The Temple of Solomon" (1659)

This frontispiece presents some Royal Arch ideas.

Right: Frontispiece to "Ahiman Rezon" (1764) including in its Upper Part the Arms of the 'Antient' Masons

By courtesy of United Grand Lodge

jurisdiction, a point easy to understand when the comparative lack of communication and transport is borne in mind. There must have been country lodges that did not even hear—or, at any rate, hear much—of the new Grand Lodge for many years, and there must have been others that were resentful and critical of any masonic body presuming to affect superiority and the right to issue orders and instructions to others. This is a most significant fact, and in it may be part of the explanation of much of the opposition to which the new Grand Lodge was subjected, and which, only a generation later, was a factor leading to the founding of a rival Grand Lodge. We know that in some quarters the Premier Grand Lodge was "not only laughed at" but brought under suspicion, and it is said (we must admit the absence of any definite proof of the statement) that only sixteen years elapsed between the issue of the first *Constitutions* and the beginning of a movement that ultimately blossomed into the 'Antients' Grand Lodge. Sixteen years was none too long a period in those days of poor communications for even a consistently wise Grand Lodge to have placated its opponents. But the first Grand Lodge had its share of failings, and there can be no doubt that its own actions contributed to the serious trouble that was to assail it by the middle of the century.

The Hiramic Degree paves the Way for the Royal Arch

The complex question of the division of the early degrees will not be entered into here. It will be simply assumed that until the 1720's there was probably but one degree or two degrees combined as one; that in a few lodges the Hiramic Degree began to be worked in the late 1720's; and that by about the middle of the century the English lodges were, in general, working a system of three degrees, of which almost invariably the first and second were conferred on the one occasion. This statement, we know, can be debated, but in general it represents the likely truth, always remembering, however, the considerable differences in custom and ceremonial among the early lodges. There is evidence that by 1750 or thereabouts the three-degree system was established in England, though in most of the lodges under the Premier Grand Lodge the Fellow Craft was still qualified to undertake any office whatsoever, and that it was not every Fellow Craft who took the trouble to proceed to the Third Degree. The rise in 1739-51 of the rival Grand Lodge—the 'Antients'—whose ceremonies were closely watched and sometimes adopted by their opponents, helped to bring about a condition in which the "skilled" and qualified mason was never less than the third-degree mason—the Master Mason.

The general adoption of the Hiramic Degree throughout English freemasonry by the middle of the eighteenth century should be emphasized because it means much to the R.A. mason. Failing its introduction, the R.A. might never have become a part of the masonic Order. Let it be remembered that the mason of the early lodges was in general a religious and relatively simple soul. The story unfolded by the Hiramic legend prepared his mind for yet another story, this one serving to make good two things that were absent from the earlier degrees. The three-degree system, ending in what may *appear* to be disappointment and anticlimax, prepared the way for the introduction of a degree which, new or otherwise, was accepted particularly by the opponents of the Premier Grand Lodge as part of an ancient system. It is a point of the greatest significance that it was these opponents that adopted and developed not only the R.A. ceremonial but also the Craft Installation ceremony which, in its sequel, became a bridge from the Craft lodge to the chapter, and still serves in that way in some jurisdictions overseas.

The author's earlier work mentions the considerable public interest aroused by freemasonry in the 1720's. This, in particular, led to the publication of irregular prints, the so-called 'exposures,' notably Prichard's *Masonry Dissected* (1730), which purported to give the ritual and secrets of freemasonry and had a most amazing sale in England and in all English-speaking countries, being reprinted many scores of times during the eighteenth century. Prichard's book had a lasting effect and a very complex one. It was freely bought by masons, and must have influenced lodge ceremonial in a day when the ritual was handed down by word of mouth without the help of printed *aides-mémoire*; thus it played into the hands of impostors who could set themselves up to 'initiate' credulous people on payment of a few shillings. There is no doubt that its publication frightened the Grand Lodge into making a grave and unfortunate decision (the transposition of the means of recognition in the First and Second Degrees), a decision which brought about serious trouble. In the course of that trouble arose the rival Grand Lodge—the 'Antients'—a development which was the greatest of all factors in the introduction and rise of the Royal Arch.

How did the Royal Arch come to be Accepted?

Whether the 'new' degree was entirely an innovation or whether it was an amplification of time-immemorial elements, however and wherever it arose, some explanation is needed of how it came to be so enthusiastically adopted by the 'Antients,' who prided themselves on working a truly ancient ritual, and who were quite convinced that the innovators were their opponents.

How came these conservatively minded Brethren to accept a degree which, however it was presented, must, one would suppose, come as at least partly an innovation? Of course, the degree could not possibly have been presented to them as merely an attractive ceremonial. It could have come only in the guise of a truly ancient ceremony, which they accepted as a true part of the masonic scheme. Those 'Moderns' too who unofficially welcomed it must have regarded it in the same light.

As the author sees it, only one course was possible. In the days between 1717 and the rise of the Committee that ultimately flowered into the 'Antients' Grand Lodge there must have been, as already said, quite a number of lodges that did not recognize the Premier Grand Lodge—lodges possibly several days' journey by horse or coach from London, lodges which in some unknown way had arisen here and there and which, while probably conforming in essentials one with another, almost certainly practised many variations of ceremonial. Such lodges could and did please themselves. If to them were introduced an addition, a detail, a ceremony, that struck them as having merit and in which they saw (rightly or wrongly) evidence of what they would regard as the original pattern of freemasonry, then those additions, details, and ceremonies they would adopt. There was nobody either to criticize or obstruct their intention.

We can easily picture the attractive ceremony of the R.A. coming to these lodges. It would offer itself as a hitherto neglected rite; it would follow in the Christian tradition to which its members were well accustomed; and it would bring to them that which they had learned had been lost. Many of the lodges which ultimately found themselves under the 'Antients' banner must have been lodges of that order—more or less detached, independent or semi-independent, and composed of simple-minded, religious men none too critical of their ritual so long as it gave the impression of time-immemorial usage. One lodge would learn from another, and very quickly, too, because there was something about the Royal Arch that rapidly assured its popularity, and by the time the 'Antients' Grand Lodge was founded there would be, all ready for general adoption, a ceremony, even a fully fledged degree, highly attractive to the mason of that day. And if, as we may well conclude, any correspondence between the Third Degree and the Royal Arch was in places far closer than now is the case, all the better in the eyes of the Brethren of the day.

Section Three

THE EARLY YEARS OF ROYAL ARCH MASONRY

By drawing together many early allusions and references this section will attempt to tell the story of the formative days of the Royal Arch up to 1766, the year that saw the founding of the first Grand Chapter and so became a milestone in the history of the Order.

Deferring any account of the traditional history to Sections 11 and 12 and coming down to the late Middle Ages, we find that there are in manuscript and print many allusions and references which may be interpreted as relating to the main idea or dominant *motif* of the Royal Arch. Perhaps the earliest was an endorsement (now lost) on one of the Old Charges, one known as the Grand Lodge No. 1 MS., bearing the date December 25, 1583. The handwriting does not suggest the sixteenth century, but the endorsement, for what it is worth, is here given: "In the beginning was the Word and the Word was with God and the Word was God." (St John, i, 1.) In another of the Old Charges—the Dumfries No. 4 MS., of the year 1710—are two references to the "Royal secret," the actual phrase being: "No lodge or corum of masons shall give the Royal secret to any suddenly but upon great deliberation." It has been suggested that the significance of the word "Royal" is the same as that in the Royal Arch. (In the Graham MS. of 1726 or earlier a secret is described as "holy.")

Some Allusions and References of the 1720's

The *Constitutions* of 1723 mention an "Annual Grand Assembly wherein . . . the Royal Art" may be "duly cultivated, and the *Cement* of the Brotherhood preserv'd; so that the whole Body resembles a well built *Arch*." While it might be easy to give the word "Arch" a special significance, frankly it is not thought that the phrase alludes to the Royal Arch, but is rather a figure of speech suggesting that the masonic Order forms one strong, solid structure.

The term "Royal Art" occurs twenty-three times in the *Constitutions*, the initial letters being printed in capitals or the words themselves in italics. But there seems no reason to invest this usage with particular significance, and it is easy to be misled by the similarity in sound between "Royal Art" and "Royal Arch." It is important to remember that Anderson's words are concerned with architecture, an art supported and encouraged by kings, hence a Royal Art. When the term is used to-day it connotes a mystical conception of freemasonry—an art by which is built the "spiritual house," the invisible temple. (By the way, Jonathan Swift said in 1728 that "mathematics resemble a well built arch; logic, a castle; and romances, castles in the air," but here again, although Swift was possibly a freemason, it is unwise to read special significance into his words.) The *Constitutions* of 1723 give, in Regulation II, the Master of a lodge

> The Right and Authority of congregating the Members of his Lodge into a *Chapter* at pleasure, upon any Emergency or Occurrence.

Further, Regulation X says:

> The *Majority* of every particular *Lodge*, when congregated, shall have the privilege of giving *Instructions* to their *Master* and *Wardens*, before the assembling of the *Grand Chapter*, or *Lodge*, at the three *Quarterly Communications* hereafter mention'd, and of the *Annual Grand Lodge* too; because their *Master* and *Wardens* are their Representatives, and are supposed to speak their Mind.

But is the term "Grand Chapter" in this quotation anything more than a rather fine term for an assembly, congregation, or convocation, particularly bearing in mind that the word 'chapter' had been in general use for hundreds of years? The monks in medieval days met in an assembly, a chapter, presided over by the head of their house. We admit the possibility that a few lodges might have found the word 'chapter' attractive because of its religious associations—for example, only a few years later the minutes of Old King's Arms Lodge, No. 28, referred in 1733 to "the last chapter" of this lodge, and other instances might be given, but we are far from supposing that this usage implies any knowledge of the Royal Arch. We first learn definitely of Royal Arch chapters in the 1750's.

Much has been made of the following reference in a manuscript catechism of 1723—quite an early date:

> If a Master Mason you would be
> Observe you well the Rule of Three.

And three years later appeared an advertisement mentioning "the necessity there is for a Master to well understand the Rule of Three." The possibility that "the Rule of Three" refers to a well-known feature of the Royal Arch ritual has, of course, been raised, but the phrase had more than one Craft implication.

More to the point is a passage in *The Whole Institutions of Free-Masons Opened* (Dublin, 1725):

> Yet for all this I want the primitive Word, I answer it was God in six Terminations, to wit I am, and *Johova* is the answer to it, ... or else Excellent and Excellent, Excellency is the Answer to it, ... for proof read the first of the first of St *John*.

Here we have a clear reference to words and ideas with which the Royal Arch mason is familiar. The word "Excellent" has been in use in Royal Arch ritual and custom for more than two centuries, and we shall later meet pointed examples of the word occurring in the 1740's and in the following decades. We find the words "the excellency of excellencies" occurring in another irregular print only one year later. A newspaper skit entitled "Antediluvian Masonry" (date about 1726), intended to throw ridicule upon freemasonry, mentions "moveable letters" and sends our thoughts forward to the Imperial George Lodge, which in a minute of 1805 recalls that a "set of movable letters was bought." An irregular print of 1725 mentions "a Compound Word" consisting of three (unintelligible) syllables, while a pamphlet of the year 1724, possibly written by Jonathan Swift, itself a skit on an alleged exposure of masonry that had recently appeared, says that freemasons attach great importance to "three pairs of Hebrew letters ... by which they mean that they are united as one in Interest, Secrecy and Affection."

From other irregular prints of the 1720's come these questions and answers:

Q. Whence is an Arch derived?
A. From architecture.
Q. Whence comes the pattern of an arch?
A. From the rainbow.

Probably the allusion in the second question is to a phrase in Genesis in which the rainbow is given as the token of God's covenant with man (there are other significant Biblical texts), and, jumping a few decades, it may be mentioned that a cavern and a rainbow are among the symbols illustrating a French rite of the 1760 period.

In the Graham MS. (1726 or earlier) already mentioned is a number of references to the "trible voice," and two of them, especially, may be quoted:

> Bezalliell ... knew by inspiration that the secret titles and primitive pallies of the God head was preservativ and ... agreed conditionally they were not to discover it without another to themselves to make a trible voice.

> ... now after [Bezalliell's] death the inhabitance there about did think that the

secrets of masonry had been totally Lost because they were no more heard of for none knew the secrets thereof. Save these two princes and they were so sworn at their entering not to discover it without another to make a trible voice.

The above quotations might well imply association with the Royal Arch *motif*, and cannot be lightly brushed aside. Neither can a reference in a lecture on December 27, 1726, delivered to the Grand Lodge of ALL England, at York, in the presence of the Grand Master, Charles Bathhurst. This reference was to Josiah and repairs to the Temple, including the re-building of the Temple by "Zerubbabel and Herod."

The More Definite References of the 1730's

Stress has sometimes been laid on the fact that the earliest seal in use by the Premier Grand Lodge in the 1730–33 period bore in Greek the words taken from St John i, 1: "In the beginning," etc. The seal itself has not survived, but its impress is seen upon the deputations to constitute various lodges in 1732 and 1733. In weighing this evidence we must bear in mind that the Premier Grand Lodge was hostile to the Royal Arch until the early nineteenth century, and it is therefore almost unbelievable that, assuming for one moment the Royal Arch to have been at work in the 1730 period, Grand Lodge would have chosen a motto known to be representative of a degree whose status it steadily refused to recognize. No, the adoption of the motto is most unlikely to be evidence of the existence of the Royal Arch at that date, but it certainly does suggest that the Craft degrees then included a mention of "the Word," a mention that in a brief score or so of years was to be considerably amplified.

'Scotch' or 'Scots' Masonry

There is a strong case for assuming that at the time when the Hiramic Degree had only recently found its way into masonic working, and but few lodges were capable of conferring it, some of the Fellow Crafts who aspired to be Master Masons went to Masters' Lodges. These came into existence in the 1730's, and are believed to have devoted themselves to working the Hiramic Degree, although they might also, perhaps in later years, have been working degrees that were not of a truly Craft nature. Nothing is known for certain, but it is a point of particular interest that the earliest recorded Masters' Lodge (No. 115, meeting at the Devil Tavern, Temple Bar, London) is described in the Engraved List (at that time the only approved list of lodges) as "a Scotch Masons Lodge." This description is thought to mean not that its members were Scots, but rather that the ritual or ceremony worked was known as "Scotch masonry," which may possibly (not *probably*) have been originated in France by Jacobites, political refugees from Scotland. According to the historian Gould (who appears to have known something of the ritual), Scotch masonry had as its *motif* the discovery in a vault by Scottish Crusaders of the long-lost and Ineffable Word. So if the lodge at the Devil Tavern was actually working a degree of French origin, then obviously a strong likelihood exists that some primitive form of the Royal Arch rite was actually being worked as early as 1733. The many rituals known, says Gould, exhibit much diversity, but running through them all is the main idea of the discovery of a long-lost word, while in the search leading to that discovery the Crusaders had to work with the sword in the one hand and the trowel in the other. That the discovery is made in the Middle Ages by Crusaders and not in pre-Christian days by the Jews returned from exile need not unduly concern us, for we must be prepared for considerable differences between any prototype Royal Arch ceremonies and those which were later developed.

The Scots Master claimed to be "superior to the Master Mason; to be possessed of the true history, secret and design of Freemasonry; and to hold various privileges . . . he wore distinctive clothing, remained covered in a Master's Lodge, and in any lodge, even as a visitor, ranked before the W.M." He claimed that at any time or place he could personally impart, either with or without a ceremony, the secrets of the three Craft degrees, and if, as a member of a lodge, his conduct came into question, only fellow Scots masons could adjudicate upon it. This is more or less the case which Gould presents, but it is not fully acceptable. So much depends upon the *date* when the Scots mason was making his exaggerated claims, and it is by no means clear that when Gould was speaking of the Crusaders' ceremonies he had in mind any that were worked as early as 1733, the year in which the first Scots Masters' Lodge is known to have been meeting in London. Frankly we do not really know that the Scots lodge was at that time working the Crusaders' ritual, and we suspect that Gould is talking of degrees that were worked at a rather later date.

It has often been advanced that the early 'Scots' degrees contained matter which to-day is found not only in the R.A., but in the Mark Degree. There seems little doubt that in the 1740's the Scots Degree (or degrees) was a 'fourth' ceremony, one dealing with the rebuilding of the Temple of Zerubbabel and bringing into prominence the occasion when builders worked with sword in one hand and trowel in the other. But then, by that time, the R.A. itself was known to be working in England, and it cannot be said with certainty whether the Royal Arch had learned from the Scots degrees (which is the way the evidence points) or *vice versa*.

The possibility that English freemasonry was subjected to Jacobite influence in the period following 1717 has often been raised. The broad suggestion is that Jacobites resident in France brought into existence the degrees known in England as 'Scots masonry' and in France as '*Maçon Écossois*,' '*Maître Écossois*,' '*Maçonnerie Écossois*,' and so on and that the English Jacobites introduced this Scots masonry into England as providing convenient, safe, and secret opportunities for their fellows and adherents. This does not strongly appeal to us, although the probability that Scots masonry was an importation from France may have to be conceded. It is not known that any rituals connected with the Royal Arch have ever contained any certain mark of Jacobite origin.

The Fifth Order

Coming now more particularly to the year 1734, we find a somewhat facetious reference to the "Fifth Order" occurring in a letter on masonic matters, signed "Verus Commodus," and believed to be referring to Dr Desaguliers, third Grand Master. The letter says he "makes a most Illustrious Figure . . . and he makes wonderful brags of being of the Fifth Order." This has been thought to allude to the Royal Arch, but no one can be sure that it does.

At the New Year, 1735, Mick Broughton, not himself a freemason and at the time a member of a house party including Dr Desaguliers and other masons staying with the Duke of Montagu at Ditton, Surrey, wrote the second Duke of Richmond a letter in which he states that

> Hollis and Desaguliers have been super-excellent in their different ways. . . . On Sunday Night at a Lodge in the Library St John, Albemarle and Russell [were] made chapters: and Bob [Webber] Admitted Apprentice.

To the natural inference that three individuals were made Royal Arch masons the use of the word "super-excellent" lends particular force. While the letter is obviously written in facetious terms, certain words in it could have had special meaning for the recipient, an active mason, who had been Grand Master ten years earlier, and, by way of comment on the fact that the meeting took place on a Sunday, let it be remembered that this was a favourite day for the holding of Masters' Lodges and, much later, of Royal Arch lodges and chapters.

Chevalier Ramsay

A statement attributed to Andrew Michael Ramsay, a Scot born in Ayr, who had passed many years in France, where he had acquired the courtesy title of Chevalier, has helped to make history. Ramsay, a Roman

Catholic, was a freemason, and is alleged to have made a speech containing certain significant words at a Paris convocation of the Grand Lodge of France on March 21, 1737. There is some doubt as to whether he ever delivered the speech, but none that he wrote it and that it was printed, probably in the same year and certainly in 1739 and later. The following literal translation of the part of the speech that particularly matters to the present reader was prepared, we believe, by *Miscellanea Latomorum*:

> We have amongst us three classes of confrères, the Novices or Apprentices; the Companions or Professed; the Masters or the Perfected. We explain to the first the moral virtues; to the second the heroic virtues; and to the last the Christian virtues; in such sort that our Institution encloses all the Philosophy of the Sentiments and all the Theology of the heart.
>
> This union was after the example of the Israelites, when they raised the second Temple. During this time they handled the trowel and the mortar with one hand, whilst they carried in the other the sword and buckler.

Undoubtedly Ramsay's is the most likely early allusion yet brought to light, but on it has been built rather too much. Dr Oliver, whose unreliability as a masonic historian has already been commented on, definitely asserts that Ramsay, about 1740, came from Paris to London and brought with him the rituals of some so-called high grades, among them being the Royal Arch; that his visit was "for the purpose of introducing his new degrees into English masonry; and his schemes being rejected by the Constitutional Grand Lodge, nothing appears more likely than that he would throw himself into the hands of the Schismatics."

The masonic student of to-day rejects Dr Oliver's statement, as well as his use of the word 'Schismatics.' Altogether too little is known about Ramsay to father upon him the introduction of the R.A. into England. W. J. Hughan points out that "so much has been said about Ramsay and his 'manufacture of masonic degrees' that it would be quite refreshing to have proofs of his having actually arranged or permitted one particular ceremony additional to those worked prior to his initiation," and William Watson has well said that "Ramsay was not a factor in the origin [of the R.A. Degree] and Oliver's statements are misleading, unreliable, . . . practically worthless."

Associated with the name of Ramsay (but probably quite wrongly) is the *Rite Ancien de Bouillon*, attributed to Godfrey de Bouillon, which had a Royal Arch-cum-Templar complexion and may or may not have been worked in London about 1740, but was possibly known in France at a much later date. It is said to have had six grades—Apprentice, *Compagnon* (Fellowcraft), Master, Scotch Master, Novice, and *Chevalier du Temple* (Templar). Some little inquiry into it has not proved very rewarding.

While it does seem likely that Ramsay had experience of a degree corresponding to the Royal Arch, the *only* evidence of any kind supporting the likelihood of his having introduced a degree is the fact that he wrote his oration, possibly delivered it, and that the oration itself contains a phrase that appears in almost the same form in to-day's ritual.

John Coustos and his Sworn Evidence

We have said that Chevalier Ramsay was both freemason and Roman Catholic. In his day many Continental and other masons were Catholics. Pope Clement's first Bull against freemasonry was issued in 1738, and needed to be backed up by later Bulls, as there was a disinclination on the part of many Catholics to observe the Pope's prohibition. The hostility of the Governments in Catholic countries to freemasonry, even in modern times, is well known. In 1954, for instance, a Spanish tribunal imposed prison sentences on five men accused of practising freemasonry. (By the way, Spain was the first Continental country to have a masonic lodge constituted in it by or on behalf of the Grand Lodge of England—that of the Duke of Wharton, which he founded in his own apartments in Madrid in 1728 and which, as originally constituted, had a life of forty years.)

Portugal, in 1738, had two Lodges in Lisbon, one of mainly Irish Catholics; another, under English Warrant, was composed of Protestants. In that year, Charles O'Kelly, a Dominican theologian at the Irish (R.C.) College of Corpo-Santo, was summoned to reveal to the Inquisition what he knew of the Catholic Lodge. He was not a Mason but was Confessor to many of the members and he made the strong point that all members—they included three Dominican monks—were excellent Catholics.

Later, in October 1742, John Coustos, a Protestant and Master of a Lisbon Lodge of mainly French Catholics, was denounced to the Inquisition as chief of a "sect" called Free-Masons that had been condemned in the Papal Bull of 1738. Coustos, a Swiss by birth and English by adoption, had apparently been initiated in London in 1730; then moving to Paris, he became Master and later Deputy Master of Lodge Coustos Villeroy there, before going to Lisbon where he practised his trade as a master diamond cutter.

In the hands of the Inquisition, Coustos gave evidence under solemn oath on a number of occasions, and on April 25, 1744, was tortured on the rack in Lisbon for more "than a quarter of an hour," being afterwards sentenced to serve four years in the galleys. On the intervention of the British Minister at Lisbon he was liberated in October 1744, and reached England on December 15 of the same year. Hitherto we have had, in a book which he wrote and published in England in 1746, a not quite reliable account of his tribulations (he can be forgiven much, poor fellow!), but fortunately the original Inquisition documents were discovered in the Torre do Tombo archives and translated, in part, by Mr A. Walford, a member of the then Lisbon Branch of the Historical Association and reproduced by John R. Dashwood in *A.Q.C.* (vol. lxvi, pp. 107–123). These documents show that Coustos made a "confession" on two days of March 1743, and in this he gave a fascinating account of the Craft masonry known to him, a tiny portion of this account being here reproduced[1]:

> ... when the destruction took place of the famous Temple of Solomon there was found below the First Stone a tablet of bronze upon which was engraved [a familiar Biblical word meaning] 'God,' giving thereby to understand that that Fabric and Temple was instituted and erected in the name of the said God to whom it was dedicated, that same Lord the beginning and the end of such a magnificent work, and as in the Gospel of St John there are found the same words and doctrine they, for this reason, cause the Oath to be taken at that place.

John Coustos declared this and many other things under oath on March 26, 1743, and it will be particularly noted that the legend or ritual revealed by him, including St John's reference to the 'Word,' must[2] have been that of one or two lodges under the premier Grand Lodge during the 1730's. As the authenticity of the quoted passage does not admit of any doubt, it is beyond question that in the 1730's a Craft ritual—that is, the ritual of a lodge in London or Paris, not necessarily of all, by any means—contained elements which now are unknown to the Craft, but which, in an elaborated form, are present in to-day's R.A. ritual.

The Coustos documents (which, we must insist, to be read are to be believed) afford evidence that some elements of the R.A. legend were probably known to a few English or French lodges at an early date, within their three degrees, and this is a fact that must necessarily affect hitherto accepted views on the early history of the R.A.

It should be noted that Coustos considered himself competent to conduct the Lisbon lodge as Master, and he may well have been the actual Master of a London lodge before he left England. By the year 1732 he was a member of Lodge No. 75, at the Rainbow Coffee House, York Buildings, London (now the Britannic Lodge, No. 33), and a founder, in the year mentioned, of Lodge No. 98, at Prince Eugene's Coffee House, St Alban's Street, London (constituted 1732 and known as the Union French Lodge in 1739; ceased to exist, 1753).

The Coustos reference to something hidden below a stone has an echo in an Irish folk-song, *An Seann-Bhean* ("The Poor Old Woman"), which includes these two lines:

> Or is it true that the promises were written which Moses gave to the Jews,
> And which King David placed timidly under the stone?

[1] See also "John Coustos", in *A.Q.C.*, vol. lxxxi, by Dr S. Vatcher and Rev. N. B. Cryer.
[2] 'must' is doubtful; Coustos may have learned this in France.

In another version "King David" is replaced by *An Da Ri* ("The Two Kings"). J. Heron Lepper suggests that we have here a piece of folklore—a use of the *motif* of the buried book. There must be many such or similar references in the world's literature. One further example is contained in a third-century papyrus, *The Sayings of Jesus*, a non-canonical Gospel found on the site of an ancient Egyptian city, Oxyrhynchus:

> Lift up the stone and there shalt thou find me;
> cleve the wood and I am there.

Minutes and Printed References of the 1740's

The first printed reference to the term 'Royal Arch' is forthcoming in the year 1743. It is in a newspaper, *Faulkner's Dublin Journal*, for January 10–14, 1743–44, and occurs in an account of a masonic procession at Youghall, County Cork, Ireland, on St John's Day in Winter (December 27), when the Master of Lodge No. 21 was preceded by "The Royall Arch carried by two Excellent Masons." We wish we could be certain that this "Arch" was not a mere piece of added ornament—arches are not uncommon in public processions—but certainly the inclusion of the term "Excellent Masons" does incline us to the inference that the procession was indeed one of R.A. masons.

On the heels of the first printed mention comes a second and most important reference to the R.A. as a *degree*. In 1744 was published a book by Fifield Dassigny (D'Assigny), M.D., Dublin, entitled *A Serious and Impartial Enquiry into the Cause of the present Decay of Free-Masonry in the Kingdom of Ireland*. Until 1867 this book was known only through a quotation in *Ahiman Rezon*, but in that year one of the few surviving copies was discovered by the well-known masonic student W. J. Hughan, who caused it to be reprinted in facsimile in 1893; there are copies also in the G.L. and W. Yorks. Masonic Libraries. Dassigny says in a roundabout way that, a few years earlier, a Brother of probity and wisdom had been made a R.A. mason in London. Here is part of the paragraph including the significant words:

> ... a certain propagator of a false system some few years ago in this city [Dublin] who imposed upon several very worthy men under a pretence of being Master of the Royal Arch, which he asserted he had brought with him from the city of York; and that the beauties of the Craft did principally consist in the knowledge of this valuable piece of Masonry. However he carried on his scheme for several months and many of the learned and wise were his followers, till at length his fallacious art was discovered by a Brother of probity and wisdom, who had some small space before attained that excellent part of Masonry in London and plainly proved that his doctrine was false.

The above can be very simply put by saying that somewhere about 1740, some one in Dublin, pretending to be Master of the Royal Arch, was proved to be an impostor by a Brother who had been made a member of the degree in London. Dr Dassigny's book refers to R.A. masons assembling at York in 1744 as "he was informed"; says that some of the fraternity did not like "such a secret ceremony being kept from those who had taken the usual degrees"; refers to members who had "passed the chair" and were "excellent masons"; and states that the R.A. was "an organised body of men who have passed the Chair and given undeniable proofs of their skill."

Some students have sought to cast reflections upon Dassigny's reputation, and have suggested that his words should be handled with caution and reserve, but nothing is known against him. Dermott, the greatest figure in the 'Antients' Grand Lodge, refers to him as "our Worshipful Brother, Dr Fifield D'Assigny"; among the four hundred subscribers to his book were many important people; and there seems no reason to doubt that he was speaking the truth and knew what he was talking about. He evidently was sure that the Royal Arch Degree existed. Indeed, J. Heron Lepper, who, in coming to a conclusion on the antiquity of the R.A., based himself very largely upon Dassigny's statements, held that Dassigny had had experience of it at first hand. Certainly there is a general consensus of opinion that his statement is sound evidence of an early R.A. Degree in working order, even at a date a few years earlier than 1744.

The 1740's afford reasonable evidence that an R.A. ceremony was worked in Stirling, Scotland. There are two dates, 1743 and 1745, and it is claimed that in the earlier year the minute here given shows that two men were admitted R.A. masons:

STIRLING, *July* 30*th*, 1743.
Which day the Lodge of Stirling Kilwinning being met in the Brother Hutchison's house, and being petitioned by Mungo Nicol, shoemaker and brother James McEwan, Student of Divinity at Stirling, and being found qualified, they were admitted Royal Arch Masons of this Lodge, have paid their dues to the Treasurer, John Callendar, R.W.M.

In 1745 occurs another minute (given below), which unfortunately is almost a repetition of the earlier one. A sworn declaration that the R.A. had been worked in Stirling in 1743, based upon the original record then existing, was deposited in 1818 with the Grand Scribe E. of the Grand Royal Arch Chapter of Scotland in Edinburgh, but the first minute-book of Stirling Rock R.A. Chapter, No. 2, is not available. The minutes of Lodge Ancient, No. 30, state that no such minute as that above attested is to be found in the minute-book for 1743 and that John Callendar, signing as Right Worshipful Master, was not Master of the Lodge until 1745; so it may be that 1743 is an error for 1745 or, alternatively, that John Callendar, although not Master of the Lodge, may have presided in a Royal Arch lodge attached to the Craft lodge in the earlier year.

The minute of 1745 is as follows:

STERLING *July* 30, 1745.
The Which day the Lodge of Sterling Kilwinning having meet in Brother Hickson's hous And being Petitioned by Mr. Mungo Nicholl Shoe Maker & Mr. James McEuen Student of Devenitie at Sterling & they being found qualified were accordingly Admitted as prenticess & payed the accustomed dues accordingly to the trer:—Jo. Callendar M.

Obviously, if the minute of 1743 is beyond question, it could be truthfully affirmed that the R.A. was being worked at Stirling in 1743, but W. J. Hughan did not think that Stirling's claim was either substantiated or confirmed, and other students have expressed themselves in similar manner; on the other hand, George S. Draffen, formerly Grand Librarian of the G.L. of Scotland, says that, having examined the old records of six of the twelve senior chapters on the Scottish Roll (Nos. 3, 6, 7, 8, 9, and 12 in the Province of Angus and Mearns), he has found the dates to conform exactly to those assigned by the Seniority Committee of the Supreme Grand Royal Arch Chapter of Scotland, and he is therefore of the opinion that the date of 1743 assigned to Stirling was supported by written evidence in 1817.

Progress in the 1750's and 1760's

The remaining pages of this section will indicate some of the progress made in the 1750's and the 1760's up to a point in the second of those decades marking the foundation of the first Grand Chapter in the world, that erected by Lord Blayney, Grand Master of the 'Moderns,' by means of his celebrated Charter of Compact.

The earliest date on which we have definite and undisputed knowledge of the Royal Arch in England is March 4, 1752 (see p. 59). The earliest existing minutes (other than in Scotland) recording what was then known as the raising of a Brother to the Royal Arch are of the period between 1752 and 1758. In Ireland the first exaltee was in 1752; in America (not yet the U.S.A.) in 1753; in Scotland in 1756 (but if the Stirling record is accepted, then in 1743 or 1745); in England in 1758; and in London in 1767. These four countries will be taken in the order above given.

Ireland. Lodge No. 123 was warranted in 1741 at Coleraine, County Derry, by the Grand Lodge of Ireland, and must very soon have been working the R.A. A list or register of members contained in a minute-book covering the years 1763–83 shows that of twenty Brethren initiated between May 1741 and December 1759 sixteen were made R.A. masons, but there is no confirmation of this in the minutes themselves. John Holmes, included in the list, was exalted two weeks after his Initiation in May 1746, and reached the chair eight years later. Another, the Rev. Wm Bristow, was initiated in 1757, became Master of the Lodge in 1759, and was exalted immediately following his leaving the chair six months later. It is not known whether the other exaltees were actual Past Masters of this or any other lodge, but the inference in many of the cases is that they were not. Dated April 16, 1752, is the following Coleraine minute of historic importance, one that antedates by twenty months a minute of a lodge at Fredericksburg, Virginia (which, however, is still the oldest undisputed written record of the *actual making* of R.A. masons).

> At this lodge, Bro^r Tho Blair propos'd Samson Moore a Master & Royal Arch Mason to be admitted a Member of our Lodge.

Only one other minute of the Coleraine Lodge mentions the R.A.:

> 1760. Jany. 14th—Br Armstrong requests the favour of the Lodge to admitt him a Royal Arch Mason.

At Youghall, County Cork, there had been founded in 1734 a lodge which made no mention in its minutes until 1759 of the Royal Arch, and, curiously, for half a century after that year did not again allude to it. In that year, on July 30, 1759, occurs a minute of which the following is part:

> Then proceeded to the passing of Spencer Scannaden and Samuell Gardner to the dignity of Royal Arch Masons, they being proper Officers of the Lodge, That is, Bro. Scannaden Senr Warden and Samuel Gardner Junr Deacon.

It is extremely likely that the Craft freemasonry practised in the Youghall lodge stemmed directly from the English system, the sea connexion between Bristol and many Irish ports being much closer early in the eighteenth century than the road connexion between Bristol and many inland English towns. The Royal Arch has a long and important history in Ireland, as will be seen in a later section.

America. What is still thought to be the earliest minute definitely recording a Royal Arch Exaltation is of "Lodge of Free and Accepted Masons" in Fredericksburg, Virginia, of the year 1753 (year of Masonry 5753), and to the eye of the present-day mason must appear to be of a singular character:

> Decemb^r 22^d 5753 Which Night the Lodge being Assembled was present
> Right Worshipful Simon Frazier G.M.,   ⎫ of Royall
>   Do.   John Neilson S. Ward^n   ⎬   Arch
>   Do.   Robert Armistead Ju^r Ward^r ⎭   Lodge.

PLATE IV

THE CHARTER OF COMPACT
This document erected the very first Grand Chapter. Its true date, 1766, is the subject of a note at p. 74.
By courtesy of United Grand Lodge

PLATE V

CADWALLADER, NINTH LORD BLAYNEY (1720–75)
Lord Blayney was " Grand Master of Free and Accepted Masons," 1764–66, and the first " Grand Master of the Royal Arch of Jerusalem " (1766).
By courtesy of United Grand Lodge

Transactions of the night

> Daniel Campell
> Robert Halkerston
> Alex^r Wodrow

Raised to the Degree of Royall Arch Mason.

Royal Arch Lodge being Shutt, Entered Apprentices Lodge opened.

It is believed that Simon Frazier, given in the minute as "Grand Master," was a visitor, and that he became a member in the following month. The Wardens assisting him and named in the minute were the Senior Warden and the Temporary Treasurer respectively of the lodge. It is to be noted that Daniel Campbell, the first of the exaltees, was actually the Master of the Craft Lodge; the second candidate, Dr Robert Halkerston, was the actual Junior Warden; and the third was the Secretary. The Craft Lodge itself was not at that date, 1753, warranted by any recognized Grand Lodge, but it received a charter from the Grand Lodge of Scotland in 1758. (A statement once made that it was an Irish lodge is not substantiated.) The Lodge charter is, we believe, still preserved, and the Lodge was reported at the end of the nineteenth century as being "happily vigorous and active"; its place in history is well assured, for in it on November 4, 1753, was initiated George Washington, later to become the first President of the United States of America.

Scotland. Scotland deservedly claims a long history of the R.A., beginning with the Stirling records already dealt with. So far back as 1755 a lodge bearing the name of Royall Arch was chartered at Glasgow, apparently bearing the number 77, and was erased in 1816. Other Royal Arch lodges were at Edinburgh in 1765 and at Stirling in 1759.

One of the most important of the early Scottish dates concerns a minute of the Thistle Lodge, Dumfries (now No. 62), founded in 1754.

4 March, 1757
The Briting Bieng met & opening the Lodg in deu order Johen Patten was past from aprent[s] To the Care of Adoniram and John McKewn James Marten was med Exlant & Super Exlant and Roiel Arch Men as witness.

[Three signatures]

This is the first *undisputed* Scottish minute recording raisings to the Royal Arch Degree. In a record of "the Royal Arch Masons and their Passing to that" at the end of the minute-book the first name is dated November 7, 1756.

Lodge Kirkwall Kilwinning, No. 38[2], founded in 1736 by masons from the Lodge of Stirling and the Lodge of Dunfermline, is believed to have been working the Royal Arch in the 1754–60 period. A minute of 1759 mentions "Royall Arch King Solomon's Lodge, Number 2, New York." The Kirkwall Lodge owns a famous scroll, crudely depicting the emblems of various degrees, the Royal Arch prominently among them. (See Plate VII.)

A lodge at Banff has early minutes relating to the Royal Arch Degree. Hughan says that on January 7, 1765, it was agreed that "any member who wants to attain to the parts of Royal Arch and Super Excellent shall pay two shillings and sixpence to the Publick Fund *for each part*." On January 7, 1766, Brother William Murray, who joined the lodge, is styled "*Master and Royal Arch*." On January 1, 1778, seven Brethren paid two shillings and sixpence each "for that branch of Royal Arch," and three of these were charged additional half-crowns each "for that Branch of Super Excellent."

England. Of the English definite records the oldest, either 'Antients' or 'Moderns,' are not earlier than the 1750's. At a meeting of the Grand Committee of the 'Antients' on March 4, 1752, some Brethren made formal complaints that two individuals, Phealon and Mackey, "had initiated many persons for the mean consideration of a leg of mutton," and had pretended "to have made Royal-Archmen." (This subject will be returned to in the next section.) The complaints were received at a meeting at which Laurence Dermott acted for the first time as Secretary. Later in the 'Antients' minutes of this same year occurs another reference:

> September 2nd, the Lodge was Opened in Antient form of Grand Lodge and every part of Real Freemasonry was traced and explained; except the Royal Arch.

These matters are more particularly dealt with in a later section.

We have Thomas Dunckerley's own assertion that he was exalted in a Portsmouth lodge in 1754 (probably in his mother lodge). The 'Antients' were, of course, at this time very busy with the Royal Arch, and we find in 1757 a minute of their Grand Lodge summoning "The Masters of the Royal Arch" to meet "in order to regulate things relative to that most valuable branch of the Craft."

The first-known English minute recording the raising of a Brother to the R.A. is, perhaps unexpectedly, of a '*Moderns*' lodge at Bristol, in 1758, but it would be wrong to rush to the conclusion from this isolated evidence that the 'Moderns' worked the Royal Arch earlier than the 'Antients.' The Lodge, No. 220, was short-lived. It was constituted in February 1757, at Lord Blakeney's Head, Temple Street, Bristol, but by the time its minute-book was begun had already moved to the Crown in Christmas Street. Although a 'Moderns' lodge, it yet worked an 'Antient' ritual, being of that class of lodges which J. Heron Lepper, in a noteworthy paper published in *A.Q.C.*, vol. lvi, described as Traditioner lodges—that is, lodges owning allegiance to the Premier Grand Lodge, but in their ceremonial following closely the 'Antients' working. A Lodge of Emergency was held on Sunday, August 13, 1758, by desire of Brother William Gordon, who, at a regular meeting held some days earlier, had been proposed "to be raised to the degree of a Royal Arch and accepted"; at this Sunday evening meeting he and another were 'raised' to the R.A. Degree. By May 6 of the next year seven R.A. meetings had been held and thirteen Brethren so 'raised,' all of whom were taking the step quite shortly after becoming Master Masons.

Of the many R.A. records in the 1760's the earliest, so far as is known, relating to an actual 'raising' of a Brother to the R.A. is particularly historic. On Sunday, February 7, 1762, a Royal Arch lodge was opened at the Punch Bowl Inn, in Stonegate in York, by members of the Punch Bowl Lodge, No. 259, founded in the preceding year (and expiring in its seventh). Four members, all of them actors and members of the York Company of Comedians, opened the Royal Arch lodge, so providing an early instance of a separate organization especially formed for the working of the Royal Arch ceremonial. Under the 'Antients,' and legally so, that ceremonial was worked in their Craft lodges, while under the 'Moderns' at that time the Royal Arch Degree was irregular and, if worked, quite unofficial. But this was not a 'Moderns' lodge! It was held under the authority of the Grand Lodge of ALL England, a Grand Lodge erected by an old City of York lodge in 1725 and holding sway actually in parts of Yorkshire, Cheshire, and Lancashire. The separate organization had a minute-book entitled *Minute Book Belonging to the Most Sublime Degree or Order of Royal Arch appertaining to the Grand Lodge of ALL England, held at the City of York, 1762.* (This lodge or chapter became in the course of time a Grand Chapter.) The first minute recorded relates to the meeting of Sunday, February 7, 1762, already mentioned, and states that "Brothers Burton, Palmes, Tasker and Dodgson petition'd to be raised to the Fourth Degree of Masonry, commonly call'd the Most Sublime or Royal Arch, were accepted and accordingly made."

Section Four

THE 'ANTIENT' MASONS AND THE ROYAL ARCH

THE rise and development of the Royal Arch, and indeed its ultimate position in the whole masonic Order, were immeasurably affected by the bitter quarrel between the premier Grand Lodge, founded in 1717, and another Grand Lodge—the 'Antients'—thought to have been in course of formation from *c.* 1739, and taking its place in 1751–53 as a Grand Lodge with all powers to warrant private lodges. Only as much of the story need be given here as will explain the circumstances in which the 'Antients' came into being and the attitudes of the two opposed bodies to the Royal Arch. Actually, during the years of the formation of the 'Antients' Grand Lodge the Royal Arch had been quietly progressing towards general adoption. The quarrel lasted for sixty years or so, and the present position of the English Royal Arch relative to the Craft is a reflection of that quarrel.

The masonic historian Gould looked upon the formation of the 'Antients' Grand Lodge as a schism, the work of seceders from the original plan of freemasonry, but his great work was written in the 1880's, before research had revealed that, while there must have been many discontented masons who left the 'Moderns' lodges to throw in their lot with the opponent, it was not seceders who built the rival body, but, chiefly, Irish and Scottish masons residing in England, who naturally welcomed the help of any of the English malcontents.

The premier Grand Lodge had contributed to or even brought about many of its own troubles by its lack of zeal and discretion and its ignorance of the art of government, faults accelerated by its assumption of superiority to its sister Grand Lodges of Ireland and Scotland. It signally failed to meet the challenge offered by the appearance of certain irregular prints, particularly, as already stated, that of Samuel Prichard, whose *Masonry Dissected*, published in 1730, was reprinted scores of times in English-speaking countries. It is not unfair to say that the publication of this and similar works caused the 'Moderns' Grand Lodge such great concern and nervousness that, afraid to give itself time properly to consider the matter, it rushed into a great mistake from which it long suffered, for somewhere in the 1730 period (the exact date is in doubt) it instructed the private lodges, as we have already said, to transpose the forms of recognition in the First and Second Degrees, with the intention of placing a shibboleth in the way of any clandestine mason attempting to enter its lodges. (In at least one Continental system that stemmed from English masonry about that time the means of recognition remain still transposed, although in England the matter was remedied immediately before the Union, 1813.) The transposition was regarded with horror by a great many masons, who charged the Grand Lodge with having grievously and wholly improperly interfered with a landmark.

This alteration came to be by no means the only difference between the working of the 'Moderns' lodges and that of the independent lodges and still later, lodges of the 'Antients' persuasion. With the passage of time the 'Moderns' Premier Grand Lodge was charged, not in all instances fairly, with omitting prayers; de-Christianizing the ritual; ignoring saints' days; failing to prepare Candidates in the traditional manner; abbreviating or abandoning the lectures (catechisms); abandoning the Ancient Charges; causing the ceremonies, particularly Initiation, to be more austere; allowing the esoteric Installation of the Master to fall into disuse; arranging their lodges in a different manner; etc., etc. Undoubtedly the greatest of these 'etceteras' was the refusal to recognize and acknowledge officially the antiquity of the Royal Arch, a ceremonial regarded by the 'Antients' as having come down to them from time immemorial. A few of these accusations may have been well founded, but many were not, and even those that were true did not apply to all 'Moderns' lodges and at all times between, say, 1740 and 1813. We know, of course, that Dr Anderson's *Constitutions* of 1723 did in effect de-Christianize the ritual; there is no doubt that the 'Moderns' had not, in all cases, retained the affection for saints' days; it is likely that they tended to shorten the catechisms and to omit recitals of the Ancient Charges; but whether, for instance, they 'omitted' the use of the sword in the Initiation ceremony or 'abandoned' the esoteric Installation of the Master—these are open to serious question. Indeed, the accusations are almost certainly false. It was not the 'Moderns' who ignored a time-immemorial practice and discontinued the use of the sword; it must have been the unattached lodges, and following them the 'Antients,' who, in adopting the use of the sword, simply borrowed an idea from the French. It is thought to be impossible that the 'Moderns' or anybody else, at the founding of the first Grand Lodge, knew of an esoteric Installation of the Master; consequently the accusation that they had 'abandoned' it had no foundation. It must have been the unattached lodges and, in due course, the 'Antients' who adopted that ceremony, confident, we can well admit, that it was a part of the original masonic tradition.

But, however, the differences came, there they were and there they stayed, to distinguish so many of the 'Moderns' lodges from so many of the 'Antients.' Both sides made great capital out of them, and we find the second edition of Laurence Dermott's *Ahiman Rezon* (the 'Antients' Constitutions) attacking the 'Moderns' ritual and underlining the changes which the 'innovators' were accused of having made. But as we reflect upon the matter we ask who were the innovators? More and more we realize that, although innovators the 'Moderns' undoubtedly were in one serious and unfortunate respect, in nearly all others it was the 'Antients' who permitted and encouraged the positive variations that in the second half of the eighteenth century distinguished the two bodies.

It should be remembered that there was not in the eighteenth century anything that could be regarded as a cast-iron ritual, even remotely so. All through that century the rituals were being made, borrowed from, and added to; were being developed in different localities and in different ways; and the many variations were, in due time, to give a real headache to the bodies charged with the preparation of agreed rituals following on the Union of the Craft and later that of the Royal Arch. So when we try to estimate the differences between the rituals of the 'Antients' and the 'Moderns' we shall do well to remind ourselves that there was no one ritual precisely followed by everybody; there was no brand-new ritual adopted in the 1730 period by the 'Moderns' and imposed by them on their lodges. There was one continuous process of development and modification under both of the two Grand Lodges through much of the century, although possibly not always perceptible to those immediately concerned in it.

Douglas Knoop, a trained historian, believed that the Craft lodges had no formal openings or closings in the 1730 period; that later there was, in many lodges, no opening in the Second and Third Degrees and no closing in any degree; and that ceremonial methods of opening and closing grew up gradually among both 'Antients' and 'Moderns,' and obviously could not be identical in all lodges in all places. This must apply also to many of the features that distinguished the two bodies, the differences being more marked in some places than in others. A process of assimilation between the two bodies was always at work, and it is to be expected that this chiefly took the form of tempering the early austerity of the 'Moderns' ceremonies. It is believed that towards the end of the century the differences in some localities between the two systems were only slight. Evidence in the matter is conflicting, but we have the instance of Robert Millikin, of Cork, who visited a 'Moderns' lodge in Bristol about 1793 and, beyond a few phrases in opening the lodge, discovered no difference from his own 'Antient' ritual. However, between the *extreme* lodges of each body there must still have been some considerable differences, which must have caused the Lodge of Reconciliation plenty of trouble following the Union (see p. 115).

By the end of the century the assimilation that had been fostered in lodges of the Traditioner type (see p. 50) had made a considerable effect in some localities, and it is now certain that for years prior to 1813 many devoted masons on both sides were quietly working to bring about union. In the minds of such men the Royal Arch must have occupied a big place. A spirit of toleration and understanding had been steadily growing up between the two bodies, but there were still many masons of the type of the Deputy Grand Secretary of Ireland, who, in a letter written in 1790 to an Irish lodge, said that "A Modern Mason cannot or ought not to be admitted into a lodge of Antient Masons without passing the courses over again as if the same had never been performed—their mode and ours being so different."

"Without passing the courses over again"! One of the customs commonly practised during the quarrel was that of 'remaking,' said to have been originated by the 'Moderns,' who insisted that certain Irish masons should be 'remade' before they could be admitted to their lodges as Brethren. Both sides practised it over a long period, so causing many anomalies and ridiculous instances, as related in the author's earlier volume.

The Union—not immediately it came, but in the course of a few years—brought to an end the quarrel between the two sections of the Craft and had an immediate and marked effect upon the fortunes of the Royal Arch.

The 'Antients' Grand Lodge

The 'Antients' Grand Lodge was functioning as such from about 1751, although officially it still called itself in February 1752 "The Grand Committee of the Most Antient and Honourable Fraternity of Free and Accepted Masons," and the term "Grand Lodge" appears in its minutes for the first time in 1753. By the time of the Craft Union (1813) its name had become "The Most Antient and Honourable Fraternity of Free and Accepted Masons according to the Old Institutions." Care must be taken not to confuse this with a much later Grand Lodge, centred in Wigan, "of Free and Accepted Masons of ALL England according to the Old Institutions," formed in 1823 by four lodges that had been erased by the United Grand Lodge. The first 'Antients' Grand Master was Robert Turner; the second the Hon. Edward Vaughan; and the third, from 1756 to 1759, the first Earl of Blesington, writing to whom in December 1756, to thank him for consenting to become Grand Master, Laurence Dermott spoke of "the great honour your Lordship has done the Fraternity in condescending to fill SOLOMON'S CHAIR"! Two Grand Masters of Ireland and three of Scotland were among the 'Antients' Grand Masters. The third Duke of Atholl served from 1771 to 1774, and on his death was succeeded by his son; altogether the Atholls served as Grand Masters for over thirty years, both of them being at some time Grand Master of Scotland, so it is easily understandable why the 'Antients' Grand Lodge in its last forty years was generally known as the Atholl Grand Lodge.

On the retirement of the 'Antients' first Grand Secretary in 1752 there was elected in his place Laurence Dermott, age thirty-two, "a man of remarkable quality and tremendous energy," to whose "forces of character and administrative ability" must be attributed much of the 'Antients' success. He became the greatest personality in the 'Antients' Grand Lodge and one whose importance in the history of the English Royal Arch can never be questioned. He was born in Ireland in 1720, initiated in 1740 in Lodge No. 26, Dublin, of which he became Master and Secretary, and came to England about 1747–48. It is highly probable that at some time prior to this he had been a member of a 'Moderns' lodge, and he is thought to have become a Royal Arch mason in his Irish lodge in 1746. By trade he was a journeyman painter, and never grew ashamed of his "mecanic" origin, but he was to reply in a few words of Latin, a few years later, to the Grand Master, who had nominated the text for a sermon to be preached at St Clement's Church, London! He received a whole succession of compliments and honours during his masonic career, but with the ever-increasing dignity of office he never lost his head, and his bookplate names him "Lau. Dermott, G.S., Painter, London," although by now he was using the heraldic arms of the MacDermotts, chiefs of Moylurg, County Roscommon. In 1772 in his Grand Lodge minutes he becomes "Lau. Dermott, Esq.," but in that same year, in an official letter addressed to him from the Deputy Grand Secretary, Ireland, he is called "Lau. Dermott, Wine Merchant, London."

In 1756 Dermott issued the first edition of the 'Antients' Constitutions, largely based upon Anderson's *Constitutions* of 1723, and gave them the extraordinary title of *Ahiman Rezon*, which he may have built up from two words in the Geneva or "Breeches" Bible of 1560, which gives "Ahiman" as "a prepared Brother, one of the sons of Anak," and "Rezon" as a "secretary" or "Prince." It has been suggested that the name means "Brother Secretary," "The Brother's Secret Monitor," etc., but nobody really knows the meaning or whether the two Hebrew words in conjunction have any. Many editions of *Ahiman Rezon* were published in England, Ireland, and America. The English edition of 1764 includes "a prayer repeated in the Royal Arch Lodge at Jerusalem," and states the compiler's belief that the Royal Arch was "the root, heart and marrow of Masonry."

Dermott was an invalid for many years, and there are references to the subject in the 'Antients' Grand Lodge minutes: in an entry of June 6, 1770, occurs the statement that he "was so ill with the gout that he was oblidg'd to be carried out of his bed (when incapable to wear shoes, stockings or even Britches) to do his duty at the Steward's Lodge," and rather more than seven years later, when he was resigning as Deputy Grand Master, he pleaded "his age, infirmities and twentysix years service," although actually he was to give many more years of service to the work that he loved. It was resolved on that occasion that a gold medal be struck and presented to Dermott, who had resigned as Secretary in 1771 and been appointed Deputy Grand Master. It was Dermott who was principally responsible for dubbing his opponents the 'Moderns,' although, from to-day's point of view, which side was the 'Moderns' and which the 'Antients' quite eludes the present writer, whose mood is echoed in John Byrom's Jacobite verse (late eighteenth century):

> God bless the king, I mean the faith's defender;
> God bless—no harm in blessing—the pretender;
> Who that pretender is, and who is King,—
> God bless us all,—that's quite another thing!

The Royal Arch mason will be especially interested in the frontispiece to Dermott's second edition (1764) of *Ahiman Rezon* reproduced in this volume as Plate III. In this are depicted two sets of armorial bearings, in one of which, described as "The Arms of ye most Antient & Honourable Fraternity, of Free and Accepted Masons," we find the Lion, Ox, Man, and Eagle, with the Ark as crest, and the Cherubim as supporters. The lion represented strength; the ox patience and assiduity; the man intelligence and understanding; and the eagle promptness and celerity—four emblems implying, we may reasonably conclude, that to the 'Antients' the Royal Arch was an integral part of the masonic Order.

The 'Antients,' as we have already indicated, had a most profound respect, amounting to warm affection, for the Royal Arch, the "root, heart and marrow" of their masonry. We are clearly led to assume that they were the first to practise it, but this assumption, as we have already said, does not rest on definite evidence. They liked it as individuals, but they liked it, too, officially as an asset in the quarrel between themselves and the 'Moderns'; it gave them the advantage of offering a fourth degree, and, indeed, their Grand Lodge became known as "the Grand Lodge of Four Degrees," a fact which was undoubtedly well in the mind of the 'Moderns' Grand Master, Lord Blayney, and his advisers when he erected in 1766 the Charter of Compact, constituting the first of all Grand Chapters. That the Royal Arch was often a considerable attraction to the 'Modern' mason is an easy inference, and we have such evidence as the instance of a 'Moderns' lodge in Bristol transferring its allegiance in 1768 because the Premier Grand Lodge had forbidden it to continue to practise the Royal Arch.

Many authors have boldly stated that the 'Antients' designed or adopted the Royal Arch as a mark of hostility to the 'Moderns' or as a means of gaining an advantage over its opponents. Quite a mild version of the accusation is the statement that the Royal Arch was "the second part of the old Master's grade, which Dermott made use of to mark a supposed difference between the 'Antients' and the 'Moderns.'" What is the statement worth? Dermott was exalted in Dublin, at a time (say, 1746) when the degree was already in existence and making progress in England.

As an Irish Royal Arch mason he is likely to have been introduced to the narrative of the *repair* of the Temple, whereas the English narrative was the *rebuilding*. It is difficult to avoid the conclusion that if Dermott had been responsible for the introduction or adoption of the Royal Arch in England the English tradition throughout two hundred years would have been in accordance with the Irish system. All the evidence is against accepting any suggestion that the 'Antients' devised the Royal Arch; they found it conveniently to their hand, warmly embraced it, and later recognized it as an asset in waging their quarrel with their opponents.

It is often commonly stated that under the 'Antients' Grand Lodge every private lodge was empowered by its charter to confer the Royal Arch Degree. Only in a sense is this true. The Royal Arch was not *specified* in the lodge charter, but was regarded as such a completely integral part of the masonic scheme as not to need mention. It was just taken for granted. And to that statement must be added a further one: under their ordinary charters or warrants, the 'Antients,' the Irish and many of the Scottish lodges, and some few of the 'Moderns' lodges believed they had the right to confer any and every masonic degree they pleased!

What is claimed to be the oldest 'Antients' warrant in existence, quite typical in its references to Installation and St John's Day, is of the date 1758, and was issued to Kent Lodge, then No. 9 (now No. 15), founded in 1752 at Spitalfields, London. It empowers the founders "to form and hold a Lodge of Free and Accepted (York) Masons... and in such Lodge, admit, Enter, and make according to the Honourable Custom of the Royal Craft... to nominate, Chuse and Instal their Successors, etc., etc., etc., such Instalations to be on every St John's Day, during the Continuance of the Lodge for ever." But the *laws* and *regulations* of the 'Antients' Grand Lodge made good any possible omission from its charters, for in them the Royal Arch was designated the "fourth degree." Towards the end of the century it was laid down "that Members of Grand Lodge, and all warranted Lodges, so far as they have the ability and numbers, have an undoubted right to exercise all the degrees of the Antient Craft."

The first official reference to the Royal Arch Degree is in the 'Antients' minutes of 1752. The Grand Committee had met at the Griffon Tavern, Holborn, London, on March 4 of that year, with John Gaunt, Master of Lodge No. 5, in the chair and Dermott acting for the first time as Grand Secretary. It is the second meeting recorded in the minute-book. The one and only minute of the meeting voices a formal complaint brought by five Brethren against Thomas Phealon and John Macky (Mackey) that they had

> initiated many persons for the mean consideration of a leg of Mutton for dinner or supper, to the disgrace of the Ancient Craft, that it was difficult to discover who assisted them if any, as they seldom met twice in the same Alehouse. That Macky was an Empiric in phisic; and both impostors in Masonry. That upon examining some brothers whom they pretend to have made Royal-Archmen, the parties had not the least Idea of that secret. That Doctor Macky (for so he was called) pretended to teach a Masonical Art by which any man could (in a moment) render himself Invisible. That the Grand Secret[y] had examined Macky, at the house of Mr. James Duffy, Tobacconist, in East Smithfield who was not a Mason and that Macky appear'd incapable of making an Apprentice with any degree of proprety. Nor had Macky the least Idea or knowledge of Royal Arch Masonry. But instead he had told the people whom he deceived, a long story about 12 white Marble stones &.& and that the Rain Bow was the Royal Arch, with many other absurdities equally foreign and Ridiculous—The Grand Committee Unanimously Agreed and Ordered that neither Thomas Phealon nor John Mackey be admitted into any Antient Lodge during their natural lives.

Another of the very early references occurs later in this same year, a Grand Lodge minute of September 2, 1752, stating that, "The Lodge was Opened in Antient Form of Grand Lodge and every piece of Real freemasonry was traced and explained: except the Royal Arch, by the Grand Secretary."

Seven years later, on March 2, 1759, we get a hint of the coming of regulations; a general meeting of Master Masons having been "convened to compare and regulate things," it was ordered that "the Masters of the Royal Arch shall also be summoned to meet and regulate things relative to that most valuable branch of the craft."

Some early evidence of the undoubtedly long and close association of the 'Antients' with the Grand Lodge of Ireland is afforded by a Grand Lodge minute of June 2, 1762: "Order'd that a Constant Correspondence shall be kept with the Grand Lodge of Ireland." The minute further recited that, the Irish Grand Lodge having agreed not to admit any Sojourner from England (as a member, petitioner, etc.) without a certificate of his good behaviour under the seal of the 'Antient' Grand Lodge in London, it was now agreed that an Irish Sojourner should likewise produce a proper certificate before he could be admitted as a member or receive any part of the General Charity. This reciprocal arrangement was aimed at ensuring that only Brethren of 'Antient' persuasion, whether English or Irish, should be admitted or helped, and it is fully in keeping with the seventh regulation in the edition of *Ahiman Rezon* published two years later (1764), given in the form of question and answer:

> *7th.* Whether it is possible to initiate or introduce a Modern Mason into a Royal Arch Lodge (the very essence of Masonry) without making him go through the Antient ceremonies?
> *Answer.* No!

The close correspondence and association between the 'Antients' on the one hand and the Irish and Scots Grand Lodges on the other was not free from anomalies (very little in the relationship of the 'Antients' with other masonic bodies was). The Irish and Scots viewed the 'Antients' with a friendly eye, but looked askance at the 'Moderns,' and at this distance of time, when so much is hidden from us and so much of what we do see is possibly misunderstood, we may blame chiefly the affectation of superiority by the Premier body and its most unfortunate transposition of the signs of recognition, for in their *official* attitude to matters of ritual the 'Moderns' agreed much more closely with the Irish and Scots than the 'Antients' did, strange as this may seem.

It might well be asked: If the 'Antients' became innovators—at any rate, in the eyes of the 'Moderns'—by adopting certain ceremonies which officially were not recognized or practised by the 'Moderns,' must it be taken for granted that in matters of ceremonial and the working of degrees the Irish and the Scots followed the example set by the 'Antients'? Otherwise how could it come about that the 'Antients,' the Irish, and the Scots were all three in accord—an agreement that is so very obvious when reading at first hand the minutes of the 'Antients' Grand Lodge? How came it that, of the four, the 'Moderns' were the 'one out'? It is true that the Irish and the Scots *appear* to have approved the 'Antients' ceremonials, but—a big but, too—while the Irish worked the Third Degree and gave to certain added degrees what might seem to be their natural home, it was a long time before they would *officially* countenance the Royal Arch. This is proved by the first officially recorded notice taken by the Irish Grand Lodge of that ceremonial, to be found in a resolution of 1786: "that it is highly improper for a Master Masons' Lodge... to enter upon their books any Transactions relative to the Royal Arch." This might have meant merely that it was desirable for two sets of transactions to be kept in two separate books, but it does not read quite so sweetly as that, and in any case it indicated far more sympathy with the 'Moderns' than with the 'Antients' point of view. (Indeed, the 'Moderns' had issued similar instructions eighteen years before, as mentioned in the next section.) Should the reader instance against this assumption that the Royal Arch had been worked in Ireland during much of the eighteenth century, then it must be made clear that such history is largely of *unofficial* happenings in certain lodges that felt themselves able to disregard the wishes of their Grand Lodge. And this applies with equal force to Scotland, in which country the lodges were slow and far from unanimous in adopting even the Third Degree and, further, were mostly bitterly opposed to the Installation ceremony. (Scots lodges adopted that ceremony as late as 1865, under an instruction from their Grand Lodge.) Not until 1816 did the Scots have a Grand Chapter, not till 1829 the Irish.

Before we can discuss further the attitude of the 'Antients' we must take a fairly comprehensive view of the 'Moderns' in their relationship to the Royal Arch.

Section Five

THE 'MODERNS' MASONS AND THE ROYAL ARCH

THE Grand Lodge of 1717 was generally known by its opponents as the 'Moderns,' and by that unfortunate name history still knows them. Their official attitude of indifference to the Royal Arch may have largely turned, as the years went by, upon the zealous adoption by their opponents of the 'new' ceremonial. Officially they regarded the 'Antients' as 'irregular' and 'illegal,' would not therefore countenance them, and threatened any of their own members with the 'severest censure' for associating masonically with them. Visitors to 'Moderns' lodges were compelled to take an oath on the V.S.L. that they had been regularly made in a lodge constituted under the premier Grand Lodge, or, if they had not been so made, to submit to be reinitiated. Naturally the 'Antients' bitterly retaliated in the same way.

In such an atmosphere as this it was unlikely that the 'Moderns' Grand Lodge would look with a kindly eye upon a degree with which the rival body was closely identified, and there is an indication of this in some curious happenings centred around a lodge that met in 1755 at Ben Jonson's Head, Pelham Street, Spitalfields, London. This lodge, founded as far back as 1732 at the Nag's Head, South Audley Street, West London, must have had a somewhat chequered career, and was erased in 1755. The happenings are mentioned in the 1787 edition of *Ahiman Rezon*, while in Dr George Oliver's *Revelations of a Square* (1855) are given further details, although these must be looked at somewhat narrowly. We have drawn upon both of these sources, and believe that the story as now told represents the approximate truth. Certain members of the lodge "had been abroad and had received extraordinary benefits on account of Antient Masonry." This Dr Oliver embroiders, and says (on unknown evidence) that these Brethren brought back with them certain rituals, including that of Ramsay's Royal Arch, and these they practised secretly every third lodge night under the designation of 'Antient Masonry.' Dr Oliver's story is that Dr Manningham, the Deputy Grand Master, was reluctantly admitted on one of these occasions, and he in due course reported that the ceremony he had witnessed was a reconstruction of Ramsay's Royal

Arch (how could he know this?) to which had been transferred the real landmarks of a Master Mason. W. J. Hughan, much more cautious, says that the working in the Ben Jonson Lodge probably referred to the Royal Arch and that the necessary changes would be in the Third Degree, but even his statement is nothing more than guesswork. Another version is that Dr Manningham with other Brethren called at the lodge and was refused admission; consequently a complaint was made at the next meeting of Grand Lodge, and as a result the lodge was severely censured and instructed that any Brother should be eligible for admission as a visitor on any of its regular nights. The lodge resented the censure, issued a manifesto accusing the Grand Lodge of partiality, innovation, and deviation from the ancient landmarks, and publicly renounced allegiance to it. The sequel was an unanimous resolution of Grand Lodge on St John the Baptists' Day 1755 to erase the lodge from the list. This is a celebrated case, but amounts to just this: the Ben Jonson Lodge insisted on working a ceremonial unknown to the 'Moderns'—possibly and even probably an early form of the Royal Arch—and, in consequence, was erased.

The official attitude notwithstanding, many 'Moderns' lodges did work a Royal Arch ceremonial, evidence thereof being the oldest English minute recording the raising of Brethren to the Royal Arch Degree. This minute is of a 'Moderns' lodge, then No. 220, meeting at the Crown, Christmas Street, Bristol, in 1758, obviously a lodge of the Traditioner type (see p. 50). Grand Lodge is not known to have taken any steps against this lodge, and we may safely assume that from some such period as this, or even earlier, many 'Moderns' lodges were working the Royal Arch. As an indication that their Grand Lodge could not have been unaware of what was going on but thought it better to adopt an attitude of studied indifference, let us adduce one of the most quoted phrases in the history of freemasonry. It occurs in a written reply by Samuel Spencer, the 'Moderns' Grand Secretary in 1759, to an Irish Brother who asked for charity: "Our Society is neither Arch, Royal Arch or Antient, so that you have no right to partake of our Charity"—a statement which may have been icily correct, but was just a gift to his opponents, whose Grand Secretary, Laurence Dermott, gladly incorporated it in his records. The petitioner, William Carrall or Carroll, "a certified sojourner in distress," coming from Dublin and possibly unaware of the division in English freemasonry, petitioned the Premier Grand Lodge for help, which unfortunately was not given him. But let us be fair in this matter; in view of the reciprocal agreement mentioned in the preceding section (see p. 60) would any English 'Modern' have fared any better in Dublin either then or, say, only three years later? The same Grand Secretary, Spencer, wrote in 1767 to a Brother in Frankfurt who was making inquiries: "The Royal

Arch is a society which we do not acknowledge and which we hold to be an invention to introduce innovation and to seduce the brethren." There speaks the *official* Spencer, but the unofficial Spencer had been exalted and admitted a joining member of a prominent chapter the year before! And the anomaly is all the more marked when we bear in mind that Samuel Spencer's Grand Master, Lord Blayney, had only recently erected the first Grand Chapter.

In 1768 Samuel Spencer's successor, Thomas French, in a letter to the Master of Sun Lodge, Bristol, said:

> There is only one circumstance in your minutes which you are requested to correct, and that concerns Royal Arch Masonry, which comes not under our inspection. You are desired never to insert the transactions thereof in your Regular Lodge Books, nor to carry on the business of that degree on your stated Lodge nights.

The Charter of Compact carries French's signature. Another signatory of the Charter, James Heseltine, one of the best of the Grand Secretaries of the day and at one time an officer of the Grand Chapter, writing to J. Peter Gogel, Past Grand Master of Frankfurt in 1774, did, indeed, acknowledge that the Royal Arch is "part of Masonry"; he clearly puts the anomalous position in which he found himself:

> It is true that many of the Fraternity belong to a Degree in Masonry which is said to be higher than the other, and is called Royal Arch . . . I have the honour to belong to this Degree . . . but it is not acknowledged in Grand Lodge, and all its emblems and jewels are forbidden to be worn there. . . . You will thus see that the Royal Arch is a private and distinct society. It is part of Masonry but has no connection with Grand Lodge and this is the only further Degree known to us in England.

And only twenty-one years before the Craft Union we find the 'Moderns' Grand Lodge resolving (November 21, 1792) "That this Grand Lodge do agree with its Committee that Grand Lodge has nothing to do with the proceedings of the Society of Royal Arch Masons."

The Unofficial Attitude

Many students of repute have held the opinion that the 'Moderns' worked the Royal Arch in London and perhaps in the provinces long before the 'Antients' did so. Henry Sadler thought that, "notwithstanding that the Royal Arch was first mentioned by Dermott in the records of the 'Antients,' it was not generally adopted by them until some years after it had become exceedingly popular with the 'Moderns.'" Alas! where is the evidence in support? We simply do not know who first

PLATE VI

TWO DECORATIVE APRONS OF THE LATE EIGHTEENTH CENTURY

Left: On flap, the arms of the 'Moderns'; on apron itself, the five-pointed star of the 'Antients.' *Right:* Printed apron (dated 1795) popular in its day and comparable with banner shown in Plate XIV. The original is hand-coloured.

By courtesy of United Grand Lodge

PLATE VII

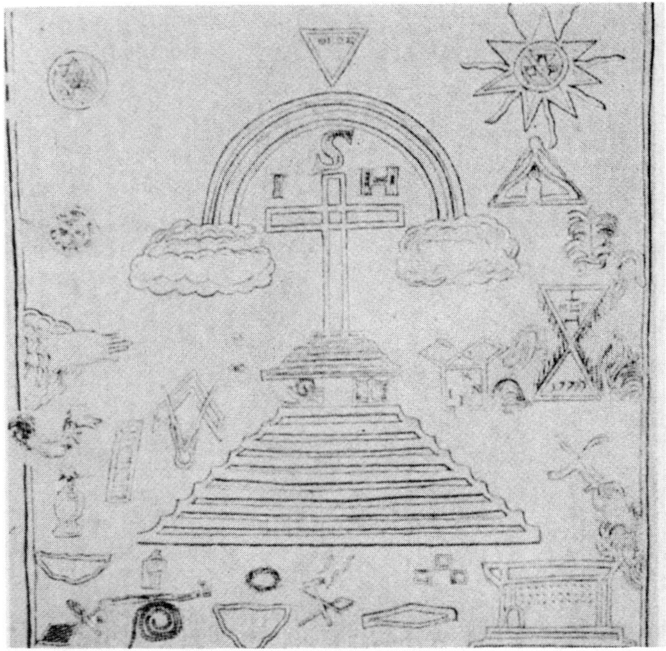

THE KIRKWALL SCROLL

Small portions of a scroll painted in colours (date, 1760–80), the property of Scottish Lodge Kirkwall Kilwinning, No. 38[2], founded 1736. (See p. 241.)

By courtesy of Quatuor Coronati Lodge

worked the Royal Arch, but, judging from the known circumstances, the present author tends to give the 'Antients' the credit. Their Grand Lodge minutes of 1752 (already quoted) cannot be forgotten, but we certainly find the oldest record of the raising of Candidates, in England, in connexion with a 'Moderns' lodge—that at the Crown Inn, Christmas Street, Bristol, to which reference has been made at p. 50. The day was Sunday, the date August 13, 1758; four other meetings of this lodge were held, also on Sundays, during the next twelve months, but there are no later mentions of the Royal Arch in these minutes, and it is possible that Grand Lodge had warned the lodge not to continue in its new course. It is known that some or many lodges owning allegiance to the 'Moderns' practised an 'Antient' form of working and had considerable respect for their opponents' customs and traditions, a feeling that was far from being reciprocated, and it is not without significance that a Brother in Wakefield wrote to somebody apparently connected with the 'Moderns' Grand Lodge in London, asking to be sent a copy of *Ahiman Rezon* (the 'Antients' Constitutions).

Much has always been made of the fact that the 'Antients' worked the Royal Arch without specific authorization in their warrants. But what of the 'Moderns'? Did they not (until such time as the separate chapter became the vogue, say, in the 1770's or even later), did they not work the Royal Arch in their private lodges? They too had no specific warrants! The only difference is that in one camp the lodges were doing it with implied and understood authority and in the other without! Thomas Dunckerley, a high officer and the opposite number to Laurence Dermott ('Antients' Grand Secretary), conferred the Royal Arch Degree in private lodges which could not possibly have been authorized to work it; a certificate issued to him in February 1768 by a lodge in Plymouth Dock (Devonport) states that he had presided as Master for two years, "during which time his Masonic skill, knowledge and experience hath been manifested in the care he hath taken in Governing, Instructing and Improving said Lodge in the several degrees of E.P. ∴ F.C. ∴ ∴ M.M. ∴ ∴ ∴ & R.A. ∴ ∴ ∴ ∴." The lodge issued this certificate at a time before the Grand Chapter had begun to issue warrants for private chapters: quite obviously Dunckerley was doing as many other Masters and lodges were doing—he was working the Royal Arch ceremony in his Craft lodge and taking for granted the complete regularity of his course.

As from the erection of the Grand Chapter in 1766 Brethren could regularize themselves by taking a warrant from the Grand Chapter and founding a private chapter. But the lodges showed no undue haste to put themselves right in this way, for even seven years after the coming of Grand Chapter the warranted private chapters were only twenty or so, surely a small number in relation to the Craft lodges which continued, on their own authority, to confer the degree. As definite instances we may quote the Anchor and Hope Lodge, No. 37, Bolton, founded in 1732, which worked the degree from 1767 until a warrant for a chapter was issued in 1785, and the Lodge of St John, No. 191, founded in Manchester in 1769 (meeting in Bury since 1845), which at a very much later date was continuing to work the degree in lodge, and did not have at any time a chapter associated with it.

There is a sequel to all this in the warranting of chapters in considerable number in the closing years of the eighteenth century, but that is a matter for a later section.

Masters' Lodges

It has commonly been advanced that Masters' Lodges, of which first recorded mention is made in the 1730's, played a part in the early development of the Royal Arch. It is accepted that these lodges came into being to meet a need of their day—namely, to raise Fellow Crafts to the Third Degree, the Hiramic Degree having only late in the 1720's reached some of the lodges, few of which knew it well enough to be able to confer it. It is reasonably assumed that Fellow Crafts wishing to be 'passed' to the Master Mason's grade often resorted to the Masters' Lodges, where the ceremony was worked by particularly keen and knowledgeable Brethren, but as from the middle of the eighteenth century the ordinary lodges were able to work the degree. Consequently, as Third Degree lodges pure and simple, the Masters' Lodges had now served their purpose, and if and where they continued to exist they had to find other employment.

What that employment was nobody knows. There has been plenty of guessing, plenty of downright assertion, but (and here the writer is supported by J. Heron Lepper, no mean student of Royal Arch history) we have no evidence—no positive, definite evidence—that it was the conferment of the Royal Arch Degree. Only a relatively small number of Masters' Lodges were at work in the second half of the eighteenth century. Between 1760 and 1780, for example, the most likely period of their being used as Royal Arch lodges (if they ever were so used), seven are on record in the 1760's, of which six met once a month and one every two months, and only six in the 1770's, of which five met once a month and one quarterly. So in one decade, so far as is known, only seventy-eight and in the other only sixty-four Royal Arch meetings could have been available in each year to Brethren looking to the Masters' Lodges for Exaltation—this at a time when both the lodges and increasingly the chapters of the 'Moderns' were exalting Brethren in numbers. (The

'Antients,' making their Royal Arch masons in their ordinary lodges, had no use for Masters' Lodges.)

There is a feeling that late in the century Master Masons could have gone to the Masters' Lodges to be made *virtual* Past Masters for the purpose of qualifying them as Royal Arch Candidates, but there is no evidence of it. At different times in, but not all through, the thirteen years immediately preceding the Union five Masters' Lodges met monthly and six quarterly, all of them apparently disappearing with the Union. Even if the possibility is conceded that Masters' Lodges worked the Royal Arch in the second half of the eighteenth century it is fair to assume that any part they played in the history and development of the Royal Arch was negligible. It is likely (again no evidence) that they worked some of the many added degrees known late in the eighteenth century.

The student may be informed that the "somewhat tantalizing" subject of the Masters' Lodges is well treated by John Lane in *A.Q.C.*, vol. i, while the present author offers in vol. lxvii of the same transactions a review of the existing evidence.

'*Arching*'

'Arching' was a commonly used term to signify what is now called 'Exaltation,' and an early use of it is in the minutes of a Bolton lodge in 1766, where from each of nine Brethren 5*s*. 3*d*. was "Received for Arching." Unanimity Lodge, Wakefield, charged a Brother a fee "for the Arches" in 1766, the plural form agreeing with an idea quite general in that day and one that is exemplified on many old Royal Arch jewels. An old manuscript ritual of Sincerity Chapter, Taunton (warranted 1819), contains many references to candidates "passing through the Arches and back again." There must be many available references on similar lines.

Section Six

THE PREMIER GRAND CHAPTER

THE erection of a Grand Chapter some time late in the eighteenth century was more or less inevitable, but it came sooner and somewhat differently from what might have been expected. It is obvious that late in the 1760's many distinguished Brethren of the 'Moderns' were entering the Order, but in what might be regarded as an irregular manner, for there was no authority that could issue charters to chapters, and the 'Moderns' Grand Lodge would have been horrified at any suggestion that it should do anything to regularize the increasingly common practice of making Royal Arch masons in its Craft lodges. Meanwhile 'Antient' Brethren were being quite regularly and properly exalted in their ordinary lodges, solidly behind them being their Grand Lodge, enjoying the kudos and solid advantage of being known as the "Grand Lodge of the Four Degrees." 'Modern' Masons had a need for a Grand Chapter, both to regularize a growing practice and to meet the competition of their earnest and energetic rivals. And that Grand Chapter came in 1766, probably as warmly welcomed by the rank and file as it was keenly resented by some of their leaders and officials.

Lord Blayney, Grand Master of the 'Moderns', recently exalted in a new chapter—later the Excellent Grand and Royal Chapter—entered into a Charter of Compact which brought into existence the first Grand Chapter of Royal Arch masons, the first not only in England, but in the world. That Charter was signed in 1766, although in masonic literature the date has, until very recently, been given as one year later, and it will therefore be necessary to explain the circumstances in which it is thought that the date became altered, probably within a year of the signing of the Compact.

The reader may excusably confuse one Grand Chapter with another. Let us briefly recapitulate them. The first Grand Chapter was that promoted by Lord Blayney, Grand Master, in 1766 under the title of "The Grand and Royal Chapter" or "The Excellent Grand and Royal Chapter." In 1795–96 the title was altered to "The Grand Lodge of Royal Arch Masons," and in 1801 again altered, this time to "The Supreme Grand Chapter." The 'Antients' founded a so-called Grand Chapter (see Section seven) in 1771. Another was the short-lived York Grand Chapter or Grand Chapter of All England (its one minute is dated 1778). The present "Supreme Grand Chapter of Royal Arch Masons of England" was formed by a union in 1817 of the original Grand Chapter of 1766 and the Royal Arch masons under the former Grand Lodge of the 'Antients.' Ireland founded its Grand Chapter in 1829 under the title of "The Supreme Grand Royal Arch Chapter of Ireland," and Scotland its Grand Chapter in 1817 under the title of "The Supreme Grand Royal Arch Chapter of Scotland."

"The Excellent Grand and Royal Chapter"

Most of the hitherto accepted stories of the way in which the first Grand Chapter came to be erected by Charter of Compact are, it is feared, somewhat inaccurate. The most reliable account available is that given in two valuable contributions to *A.Q.C.* (vols. lxii, lxiv) by J. R. Dashwood, to whose reproduction of the Grand Chapter minutes with his notes thereon, and to A. R. Hewitt's Address to Grand Chapter in 1966, we are indebted for much of the information that follows.

It has been commonly understood that the first Grand Chapter came into being as a result of Lord Blayney's constituting the Caledonian Chapter into a Grand and Royal Chapter; the present author fell into the same mistake. It is true that the Caledonian Chapter had much to do with the bringing into existence of the new Chapter whose members entered into the compact with Lord Blayney; both of these chapters had a close connexion with the Caledonian Lodge, which started life as an 'Antients' lodge, but seceded in its second year and in 1764 obtained a charter from the Premier Grand Lodge, its then number being 325 and its present one 134. The first Caledonian Chapter, which may possibly have antedated the lodge of the same name, did not have a long life and a new Caledonian Chapter was in existence by 1780, but even that one is not to-day's, the present one dating back only to 1872 and being attached to Caledonian Lodge, No. 134; this lodge has a distinguished history, among its members in early days being William Preston, the famous masonic author and lecturer.

The first minute-book of the Excellent Grand and Royal Chapter covers the period from March 22, 1765, to December 11, 1767, inclusive, the writer of the minutes being the first Scribe E., Francis Flower, who died within a few days of the last entry. The Chapter had at first no specific name. In contradiction of many earlier and inaccurate accounts it is well to say that, although this Chapter might appear to be a reincarnation of the Royal Arch activities of the Caledonian Lodge, this is now known to be impossible. Of twenty-nine original members of that lodge whose names are known not one is included among the early members of the new Chapter—not even the name one might most expect to find there, that of William Preston. By-laws of February 12, 1766, make it plain that the new Chapter was not the Caledonian Chapter, although it was under some obligation to that body.

We can well suppose that the new Chapter was formed for the definite purpose of being erected at an early date into a Grand Chapter. Its name at its inception, as already said, is unknown, and it is convenient to call it straight away the Excellent Grand and Royal Chapter, although it could not have functioned as such until it had received its authority from the Charter of Compact signed in its second year.

In the early pages of its first minute-book is a self-conferred charter under which the new Chapter considered itself entitled to act; this appears to have been agreed at a meeting on June 12, 1765, and it was signed by twenty-nine Brethren at the next meeting (July 10), a further fourteen signatures being appended from time to time up to March 11, 1767. The manifesto recited that the Companions had resolved to hold a chapter at the Turk's Head Tavern, Gerrard Street, Soho, London, on the second Friday ("Wednesday" was crossed out) of every month at six o'clock in the evening, and that every member should pay two guineas ("twentysix shillings" crossed out) annually towards expenses:

> Every Brother who desires to pass the Arch, or to become a Member of this Chapter must be regularly proposed in open Chapter: and it is expected that the Member proposing such a One, be able to give a satisfactory account of the Brother so proposed. Any Member may without offence demand a Ballot: and if on being had there shall be found more than two negatives against such Brother, he shall not be permitted to pass the Arch in, or become a Member of, this Chapter.

"Every Brother passing the Arch in this Chapter" and also every joining member paid two guineas ("one guinea" crossed out), while visitors admitted "on very particular occasions" paid half a guinea each to the current expense. The penalty for behaving indecently or disorderly in the Chapter or being intoxicated with liquor therein was admonishment or, if incorrigible, expulsion. A Brother in arrears later than the fourth meeting of the current year was no longer deemed a member. Officers were elected at the first meeting after the Feast of St John the Evangelist every year, and continued in authority one whole year:

> And if any Officer is absent on any night of meeting, the E:Z.L: shall appoint any able and experienced Brother to supply his place for that Night.

And if the E:Z.L: shall unavoidably be absent, the next Officer in Authority shall officiate for him, or appoint who he judges proper to do it. And the Brother so officiating shall in all respects have ample Authority for that Night.

(Obviously, then, at that early date there was no esoteric Installation of Principal Officers.)

The manifesto with its regulations was followed by a set of seven resolutions, evidently of the same date (1765), and it is of advantage to give these exactly as they appear in the minute-book:

> 1st On Chapter night, the Companions being discreetly convened in the Antichamber, the P.H.Z.L. & L. together with the E. & N. and the Principal S^r. shall go into the Chapter Room, and being properly invested shall open the Chapter in due form. After which they shall come forth to the Companions in Order, who shall receive them with proper respect. And immediately the procession shall begin.
>
> 2nd That the E.G.s be clothed in proper Robes, Caps on their Heads, and adorned with proper Jewells.—No Aprons.
>
> 3rd That the S^{rs} appear with the emblems of their employment.
>
> 4th That the Secretarys be adorned with proper Jewells, etc. [The word "Robes" has been interpolated at a later date.]
>
> 5th That all the Companions wear Aprons, (except those appointed to wear Robes) and the Aprons shall be all of one sort or fashion. Vis. White Leather Indented round with Crimson Ribbon and strings of the same, with a TH in gold properly displayed on the Bibb. & Purple Garters Indented with Pink.
>
> 6th The Secretarys shall order all Liquor and refreshments and take proper account of the same. But no Liquor &c. shall be brought into the Chapter room, during Chapter, on any pretense whatsoever.
>
> 7th The Officers shall preserve their stations and Authority during the remainder of the Evening, after the Chapter is closed, for the sake of good order, etc.

A later by-law seems to give an advantage in fees, either as a joining member or a visitor, to Brethren exalted before June 12, 1766, or in the Caledonian Chapter or in a chapter in the country, or beyond the seas. From this it is plain that the Excellent Grand and Royal Chapter was *not* the Caledonian Chapter, and that it dated its own inauguration from June 12, 1765, and that any earlier meetings were preliminary meetings, but later minutes strongly support the suggestion that there was a close amity between the new Chapter and the Caledonian Chapter.

Many Exaltations took place, including one in April 1765, of Dr John James Rouby, whose Royal Arch jewel, now in the Grand Lodge museum in London, is the earliest at present known and bears the date

1766, although he was exalted a year earlier (see Plate VIII). At the meeting of June 12, 1765, officers were elected, their appellations being:

Bro^r. Keck Senr.	P.H.	⎫
Bro^r. Maclean	P.Z.	⎬ Excellent Grands
Bro^r. Aynson	P.I.	⎭
Bro^r. Galloway	Principal Sojourner	
Bro^r. Flower	E.	⎱
Bro^r. Jno. Hughes	N.	⎰ Secretaries.

It will be noted that P.Z. comes second in the list, although it is known that Maclean ruled the Chapter, but the order above given is the same as that found in the Toast in the 'Antients' *Ahiman Rezon*, 1756, and as used much later by the York Chapter in 1772. Elsewhere in the minute-book of the Excellent Grand and Royal Chapter the method of designating the Three Principal Officers varies considerably, and in the one year, 1766, we find the first two officers are P.Z. and P.H., but the third is given in one case as P.I., in another as J.P., and in still another as I.H.P. In all these titles the letter P stands for "Prince, Prophet, and Priest."

In expenses endorsed by an Audit Committee on March 21, 1766, occur these items: Robes, £8 2s.; 24 Aprons, £5 4s.; "Copper Plate and 1000 Bills" (presumably Summons blanks), £3 6s.; 3 Candles, 2s. 6d.; Painting the Lodge, 10s. 6d.; Brass Letters, £1; Floor Cloth, 17s. 6d.; Inkstand and Stationery, 10s. 6d.; and a "Cable Tow 15 yd. long made of Purple Blue & Scarlet Worsted, and a Tassell," £1 1s. (The 'Lodge' was probably the lodge board, the tracing-board.)

At the anniversary feast Thomas Dunckerley attended the Chapter for the first time, was promptly elected a member, but paid no joining fee; he has been assumed to have been the moving spirit in the new Chapter, but this is not supported by available evidence. The Chapter was seven months old when he became a member; he was immediately elected Third Principal, but made very few attendances, even after he had gone through the Principal Chair.

Lord Blayney Head of the Royal Arch

A most important era in Royal Arch masonry began on June 11, 1766, on which day twenty-seven companions witnessed the Exaltation of Cadwallader, Lord Blayney, in the new Chapter. Automatically, it appears, he immediately became head of the Royal Arch and First Principal of the Chapter, and he did in fact preside at the next three meetings, all held in July, the first of them on the 2nd of the month, being the day on which James Heseltine, then Grand Steward, and three others were exalted.

Heseltine became Grand Secretary in the Craft three years later and was a keen spirit in the Chapter.

Cadwallader, ninth Lord Blayney, an Irishman, 'Moderns' Grand Master from 1764 to 1766, was born in 1720, succeeded to the family title in 1761, was by profession an army officer, was a Major-General in 1765 and later Commander-in-Chief, Munster, which office he held at the time of his death in 1775. He was initiated when young, but in which lodge is not known, and served in 1764 as Master of the ('Moderns') New Lodge, Horn Tavern, Westminster, No. 313, which took the name Royal Lodge in 1767 and in 1824 united with the Alpha Lodge (founded in 1722), now the Royal Alpha, No. 16. The inspiration and driving force behind him may have been Thomas Dunckerley; these two with Laurence Dermott of the opposite camp are the three great names in the formative period of the Royal Arch. But we are very much in the dark as to the parts played by some of the signatories to the Charter of Compact, and it is possible that a few of them—notably John Maclean and James Galloway—did as much as Dunckerley, or even more, to make possible the founding of a Grand Chapter. Lord Blayney was elected Grand Master of Ireland on May 6, 1768, but resigned before June 24 of the same year.

Lord Blayney proved a good Grand Master in the Craft, and during his office constituted seventy-four lodges, of which nineteen, bearing honoured names, are in to-day's list. In his presence the Duke of Gloucester was initiated in Lord Blayney's lodge at the Horn Tavern, Westminster, the first Initiation of a Royal Prince on English soil since that of Frederick, Prince of Wales, in 1757. Lord Blayney obviously had a great regard for Thomas Dunckerley, appointed him to high office, and we can well suppose regarded him as his chief masonic mentor. Blayney was strongly 'Antient' in sympathies, and evidently favoured the softening of the 'Moderns' austere working. In support of that statement may be adduced his action—after witnessing in the Old Dundee Lodge, then No. 9, an Initiation not altogether to his liking—in requesting the members to alter their ceremonial in some particular, a request agreed to, but not without demur.

He was the first 'Moderns' Grand Master to acknowledge and foster the Royal Arch, but not the first Grand Master to become a Royal Arch mason, for the Hon. Brinsley Butler (later Earl of Lanesborough) was exalted during his year of office as Grand Master of Ireland, an equally difficult event to understand from any official point of view, for the Irish Grand Lodge had officially no more use for the Royal Arch than the Premier Grand Lodge of England had shown itself to have.

The Charter of Compact, 1766

Out of the new Chapter in which Lord Blayney had been exalted came, under his direction, the Grand Chapter of England, and it came in 1766, and not, as all the historians—Gould, Hughan, and Sadler among them—have stated, in the next year 1767. Masonic writers, including the present author, have helped to continue the mistake. Before explaining how the mistake arose it should be said that, although the major credit for the erection of England's first Grand Chapter has customarily been given to Lord Blayney, the most likely truth is that a few keen spirits, among them Thomas Dunckerley, promoted the scheme, and the Grand Master gave it his encouragement and personal authority, without which the scheme would have had but small chance of success.

At Lord Blayney's second meeting of the Chapter in which he had been exalted the famous Charter of Compact must have been decided upon, this being clear from indications in the minutes and in the Charter itself. The Charter, dated July 22, speaks of Lord Blayney as Grand Master. He was Grand Master in 1766, but not in 1767. The Charter is signed by the officers of the year 1766, not of the year 1767. "July 22" must have been of 1766 because there was no meeting of the Chapter on July 22 of 1767, nor did Lord Blayney attend the Chapter after July 30, 1766.

It is J. R. Dashwood's contention (see *A.Q.C.*, vol. lxiv) that the original Charter itself displays evidence that the dates have been tampered with, the effect being that "1766" is a trifle clumsily made to appear as "1767." The cost of engrossing the Charter, a very beautiful piece of work, was two guineas. The draft of the Charter was probably approved on July 22, and the engrossment was ready for signing by Lord Blayney and the officers present, other officers signing at a later date.

A further alteration was, quite skilfully, to insert the letter "P" before the words "Grand Master," the whole tenor of the document proving that this is an interpolation. J. R. Dashwood's suggested explanation of the true inwardness of the matter is that, although many Grand Officers had been exalted, it is well known (as reiterated in this book) that the 'Moderns' officially did not regard the Royal Arch with favour; it is reasonable to suppose that they may have heard with horror that their Grand Master had allowed himself to be exalted during his period of office, that he had become a Principal Officer of his Chapter, had entered into a Charter of Compact setting up a Grand Chapter with power to grant charters, and had even consented to be named as the M. E. Grand Master of Royal Arch Masonry. J. R. Dashwood thinks that some persons were determined to undo the worst of the damage by making it appear that Lord Blayney had acted not *officially* as Grand Master, but in his *private* capacity after he had laid down that office, and the easiest way of doing this was by postdating the Charter by a year, the letter "P" being inserted in front of the words "Grand Master" to suggest that Lord Blayney was no longer in office and was acting individually. The matter is dealt with at length in *A.Q.C.* at the references already given, and the interested reader can there study the matter and form his own judgment.

The Charter of Compact, a "Charter of Institution and Protection," instituted and erected

> [certain Excellent Brethren and Companions] to form and be, The Grand and Royal Chapter of the Royal Arch of Jerusalem ... with full power and absolute Authority ... to hold and convene Chapters and other proper Assemblies for the carrying on, improving and promoting the said benevolent and useful Work. And also to admit, pass and exalt in due form and according to the Rites and Ceremonies Time immemorial used and approved in and by that most Exalted and sacred Degree, and as now by them practised, all such experienced and discreet Masters Masons as they shall find worthy. ... And also to constitute, superintend and regulate other Chapters.

The Charter itself is a handsomely illuminated and engrossed document, twenty-five inches wide and thirty deep (see Plate IV). The faded writing is quite legible. It bears three coats of arms (Royal, Premier Grand Lodge, and Lord Blayney's), three hexalphas, nine triangles, the 'T-over-H' device, etc. It has thirty signatories, of whom nine, including Lord Blayney, Dunckerley, Allen, and Thomas French, affixed their seals. At or near the head of the Charter are the words commonly found on the early Grand Chapter documents, "The Most Enlightened East." In a central triangle appear the letters "I.N.," which some students have thought stand for the "Ineffable Name," but which more probably might represent "Jesus of Nazareth." The triangles, in their curious disposition, are held to represent the positions of the Three Principals, the Three Sojourners, Scribe E., Scribe N., and the Altar. Framed and glazed, it hangs in the Librarian's office in Freemasons' Hall, London, as becomes such a most important document.

John Allen, attorney of Clement's Inn, who at times acted as Deputy Grand Master in the Craft and whose seal and signature the Charter bears, not only, it is thought, drafted the document, but apparently retained it, for after his death it was found among his papers. Some time in the nineteenth century it was placed in a storeroom in Freemasons' Hall, where late in the century it was discovered.

The Charter bears the (altered) date "1767," the ordinary calendar year reckoned from the birth of Christ, and also a second date formed by adding 1767 to 4004 = 5771. Nowadays the year *Anno Domini* is converted to *Anno Lucis* by adding 4000.

The eighth 'clause' of the Charter states "that none calling themselves Royal Arch Masons shall be deemed any other than Masters in operative Masonry" (a term which in this connexion must obviously mean "Craft Masonry"). This assumption appears to echo the claim to superior status made in earlier years by the 'Scotch Masons' (see p. 39), and its presence in the Charter, besides strengthening any supposition that the earlier rite was related to the later one, may help us to arrive at an answer to a difficult question: how came it about that the new Grand Chapter, with no experience of esoteric Installation, was so soon to insist on a Past Master qualification in its Candidates? Is the answer, or some part of it, that, regarding itself as an association of Masters, it eagerly took a leaf from its opponent's book to ensure that only Masters entered into its membership? The argument may not be quite watertight, but the truth may well be somewhere in it!

Thomas Dunckerley

Thomas Dunckerley (or Dunkerley) is credited with being the 'master mind' that continued Lord Blayney's policy. Born in London in 1724 and later acknowledged as the natural son of the Prince of Wales, afterwards George II, "to whom he bore a striking resemblance," he died in Portsmouth in the year 1795. In a book-plate known to the Rev. A. F. A. Woodford he gives his name as Thomas Dunckerley Fitz-George. He is believed to have been initiated in 1754 in Lodge No. 31, meeting at the Three Tuns, Portsmouth. He was called to the bar at about fifty years of age, but probably did not practise, and as the circumstances of his birth had by this time become common property he was now admitted into high social circles. In his last days he was reduced to penury by the profligacy of his son, and on his death in 1795 his estate was valued for probate at only £300, although he had been living free in apartments in Hampton Court Palace and had received from the King a pension of £800 *per annum*, quite a sum in those days.

Dunckerley acquired considerable masonic experience, was a loyal officer of the premier Grand Lodge, although in sympathy with the 'Antients' working, and at various times was the Grand Master of eight different provinces and Grand Superintendent in the Royal Arch of twenty-eight counties.

There were early authors who credited Dunckerley with being the founder of Royal Arch masonry, obviously a ridiculous claim, but he did indeed take a leading and active part in its development. In his capacity of Provincial Grand Superintendent he took to Portsmouth in 1769 the warrant of constitution for a chapter in connexion with Lodge No. 259, and, while there, conferred for the first time on record the degrees of Mark Man and Mark Master Mason, which he himself had only recently received. He had some of the faults of the highly energetic worker, his zeal being inclined to run away with him, and we know that in 1777 the Grand Chapter criticized his action in exalting Brethren in Colchester otherwise than in a chartered chapter, and that in May 1780 he was again in trouble for having exceeded his powers ("with the utmost respect for Companion Dunckerley"), and it was finally decided to draw up a regular patent defining the powers of Grand Superintendents.

When the Provincial Grand Chapter for Dorsetshire, with Dunckerley as its Provincial Grand Master, met in 1781 to honour the birthday of the Prince of Wales the choir of St Peter's Church of that city sang a special hymn written for the occasion by Dunckerley. Of its seven verses here are two having clear Royal Arch implications:

> Thou who didst Persia's King command
> A Proclamation to extend;
> That Israel's sons might quit his land
> Their holy Temple to attend.
>   All hail! great Architect divine!
>   This Universal Frame is thine.

> Thy *watchful Eye* a length of time,
> That wond'rous CIRCLE did attend;
> The Glory and the Pow'r be thine,
> Which shall from Age to Age descend.
>   All hail! great Architect divine!
>   This Universal Frame is thine.

The attorney John Allen is believed, as already said, to have had a considerable hand in the drafting of the Charter of Compact. Of the highest standing, he was entrusted with the legal business of Grand Lodge in the 1770–80 period, and is thought to have prepared the conveyance of the property in Great Queen Street (including part of the site of the present Freemasons' Hall) which Grand Lodge bought in 1774.

Successors to Lord Blayney

While Lord Blayney was absent in December 1768 in Ireland on military duties he was continued or re-elected as "Grand Master of the Most Excellent Chapter or Fourth Degree," but was not able to attend to his duties. The Duke of Beaufort, who followed Lord Blayney as Grand Master in the Craft, was also inclined to the 'Antients' working, so much so that he encouraged the introduction of an esoteric Installation ceremony for Masters of Lodges, but it was not officially adopted until long afterwards. It will be shown in later sections how great a part the Craft Installation ceremony played in the development of the Royal Arch.

Owing to the continued absence of Lord Blayney, the Hon. Charles Dillon was elected in 1770 Grand Master of the Royal Arch, he being, at the same time, Deputy Grand Master in the Craft, but he did not attend Grand Chapter after his election and, as a consequence, in succeeding years the Grand Chapter elected not a Grand Master, but a Patron, who had the right to preside when present, although a Zerubbabel was elected to preside in his absence. Rowland Holt, Grand Warden in 1768 and later Deputy Grand Master, was the first Patron, and held that office until the Duke of Cumberland replaced him in 1774.

Many Grand Officers were exalted, among them Sir Peter Parker, Grand Warden, who became Deputy Grand Master of the Craft fifteen years later. H.R.H. the Duke of Cumberland, exalted December 12, 1772, became Patron a year or so later, and from 1782 to 1790 was Grand Master in the Craft.

The Earliest Warranted Chapters

The first eight chapters warranted by the Grand Chapter, all in 1769, are as follow:

1. The Restauration Lodge or Chapter of the Rock Fountain Shilo (at Brother Brooks' House in London).
2. The Euphrates Lodge or Chapter of the Garden of Eden (at Manchester).
3. The Lodge of Tranquility or Chapter of Friendship (at Portsmouth).
4. The Bethlehem Lodge or the Chapter of the Nativity (at Burnley, Lancs.).
5. The Cana Lodge or Chapter of the First Miracle (at Colne, Lancs.).
6. The Most Sacred Lodge or Chapter of Universality (at London).
6b. The Lodge of Intercourse or Chapter of Unanimity (at Bury, Lancs.).
7. The Lodge of Hospitality or Chapter of Charity (at Bristol).

(Some chapters must have worked under the authority of a dispensation until granted a proper warrant; as an example, a dispensation to form the Union Lodge and Chapter of Harmony at the Bedford Head, Maiden Lane, issued in 1770 by John Maclean of the Grand Chapter, is preserved at Freemasons' Hall, London.)

An important point arising from the consideration of this list has already been touched upon. The Royal Arch 'lodge' was in the course of becoming a 'chapter,' and it certainly looks as though the double title given to each body in the above list is meant to cover the eventual or inevitable translation. Obviously the Grand Chapter had no right or even a wish to establish Craft lodges. Its authority could not extend farther than the setting up of bodies devoted to the working of the Royal Arch. But there enters an anomaly or a serious question (as in so very many details of masonic history), for the *Craft* Lodge of Hospitality, Bristol, the last entry in the list, was warranted by the premier Grand Lodge under a dispensation of July 22, 1769, confirmed by a warrant of August 12. This is now the Royal Sussex Lodge of Hospitality, No. 187, meeting in Bristol, while the Chapter of Charity was given its charter from the Grand Chapter on December 8, 1769, and, bearing the same name, is still at Bristol and still anchored to Lodge No. 187. Curiously and nevertheless, the Royal Arch Charter authorized the double body "by the Title of the Lodge of Hospitality or Chapter of Charity," which is extremely difficult to understand, but there it is! It may, of course, be that the lodges named were the Craft lodges to which the chapters were attached or with which they were associated, but Lane's *Masonic Records* mentions only the last of them, the Lodge of Hospitality, and it is certain that the first of them, the Restauration Lodge, was never officially other than a chapter, and twenty-six years later was so called.

The rules of the Grand Chapter erected by Charter of Compact are practically those of the original Excellent Grand and Royal Chapter, and were written into the Compact itself (see the Appendix), but were revised and published many years later.

Events after the Founding of Grand Chapter

Following the founding of the first Grand Chapter came a formative period, one of considerable growth and development both in the 'Moderns' and the 'Antients' systems. The ritual continued to develop and by 1800 the Grand Chapter had issued 116 Warrants. Certain masonic terms were changing; the 'lodge' was in the course of becoming a 'chapter,' the Royal Arch 'Brother' of becoming a 'Companion'; and—but not very quickly or generally—the 'Candidate,' instead of being 'raised,' would be 'exalted.' The Grand Chapter began to issue charters to lodges authorizing them to work the Royal Arch, the charter to be attached to the warrant of the Lodge and so setting a pattern or custom in that respect strictly followed to-day.

In the Grand Chapter itself the Zerubbabel was, according to the minutes, "appropriately Invested and Installed," but we have no means of knowing what the Installation ceremony actually was, although it is strongly held that the Zerubbabel chair carried no secrets with it until the turn of the century, and in most places much later. At an Installation meeting on St John's Day in Winter in 1768

> the Officers resigned their several stations and delivered their Ensigns of Office to the M.E.Z. ... Brother Galloway was elected by Ballot into the Office of Z. ... and was appropriately Invested and Installed,

And on January 12, 1770,

> Brother Heseltine was by Ballot Elected into the Office of Z. ... and was duly Invested and Installed accordingly, making a most solemn promise on the occasion, according to ancient usage.

Some prominent masons were exalted in the Grand Chapter, among them Chevalier Bartholomew Ruspini in 1772, becoming its M.E.Z. in 1780. Ruspini's is the greatest name in the history of the masonic charities, for the Royal Cumberland Freemasons' School, from which developed the Royal Masonic Institution for Girls, the senior charity, was established in 1788 mainly by the exertions of this influential and energetic mason, who in private life was a well-established dentist. At a committee meeting held in 1777 Ruspini produced drawings of proposed new robes for the Principals. These drawings, with some alterations, were approved.

Some trouble behind the scenes must have prompted the Grand Chapter in 1773 to resolve unanimously

> that the Royal Arch Apron be disused in this Excellent Grand and Royal Chapter until the Grand Lodge shall permit the Companions of this Chapter to wear them in the Grand Lodge, and in all or private Freemasons' Lodges.

Which looks as though a fight to determine a higher status of the Royal Arch mason was proceeding; if this were the case the fight was lost, for there are no further minutes on the subject, the resolution was apparently quietly ignored, and the Companions soon resumed the wearing of their aprons in chapter.

James Heseltine had been exalted in the Excellent Grand and Royal Chapter and had signed the Charter of Compact, but this did not prevent his writing as Grand Secretary to a foreign correspondent in 1774 in the following terms:

> It is true that many of the Fraternity belong to a degree in Masonry which is said to be higher than the other, and is called Royal Arch. I have the honour to belong to this degree ... but it is not acknowledged in Grand Lodge, and all its emblems and jewels are forbidden to be worn there. ... You will see that the Royal Arch is a private and distinct society. It is a part of Masonry, but has no connection with Grand Lodge.

THE DEVELOPMENT OF THE ROYAL ARCH EMBLEM AND JEWEL

Left: Dr J. J. Rouby's jewel, the earliest known, made in 1766, the year in which it was authorized. *Right*: Jewel made by Thomas Harper, about sixty years later, by which time the T-over-H had become the triple tau.
By courtesy of United Grand Lodge and Quatuor Coronati Lodge respectively

PLATE IX

ANCIENT METAL PLATE
This plate was discovered in Northern India by Norman Hackney and bears hexalphas and Sanskrit words expressing Divine attributes. (See p. 243.)
By courtesy of the photographer, Norman Hackney

THE ALL-SEEING EYE IN WROUGHT-IRON ORNAMENT
From a chemist's shop in Vienna, date 1720 or earlier; suggestive of the eminence of this symbol in alchemy. (See p. 238.)
By courtesy of the photographer, Rudolph Halama, Vienna

Next year we find him writing:

> I have already told you a further degree, called Royal Arch, is known in England, in which the present Grand Officers are mostly members of the Chapter. They belong to it as a separate Society, without connection with Grand Lodge, and its explanations of Freemasonry are very pleasing and instructive.

During the period of the first Grand Chapter masonic meetings were occasionally convened by means of public advertisements. An announcement in an unidentified London newspaper states that a "Chapter will be held on Sunday evening next, at the house of Brother John Henrys, the Crown and Anchor in King Street, Seven Dials." Another advertisement calls a meeting of the Grand Chapter for the following Sunday, again at the Crown and Anchor, "in order for a Grand Installation."

Grand Chapter soon left the Turk's Head Tavern in Gerrard Street, Soho; in 1771 it went to the Mitre in Fleet Street, but moved four years later to the Freemasons' Coffee House, Great Queen Street, which stood upon some small part of the site now occupied by Freemasons' Hall and Connaught Rooms. The Chapter went into its new quarters in December 1775, in the May of which year had been laid the foundation stone of the first Freemasons' Hall.

The "Most Enlightened East" appears as the heading of the minutes in January 1776, and is also the heading of charters and certificates of that period, although the more usual heading of the minutes up to 1793 is "Grand and Royal Chapter of the Royal Arch of Jerusalem."

Grand Chapter had a strong social side, for in its early years its annual festival was followed by a ball and supper to which apparently not only Royal Arch masons but Master Masons and their ladies were invited; and of one of these occasions the Secretary's minutes related that "after an elegant supper, the evening concluded with that Harmony and Social Mirth which has ever been the peculiar criterion of Masons and True Citizens of the World." At a ball held in January 1782 "four hundred ladies and gentlemen were present," Ruspini acted as Master of Ceremonies, and Companion Ayrton composed the ode sung on the occasion.

To "form a complete code of laws and regulations not only for this Excellent Grand and Royal Chapter, but also for the subordinate Chapters," a committee was appointed, and its report was received in May 1778; the laws were finally approved in the following October, and copies are in existence. The laws and regulations were revised and reprinted in 1782; other editions were produced in 1796 and 1807, and a further edition appeared after the 'union', 1817.

Four Most Excellent Companions were appointed in 1778 to hold the Great Seal in Commission and to act as Inspectors-General, Thomas Dunckerley being one of them.

The Grand Officers in 1778 included a Patron (H.R.H. the Duke of Cumberland), three Grand Masters, a President of the Council, four Inspectors-General, a Correspondent General, a Treasurer, three Superintendents of Provinces, Past Masters Z., H., and J., a Chaplain, three Sojourners, two Scribes, two Stewards, a Standard Bearer, a Sword Bearer, an Organist, a Senior Janitor or Messenger, and a Junior Janitor or Common Door Keeper.

Appointments to the "past rank of Z." were made in 1778 and following years, a matter more particularly dealt with at p. 179.

An extraordinary petition for relief was received in 1784 from "John Vander Hey, Esq., Privy Counsellor to His Majesty of Prussia. Late Master of the Lodge Virtutis et Artis Amici at Amsterdam." He was voted five guineas.

The first of the stated Communications was apparently the general convention in 1785 of all Royal Arch masons in English chapters under the obedience of the Grand Chapter. It was attended by members of six chapters—namely, Cumberland, Caledonian, Fortitude, Canterbury, Philanthropic, and Colchester.

Unknown trouble must have lain behind a serious attempt made in 1793 by the Chapter of Emulation to induce Companions to withdraw from Grand Chapter. At a Grand Convention held on May 10 it was resolved

> that the thanks of Grand Chapter be transmitted to the several Chapters that have expressed in such handsome terms, their determination to preserve inviolate the union subsisting between them and the Grand and Royal Chapter of the Royal Arch of Jerusalem, in opposition to the Innovation proposed in the circular Letter sent to those Chapters by the Chapter of Emulation.

Emulation Chapter, No. 16, founded in London in 1778, had issued a 'Memorial' in the form of a circular letter, and for its attempt to create schism in the Order paid the penalty of being erased by vote of Grand Chapter.

Masonic Union in Contemplation?

The Excellent Grand and Royal Chapter had a double existence. On the one hand it was a private chapter; on the other a Grand Chapter using its authority to warrant private chapters. But it will have been noted that the very first private chapter warranted was the Restauration Lodge or Chapter of the Rock Fountain Shilo, and it is more than likely that this may have been regarded up to the 1790's as contained within Grand Chapter. At any rate, in the December of 1795 Grand Chapter, recognizing the need for a separation, revived Restauration Chapter, No. 1, as an "exalting chapter," and (surprisingly, from our point of view) then styled itself "The Grand Lodge of Royal Arch Masons." This title was an obvious misfit, and soon gave way (1801) to "The Supreme Grand Chapter," although when the Duke of Sussex became in 1810 the highest officer of the Order he was styled "The First Grand Master of Royal Arch Masons." From all this it will be seen that the change from 'lodge' to 'chapter' and from 'Master' to 'Principal' was by no means a simple, automatic process.

Lord Moira, who, it is to be expected, was already quietly playing a part in preparing the minds of his Brethren for the coming Union, was exalted in June 1803, in Supreme Grand Chapter, "having been obligated prior to the ceremony in the Chapter of St James." In 1810 he, as M.E. Zerubbabel, proposed for Exaltation H.R.H. Augustus Frederick, Duke of Sussex, who, having been exalted and Lord Moira having immediately resigned office, was elected and consecrated M.E. Zerubbabel, taking the title, as already mentioned, of "First Grand Master of Royal Arch Masons." The Investment and Installation of the Second and Third Principals followed. The Duke's introduction into Royal Arch masonry was doubtless influenced by a prospect of the Craft union of the opposed bodies, particularly bearing in mind that in 1813, the year of Union, he would find himself Grand Master of the 'Moderns' and his Brother, Edward, Duke of Kent, Grand Master of the 'Antients,' and that in the negotiations for the settlement the future of the Royal Arch would be a very considerable factor.

By 1800 the premier Grand Chapter had warranted 116 chapters, some of which were not working (in addition, many 'Antient' lodges were working the R.A.), but we see what is probably a move in the direction of the union of the two systems in a regulation of 1798 to the effect that no Royal Arch mason exalted in lodge, as distinct from chapter, could be admitted as a member of or visitor to a chapter. Obviously, at this date, there were still 'Modern' lodges working the Royal Arch ceremonial, and, although the regulation was not everywhere observed, it does suggest that there was a growing feeling that the 'regular' Royal Arch mason was one who had received the degree in chapter, not in lodge.

The coming into force, late in the 1790's, of the law against seditious meetings (39 Geo. III, Ch. 79) brought uncertainty into masonic administration and affected the warranting of new lodges. The Grand Chapter, however, continued to warrant chapters during the period of uncertainty.

Sunday Meetings

Sunday meetings (often in private rooms) were, over a long period, regarded with great favour by Royal Arch masons. In Lancashire, for example, it was almost a general custom for chapters to meet on that day, and Norman Rogers has pointed out that when the Burnley and Colne Chapters were compelled to give up Sunday meetings the small attendance almost broke up the chapters, and it took a few years to recover from the change. This followed the official ban in 1811, when Grand Chapter decided that in future no warrants should be granted to chapters intending to hold Sunday meetings, and that chapters already meeting on a Sunday should be advised to change their day. Following the 'union' of 1817, Supreme Grand Chapter expressed its disapprobation of Sunday meetings. In any case, it appears that Sunday meetings on licensed premises were illegal, for in 1806, as one example, the Bolton magistrates fined a landlord twelve shillings for permitting a chapter to meet at his inn on a Sunday.

A Masonic Pantomime

An almost forgotten event is the presentation of a masonic pantomime at the Drury Lane Theatre, London, the first performance being on December 29, 1780. Altogether there were sixty-three performances at somewhat irregular intervals, the last of them being in December 1781. It was by no means the only theatrical performance presenting a masonic subject, but from the present point of view it was notable in that it included two features having direct reference to the Royal Arch.

The words and music were mostly written and composed by Charles Dibdin, a great figure in the theatrical and musical life of the eighteenth century and best remembered as the author of the song "Tom Bowling"; the vocalists were well-known singers of the time. The *Morning Post* spoke of the absurdity of this kind of performance, but the Press in general, as well as one or two authors since that day, spoke well of it. The modern critic would not have had a very high opinion of its versification. The pantomime included a "Procession of the Principal Grand Masters from the Creation to the Present Century," the procession consisting of twenty different banners, with actors telling the story of each banner. The sixth banner was of Darius Hystaspes, "who married a daughter of Cyrus, confirmed his decree to rebuild the Temple of Jerusalem: and in the 6th year of his reign his Grand Warden, Zerubbabel, finished it." Two actors accompanying the banner bore the Temple of the Sun. The nineteenth banner was of the Royal Arch, and was attended by "Six Gentlemen Masons, Two bearing a Pageant." It is thought that the word "Pageant" in this connexion meant a painted representation, perhaps a subsidiary banner. The pantomime included a well-known masonic song beginning with the line—

> Hail masonry, thou Craft divine

In the Craft *Constitutions* of 1723 this song had been attributed to Charles Delafaye "To be Sung and Played at the Grand-feast." The presentation of this pantomime at such a well-known theatre is clear evidence of the considerable public interest taken in freemasonry late in the eighteenth century.

Notes on a Few Early Chapters

The following notes relate to some of the chapters at work towards the close of the eighteenth century.

Chapter of Friendship, Portsmouth. Of the first three chapters warranted by Grand Chapter in 1769 Friendship was third on the list. The first two are now extinct and Friendship can claim the distinction of being the oldest warranted chapter in the world. It is attached to Phoenix Lodge, No. 257.

Britannia Chapter, Sheffield. In Lancashire the Royal Arch made great progress in the 1760's. Norman Rogers has brought to light that the first record of a Lancashire Royal Arch mason appears in the minute-book of the Britannia Lodge, Sheffield (now No. 139), thus: "June 25, 1764. Thomas Beesley, Hosier, Royal Arch from Lodge 45, Liverpool." Lodge No. 45 was 'Antients' (founded in 1755), and Thomas Beesley was visiting a lodge of the same persuasion. Britannia Lodge had started as an 'Antients' lodge, No. 85, in 1761; it absorbed another lodge, No. 75, of the same kind in 1764, and immediately afterwards applied to the 'Moderns' for a warrant, which was granted in 1765! While still a 'Moderns' lodge in 1796, it is said to have amalgamated with the 'Antients' Lodge No. 72 and, not surprisingly, to have worked under the two systems. The chapter attached to Britannia Lodge, No. 139, has had the name Paradise since it was warranted in 1798.

Lodge of Lights, Warrington. The Royal Arch must have been worked at Warrington, Lancashire, in the 1765 period. The town's oldest lodge (now No. 148) was warranted in 1765, received its name Lodge of Lights in 1806, and apparently worked the Royal Arch from its earliest days, for in December 1767 three members of the Chapter of Concord, No. 37, Bolton, visited Warrington to acquaint themselves with the ceremonial.

References to the Royal Arch activities of the Lodge of Lights appear on other pages of this book.

Anchor and Hope Lodge, Bolton. An early chapter formed in the Anchor and Hope Lodge, No. 37, Bolton, Lancashire, has a notable place in Royal Arch history. Before the years 1767-74 inclusive it exalted twenty-four Candidates, as we learn from a manuscript account of Royal Arch masonry in Lancashire by Norman Rogers, to whom the following information is due. The chapter above referred to became eventually (in 1836) the Chapter of Concord, No. 37, which is still attached to the same lodge, which dates back to 1732 and offers an outstanding example of Traditioner working (see p. 50). A 'Moderns' lodge, it was considering in 1765 the possibility of taking an 'Antients' warrant, and in December 1768 it "crafted and raised" three members of the friendly Lodge of Relief (Bury), "they being before Modern Masons." These same three "were made Royal Arch Masons" in the following month after the "Royal Arch Lodge assembled in due form." Now, all three—Ralph Holt, Elijah Lomax, and James Wood—had gone through the chair of their 'Moderns' Lodge of Relief, in the neighbouring town of Bury, and yet had been compelled to submit to reinitiation in another 'Moderns' lodge.

In November 1769 the same three Brethren were granted a warrant (number 6b issued by the new Grand Chapter) for the Unanimity Chapter or Lodge of Intercourse, Bury.

In the records of the Bolton lodge is a reference, dated December 1767, to "Expenses at Warrington in making Three Arch Masons... £1. 11. 6." Three Brethren were named, all of whom were Past or Present Masters of their lodge, and had apparently been sent to the Lodge of Lights, Warrington, as Candidates for the Royal Arch. We learn of 'passing the chair' (see Section 16) in a minute of November 30, 1769: "A Lodge of Emergency when Bror. John Aspinwall, Bror. Jas. Lever and Bror. Richard Guest were installed Masters and afterwards Bror. Jas. Livesey Senr. was re-installed." Subsequently all four were made Royal Arch masons. Now, Livesey had gone into the chair of the lodge in the preceding June, and yet had to be installed before he could be exalted. Why? Apparently because the mere fact of being made Master of a 'Moderns' lodge did not at that time bring with it the conferment of any particular secrets, whereas 'passing the chair' was either in itself the 'Antients' ceremony of Installation or a development of it. This was a Traditioner lodge, it must be remembered, strongly influenced by 'Antients' ideas. Indeed, so 'Antient' in its ways was it—so convinced that its lodge masonry comprehended the Royal Arch—that when this Bolton chapter decided in 1785 to obtain a warrant from the premier Grand Chapter many members objected, and the membership fell from seventeen to seven.

The first entry in the minutes of the newly warranted chapter is as follows:

> Bolton, 5th October, 1785. At a General Encampment of Royal Arch Superexcellent Masons, held in due form, Bro. M. J. Boyle in the chair, the following Royal Arch Brethren were properly instructed and afterwards Initiated into the higher degree of Masonry [five names follow].

The minute is signed by Mich. James Boyle, who, quoting Norman Rogers, was probably a member of the King's Own or 3rd Dragoons, and in the minutes of Paradise Chapter is termed a "Mason of the World."

The Cana Lodge or Chapter of the First Miracle, Colne. A Lancashire lodge or chapter as here named received the fifth warrant (May 12, 1769) issued by the new Grand Chapter. It is now Cana Chapter, attached to the Royal Lancashire Lodge, No. 116, a lodge founded at the Hole in the Wall, Market Street, Colne, in 1762, possessing minutes going back to 1760, and known to have been at work earlier still. Norman Rogers has pointed out that, before the printing in separate form for distribution of the laws, etc., of the first Grand Chapter or those contained in the Charter of Compact (1766), it is obvious that some kind of written instructions must have been sent out to chapters with the early warrants (from 1769), evidence of which, he thinks, exists in the "Principia" preserved in the Cana Chapter. The full title is "The Principia to be observed by all regular constituted Chapters of the Grand and Royal Chapter," and at the foot of the document is written: "This Principia is the oldest known copy of Grand Chapter Bye-Laws, and is the work of the same hand as the Chapter Warrant, which is dated 1769." *Principia* is Latin, the plural of *principium*, and means the beginnings or foundations, also the chief place, and, in a Roman camp, often the open space where speeches were made to the soldiers. In the Cana document the word can only mean "rules and regulations." They are here given as in the original:

> *1st.* That as soon as the Chapter is duly formed, an account shall be transmitted to Grand Chapter containing the names of each respective Officer and Companion, and that this be done annually immediately after election.
> *2nd.* That they have full power to make Bye-Laws for their own government, provided they don't interfere with the fundamental ones of the Most Excellent Grand and Royal Chapter.
> *3rd.* That their jewels and ornaments be such as are in use in Grand Chapter.
> *4th.* That they make no innovations in the business of the chapter, and if any doubts should arise, they must always be referred to the Grand and Royal Chapter for decision.
> *5th.* That they should contribute annually to the Grand Chapter so much as they reasonably can towards raising a fund to be employed to the most truly benevolent and advantageous purposes.

6th. That no man of bad or immoral character be admitted a Companion, nor anyone until he hath passed through the several probationary degrees of craft Masonry and thereby obtain the necessary passport as a reward for his services.

7th. That no man be admitted for an unworthy consideration, or for a less sum than is usually paid for the three previous degrees.

8th. That they take every method to forward the true purpose of our Order, which is to promote all the useful arts and sciences and create universal peace and harmony, and that every Companion do consider it as his duty to lay before the Chapter whatever may tend to such salutary purposes.

9th. That any new discovery or any other matter thought worthy of observation be communicated to the Grand and Royal Chapter, which will always be ready to support and forward whatever may be found useful to the public in general or that Chapter in particular, not repugnant to the common welfare.

Lodge Probity and Paradise Chapter, Halifax. The earliest record of a Royal Arch chapter in Yorkshire (other than at York, then in abeyance) is in the minutes of Probity Lodge, Halifax—a resolution dated January 9, 1765, to form a chapter. The first meeting was twenty-one days later. In the list of twenty-nine lodge members for 1765 sixteen have the T-over-H symbol appended, and of these only two, plus the Master, had been in the lodge chair. But the Royal Arch had been worked earlier than this, for in the cash account for the second term of 1764 are references to two Brethren who had been "made Roy^l Arch," at a fee of 10s. 6d. each, on October 18, 1764.

Unanimity Chapter, Wakefield. References to the historic chapter at Wakefield appear on other pages, in particular one (p. 159) to its ancient ritual, the like of which is not revealed by the records of any other chapter. Two books or journals contain the minutes of all meetings held from 1766 to 1793 of this chapter—Unanimity—whose minutes are confused for a period as from 1844 with those of the Wakefield Chapter, now No. 495. In 1865 separate records started, and these continue to 1920, when Unanimity moved to Meltham, where it is attached to Lodge of Peace, No. 149. Unanimity's beautiful and distinctive old jewels (Plate XXIV) were discovered after a long repose among "the accumulated rubbish of years," and then, early in the 1940's, two pages of a minute-book of the 1776 period were restored to the chapter, these having been found among some old prints in a dealer's shop. J. R. Ryland's papers in *A.Q.C.*, vols. lvi and lxv, are a fund of valuable information on Wakefield's Royal Arch activities. From them it appears that the early meetings of the chapter were actually held in a Craft lodge which, for the occasion, called itself a "Royal Arch Lodge Night," or "Royal Arch Lodge," and frequently the three Masters of the Royal Arch lodge were the Master and

Wardens of the Craft lodge. In the minutes of the February 3, 1768, meeting the initials M., S.W., and J.W. were put against the names of the Three Principals respectively, but then crossed out and "Mr." substituted in each case. At this meeting two Brethren were made "Excellent Royal Arch Masons." At an emergency meeting of the Royal Arch lodge on July 30, 1776, four Brethren "propos'd themselves to be rais'd Royal Arch Masons—the next Lodge Night—balloted for and pass'd in ye affirmative." (They were raised accordingly at the next meeting.) It is likely that these Brethren proposed themselves in the Craft lodge, which then resolved itself into a Royal Arch lodge. It was quite common in the early days for a Brother so to propose himself or be proposed by somebody else. A Candidate received the "Superlative Degree of R.A. Mason" on February 24, 1783. In February 1807 the chapter agreed to hold six meetings in the winter months, all of them on Sundays.

Richard Linnecar, referred to at p. 159, was a revered and prominent member of Unanimity Chapter, and was held in honour throughout his province and beyond. Among his many claims to attention was his book (1789) containing plays, songs, poems, and his "Strictures on Freemasonry" (comments, not adverse criticism as the word "strictures" would now imply). His poems may not have been of great worth, but certainly his "Hymn on Masonry" as well as a song written by him were popular and probably much sung. We learn from his "Strictures" of the curious legend of masons entreating St John the Evangelist, then Bishop of Ephesus, to honour with his patronage a lodge meeting in the city of Benjamin following the destruction of Jerusalem by Titus, A.D. 70. "St. John told them, he was very old, being turned of ninety, but to support so good and ancient an institution, he would undertake the charge—and from that day, all lodges are dedicated to him." The story is, of course, a myth which attempts to explain (what never has been explained, so far as we know) why lodges are dedicated to St John, and why not only lodges but Craft masonry in general came to be associated with his name, and associated so closely that his festival, December 27, was regarded as a sacred occasion by the early Brethren. Possibly the old custom of reading from (or opening the Bible at) the first verses of St John's Gospel is the only explanation now possible.

Loyalty Chapter, Sheffield. Surprisingly many of the chapters founded in the late years of the 1800's had but a short life, a marked instance being that of the Chapter of Loyalty, No. 95, Sheffield's first regularly constituted chapter, warranted in 1795 with a notable local mason, James Woolen, as its first Z. and associated with the Royal Brunswick Lodge. It did not keep records or make returns to Grand Chapter, and as it was erased in 1809 its rather poor life did not exceed about fourteen years. A letter written in 1820 by Joseph Smith to Supreme Grand Chapter acknowledging a notice that Loyalty Chapter had been erased says:

> I have enquired into the proceedings of the said Chapter & find that there were only three exalted by the Comp^{ns}. who obtained the Charter . . . & two of them are no more & the third resign'd & all three without being registred —& it also unfortunately happened that Two of the Principals for whom the Charter was obtained died in a few years after & consequently put a stop to the complete Knowledge of the Art.

(Since James Woolen did not die until 1814, there were two Principals alive at the date of the erasure.) A resuscitated Loyalty Chapter received a new warrant in 1821, this being attached to the Royal Brunswick Lodge, now No. 296, a lodge of which James Woolen had been Master thirteen times between 1793 and 1811.

Unity, Leeds. One of Yorkshire's oldest chapters, the Chapter of Unity, No. 72, Leeds (now Alfred Chapter, No. 306), was warranted in 1790 at a time, it is thought, when there was no Craft lodge in its town, although possibly the Loyal and Prudent Lodge was meeting by dispensation there. Although warranted in 1790, it did not meet for business until six years later, and in the interval three Craft lodges had come into being in Leeds. It met on the third Sunday of every month, and the Janitor had the duty of delivering the summons to each member. Candidates "must have duly passed the Chair" and be not less than twenty-three years of age, although the son of a Companion or a Master Mason of two years' standing was admitted at twenty-one! The Exaltation fee was £2 2s.

Rules agreed to in 1796 included the unusual one that the "master of the house" should light a fire in the chapter-room in the winter season at least one hour before the time of meeting, at a cost of half a guinea each year, any failure involving him in a "forfeited sixpence." In 1819 the chapter obtained a new Charter and became attached to Alfred Lodge.

Vigilance Chapter, Darlington. Brethren of the Darlington (Durham) Lodge (founded in 1761 and soon to be known as Restoration Lodge—now No. 111) acquired from an unknown source some knowledge of the Royal Arch, and proceeded to establish in 1769 "The Lodge of Royal Arch Masons," which must have been one of the oldest examples of a self-contained and unrecognized body working the degree. It met regularly, and in 1787 asked Grand Lodge whether it approved of what it was doing and inquired as to the charge for a warrant. The request was passed to Dunckerley, who arranged for a warrant to be issued, the members consenting to his request to be exalted (that is, re-exalted) in Concord Chapter (now No. 124), founded in the previous year at Durham, the county town, rather less than twenty miles north of Darlington. The new chapter, Vigilance, now No. 111, was regularly constituted in February

1788 after apparently nineteen years of irregular working. The minute-books are complete of "the Royal Arch Masters" up to 1788 and forward from that date of the warranted chapter.

William Waples, in a manuscript placed at the author's disposal, gives much further information relating to the old lodge and chapter. "The Lodge of Royal Arch Masons" was known at one time as "The Hierarchical" Lodge, associated with a priestly order of the same name of which little is known. The lodge had a "Dedicated Arch," which may possibly have been a floor-cloth displaying Royal Arch emblems and carried in processions. William Waples believes that, following the Union, some of the symbols of the Royal Arch were carried over into the Master Mason's Degree as practised by Restoration Lodge, with which the chapter was associated. As likely evidence of the early working of the veils ceremony, it is recorded that in 1769 the sum of £2 5s. 9d. was paid for sixty yards of 'tammy' (otherwise tamine or taminy, a glazed woollen or worsted fabric used for curtains), and at the same time curtain rods and rings were bought.

Chapter of St James, London. The many notes on this historic chapter (now No. 2), both those following and on other pages, are mostly from W. Harry Ryland's history of the chapter issued in 1891. The ornate warrant, headed "The Almighty Jah," was granted in 1788, and is signed by James Heseltine as Z. of Grand Chapter. The chapter records are almost continuous from 1791 to date as, although the minutes for 1812–29 have been lost, records for those years do exist in rough form. Originally the chapter met in Old Burlington Street or its immediate neighbourhood, but since 1797 has met at Freemasons' Tavern or Freemasons' Hall. Its early meeting-places may in part explain how it came to draw many of its early members from Burlington Lodge, now No. 96 (founded 1756), and the still earlier British Lodge, now No. 8 (founded 1722). It is attached to the time-immemorial lodge, Antiquity, now No. 2.

As from at least as early as 1791, and continuing for the greater part of the nineteenth century, the First Principal, and very often the Second and Third, held his chair for two years. The Exaltation fee in the early days was £1 1s., or, including sash, £1 5s. At an emergency meeting in 1792 two Brethren "were raised to the degrees of Master Masons," an irregularity repeated on occasions until ten years later; after that date lodges for passing Brethren through the chair continued to be held, as was the case with many other chapters.

The double-cubic stone is persistently called the pedestal in early minutes, and in 1814 comes a reference to the "mystical Parts of the Pedestal."

Caps were worn by the Principals in the 1797 period, as becomes evident from the purchase in that year of a trunk in which to keep them; in

1802 there is an item of 17s. 6d. for repairing them. Actually, over a very long period, the First and Second Principals have worn crowns, as they still do, and the Third Principal a mitre.

A sidelight upon the etiquette observed in forms of address at the turn of the century is afforded by a list of nine Brethren exalted at a special meeting on a Sunday in May 1797; the list includes two "Reverends," one Colonel, three Esquires, one "Mr.," one "Brother," and one plain "David."

Stewards are mentioned as assistants to the Sojourners in 1801. Both in lodge and chapter—at any rate under the 'Moderns'—Stewards had ceremonial duties well into the nineteenth century, and in general were of higher status than they are to-day. A floor-cloth was in use in the early years, for it is recorded that the sum of £1 10s. was paid for the painting of one in 1810. The Lectures (catechisms) had a big place in the early ceremonies, just as they had enjoyed in the Craft, and in 1811 the minutes record the appointment of three Sojourners as lecturers. In the chapter, on a pedestal near the Second Principal, is a carved and gilded eagle some 15 inches high.

At least twice in its history the chapter has been concerned with the activities of charlatans. Its Z. in the year 1792 attended Grand Chapter to report Robert Sampson, watchmaker, of Petty France, Westminster, "for pretending to exalt several Masons." Sampson had been expelled from his chapter and had "formed an independent Society at his own house where he professed to exalt Master Masons for 5/–." Then, in 1808, the chapter heard—probably not for the first time—of another impostor, William Finch. Three Companions had been proposed as joining members in that year, but were found to have been irregularly exalted by Finch; however, they were allowed to attend as visitors on their consenting to be exalted in regular manner, and they became members two months later. Finch, a breeches-maker, initiated in Canterbury, was to some extent a real student of masonic ritual. He became an author and publisher of masonic books and made a practice of selling rituals—of very doubtful authenticity. His troubled career included an action which he brought in the courts of law and in which the Grand Secretary of that day gave evidence not in Finch's favour. He died in 1818 at the age of about forty-six. His story, putting him in a rather better light, is told by Colonel F. M. Rickard in *A.Q.C.*, vol. lv.

A report in the *Lewes Journal* (Sussex) of October 5, 1801, speaks of a Royal Arch chapter that had just been held in the Old Ship Tavern, Brighton, under a deputation from St James's Chapter, "when nine MASTERS of ARTS were exalted." It should be explained that 'virtual' Masters were commonly so designated.

Section Seven

THE SO-CALLED 'ANTIENTS' GRAND CHAPTER

SOON after the erection of the premier Grand Chapter it seems likely that the 'Antients' for the first time found the scales tilted against them, and, although to them any separate control of the Royal Arch was of no advantage, they obviously felt compelled to counter the efforts of their rivals by creating their own Grand Chapter. So, in 1771, they replied to Lord Blayney's gesture, but their Grand Chapter was nothing more than a nominal body; it is not known to have had minutes before 1783, and it is doubtful whether for a long time it had even the semblance of a separate organization, certainly never an independent one such as that of the first Grand Chapter. The explanation is simple enough: the 'Moderns' had formed their Grand Chapter in the face of official dislike; it had to be separate and distinct, or otherwise could not have existed at all. On the other hand, the 'Antients' system embraced and comprehended the Royal Arch; its Brethren loved it, respected it, believed it to be an integral part of the masonic Order; any independent organization for its control was superfluous. Nevertheless, they felt obliged to make a positive reply to Lord Blayney's move, for they had enjoyed in the Royal Arch a considerable asset which now might tend to disappear, so they founded a 'Grand Chapter.' Very slowly at first, but quite definitely in the course of a generation or so, the 'Antient' Brethren would be looking not to the lodge, but to the chapter when they wished to be exalted, but for years to come they would view with disapproval the setting up of any authority, even a shadowy one, coming between their Grand Lodge and the working of the R.A. in their lodges. There continued for many years a most distinct 'oneness' between their Grand Lodge and their Grand Chapter; indeed, in general, it was impossible to distinguish between them.

That the arrival of the first Grand Chapter forced their hands is obvious from many minutes of the 'Antients' Grand Lodge. Consider the proceedings of September 4, 1771, when Laurence Dermott, the new Deputy Grand Master, was in the chair. The Grand Secretary (Dicky) asked whether his Grace, the Duke of Atholl, was Grand Master "in every respect." The meeting unanimously answered the question in the affirmative. Then the Grand Secretary said he had heard it advanced that the

Grand Master "had not a right to" inspect into the proceedings of the R.A.; that he, the Grand Secretary, had "with regret perceived many flagrant abuses of this most sacred part of Masonry; and therefore proposed that the Master and Past Masters of the Warranted Lodges be conven'd as soon as possible in order to put that part of Masonry on a Solid Basis".

In this same year, 1771, matters relating to the R.A. having come before it, the 'Antients' Grand Lodge "considered that as several members of Grand Lodge were not Royal Arch masons, the Chapter were the 'properest' persons to adjust and determine this matter"; it was then agreed that the case be referred to their Chapter "with full power and authority to hear and determine and finally adjust the same." In November 1773 it was resolved in Grand Lodge "that this Chapter perfectly coincided and agrees that Masters and Past Masters (Bona-fide) only ought to be admitted Masters of the Royal Arch." Then, in the next month, December, we find the Grand Lodge deciding when the Grand Chapter is to meet, the actual resolution being

> that a General Grand Chapter of the Royal Arch shall meet on the first Wednesday of the Months of April and October in every year to regulate all matters in that branch of Masonry, and that at such meetings a faithful copy of the Transactions with a list of all the Royal Arch Masons of the respective Lodges shall be returned to the Grand Secretary to be Inrolled.

At this very same meeting we hear what is undoubtedly an echo of the disquiet created in the 'Antients' ranks by the formation of the first Grand Chapter:

> The Master 193 reported that several Members of His Lodge was very refractory, insisting that the Grand Lodge had no power to hinder them from being admitted Royal Arch Masons, and that they was countenanced in such proceedings by Bro[r]. Robinson, the Landlord of the House they assembled in.

Then follows an attack on this Brother Robinson, who was summoned to attend the next Steward's Lodge. (In the 'Antients' system, the functions of the Steward's Lodge somewhat resembled those of to-day's Board of General Purposes.)

There is further evidence of the close association of the two bodies when in 1788–89 it was resolved that copies of the R.A. regulations should be included in the Circular Letter of the Year. This followed an inquiry by a select committee into a report that many and gross abuses had been practised; so seriously was the matter regarded that, pending the completion of the inquiry and thorough reform, no R.A. masons could be made without consent of Grand Lodge officers. Later, in 1791, we find the

Grand Lodge confirming a "report of the General Grand Chapter and Committee of the Holy Royal Arch" and agreeing to circulate it to all lodges under the 'Antients' constitution. At about this period there are references in the minutes to "A Book of the Royal Arch: Transactions," but it is not known whether a copy of this book is in existence. In the years 1796–97 Grand Lodge read the minutes of the last Grand Chapter of the R.A. and passed them unanimously. A minute of June 3, 1807, of the 'Antients' Grand Lodge, recorded that fees received on *exaltees* had been finally paid into Grand Lodge. More complete evidence of the real identity of the two bodies is hardly possible.

Rules and Regulations

No rules relating to the Royal Arch appear to have been made in the early years by the 'Antients' Grand Lodge, whose book of constitutions, *Ahiman Rezon* for 1756 and 1778, did not include any, although having borrowed a phrase from Anderson's first *Constitutions* (it helped itself cheerfully from any useful source), its rule No. 2 stated that "the Master of a particular Lodge has the right and authority of congregating the members of his own Lodge into a Chapter upon any emergency or occurrence," but, as stated earlier, it is extremely unlikely—practically impossible—that "Chapter" in Anderson's instance had anything to do with the R.A. In 1783, however, the 'Antients' Grand Lodge ordered a register of the Excellent Royal Arch Masons returned by lodges to be made, and more than ten years later, in 1794–95, they went through the rules and regulations on which they had been working and issued them in revised form as a set.

The earliest-known 'Antients' register of R.A. masons dates back to 1782–83, but, to tell the truth, it is not a live, current register, but more in the nature of a list of Brethren known to be (or have been) R.A. masons, for it includes in an early entry Laurence Dermott's name, to which is appended "D.G.M. No. 26, 1746" (Laurence was not Deputy Grand Master until many years later). The names of other prominent masons appearing in the list could not have been compiled from any normal returns.

The rules and regulations of 1794 are stated to be:

For the Introduction and Government of the Holy Royal Arch Chapters under the Protection and Supported by the Antient Grand Lodge of England Made at Several Times. Revised and corrected at a Grand Chapter, October 1st, 1794. Confirmed in Grand Lodge, December 3rd, 1794.

The outstanding points of the rules are:

1. That every chapter shall be held "under the authority and sanction of a regular subsisting warrant granted by Grand Lodge according to the Old Institution."

2. That six regularly registered Royal Arch masons be present at the making of an R.A. mason.

3. "That no Brother shall be admitted into the H.R.A. but he who has regularly and faithfully passed through the three progressive degrees, and has filled and performed the office of Master in his Lodge to the satisfaction of his Brethren, to ascertain which they shall deliver up to him in open lodge, held in the Master's degree, a certificate to the following purport:

> To the presiding chiefs of the Chapter of Excellent Royal Arch Masons under the Lodge.... No.... Whereas our truly well beloved Brother... a geometric Master Mason, every way qualified so far as we are judged of the necessary qualifications for passing the Holy Royal Arch, we do hereby certify that the said trusty and well beloved brother has obtained the unanimous consent of our Lodge No.... for the recommendation and the signing of this certificate.
>
> Given under our hands this ..... day of .....
> W.M.
> S.W.
> J.W.

Secretary................"

4. "That a general Grand Chapter of the H.R.A. shall be held half yearly, on the first Wednesday in the months of April and October in each year, that every warranted Lodge shall be directed to summons its Excellent Royal Arch Members to attend the same, and that none but members of warranted Lodges and the present and past Grand Officers (being Royal Arch Masons) shall be members thereof, and certified sojourners to be admitted as visitors only."

5. That Scribes shall keep a register of all Brethren admitted to the Degree and make due return half-yearly.

6. That general Grand Chapters of Emergency may be called, on application being made to the Grand Chiefs by at least six Excellent Masons.

7. "That on the admission of a new brother the form of the return to General Grand Chapter shall be as follows:

> We, the three Chiefs, whose names are hereunto subscribed, do certify that in a Chapter of Holy Royal Arch, convened and held under the sanction and authority of the Warrant of the Worshipful Lodge No. . . . our well beloved

PLATE X

THE CRYPT OF YORK MINSTER
As depicted on summonses of York Lodge, No. 236, commemorating the assembly of " Royal Arch Brethren " in a " sacred recess,"
May 1778.
By courtesy of United Grand Lodge

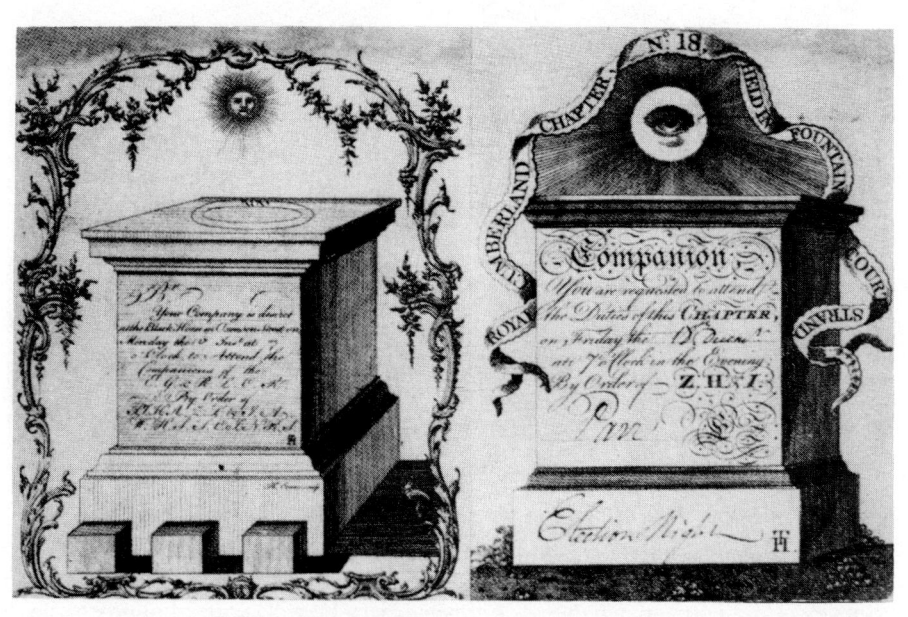

TWO TYPICAL SUMMONSES, LATE EIGHTEENTH CENTURY
By courtesy of Quatuor Coronati Lodge

PLATE XI

SOME EARLY VARIATIONS OF THE ROYAL ARCH JEWEL

Top left : Dated 1788 ; made by Beavon of Marylebone. *Top right :* Dated 1790 ; includes many Craft emblems. *Bottom left :* Dated 1798 ; silver gilt jewel of Caledonian Chapter. *Bottom right :* Dated 1822 ; thought to be of Royal Preston Lodge, now No. 333.

By courtesy of United Grand Lodge

Brethren, G.H., I.K., and L.M., having delivered to us the certificate hereunto subjoined and proved themselves by due examination to be well qualified in all the three degrees of Apprentice, Fellowcraft and Master Mason, were by us admitted to the supreme degree of Excellent Royal Arch Masons. Given under our hands and Masonic Mark in Chapter this . . . . . day of . . . . . in the year of Masonry . . . . . and in the year of our Lord . . . .

. . . . . . Z.
. . . . . . H.
. . . . . . J.

Scribe . . . ."

8. "That all registered Royal Arch Masons shall be entitled to a Grand Royal Arch certificate on the payment of three shillings, which shall be a perquisite of the Grand Scribe, they paying the expense of printing, parchment, ribbon, etc. etc."

9. "That the expenses of General Grand Chapter for Tylers, summonses, etc. shall be borne from the Grand Fund as formerly ordered by Grand Lodge."

10. That London Brethren, on admission, shall pay a fee of half a guinea, of which two shillings shall be paid to the general Grand Fund on registration and one shilling to the Grand Scribe; country, foreign and military chapters may charge a smaller fee but make the same payment on registration.

11. That a member of any particular lodge in London recommended by the Master, Wardens, and Secretary in open lodge assembled, and after due examination by any of the Three Grand Chiefs, or the Two Grand Scribes or any two of the same, the brother, being a Master Mason and duly registered at least twelve months as shall appear under the hands of the Grand Secretary, and having passed the chair, shall, if approved by the R.A. chapter to whom the brother is recommended be admitted to the sublime degree of Excellent or Royal Arch Masons.

12. The foregoing rule is adapted to Brethren in country or foreign lodges.

13. That the names of exaltees be duly returned.

14. That Excellent Brothers from country and foreign lodges "the two Scribes or any two of them" be entitled to be registered and receive a certificate.

A note laid down that nine Excellent Masters, to assist the Grand Officers in visiting lodges (chapters), etc., were to be elected in October of each year: "That the general uniformity of Antient Masonry may be preserved and handed down unchanged to posterity." These nine Brethren have come down to history as the "Nine Worthies," and they soon had duties, and very important ones, in addition to those originally named

They wore a special jewel (Plate XXXI) whose chief motif was three arches, one within the other, these jewels being among the most distinctive of those made in the latter part of the eighteenth century. The names of these "Worthies" were kept in a special register, and one of their particular duties was to examine all persons undertaking to perform R.A. ceremonies, install Grand Officers, "or as to processions." The "Nine Worthies" developed in the course of time into a Committee on the lines of to-day's Board of General Purposes; thus we find that in 1797 the question of estimating and reporting the expense of proper clothing and regalia for the Grand Chapter was referred to them. Probably all the "Worthies" were preceptors of considerable experience. One of them, J. H. Goldsworthy, appointed a few years later, was Lecture Master, had some part in bringing about the Union, and, living to be nearly eighty years of age, was a Senior Grand Deacon in 1845 and a member of the Board of General Purposes as late as 1850. He died eight years later.

Further laws and regulations for the Holy Royal Arch Chapter were agreed in April 1807: "Revised, amended and approved in General Grand Chapter at the Crown and Anchor Tavern, Strand, London, April 1st, 1807." They are included in the seventh edition of *Ahiman Rezon*, 1807, and the preamble to them (somewhat repeating that of the 1794 version) so clearly points to the 'Antients' high regard for the Order that it may well be reproduced here:

Antient Freemasonry consists of four Degrees—The three first of which are, that of *Apprentice*, the *Fellow Craft*, and the sublime degree of *Master*; and a Brother being well versed in these degrees and otherwise qualified is eligible to be admitted to the fourth degree, the *Holy Royal Arch*. This degree is certainly more august, sublime and important than those which precede it, and is the summit and perfection of Antient Masonry. It impresses on our minds a more firm belief of the existence of a Supreme Deity, without beginning of days or end of years and justly reminds us of the respect and veneration due to that Holy Name.

Until within those few years, this degree was not conferred upon any but those who had been a considerable time enrolled in the Fraternity; and could, beside, give the most unequivocal proofs of their skill and proficiency in the Craft.

It must of consequence be allowed that every regular and warranted Lodge possesses the power of forming and holding Meetings in each of these several degrees, the last of which, from its pre-eminence, is denominated, among Masons, a *Chapter*. That this Supreme degree may be conducted with that regularity, order and solemnity becoming the sublime intention with which it has from time immemorial been held, as an essential and component part of Antient Masonry, and that which is the perfection and end of the beautiful system; the Excellent Masons of the Grand Lodge of England, according to the Old Constitutions, duly assembled and constitutionally convened in General Grand Chapter, have carefully collected and revised the regulations.

The rules of 1807 are in general effect the same as those of 1794 just given, but there are a few significant changes.

Rule No. 1 states that, agreeably to established custom, the Officers of the Grand Lodge for the time being are considered as the Grand Chiefs; the Grand Secretary and his Deputy for the time being shall act as Grand Scribes; and the said Grand Officers and Grand Scribes are to preside at all Grand Chapters, according to seniority; they usually appoint the most expert R.A. companions to the other offices; and none but Excellent R.A. masons, being members of warranted lodges, in and near the Metropolis, shall be members thereof. Certified Sojourners may be admitted as visitors only.

Rule No. 4 provides that, as from this date, every chapter under the authority of the Grand Chapter must have a "regular subsisting warrant of Craft masonry granted by the [Antients] Grand Lodge or a Charter of Constitution specifically granted for the purpose." (Thus, the day in which the R.A. could be worked under the inherent authority of the Craft lodge appears to have closed.)

By Rule 10 the *minimum* fee for Exaltation is one guinea, out of which the chapter shall pay to the Grand Scribe three shillings, two shillings shall go to the general Fund of Grand Lodge, and to the Grand Scribe as a perquisite for his trouble, etc., one shilling.

It is expressly laid down in Rule 6 that the Candidate for the R.A. must have attained three progressive degrees; have passed the chair; been registered in the Grand Lodge books, as a Master Mason, for twelve months at least; and have been approved on examination by some one of the Grand Chiefs or Grand Scribes, to ascertain which a certificate must be given and signed in open lodge and further attested by the Grand Secretary.

There is little or nothing to help the historian to form an opinion as to the part played by the 'Antients' Grand Chapter in preparing for and helping to bring about the 'union,' but the impression is that of itself, it did nothing, for it was part and parcel of the 'Antients' Grand Lodge, and that body spoke for both Craft masonry and the Royal Arch, integral parts of one system. The 'Antients' Grand Lodge must have had in the course of the very lengthy discussions a great deal to say about the Royal Arch, but what it said is a matter of inference and to be judged by the terms upon which peace was achieved. In the many references to the preliminary negotiations between the two high parties to be found in the 'Antients' minutes there is not, so far as the present writer is aware, any reference to the Royal Arch.

Section Eight

YORK ROYAL ARCH MASONRY

THERE is no historical basis for the claim made by the 'Antients' that they were York masons and were handing down to posterity a rite that had been worked at York for hundreds of years. The matter is gone into in the writer's earlier book, and all that need be said here is that any claim that there is a York rite of great antiquity is more a matter of sentiment than of fact. Laurence Dermott, in claiming in *Ahiman Rezon* that 'Antient' masons were called York masons because the first Grand Lodge in England was congregated at York, A.D. 926, by Prince Edwin under a Charter from King Athelstan, was not only repeating a myth, but was astutely borrowing an appellation which he rightly thought would be an asset.

The York Grand Lodge

The only Grand Lodge at York (the Grand Lodge of ALL England) was one having a drawn-out existence from 1725 to 1792. It had grown from a lodge in the city of York which had been meeting for twenty years or more, but the Grand Lodge thus brought into being had a sphere of influence limited to its own district; becoming dormant about 1740, it was revived in 1761, and was helpful to William Preston when, in his quarrel with the senior Grand Lodge, he availed himself of its help to form in London in 1779 the Grand Lodge of England, South of the River Trent, whose life was short and uneventful.

The original issue of *Ahiman Rezon* (1756) did its best to bracket the new Grand Lodge with the York masons. One of its headings was "Regulations for Charity in Ireland, and by York Masons in England," and a Warrant of Constitution issued by the 'Antients' in 1759 carries the designation "Grand Lodge of York Masons, London." But, remembering Anderson's statements that freemasonry was known at the creation of the world, we are inclined to look indulgently upon Laurence Dermott's claim to a mere eight hundred years or so of history.

T. B. Whytehead asks the following question in the preface to Hughan's *Origin of the English Rite*:

Is it not in the bounds of possibility that the Royal Arch really had its far back origin at York amongst a superior class of Operatives and was revived as a Speculative Order by those who were associated in a special manner with their Brethren the Operatives, descendants of the old Guildmen?

How gratifying and comforting it would be to be able to answer this question with a simple 'Yes.' But how impossible! There is no evidence linking the Royal Arch with operative masonry. History, some acquaintance with the English operative system, plus a little common-sense reasoning dictate a definite 'No.' We do not even know that there ever were mason operative 'guildmen.' Some of the best of the operatives were, in some cases and at some time, members of a City Company, but it is extremely doubtful whether the operative craft, by its very nature, ever lent itself to control by local guilds—for reasons explained in the author's earlier work.

Fifield Dassigny in his book (1744), mentioned at p. 45, refers to an assembly of Master Masons in the City of York and to "a certain propagator of a false system ... a Master of the Royal Arch," which system "he had brought with him from the City of York." Any basis in fact for the last statement is unknown. There is no evidence that the Royal Arch was worked in York before the year in which Dassigny's book appeared. So far as the records go, the earliest connexion with York is to be found in the Minute Book belonging to the Royal Arch Lodge of York dated 1762.

York's Earliest Chapter and its Grand Chapter

A 'Moderns' lodge, the Punch Bowl Lodge, No. 259, was formed in York in 1761. Its Brethren were actors, all of them members of the York Company of Comedians, whose principal member and a great favourite with Yorkshire audiences was its first Master, a genius named Bridge Frodsham. (Gilbert Y. Johnson's paper in *A.Q.C.* vol. lvii, to which we are indebted for much of our information, includes an entertaining character sketch of Frodsham.) Four members of the lodge proceeded to found a Royal Arch lodge, one of the earliest instances of a separate Royal Arch organization; of course, it had no warrant—there was no authority that could have issued it. Members of the Punch Bowl Lodge joined the York Grand Lodge, which took over the control of the Royal Arch Lodge and developed it in 1778 into the Grand Chapter of ALL England, usually called the York Grand Chapter. This was not blessed with long life, and is believed to have collapsed soon after the date of its last minutes —namely, September 10, 1781.

Its minutes date from 1778 and are headed "A Most Sublime or Royal Arch Chapter" (an instance of an early use of the word 'chapter'). The minute, bearing date 1778, is renowned in Royal Arch history. Its sequel is the presence of an engraving of the Crypt of York Minster on the summons of the existing York Lodge, No. 236 (see Plate X). The minute recording a meeting of the Grand Chapter of ALL England is headed "York Cathedral, 27th May, 1778," and states that:

> The Royal Arch Brethren, whose names are undermentioned, assembled in the Ancient Lodge, now a sacred Recess within the Cathedral Church of York, and then and there opened a Chapter of Free and Accepted Masons in the Most Sublime Degree of Royal Arch.

The names of nine members follow, the first three of whom have the letters S., H.T., H.A. respectively attached to their names; the fourth is Secretary and Treasurer.

A brief certificate of 1779, signed by the Grand Secretary of All England, speaks of "admitting" to the First Degree and of "raising" to the Second, Third, and Fourth, this "Fourth" being the Royal Arch. Actually the certificate mentioned one further degree, the Knight Templar, which was called the Fifth Degree, and it is worth while noting that in June 1780 (the following year) the York Grand Lodge, by arrangement with the York Grand Chapter, confirmed its authority over "Five Degrees or Orders of Masonry," the rite consisting of first, Entered Apprentice; second, Fellow Craft; third, Master Mason; fourth, Knight Templar; and fifth, Sublime Degree of Royal Arch. This does not agree with the above noted brief certificate of the previous year or with a reference dated February 7, 1762, in which the Royal Arch is distinctly termed the "Fourth Degree of Masonry." While to a great many lodges and chapters the Royal Arch was the Fourth Degree, to some others it was undoubtedly the Fifth, and it may be that some few lodges were not very consistent in the matter.

A resolution of the York Grand Chapter dated May 2, 1779, foreshadows the arrangement, made at the Union, by which Officers of Grand Lodge are given, if qualified, corresponding rank in Grand Chapter. The resolution lays down that

> in future the Presiding Officers of the Grand Lodge of *All* England shall be Masters of this Royal Arch Chapter whenever such Presiding Officers shall be Members hereof and in Case of Default they shall be succeeded by the Senior Members of the Royal Arch Chapter.

But there is still earlier evidence of the application of this principle, as, for example, the association existing from the very birth of both the premier and the 'Antients' Grand Chapters.

Some Other York Chapters

The oldest chapter still at work in York to-day is the Zetland Chapter, No. 236, consecrated January 25, 1849, and attached to York Lodge (founded as the Union Lodge in 1777), but there were much older ones—the York Grand Chapter, already dealt with; the Chapter of Unity; and the Chapter of Unanimity; the last-named was the predecessor of the Zetland Chapter.

Unity Chapter, York. In 1773 the 'Moderns' constituted Apollo Lodge, York, whose founders, two or three of whom were Royal Arch masons, had resigned in a body from the York Grand Lodge. Apollo Lodge decided to form a Royal Arch chapter, and when the senior Grand Chapter assented in 1778 to an application to grant a warrant to William Spencer, Richard Garland, and Thomas Thackray, the curious thing is that of these three only one was a Royal Arch mason—William Spencer, who joined the Royal Arch Chapter at York in 1768 and was soon appointed Superintendent for the County of Yorkshire. Neither the name of the chapter nor the names of the Three Principals were given in the application: the chapter was No. 16 in the Grand Chapter Registry, and was there called Chapter of Union at York, a mistake for Chapter of *Unity*. The chapter may possibly have never been opened, but it continued to have a place in the official list.

Unanimity Chapter, York. The 'Moderns' issued a warrant in 1799 for a Chapter of Unanimity to be founded in connexion with the Union Lodge of York, now York Lodge No. 236. The registry is at fault in some respects, but, in effect, a warrant was granted to three masons, one of whom, John Seller, was the first candidate in the new chapter. The warrant stated that the members of the chapter were to consist solely of masons belonging to the Union Lodge, but the restriction was not observed, and no other chapter warrant is known to contain a corresponding clause.

The original minutes, still in existence, show that the first meeting was held on a Sunday, February 2, but there was no ceremony of consecration. For the first few years the chapter prospered, and among its exaltees was the Hon. Lawrence Dundas, later first Earl of Zetland and Pro First Grand Principal of the Grand Chapter (his title name many years later was given to what is now York's oldest existing chapter). The chapter was soon in trouble, and was struck off the rolls in 1809 for failure to pay its dues. In 1823 only two of the old members were left, and there had been no Exaltation since 1807. As from 1831 the chapter met only about once every two years. In 1845, after exalting two candidates, it sought confirmation of its warrant by Supreme Grand Chapter, but it had not made returns or paid fees to any Grand Chapter since 1802, well over forty years before, had been struck off the rolls in 1809, and none of the Companions exalted during the past forty-five years had been registered at Grand Chapter and could be recognized as petitioners. There were, however, two Companions in York whose signatures as petitioners were eligible, and for the third the chapter made contact with Abraham Le Veau, a wine merchant of London, a regular visitor to York, a mason of outstanding ability, later a Grand Officer and a member of the Board of General Purposes.

The full story of the negotiations for the founding of the revived chapter is told in Gilbert Y. Johnson's paper "The History of the Zetland Chapter, No. 236," read at the Centenary Convocation in January 1939, and to that paper the present writer is greatly indebted. The revived (actually new) chapter was given the name Zetland and attached to Union (now York) Lodge, No. 236, and at its consecration on January 25, 1849, nine members of that lodge were exalted and at once made officers. All officers in this chapter were elected except Assistant Sojourners, and these were appointed by the Principal Sojourner. From 1850 the custom was for the Three Principals with the Past Principals to open the chapter and then admit the Companions. The Mystical, Symbolical, and Historical Lectures are mentioned for the first time in the minutes of 1853. It has happened that when an Installation of a First Principal had to be postponed owing to the absence of qualified Companions the ceremony was postponed indefinitely, this not affecting the status of the officer so far as the conduct of ceremonies was concerned.

Section Nine

SOME FAMILIAR TERMS

In the closing decades of the eighteenth century—the period covered by the advent and early progress of the Grand Chapters—the Royal Arch 'lodge' was becoming a 'chapter'; its 'Brethren,' 'Companions'; and its Candidates, instead of being 'passed' or 'raised' to the degree, tended to be 'exalted.'

The word 'chapter' has a long and attractive history. Masonically it is an old word, for masons met in general chapter in medieval days, as we know for certain from Act 3 of Henry VI (1425) which forbade masons to meet in chapters and congregations. The word was used in the earliest Craft *Constitutions* (1723), which gave Masters and Wardens of particular lodges the right and authority of congregating members in chapters "upon any emergency or occurrence," but that use could hardly have had any Royal Arch association (see p. 37). 'Chapter' came originally from ecclesiastical usage. When monks in medieval days met in an assembly presided over by the head of their house or by a higher dignitary they were said to be 'meeting in chapter.' Their meeting-place was the chapter-house, often lavishly decorated, attached to a cathedral or abbey. A synod or council of a cathedral's clergy presided over by the dean was a 'chapter'; the corresponding meeting of a collegiate house was a 'college,' as at Westminster and Windsor. In French the word is *chapitre*. Ernest Weekley, the philologist, has shown that the word (in Latin *capitulum*, diminutive of *caput*, a "head") had as an early meaning a section of a book, a sense which arises naturally from that of heading, as, for example, 'to recapitulate,' meaning to run over the headings of a subject. Weekley says that the word was used

> especially of the divisions of the Bible. When the canons of a collegiate or cathedral church, monks of a monastery or knights of an order held formal meetings, the proceedings began with the reading of a chapter from their Rule or from the Scriptures. Thus the gathering itself became known as the *chapter* and the room in which it was held was called the *chapter-house*.

For roughly two centuries the tendency has been to designate as chapters certain masonic bodies or gatherings outside the Craft degrees, a natural development in view of the religious and often Christian character of early chapter ceremonies. Many of the added degrees meet in chapters, as do the assemblies of knights of some of the orders of chivalry—such as the Garter and the Bath.

The tendency to substitute the word 'chapter' for 'lodge' can be traced back to the 1750 period, Laurence Dermott referring to the Royal Arch gathering as being "more sublime and important than any of those which preceded it . . . and from its pre-eminence is denominated, amongst masons, a chapter."

By-laws of the Excellent Grand and Royal Chapter (1765) freely use the word. So does the Charter of Compact in the following year. Obviously the coming of the Grand Chapters of 1766 and 1771 encouraged the change-over to what was regarded as the more appropriate, even the more reverent, term, and we see this clearly exemplified in the course pursued by the senior Grand Chapter in warranting its first chapters in 1769. Each of them is given *two* names, one of a lodge and one of a chapter, as in these two examples: (*a*) The Restauration Lodge or Chapter of the Rock Fountain; (*b*) The Euphrates Lodge or Chapter of the Garden of Eden.

There are recorded instances of Royal Arch 'lodges' transforming themselves into 'chapters.'' Thus, Unanimity Lodge, Wakefield, met as a lodge on June 24, 1788, but by the next meeting had become a chapter.

It is not to be lightly assumed, however, that the change-over from 'lodge' to 'chapter,' 'Master' to 'Principal,' and so on, was a smooth, automatic process, for, as already shown, the Grand Chapter called itself for a time in the 1790's a 'Grand Lodge of Royal Arch Masons,' and in 1801 the head of 'Supreme Grand Chapter' was a 'Grand Master.'

In Ireland the word 'chapter' was slow in coming into use. It was more common to use the word 'assembly,' and the change-over in some places was not made until the coming of the Irish Grand Chapter in 1829.

'Companion'

Following the assembly of Royal Arch masons in chapter came the practice of calling them not 'Brethren,' but 'Companions,' a term not thought to have ancient masonic status, but still most apt in its derivation and association. In his speech quoted at p. 42 Chevalier Ramsay refers to three classes of Brethren: the Novices or Apprentices; the Companions or Professed; the Masters or Perfected. He ascribes "to the first, the moral virtues; to the second, the heroic virtues; and to the last, the Christian virtues; in such sort that our Institution encloses all the Philosophy of the Sentiments and all the Theology of the Heart."

Much less to the point is a note by Dr Oliver, who, having stated that Pythagoras distinguished his pupils by calling them Companions, goes on to say that the members of the Royal Arch are denominated 'Companions' and entitled to a full explanation of the mysteries of the Order, whereas members of the former degrees are recognized by the familiar appellation of 'Brothers,' and are kept in a state of profound ignorance of the sublime secret which is disclosed in the chapter. This sounds very fine, but Royal Arch masons were still Brethren in most places until late in the 1770's and in some lodges for long afterwards.

The derivation and the associations of the word are equally attractive. The word is built up of two Latin terms, one meaning 'together' and the other 'bread,' the implication being that Companions eat bread together—that is, share their meals with one another. In some orders of chivalry a knight is termed a 'Companion.' Paul the Apostle writes to his "brother and companion in labour," and Shakespeare freely uses the word.

'Exalt'

The term 'exalted' is in the Charter of Compact in 1766 and the minutes of the Chapter of Concord, No. 124, in 1787, and probably other records round about that date would reveal other instances of its use. Its adoption by masons must have been inspired by the extensive Biblical use of the word in its various forms. Psalm lxxxix, 19, says: "I have exalted one chosen out of the people." The Magnificat (St Luke i, 52) says, "He hath put down the mighty from their seats, and exalted them of low degree." The word, which is from the Latin and signifies 'to raise or lift up' (the one so raised being an 'exaltee'), has acquired the meaning 'to raise or elevate in dignity, rank, power, or position,' and it amply sustains the particular meaning which the freemason has given it.

Editions of the laws produced by the first Grand Chapter late in the eighteen-hundreds have a lengthy preamble addressed "to all the Companions of that estate but more particularly to INITIATES." So, apparently, not until early in the nineteenth century did it become really customary to use the now familiar word 'exaltee.'

The Sojourners

The word 'sojourner' also comes from the Latin, and incorporates the word *diurnus*, meaning 'daily.' Literally to 'sojourn' is to dwell in a place for a time, to live somewhere as a stranger and not as a member of the community. Genesis xii, 10, says that "Abram went down into Egypt to sojourn there," and still more apt is a verse in 1 Chronicles xxix, 15: "For we are strangers before thee, and sojourners, as were all our fathers: our days on the earth are as a shadow, and there is none abiding." Psalm xxxix, 12, says, "I am a stranger with thee, and a sojourner." There are many similar texts. The word 'sojourner' came straight into freemasonry from the Bible, in which there are well over fifty examples of its use in one form or another.

At the time of the Royal Arch 'union,' Sojourners in many chapters were known as the Junior, Senior, and Principal Sojourners respectively, and their duties were to guard the veils. At the opening of the chapter they individually answered questions addressed to them by the First Principal and explained their duties, and we see a reflection of this in to-day's table ritual. As from the formation of the first Grand Chapter the Sojourners were among the officers who were elected annually, but there grew up in some chapters a custom by which the elected Principal Sojourner exercised a privilege of appointing his two assistants. Indeed, a rule to this effect appears in the Royal Arch Regulations of 1823, this remaining in force until 1886, when the power of election returned to the chapter.

The Janitor

In early chapters the 'Janitor' was called the 'Tiler,' as in the Craft, and it is likely that the newer term was adopted merely to make a distinction. Literally the word 'Janitor' is quite apt, for it means 'Doorkeeper,' from the Latin *janua*, 'a door.' In some of the early chapters, there were a Junior and a Senior Janitor. *The Abstract of Laws* of Grand and Royal Chapter, 1778, gives a list of officers, including the Senior Janitor or Messenger, "proper to Grand Chapter," and the Junior Janitor or Common Doorkeeper "indispensably necessary to every regular Chapter." In the Cyrus Chapter, No. 21, meeting at the Three Tuns Tavern, Southwark, in the year 1801, and in some other chapters, there were two Janitors, one within and one without. St George's Chapter appointed a 'Jager' in 1786, the word being supposed to be a corrupt rendering of 'Janitor,' by which word it was replaced a year later.

Section Ten

THE 'UNION'—SUPREME GRAND CHAPTER, 1817

How the two opposing Craft bodies came to unite in 1813 is a story that cannot here be dwelt upon at length. The present purpose is merely to show how the Craft Union affected the status of Royal Arch masonry and, together with the Royal Arch Union four years later, settled for all the years that have since elapsed the somewhat anomalous position occupied by the Royal Arch in the English jurisdiction.

By the end of the eighteenth century there was in general an assimilation of ritual between the two Craft bodies and, on the part of wise and zealous masons, an ardent wish that these bodies should unite in peace and harmony under one Grand Lodge. There was much going and coming of moderate men between the lodges and Grand lodges of the two persuasions, and a great many Brethren were undoubtedly doing their best to minimize differences and smooth the path to union.

The passage of the years had done much to make union possible, for though between extreme lodges of the two persuasions there still remained considerable differences in working, it is equally sure that between the moderate lodges the differences were tending to become few. It is known that a few lodges made Entered Apprentices, Fellow Crafts, and Master Masons by both systems—that is, they put every Candidate in each degree through the separate ceremonies of both the 'Antients' and the 'Moderns,' while a regiment stationed at Lewes, Sussex, just a few years before the Union had two Craft lodges, one of each kind, working at the same time. Between moderate lodges there was quite an amount of visiting, and it was possible, for instance, for Benjamin Plummer, Grand Junior Warden of the 'Antients,' to be admitted into a meeting of the 'Moderns' Royal Lodge, Barnstaple, and occupy the Master's chair for the evening. In some extreme lodges remakings were still insisted upon, but in the more moderate ones visitors were accepted on taking the Obligation, and it is known that both 'Antients' and Irish Royal Arch masons were admitted to the English Grand Chapter on that basis.

Behind the scenes the movement to unite the two Craft bodies certainly started at least a generation before union was achieved. In the background worked many worthy masons, and the pity is we know so very little about them. We should like to know all their names and do them honour. A great figure working for peace was Lord Moira, who held the respect and confidence not only of his 'Moderns' Brethren, but, to a remarkable extent, of his Brethren in the opposite camp; this happy condition was easier in his case than in many others owing to his Grand Mastership in 1806-7 of the Grand Lodge of Scotland, with which and the Irish Grand Lodge the 'Antients' had maintained close accord all through their history. Undoubtedly the best men on both sides wanted and worked for peace; undoubtedly, too, the Royal Arch was a factor to be most seriously borne in mind both in the preliminary negotiations and in the final settlement.

One absurd anomaly still continued. The leading 'Moderns' Grand Officers were, almost to a man, members of chapters, but the official opposition to the Royal Arch still continued, and evidence of this is provided in the correspondence passing between a former Provincial Grand Master, the Rev. Prebendary Peters, and his deputy, the Rev. Matthew Barnett, Vicar of Market Rasen. In a letter written in 1813 the Prebendary says:

> As I have known some very respectable and good characters in the Royal Arch, I do not suppose that there is anything wrong connected with it. It is not known, however, to the National [premier] Grand Lodge. That power from which I am delegated, and of which you are my deputy, knows no other denominations of Masons than Enter'd Apprentices, Fellow Crafts and Master Masons. It is dangerous to proceed further, and I have reason to believe that beyond the Royal Arch, it is impious, and when carried to the length of some weak and deluded men, approaches the Infernal.

Six years earlier, in a letter to the same correspondent, he said that the 'Antients' had had the "impudence to enter into the Witham Lodge with all their Harlequin Aprons and Badges, but Mr. Thorold much to his honour instantly closed the Lodge and went away."

The available minutes do not disclose that the 'Antients' Grand Lodge was concerned in advancing the cause of the Royal Arch in their early exchanges with the 'Moderns.' The 'Antients' proceeded cautiously, seeking for every step the full accord of the Grand Lodges of Ireland and Scotland, and insisted in the early negotiations that all their Masters and Past Masters then constituting their Grand Lodge should be members of any new and united Grand Lodge; ultimately they gave way on this point, but not until they had been made to realize that there was not a building in London large enough to hold a Grand Lodge based on such a generous qualification.

As we read through the 'Antients' Grand Lodge minutes from 1797 to December 23, 1813, which was the date of the last meeting of that body before the union, we do not light upon a single indication that the Royal Arch was a consideration in the proposed union. And yet we know it must have been. We find the 'Antients' resolving in June 1810 that "a Masonic Union . . . on principles equal and honourable to both Grand Lodges and preserving inviolate the Land Marks of the Craft would be expedient and advantageous to both," and that this be communicated forthwith to the 'Antients' Grand Master, requesting his sentiments thereon, and also to the Earl of Moira ('Moderns'), with a declaration of their readiness to concur in such measures as might assist that most desirable end.

It seems clear that, so far as preliminary resolutions of the two bodies are concerned, it was not thought necessary to bring the Royal Arch into the immediate discussion. The reason seems to be easily forthcoming. To the 'Antients' the three Craft degrees and the Royal Arch comprehended essential masonry, and it is doubtful if it would occur to them that there would be any more purpose in mentioning one than the other in the early negotiations. It is to be expected that insistence on defining the exact position and status of the Royal Arch came from the 'Moderns,' though they, as we have shown over and over again, were in a ridiculous state of division on the subject, officially opposing—perhaps, towards the end of the time, *pretending* to be opposing—a degree which as individuals they may have regarded zealously and with affection.

Taking a common-sense view of the matter, we must assume that the 'Antients' went into the negotiations with the expectation that the degree would be fully acknowledged. Opposed to them were some who had other ideas—but only some, far from all. There is much significance in a minute of the senior Grand Chapter of December 10, 1811, when the First Grand Principal worked the sections of the Lectures and in his report on approaching union stated that *four degrees* were to be acknowledged. At this very late date the Grand Chapter seems still to have been working as a Chapter as well as a Grand governing body. Negotiations spread over a considerable time, and it is in November 1813 that the immediately approaching union of the two Grand Lodges was announced in the senior Grand Chapter by the Duke of Sussex, M.E.Z., who was invested by Grand Chapter "with the fullest powers to negotiate a union of the Grand *Lodges*" in such a way as might appear to be "most conducive to the general interest of Masonry."

In the actual negotiations it can be safely assumed that the 'Antients' contended for the full recognition of the Royal Arch Degree, and that any attempt on the part of the 'Moderns' to eliminate that degree would have brought the negotiations to an end, but it may well be argued from the known result that, while the 'Moderns' were prepared to retain the

Royal Arch, officially they were not prepared for it to rank in parity with the three Craft degrees. We see in the result a compromise to which the superior negotiating ability of the 'Moderns' must have contributed.

A. R. Hewitt contends that there was no real R.A. Union comparable with the Union of the two Grand Lodges. He states:

> For the Union of the Grand Lodges a number of representatives from each had met and negotiated. In the case of the Royal Arch 'union' only Sussex was appointed to negotiate. What, if any, negotiations were carried on is not known. No formal document was executed and signed for ratification by a joint meeting. For *union* there must be two or more bodies willing to unite but there was in fact only one sovereign independent Royal Arch body, the Grand and Royal Chapter of 1766. The so-called Grand Chapter of the Antients had no existence separate from the Grand Lodge of the Antients, no independence of action. It was a part of its Grand Lodge, and when that body disappeared at the Craft Union in 1813 its Grand Chapter must of necessity have disappeared with it. With whom then did the Grand and Royal Chapter or its representative, the Duke of Sussex, negotiate? Remembering that the Duke was authorised to negotiate with the Grand *Lodge* it seems obvious that the original Grand Chapter did not acknowledge the existence of any other Grand Chapter. The minutes of the meeting held on March 18th, 1817, at which the Supreme Grand Chapter came into being, record that "The Members of the two former Grand Chapters having been summoned to meet this day they assembled in separate apartments." The occasion could more truthfully be described as a meeting not between two independent bodies about to unite but between one independent body and a number of Royal Arch Masons who had been members of the 'Antients' Grand Lodge which had disappeared four years earlier.
>
> If this is accepted then it is misleading to refer to the Royal Arch activities of 1817 as a 'union' of Grand Chapters and to have called the new body by the style and title of the United Grand Chapter, a title soon to be dropped (at the end of 1821) for that of Supreme Grand Chapter. True, at the first meeting reference was made to the "two former Grand Chapters" and to the "United Grand Chapter", expressions which it may have been thought expedient to use as a compliment to the eminent members of the former 'Antients' Grand Lodge present and about to become officers and members of the new body. That there were protracted discussions about the future of the Royal Arch during the Craft Union negotiations there can be no doubt for it is obvious that the 'Antients' Grand Lodge insisted on recognition of the Order by the 'Moderns' as an integral part of masonry, hence the inclusion in the Articles of Union of the much quoted phrase that masonry consists of three degrees and no more, viz., those of the entered apprentice, the fellow craft and the master mason, including the Supreme Order of the Holy Royal Arch. Such discussions were between brethren who, although meeting as representatives of the two Grand Lodges, were also Royal Arch Masons of distinction in their respective systems.

PLATE XII

TRACING-BOARD (COMBINED THIRD
DEGREE AND ROYAL ARCH)
OF CHURCHILL LODGE, NO. 478,
OXFORD
By courtesy of the Lodge

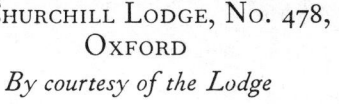

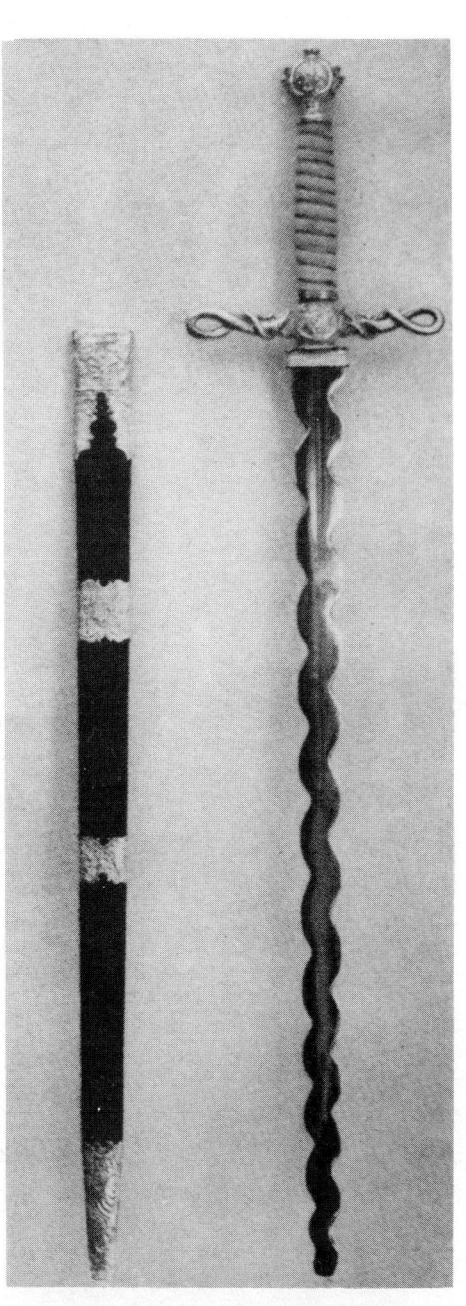

CEREMONIAL SWORD USED IN
'ANTIENTS' GRAND LODGE
AND NOW BORNE IN SUPREME
GRAND CHAPTER
By courtesy of United Grand Lodge

PLATE XIII

Apron worked on satin and ornamented in appliqué; date 1814.

Possibly an Irish apron; representative of many degrees; c. 1800.

TWO PAINTED APRONS WORKED IN APPLIQUÉ
By courtesy of United Grand Lodge

The Phrase "Pure Antient Masonry"

"What may have been meant by 'Pure Antient Masonry' in 1813 can only be guessed at, but one thing is clear—it included the Holy Royal Arch." Probably that is about the shortest and the wisest statement that has been made by the many students who have written on the subject (it is Roderick H. Baxter's), but it will not satisfy the reader seeking enlightenment, and some comments may therefore be offered in the hope of helping him.

It must be admitted that all through the nineteenth century the declaration relating to "Pure Antient Masonry" was treated by most masonic writers not as a statement of a fact, but, as Douglas Knoop remarks, "as a mythical claim, not to be taken seriously." Hughan, Gould, Findel, and others asserted that the Royal Arch was an extra or additional degree, and they could hardly have held that it was, in truth, a part of "Pure Antient Masonry." Gould asked why, if one Grand Lodge could add to the system of Ancient Masonry, another could not, and he hinted that discussion on the subject might centre upon another vexed question, that of the landmarks. G. W. Speth thought that the term "Pure Antient Masonry" could apply only to the system that was universally accepted up to 1729.

Redfern Kelly, whose lengthy paper in *A.Q.C.*, vol. xxx, is among the more important and controversial commentaries on the subject, elaborates Speth's argument that nothing beyond the Third Degree had been generally accepted before 1740, that being the approximate date when the Royal Arch first appeared in Great Britain; by the time it became generally worked by the 'Antients,' it could not, he thought, be "pure freemasonry," because the Premier Grand Lodge of England and the Grand Lodges of Ireland and Scotland had not yet acknowledged it in any way. When in 1813 the Grand Lodge of England officially recognized the Royal Arch it was much too late for that Grand Lodge to pretend to have any authority over universal freemasonry, says Redfern Kelly, at the reference above given, inasmuch as independent Grand Lodges now existed with as much right to a hearing as England herself; he thought that the limit of development in 1729 was the Third Degree, and that the only system that has ever been *universally* accepted is that of the Three Craft Degrees, which alone constitute Pure and Antient Freemasonry. But to a large body of freemasons Redfern Kelly's conclusion is hurtful and far from being necessarily correct; such Brethren do not believe that when the United Grand Lodge declared that Royal Arch masonry was part of "Pure Antient Masonry," it was offering an empty, not to say an untrue statement.

The happiest view of the matter has been offered by Douglas Knoop, who, in agreeing that it is difficult to take the declaration literally, yet says that the only way is to recognize that "Pure Antient Masonry" can be identified, not with the Three Craft Degrees alone, but rather with the esoteric knowledge associated with them, irrespective of the presentation of that knowledge in one, two, or three instalments. He holds that the claim of the Royal Arch to be part of "Pure Antient Masonry" can be judged, not by trying to trace the Royal Arch back to 1717 or so, but by considering whether the principal esoteric knowledge associated with the Royal Arch can be shown to have existed when the Premier Grand Lodge was founded (1717). If that can be shown to be the case, he says, then the Royal Arch can claim to be part of "Pure Antient Masonry" with as much justification as the Three Craft Degrees.

The crowning anomaly in the history of the Royal Arch, which is a series of anomalies, is the one implicit in the declaration of 1817 that Royal Arch masonry does not constitute a degree. It is said that the 'Moderns' Brethren were most favourably disposed to the preservation in its entirety of the Royal Arch Degree. As *Brethren* no doubt many were, but it is a curious reflection that there must still at that late date have been an amount of official opposition to complete recognition, for otherwise the Royal Arch would have kept its pre-Union status of a full degree. Nominally it failed to do that, although in effect it remains a degree, as it always was and always will be, for we must ever remember that a degree is but a step and that nobody can question that the Candidate in an Exaltation ceremony takes a step of high masonic importance. Is it not odd that what was held in 1813 to be merely the completion of a Craft degree should have been allowed to remain under the jurisdiction of a non-Craft body, even granting that the personnel of the Grand Chapter is closely identified with that of the Grand Lodge? Such an anomalous condition could come only as a result of compromise arrived at after hard bargaining—a compromise possible only in the English way of thought—but it must be admitted that the compromise, illogical as it is, has worked. Outside the English jurisdiction the Royal Arch is a separate degree.

After the Craft Union

There is no mention of the Royal Arch in the Craft *Constitutions* of 1815–47. Only in 1853 was the preliminary declaration as we have it in the *Constitutions* to-day printed by way of a preamble. The Lodge of Promulgation (1809–11), whose special and temporary task was to promulgate actually "restore," the old landmarks and to prepare masons of the 'Moderns' Craft lodges for the coming alterations in ceremonial, made plain the way for another temporary lodge, the Lodge of Reconciliation (1813–16), whose special duty was to reconcile existing Craft ceremonials and to produce what was in effect an agreed ritual.

With the object of entering into an International Compact, representatives of the Grand Lodges of Ireland, Scotland, and England met together in London in July 1814, and, but for uncertainty as to the position of the Royal Arch, obliging the Irish and Scots representatives to report back to their respective Grand Lodges, an agreement of lasting benefit to freemasonry would have been cemented. But at least one good thing came out of the conference: at its conclusion, at a meeting of the Restauration Chapter (the private chapter within Grand Chapter) held at Kensington Palace, four of the conference members were exalted—namely, the Duke of Leinster, Grand Master of Ireland; Lord Kinnaird, Grand Master-Elect of Scotland; the Earl of Rosslyn, Past Grand Master of Scotland; and Lord Dundas, Deputy Grand Master of England.

Royal Arch masonry was in a difficult position in the period intervening between the Craft Union and the so-called R.A. 'Union', in 1817. Indeed, it remained in an uneasy state for some few years afterwards, as, for reasons which are not properly understood, the Supreme Grand Chapter found difficulty in getting down to its work. The chapters, and those lodges working the R.A., were left to fend for themselves following the Craft Union. If there was still uncertainty in the Craft—and there was, of course, for some few years—how much more must there have been in the Royal Arch, left wondering from 1813 as to what exactly would happen! In support of this suggestion turn to the Twelve Brothers Lodge, meeting at the Blue Anchor Tavern, Portsea, Portsmouth, an 'Antients' lodge founded in 1808. An existing copy of its original by-laws has attached to it a letter revealing that while the lodge in 1816 was still, after the Union, holding Royal Arch meetings without a warrant from any Grand Chapter, the Provincial Grand Superintendent would not allow of admissions of Royal Arch masons made in an Irish military lodge, where the working must have been very much the same. Such anomalies as this would remain until a United Grand Chapter could bring thought to bear on the problems.

Supreme Grand Chapter, 1817

The Supreme Grand Chapter of Royal Arch Masons of England, following the example of the United Grand Lodge, was formed by the union of the two Grand bodies, the Grand Chapter of 1766 and the 'Antients' so-called Grand Chapter of 1771. This union was the natural consequence of the Craft Union, and must have been envisaged by those taking part in the earlier discussions. We know very little of the negotiations, if any, but it is on record that Augustus Frederick, Duke of Sussex, Grand Master of the United Grand Lodge and M.E.Z. of the premier Grand Chapter, had been given full power to conclude a union with the 'Antients' so-called Grand Chapter, and that the union was carried through after some delay. On March 18, 1817, members of the two former systems met, opened in separate chapters, and proceeded to a third chamber, where the M.E.Z. received them; they were then joined as one, officers of the combined Grand Chapter were elected, and a committee was formed to consider questions relating to laws and regulations, procedure, clothing, and so on.

The *Anno Lucis* date of the Union was, under the old system, 5821, but in that year the method of arriving at the year *Anno Lucis* was altered. Previously 4004 had been added to the year A.D., but in 1817 some little confusion was ended by substituting 4000 for 4004. On April 15, 1817, new Constitutions were adopted, but it was some little while before they were published. In the meantime the reconstitution of the R.A. had been formally reported to the Grand Lodge of England, which on September 3, 1817, passed the following resolution:

> That the Grand Lodge having been informed that the two Grand Chapters of the Order of the Royal Arch, existing prior to the Union of the Craft, had formed a junction, that rank and votes in all their meetings had been given to all the Officers of Grand Lodge, and that the Laws and Regulations of that body had been, as far as possible, assimilated, to those of the Craft, it was *Resolved Unanimously* That the Grand Lodge will at all times be disposed to acknowledge the proceedings of the Grand Chapter, and, so long as their arrangements do not interfere with the Regulations of the Grand Lodge, and are in conformity with the Act of Union, they will be ready to recognize, facilitate, and uphold the same.

Among the most important regulations made by the United Chapter are those acknowledging all chapters registered before December 27, 1813, and one requiring every regular chapter existing prior to that date unattached to any regular lodge to unite itself to a regular warranted Craft lodge, take its number, hold meetings at separate times from the lodge, and keep its records and accounts apart from those of the lodge. It follows that a Royal Arch chapter cannot exist under the English jurisdiction except it be attached to an existing Craft lodge itself warranted by Grand Lodge (Supreme Grand Chapter Regulation 45), though in Scotland, Canada, and the United States chapters continue to have a wholly independent existence under their own Grand Chapters. The idea behind this regulation did not have its origin in the United Grand Chapter. In the very earliest days it was understood by some that the chapter was either itself a part of the lodge or should be attached to it. It has already been shown that the earliest chapters warranted by the senior Grand Chapter were called in each case a lodge *or* chapter, although it is known that one of them, the Lodge of Hospitality or Chapter of Charity, probably comprehended two distinct bodies—a 'Moderns' lodge dating from July 22, 1769, and a chapter dating from December 8 of the same year. The Caledonian Chapter, out of which grew a new chapter that developed into the first Grand Chapter, was itself in association with the Caledonian Lodge, and this at such an early date as 1763.

The attachment of a chapter to a lodge was occasionally referred to early in the nineteenth century as the "grafting of the chapter on the lodge warrant."

The custom by which an individual lodge (or some of its Royal Arch members) applied for a charter as from the late 1760's must have fostered the very proper idea that the chapter was the natural complement of the lodge.

It is clear that the Act of Craft Union did not extend to any *lodges* the right to work the Royal Arch; this right had been enjoyed by the 'Antients' lodges up to that time, although an effort had been made in the 1790's to restrict the making of Royal Arch masons to the chapters, of which a considerable number had been founded in the decades immediately before the Craft Union.

It appears that some chapters must have had disinclination or difficulty in complying with the requirements of the United Grand Chapter, for there was considerable delay on the part of many of them in naming the lodges to which they had attached themselves. We find the quarterly communication of Grand Chapter in May 1821 requiring that such chapters as were existing prior to May 1817, and had not yet made known to which lodge they were attached, be allowed until the Grand Chapter in May 1822 to supply the information, each of them to receive a new charter free of expense. By February 1822 no fewer than ninety chapters were still in default.

Failure either to anchor the chapter to a lodge or return the information to the Grand Chapter (such failure had a way of happening in remote districts) sometimes had a most unfortunate sequel; a chapter unable after the lapse of years to satisfy Grand Chapter in a formal manner of its continuity of existence was unable to obtain a centenary warrant, although there had been no break in its meetings. There is the case, for example, of the Concord Chapter, No. 37, Bolton, actually founded in 1767, unable to qualify for its centenary warrant until 1936.

For a marked example of a chapter that met with trouble of this kind let the reader refer to the entry in the *Masonic Year Book* relating to

Chapter No. 339, at Penrith, dating back to 1830. Officially it achieved its centenary in 1930, but the centenary charter then granted refers in a preamble to the foundation of the chapter in 1788. According to Grand Chapter records its first warrant was cancelled in 1809 and, following the R.A. unification in 1817, no new warrant was issued. The chapter, however, has a minute-book dating back to January 25, 1818, and showing a succession of somewhat irregularly held meetings until the year 1823; then there comes an account of the "re-opening of the Chapter under a new Charter of Constitutions" on December 30, 1830. It then became the Chapter of Regularity, anchored to the Lodge of Unanimity, now No. 339, Penrith, the last lodge to be warranted by the 'Moderns' before the Craft Union in 1813. Although the chapter was erased in 1809, it was functioning in 1818, but officially its existence earlier than the latter year could not be acknowledged by Grand Chapter. The above details are taken from a valuable contribution to *A.Q.C.*, vol. lxvi, by Robert E. Burne, P.Z. of the chapter (who states, by the way, that there were Sunday meetings as late as 1847). In 1845 the minutes of the lodge to which the chapter was anchored show that Brother Wickham, a Doctor of Medicine, "passed the chair" in the lodge, and was proposed and seconded *in the lodge* to be exalted "to the Most Excellent Degree of Royal Arch Mason." At the next chapter meeting he was again proposed and seconded before Exaltation. Then, on April 10, 1848, again in the lodge, "in the Third Degree, it was proposed that Brother Percival be exalted to the degree of a Royal Arch Mason at the next meeting of the Chapter." Against this entry, in other writing, is the word "Irregular," and that, says Brother Burne, was "the end of proposals in the Lodge." In 1854 the Janitor of this chapter had held his office for twenty-six years, but his name had never been registered with Supreme Grand Chapter.

A chapter attached to a lodge that has become suspended or erased may be transferred to another lodge on request, subject to the approval of Grand Chapter and that of the lodge concerned; indeed, any chapter may in this way transfer to another lodge, but shall take the number and may be required to take the name of the second lodge; it thus follows that not more than one chapter may be attached to any one lodge at the same time. An example of chapters that have changed attachment is the St George's Chapter, which, attached to the Lodge of Friendship, No. 206, transferred in 1872 to the St George's Lodge, No. 140.

It is by no means unique to have a lodge and its associated chapter meeting in different towns. For example, Lodge of Freedom, No. 77, meets at Gravesend; the chapter of this number—the Hermes—meets at Sidcup. Lodge No. 1768 meets in Central London; the chapter of that number meets at Sutton.

It is obvious from the foregoing that every chapter carries a number that may have little relevance to the date of its founding, its place on the Register being determined not by its age, but by the number of the lodge to which it is attached. Whereas, after the Craft Union, the 'Antients' and the 'Moderns' Craft *lodges* 'took turns' or alternated in seniority in the list, an arrangement that looks fair but produced some startling anomalies, when it comes to *chapters* the confusion is often considerably worse. Thus the first five chapters in the list (other than the Grand Master's Chapter founded in 1886) include three going back to the eighteenth century, but not until a much later place do we reach another of that age. As examples, the Chapter of St James (year 1778) is No. 2; Chapter of Fidelity (year 1786), is No. 3; St George's (year 1785) is No. 5; Union Waterloo (year 1788) is No. 13; and then not till the twenty-eighth place comes another of the eighteenth century, the Jerusalem Chapter, No. 32 (year 1792). And so forth!

A few chapters working in Scotland under English charters that had been granted prior to the Royal Arch unification could not attach themselves to any Craft lodges in Scotland, and were permitted to continue their meetings and remain unattached. It is worth while recording their names: Land of Cakes, Eyemouth, Berwickshire (chartered 1787), became No. 15 in the Scottish Grand Chapter list in the year 1817. Similarly, Royal Bruce Castle Chapter, Lochmaben, Dumfriesshire (chartered in 1817), passed into the Scottish list in 1827 and is there No. 52[1]. Seven others are now extinct—namely, Royal Caledonian, Loyal Scots, Mount Sinai, Mount Lebanon, Royal Gallovidian, Royal St John's, and St Andrew's, the first-named dating from 1796 and the last-named from 1817.

It has been already remarked that for some years following the Union, Royal Arch masonry was in a somewhat chaotic condition. The records of a great many minute-books go to show that letters addressed to Grand Chapter were neglected, returns often unacknowledged and, perhaps as a result, failing to be made punctually in later years. There was throughout the country, particularly among the former 'Antients,' a decline in interest, leading in some cases to the (technical) lapsing of chapters and, at a much later date, to serious disappointment when a chapter sought confirmation of its continuity of existence. As from 1817, and before the new system got into working order, the 'Antients' lodges that had been conferring the degree in lodge continued to do so. Many chapters were carrying on under separate Royal Arch warrants from both 'Moderns' and 'Antients,' mostly granted many years before, and undoubtedly some bodies were working without warrants of any kind, blame for which could not always be laid upon their shoulders. Some Lancashire lodges—including Beauty,

No. 334, of Radcliffe; St John, No. 191, of Bury; and St John's, No. 348, of Bolton—petitioned repeatedly for a Royal Arch warrant (Norman Rogers remarks), and were nearly twenty years in getting it. Their failure was due in part to confusion at headquarters and also to a new policy that had come into existence with the Royal Arch Union, that of keeping the number of chapters below the number of Craft lodges, a policy which led to grievances. Cecil Adams has stated that of the eighteen chapters meeting in London in 1824 some were reported as meeting only occasionally; even so, many London petitions were rejected during the next fifty years, and even when the Royal Arch masons of the Grand Master's Lodge, No. 1, petitioned for a Charter in 1839 they failed to get one, and had to wait until 1886.

By 1823 about two hundred chapters had attached themselves to lodges, thirty-eight of them in Lancashire, seventeen in London, sixteen abroad, fourteen in the West Riding of Yorkshire and five (total) in North and East Ridings, nine in Cheshire, eight each in Devonshire, Hampshire, and Kent, six each in Somerset, Suffolk, Sussex, and Scotland, and fifty-three in other English counties. (Lodge charters had frequently been sold in pre-Union days, but as from 1823 the charter of a dissolved chapter could not be transferred without Grand Chapter's consent, and if sold or procured irregularly was forfeited and the chapter erased.)

The difficulties and delays in obtaining charters added to the bad feeling in some parts of the country where memories of the old quarrel were still fresh. Here is a typical instance, details of which have been provided by Norman Rogers. St John's Lodge, No. 348, Bolton, wrote on October 15, 1816, to the Grand Secretary saying that some of their Brethren had been made Royal Arch masons in a chapter, and others, under the 'Antients' system, in a Craft lodge. The former group looked upon the latter as illegal. The lodge asked for advice, wanted to know whether it would be justifiable to make Royal Arch masons on the 'Antients' system or whether it could have a dispensation until such times as a chapter warrant could be issued. Grand Lodge quickly pointed out that no arrangement had yet been entered upon and that, until then, former regulations should be observed. In reply to a letter sent late in 1821 the lodge was told that, owing to the unhinged state in which the Royal Arch had been for some time past, the meetings of the Grand Chapter had been temporarily suspended. Five years later the lodge asked for instructions on the manner in which it should obtain a dispensation to hold a Royal Arch chapter!

It is understandable that such unfortunate delays created exasperation in many quarters. Adding to the trouble was a suspicion of bias in appointing Provincial Officers. The practice of the Provincial Grand Master of Lancashire (suspended in 1826) of selecting his officers from what had been the 'Moderns' lodges and the failure of the Grand Chapter to issue warrants to the late 'Antients' lodges led to a bad feeling and played a part in the coming into being of the so-called Wigan Grand Lodge; this was formed by four lodges erased by Grand Lodge in 1823, was centred in Wigan and called itself "The Grand Lodge of Free and Accepted Masons of England according to the Old Institutions." Its career was not successful. After its second year or so it was in abeyance until 1838 and did hardly anything, although it continued to have an independent existence until 1913, when the only lodge surviving of the six constituted by it received a warrant from the United Grand Lodge and is now Lodge No. 3677 (Sincerity), meeting in Wigan.

The regulations of the United Grand Chapter published in 1823 did away with the Installed Master qualification in Candidates for Exaltation, and required merely that the Candidate should be a Master Mason of twelve months' standing. (The original minute is dated May 8, 1822.) In the course of time arose an arrangement by which the twelve months could be reduced to four weeks by dispensation, and in November 1893 the qualification was definitely made four weeks' standing as a Master Mason, and so it remains to this day.

To-day's Constitution of Grand Chapter

The last revision of the Royal Arch regulations was in 1955, the new regulations coming into force on January 1, 1956. The chief object of the revision was to make the regulations more compatible with modern Royal Arch conditions and also with the Craft *Constitutions*, in conjunction with which they may require to be read. The following notes are based on the new regulations.

The interests of the Order are governed by a general representation of all private chapters on the register and the Grand Officers, present and past, with the three Grand Principals at their head. This collective body is styled the Supreme Grand Chapter of Royal Arch Masons of England, and meets in convocation at quarterly intervals. First Principals, present and past, represent the private chapters, and retain membership of Grand Chapter as long as they continue to be subscribing members of a chapter. The regulations applying to Principals and their Installation are given in a later section of this book.

The Committee of General Purposes (consisting of the Grand Principals, Pro First Grand Principal, a President, and eight First Principals, present or past) meets at least four times each year; two of the eight members are annually appointed by the First Grand Principal, the six others being elected by Grand Chapter. Among its duties are to control the finances of Grand Chapter, examine and report on applications for charters, and, in general, act as a Board of General Purposes.

Regarding the appointment and election of Grand Officers, their essential qualification is that they must be the First Principal, present or past, of a chapter. The Grand Master of the Grand Lodge, if an Installed First Principal, shall be the First Grand Principal, but if he is not so qualified a First Grand Principal shall be elected annually and installed in May. Similarly, and if qualified, the Pro Grand Master is the Pro First Grand Principal, and the Deputy Grand Master is the Second Grand Principal; whom failing, then the First Grand Principal appoints the second, and, in any case, he also appoints the Third.

The Grand Secretary of the Grand Lodge, the Grand Treasurer, and the Grand Registrar occupy, if qualified, corresponding offices in the Royal Arch. Other Officers are appointed by the First Grand Principal. Grand Superintendents and Grand Inspectors are Grand Officers.

London Grand Chapter rank may be conferred on Past Principals of London chapters by the First Grand Principal. In the Provinces and Districts the Grand Superintendents are appointed, and their appointment is a prerogative of the First Grand Principal. Provincial or District Grand Chapters consist of the Grand Superintendent and other Provincial or District Grand Officers and Principals of Chapters. The appointment of the Grand Officers of a Province or District is in the hands of the Grand Superintendent.

A petition to Grand Chapter for a charter for a new chapter must be in approved form, signed by not fewer than nine Royal Arch masons, and be accompanied by a majority recommendation by the Master, Wardens, and members of the regular lodge to which the proposed chapter is to be attached. The precedence of the chapter is that of its Craft lodge.

Each chapter must be solemnly constituted according to ancient usage by a Grand Principal or some one appointed to that duty, and the chapter acts under the authority of its Charter of Constitution, which must be produced at every convocation.

A complete chapter consists of the Three Principals (considered conjointly and each severally as Master), two Scribes, Treasurer, Principal Sojourner and his two assistants, and other officers and Companions, making up the number of seventy-two. In excess of this number members may not hold the staff of office or be considered as Councillors when *more than seventy-two are present*. The officers of a chapter are appointed by the Principals if so resolved, or may be elected by ballot, except that the Three Principals and the Treasurer must be so elected. (In some chapters, even as late as the 1870's or so, the Principal Sojourner personally appointed his two assistants.)

The Installation and Investiture of officers must be as laid down in the chapter by-laws, and these, of course, must be in accord with Grand Chapter regulations. Every officer of a chapter, except the Janitor, must be a subscribing member of that chapter.

The precedence of officers is as follows: the Three Principals, Scribe E., Scribe N., Treasurer, Director of Ceremonies, Principal Sojourner, Assistant Sojourners, Assistant Director of Ceremonies, Organist, Assistant Scribe E., Stewards, and Janitor. It will be noted that the Treasurer, following an old Craft custom, ranks in precedence below the Scribe E. or Secretary, whereas in the Craft as from early in the nineteenth century the Treasurer ranks before the Secretary.

A regular convocation may not be cancelled or held otherwise than laid down in the chapter by-laws, except by dispensation, although Principals may call emergency convocations at any time. Every chapter must have by-laws, which must accord with regulations, and must make formal returns, at stated intervals, of the names of its Principals (this rule dates back to 1814) and of its members (a rule first encountered in the 1769 period).

A Candidate for Royal Arch masonry must have been a Master Mason for four weeks at least, and must produce his Grand Lodge certificate and also a certificate from his Craft lodge showing that he is a member and clear of all dues. Three black balls (less if the by-laws so provide) exclude. A member whose subscription to his chapter is three years in arrears (less if the by-laws so provide) shall cease to be a member, and can regain membership only by regular proposition and ballot. Suspension from privileges in, or expulsion from, the Craft by Grand Lodge or other competent authority applies equally to the individual's status and position in the Royal Arch, unless the proper authority declares otherwise.

Regulations relating to regalia are noted in a later section.

The Quorum

The 'Antients' had a rule "that no Chapter shall be convened and held for the purpose of exalting any person to the degree of Holy Royal Arch Mason unless six regular and registered Royal Arch Masons be present." In Bristol in the early days three Principals could open, but six more Companions had to be present to make an Exaltation regular. In 1894 the Grand Scribe E. said, in a letter, that he knew of nothing to prevent the ceremony of Exaltation being performed by the Three Principals with the assistance of two or three other Companions—strictly three. Back in 1765 and, of course, for long afterwards a quorum rather depended on the number of officers required to be present for the regular opening of the chapter, plus any Companions present after "the procession" had begun. It is understood that in Bristol no Exaltation can take place unless at least nine Companions are present, and that the Bristol Obligation includes a plain reference to the rule. Inasmuch as under Grand Chapter's Regulations of 1956 a petition to erect a new chapter must be signed by at least nine Companions, it is to be presumed that nine is the quorum.

Chapters of Instruction or Improvement

A Chapter of Instruction, often called a Chapter of Improvement, is held under the sanction of a warranted chapter or by the licence and authority of the First Grand Principal. The chapter sanctioning the Chapter of Improvement must see that its proceedings are in accordance with the regulations of the Order, and in every case an annual return to Grand Chapter must be made.

Chapters of Improvement have a long history. The first Grand Chapter arranged in 1783 for special chapters to be held for the purpose of instruction, and in the 1790's such chapters were sometimes convened by newspaper advertisements. Thus the first number of the *Morning Advertiser*, February 8, 1794, carried an advertisement of such meetings in connexion with "a Grand and Royal Chapter of this Sublime Degree" to be held on the second Thursday of every month at the King's Arms Tavern, Old Compton Street, Soho, London; it is proper to say that these meetings were probably in connexion with a non-regular chapter.

Prefixes and Styles of Address

In the minutes of Grand Chapter of December 24, 1766, the First Principal is described as the "M.E. & R.H. Lord Blayney." The early chapters were often inconsistent in these matters; one, the Chapter of Knowledge, meeting at the Dog and Partridge, Middleton, Lancs., used to conclude its summons with the words "By Order of the Eminent." Until 1811 the regulations of the premier Grand Chapter provided that the Three Principals and all Past Masters (actually Past Principals) should be styled "Most Excellent," other officers being "Excellent," the rest of the members, as well as visitors, being styled "Companions." By the then Rule VI the M.E.Z. had a casting vote. The statement relating to the Three Principals was omitted from the rules of 1817, but Rule VI was retained, and all rules issued since that date, including the revised rules of 1956, confirm that the M.E. the First Grand Principal has a casting vote.

The Three Principals in the earliest chapters were often called the Master and Wardens, and even the First Grand Principal was at times known as the Grand Master. It has long been held, and is expressly laid down in to-day's regulations, that the Three Principals of a chapter are to be considered conjointly and each severally as Master; they are equal in status and, although only one of them signs the minutes, that is purely a matter of convenience and no indication of priority. The status of the Second and Third Principals does not correspond in any sense to that of Wardens in a Craft lodge, and any one of the Three Principals can be spokesman.

The prefix 'Most Excellent' (M.E.) is nowadays accorded only to the Three Grand Principals and Pro First Grand Principal (all of them present and past). It is attached to the *titles* of Grand Superintendents and First Principals of private chapters, but not to the *names* of Companions holding such offices. In printed lists of attendances at Grand Chapter only the presiding Grand Principal is described as M.E.

The prefix 'Excellent' (E.) distinguishes Grand Officers and Principals of Chapters (all of them present and past). All other Royal Arch masons are 'Companions.' There are no salutes in Royal Arch masonry.

Section Eleven

TRADITIONAL HISTORY: THE CRYPT LEGEND

THE legend forming part of the Royal Arch traditional history is concerned with the accidental discovery of an underground chamber—a crypt on the site of the Temple of Jerusalem—and with the bringing to the light of the sun and of human knowledge certain things found within it. In the English ritual the account in the Biblical books of Ezra and Haggai and in the writings of the Jewish historian Josephus (A.D. 37–100) of the *rebuilding* of the Temple is interwoven with the legend, and the scene of the discoveries is a crypt, which, for the more convenient and dramatic course of the story, has now become an arched vault. The Sojourners (a word made familiar chiefly by Biblical usage and only occasionally found to-day outside freemasonry) may have been introduced by the early eighteenth-century arrangers for the excellent purpose of allowing the story to be unfolded by the Candidate (or some one speaking for him), he being an eyewitness of and partaker in the discoveries upon which the ceremonial depends.

In the Irish ritual the Biblical contribution is the still older story of the *repair* of the Temple and Hilkiah's discovery of the Volume of the Sacred Law, but the drama is centred on the crypt and developed in a similar way, and the symbolic interpretation is essentially the same as in the English system.

The Fourth-century Legend of the Royal Arch

It is a very old legend that provides the background of the traditional story. How old we cannot say, but in written form and in Greek it goes back to at least the fourth century. It is known in slightly different versions, apparently all derived from that of Philostorgius (who was born about A.D. 364), and can be found in a comparatively modern translation included in a famous series, the Ecclesiastical Library, published by Henry George Bohn in London in 1855. The full title of the book is: "The Ecclesiastical History of Sozoman, comprising a History of the Church from A.D. 304 to A.D. 440. Translated from the Greek: with a memoir of the Author. Also the Ecclesiastical History of Philostorgius, as epitomised by Photeus, Patriarch of Constantinople. Translated by

Edward Walford, M.A., late Senior Scholar of Balliol College, Oxford." Sozoman was an ecclesiastical historian. Photeus or Photius, a Greek scholar and theological writer of the Byzantine period, was Patriarch of Constantinople in 853 and died in 891. He compiled a *Bibliotheca* comprising a series of epitomies or digests of which the Philostorgius history was one.

All versions of the legend have necessarily a strong family likeness. A well-known and much-quoted version is that contained in Samuel Lee's *Orbis Miraculum*, published in 1659. Even a casual study of this now rare and famous book can scarcely fail to give the impression that the framers of the early Royal Arch ceremonial had access to it, and drew inspiration not only from its text but from its frontispiece (see Plate III), in which the figures strikingly suggest the appearance of Royal Arch Principal Officers in early days. (In an alchemical book of about the same period is an illustration even more strongly suggesting such a likeness.) Samuel Lee's frontispiece depicts Solomon, an obvious King, and Zadok, a priest in the Old Testament days who helped to carry "the ark of God." They hold between them a banner carrying the title of the book and texts in Greek and English—a quotation from Acts dealing with the coming out of Abraham from the land of the Chaldæans and a quotation from Hebrews dealing with certain sacrifices.

Samuel Lee was a classical scholar, born in London in 1629, Fellow of Wadham College in 1648, and at one time minister of St Botolph's, near Bishopsgate, London. In 1686 he went with his family to New England. Returning in the reign of William in 1691, he was captured by a French privateer and carried to St Malo, where he died. An edition of his book, reprinted (with some omissions) by Christopher Kelly, Dublin, in 1803 under the title *Solomon's Temple Spiritualized*, was claimed to have had the sanction and patronage of the Grand Lodge of Ireland.

Somewhere, about 1700 or perhaps earlier, the date being uncertain, was published *An Historical Catechism*, which reproduces a version of a story told in Godfrey Higgins's *Anacalypsis*, volume i, said to have been taken from a Greek manuscript, *Ecclesiastical History*, by Nicephorus Callistus, who is presumed to be a Byzantine writer of the late thirteenth or early fourteenth century; the work by Callistus had been translated into Latin and printed in 1552, and a double version giving both the Greek and the Latin text appeared in Paris in 1630. From Nicephorus Callistus is derived much or all of the *Book of God: The Apocalypse of Adam-Oannes* (Reeves and Turner, London, about 1880).

The reason for introducing all these names of authors and editors (more could have been mentioned) concerned in the publication and republication of the old legend is the desirability of preparing the reader for "discoveries" announced from time to time of extremely ancient Royal Arch legends, because such discoveries prove on investigation to be identical with, or a variant of one or other of, the versions given in the works above mentioned.

The Philostorgius Version of the Legend

Here is the legend as told in Walford's translation of the *Ecclesiastical History of Philostorgius*:

> Chap. 14. When Julian bade the city of Jerusalem to be rebuilt in order to refute openly the predictions of our Lord concerning it, he brought about exactly the opposite of what he intended. For his work was checked by many other prodigies from heaven; and especially, during the preparation of the foundations, one of the stones which was placed at the lowest part of the base, suddenly started from its place and opened the door of a certain cave hollowed out in the rock. Owing to its depth, it was difficult to see what was within this cave: so persons were appointed to investigate the matter, who, being anxious to find out the truth, let down one of their workmen by means of a rope. On being lowered down he found stagnant water reaching up to his knees; and, having gone round the place and felt the walls on every side, he found the cave to be a perfect square. Then, in his return, as he stood near about the middle, he struck his foot against a column which stood rising slightly above the water. As soon as he touched this pillar, he found lying upon it a book wrapped up in a very fine and thin linen cloth; and as soon as he had lifted it up just as he had found it, he gave a signal to his companions to draw him up again. As soon as he regained the light, he showed them the book, which struck them all with astonishment, especially because it appeared so new and fresh, considering the place where it had been found. This book, which appeared such a mighty prodigy in the eyes of both heathens and Jews, as soon as it was opened shows the following words in large letters: "In the beginning was the Word, and the Word was with God, and the Word was God." In fact, the volume contained that entire Gospel which had been declared by the divine tongue of the (beloved) disciple and the Virgin. Moreover, this miracle, together with other signs which were then shown from heaven, most clearly showed that "the word of the Lord would never go forth void," which had foretold that the devastation of the Temple should be perpetual. For that Book declared Him who had uttered those words long before, to be God and the Creator of the Universe; and it was a very clear proof that "their labour was but lost that built," seeing that the immutable decree of the Lord had condemned the Temple to eternal desolation.

The Julian referred to in the first line of the legend is the Roman Emperor Julian (331–363), surnamed the Apostate, who succeeded his uncle Constantine the Great in 361 and, in his tolerance of religion, gave the Jews permission to rebuild the Temple at Jerusalem, his motive being

PLATE XIV

BANNER PAINTED IN COLOURS, LATE EIGHTEENTH CENTURY

Once owned by an old chapter, No. 21. Note the Principals' headdresses and the breastplate worn by J. Note also the plumb-line, an association with the 'Antients' Craft Installation.

Photographed by courtesy of the Curator of the Canterbury Masonic Museum

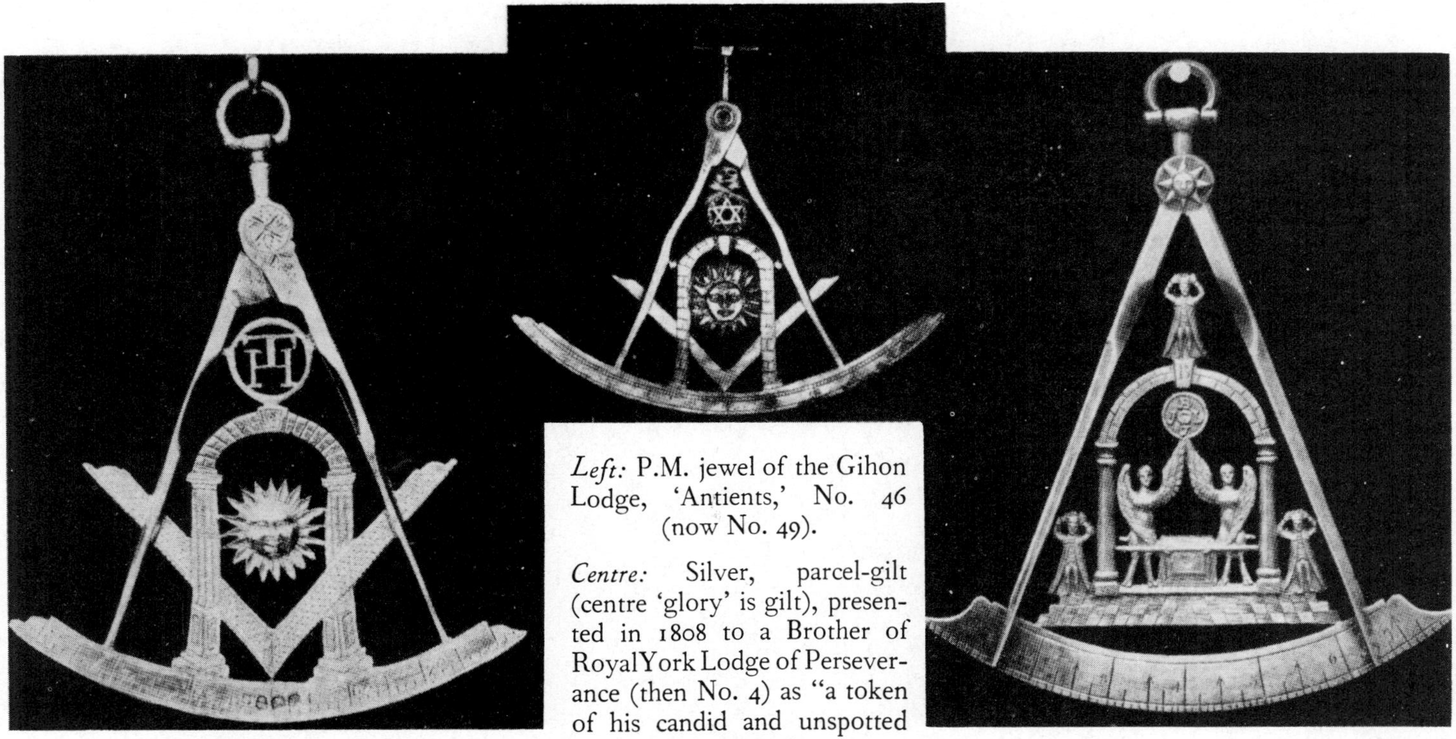

PLATE XV

Left: P.M. jewel of the Gihon Lodge, 'Antients,' No. 46 (now No. 49).

Centre: Silver, parcel-gilt (centre 'glory' is gilt), presented in 1808 to a Brother of Royal York Lodge of Perseverance (then No. 4) as "a token of his candid and unspotted behaviour."

Right: Probably Irish, P.M. and Excellent King.

COMBINED P.M. AND P.Z. JEWELS, LATE EIGHTEENTH CENTURY

to annoy the Christians, with whom, now that he had been converted back from Christianity, he had lost sympathy. From this it might appear that the actual subterranean chambers of King Solomon's Temple were disturbed not by Zerubbabel, but by Julian the Apostate, who undertook to rebuild the Temple of Herod (destroyed by Titus) in order to falsify the prophecy (Matthew xxiv, 2) that there should not remain one stone upon another: "Verily I say unto you, There shall not be left here one stone upon another." But the effect of his reopening the subterranean chambers which had been closed for centuries was that, according to one version of the fable, explosions of accumulated gas killed his workmen and still further disturbed the masonry, so that, so far from falsifying the prophecy, he, in fact, helped to fulfil it.

In Samuel Lee's *Orbis Miraculum* Ammianus Marcellinus is represented as relating the story of the Emperor Julian, who attempted at enormous cost to restore the most magnificent Temple at Jerusalem, which had been won by assault. He entrusted the work to Alypius of Antioch, but fire brought the work to an end.

The Callistus Version of the Legend

In another version of the legend, that by Callistus, it is an earthquake that interrupts the work. Here is his version much abbreviated (for an unabridged account, see *A.Q.C.*, vol. xii):

"The Jews having got together" skilled men and materials, cleansed the place and "provided spades made of silver" (at the public charge). They cleared the ground "so that there was not a stone remaining upon a stone, according to the prophecie." An earthquake the next day cast stones out of the foundation "so that many of the Jews were slain. . . . The publike buildings, also which were nearest the Temple were loosened, and falling down with great force, proved the sepulchres of those that were in them. . . . The earthquake was scarce over, but those that remained fell upon the work again, etc. But when the second time they attempted it, some fire violently issued out of the foundations . . . and consumed more than before. . . . Moreover, the fire which came down from Heaven consumed to ashes the hammers, graving tools, saws, hatchets, axes and all the other instruments which the Workmen had brought for their service, continuing a whole day together, etc., when Cyril, who was at the time Bishop of Jerusalem, saw these things: He considered in his minde the word of the Prophet *Daniel*, to which Christ also had set his seal in the Holy Gospel; He told them all, that now was the time that the Oracle of our Savour had its accomplishment; which said, That a stone should not remain upon a stone in the Temple. And when he had spoken this, a sore earthquake assiled the foundations, and cast out all the remaining stones, and dispersed them. Upon this there arose a fearful storm."

Once again fire destroyed the company of workers. The narrative continues:

> When the foundations were a laying ... there was a stone amongst the rest, to which the bottom of the foundation was fastened, that slipt from its place and discovered the mouth of a cave which had been cut in the rock. ... The Overseers ... tied a long rope to one of the Labourers and let him down ... searching every part of that hollow place, he found it to be four square, so far as he could conjecture by feeling.

Then follows the discovery in much the same words as in the first account above given.

It will be understood that in some details the versions vary one from the other, that they do not closely observe any precise order of events and that historical names are used with little or no regard for chronological sequence.

Other Versions of the Legend

The legends incorporated in the English, Irish, and Scottish rites are not the only ones by any means. The many variants cannot be given here (they belong more to certain additional degrees), but reference may be made to a vision of Enoch, father of Methuselah and the author of a Biblical book, which is known in a considerable number of versions. A. E. Waite, in a paper read before the Somerset Masters' Lodge in 1921, speaks of "The Book of Enoch," said by him to be a series of visions beheld

> by the Prophet when he was in the spirit ... a prototype of Masonic tradition ... especially reflected in the Royal Arch. It is said that God showed Enoch nine vaults in a vision, and that, with the assistance of Methuselah, his son, he proceeded to erect in the bosom of the mountain of Canaan a secret sanctuary, on the plan of which he had beheld, being vaults beneath one another. In the ninth, or undermost, Enoch placed a triangle of purest gold, on which he had inscribed that which was presumably the heart, essence and centre of the Sacred Tradition, the True Name of God.

Later in the paper the author refers "to the Royal Arch of Enoch or Knight of the Royal Arch, two titles and two forms, the second being incorporated into the long series of the Scottish rite."

The Vault

The discovery by the Sojourners is assumed to have been made on the return of the Jews from their Babylonian exile, approximately in the year 536 B.C. The crypt or vault in which the discoveries are made is not quite such a vault as might well have existed beneath the Sanctum Sanctorum, but is actually an arched vault of a construction closely associated with the medieval vaulted crypt, an architectural feature embodying a principle of construction not known until Gothic days and one well exemplified in the cathedrals of Norwich and Durham, these truly representing English Gothic architecture of the twelfth to the fourteenth centuries. The Sojourners gained entrance to the crypt by removing one or more arch stones or keystones, a job presenting considerable difficulty and involving risk both to the workers and to the structure, but obviously the story cannot stand up to critical investigation and was not intended to do so. It must be accepted for what it is—an attractive legend forming the background of a traditional history largely concerned with the efforts of the Jews returned from Babylonian exile to rebuild the Temple to the Honour and Glory of the Most High. A well-known masonic writer, the Rev. W. W. Covey Crump, once suggested that there may well be a factual basis for the legendary crypt, for he thinks that such crypts may be natural caves or survivals of structures built by Solomon and his successors; one of them, called *Bir arruah*—"the Well of Souls"—is said to be a place wherein spirits of deceased Moslems assemble twice a week for united prayer, but originally it seems to have been nothing more than a drain serving the sacrificial altar.

Symbolically the vault has always been associated with death and darkness. The Rev. Edward Young, an eighteenth-century writer, dwelling on subjects to which authors of his day were much addicted, speaks of

> The knell, the shroud, the mattock, and the grave,
> The deep damp vault, the darkness, and the worm.

Hence the imagery of the Royal Arch story, a simple allegory pointing the way from death to life, from darkness to light. With the many more elaborate symbolic explanations we in these pages are not concerned, but readers will be familiar with some of them occurring in the ritual, etc.

The crypt, of course, is an accepted hiding-place, and we have come to regard 'cryptic' things as secret things or as things that are uncovered or revealed only to the enlightened few; indeed, the word itself tells us as much, for it is a slightly corrupted form of the Greek *krupto*—"hide, keep secret."

The Arch

The arch is a very old architectural structure, but the use of the arch is not the most ancient way of covering in the space between two uprights. Much earlier than the arch is the method employed by the Babylonians, the Assyrians, the earliest Egyptians, and probably, to some extent, the Jews of Solomon's day—that of carrying beams across the opening. The arch, of course, made possible a much wider span, for the length of a beam is limited by its ability to support its own weight, and in the days of timber beams that length was not very great. Still, the arch was known in some countries at least two thousand years B.C., probably far earlier, and over a long period has been held to be an emblem of strength and beauty. Its use in symbolism has been largely inspired by the rainbow ("The triumphal arch fills the sky"), and quite early in masonic ritual (actually in 1723) we get this question and answer:

Q. Whence comes the pattern of an arch?
A. From the rainbow.

And Laurence Dermott, in his first edition of *Ahiman Rezon*, quotes:

> And to confirm my Promise unto thee,
> Amidst the Clouds my Bow a witness be;
> A heav'nly Arch.

One of two old brasses, only three inches wide and nine inches long, preserved in the Stirling Lodge, No. 30 (probably the old "Ludge of Stirlinge" and, if so, dating to long before the year 1708), carries a rough engraving depicting five concentric arches, probably based on the rainbow, although a rough arch stone is indicated; these brasses are illustrated in *A.Q.C.*, vol. vi. In a tracing-cloth or tracing-board bought in 1827 by the Chapter of Sincerity, No. 261, Taunton, a prominent emblem is a rainbow, the symbol of God's covenant with man: "I do set my bow in the cloud, and it shall be for a token of a covenant between me and the earth" (Genesis ix, 13).

Despite the insistence of the architectural idea, it must be said that many masonic writers have considered the possibility that the masonic word 'arch' originally had nothing to do with architecture, but was instead an adjective meaning 'chief,' as in 'archbishop,' 'archduke,' and 'arch-conspirator,' and some authors have suggested that the association of the word in early masonry with 'excellent' and 'super-excellent' supports that interpretation. The possibility cannot be ruled out, but the architectural interpretation is much the more likely, having regard to the close association between the arch stone and the vaulted crypt.

The suggestion has been made that, as the Greek word for 'beginning' is *arche*, it is possible to read "In the Arch was the Word ... and the Word was God." A well-known student regarded this as "an attractive possibility." It is certainly ingenious, but it must be remembered that the early and ordinary references in masonic literature to the arch relate to the noun representing a structure, and that this structure, in all probability, was introduced into freemasonry because its erection was then regarded as the work of the most highly skilled craftsmen and its invention and design a supreme achievement.

The true arch, the arch of freemasonry, derives its strength from its principle of construction. The vertical supports carry a series of tapered or wedge-shaped stones spanning the opening between them. Some strength may be provided by any cement or mortar joints between the stones, but the real strength of the arch, its ability to carry a load—and that, after all, is the usual purpose of the arch—depends on the presence of the keystone, the arch stone, the stone at the top and centre of the curve, without which the other stones must collapse. The arch stone functions independently of any cement or mortar, and transmits the weight of the superstructure through the other stones on both sides of it to the abutments or side-supports. In so doing, of course, it transmits an outward thrust that would tend to destroy the arch were it not for the supports, which have to be strong enough to resist the thrust, and are often buttressed, and were at one time often tied together for that purpose.

So the arch stone or keystone, the wedge-shaped centre stone, crowns or completes the structure and is an essential part of the true arch. It is sometimes called the cape-stone or cope-stone or coping-stone, although ordinarily a cope-stone is merely the top stone or top course of a wall, hence the stone that crowns or finishes the work. Robert Burns used the word symbolically when he spoke of "the last sad cape-stane o' his woes," and we get this same symbolism in the much-quoted phrase "The Royal Arch is the Cope-stone of the Masonic Order."

We have seen that the vault or crypt in Royal Arch masonry is a vault closed by a true arch, a catenarian arch, and it follows that the device of an arch, with arch stone removed or otherwise, is the accepted image of the vault or crypt in particular and of the Royal Arch in general. It has already been shown that it is in the highest degree unlikely that this particular form of vault or crypt could have been found in the Temple of Jerusalem, for the arch shown in masonic illustrations is the Gothic arch, taking our minds back to medieval days, when masons learned to design and build arches having a boldness and freedom unknown to those of ancient times.

We are all well aware of the anachronism involved. It is quite clear that the designers of Solomon's days were barely acquainted with the arch, still less with any means of arriving at its theoretical form, and that the catenarian idea symbolized in the Royal Arch chapter is an introduction of very much later days, being due originally, it is thought, to Galilei, who propounded it in the seventeenth century. The objection is not of much moment, for, although the traditional history based upon the Bible narrative belongs to a period a few centuries B.C., the ritual story tends largely to assume the complexion of medieval days, which, architecturally, were distinguished for one particular introduction, that of vaulting or arched roofing worked in stone.

The Catenarian Arch

While the form of the Craft or Symbolic lodge is that of an oblong square (two units long by one unit wide), that of a Royal Arch chapter approaches that of a true catenarian arch, symbolically preserving a memorial of the vaulted shrine. Further, the "impenetrable nature of this the strongest of all architectural forms" teaches various lessons which are brought to the attention of the Royal Arch mason. The word 'catenarian' is derived from a Latin word *catena*, meaning 'chain,' and in architecture

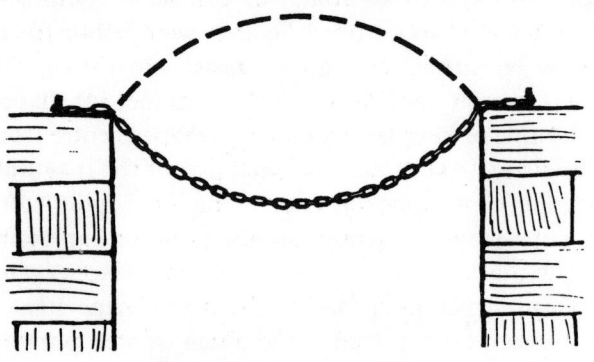

THE CATENARIAN ARCH

The dotted line indicates the curve of a catenarian arch described by the swinging chain.

refers to the curve which a chain (or a rope, etc.) naturally forms when suspended at its two ends. The curve so formed is a *catenarian* curve, and, when inverted, delineates the curve of a type of arch better able to resist forces of destruction than the earlier semicircular arch. Investigators who followed Galilei and studied the catenarian arch mathematically were able to show that a simple catenarian outline was formed by the chain suspended as already described, the length of the chain depending upon the required span and rise of the arch. More truly, the curve is given by *swinging* the chain suspended at its two ends (roughly, the skipping-rope gives the idea). It is highly probable that long before the properties of the catenarian arch had been developed by the philosophers the type of arch was known to the old freemasons who built Henry VII's chapel and other structures of about the same period.

A correspondent, aware that Sir Christopher Wren caused chains to be embedded in cement or concrete at the base of the dome of St Paul's Cathedral, suggested in *A.Q.C.*, vol. lxiv, that the term "catenarian arch" is not used as above explained, but merely implies a reference to Wren's chain. Such an implication arises from a misunderstanding. The catenarian arch is a philosopher's and mathematician's effort to produce an arch as nearly perfect as design and material could make it, one capable of supporting great weight and having a minimum destructive (sideways) thrust on the arch supports. Wren's chain has nothing to do with masonry; instead it is an engineering device for containing certain outward and destructive pressures. If Wren had so wished he could have contained those pressures in other ways, but æsthetic considerations, the need for economy of material, and any other of half a dozen reasons known to that remarkable architect led him to indulge in what was then a daring experiment.

The reader will appreciate that a chapter conforming to Wren's chain would be *circular* in plan and would not agree with the explanation in the ritual.

Reference to any architectural manual will show that the catenarian arch is one of a great many accepted arch forms.

In the Royal Arch chapter we have to use imagination to see the catenarian arch and its supports, for they exist there not in the vertical plane but in the horizontal. In the earliest Royal Arch lodges or chapters they may well have been represented by chalk lines on the floor. On the North side of the chapter are the Companions and Scribe E., forming one pillar; on the South the Companions and Scribe N., forming the other one. Those are the pillars with which we are familiar in Craft masonry. Connecting them in the East is the curved line of the catenarian arch, and at the apex of the curve are the Three Principals. In a public advertisement in London in 1754 the Scribes are referred to as the pillars, and in an old Scottish minute (Kilwinning, 1780) the Candidates are described as having "royally descended and ascended the Arch."

John Coustos in his evidence before the Inquisition in 1743 (see p. 43) said that on the floor of the London lodges were fashioned (in white chalk) two columns (those of the Temple). It is these columns which are still to be seen in the form of a Royal Arch chapter—but only by the eye of imagination!

The Triple Arch

Many tracing-boards and particularly jewels of the eighteenth century depict the arch with the centre stone removed, and in a great many cases the arch is not of single construction. Often it consists of three arches, one arch built within the other, perhaps the most notable example being the jewel worn by the Nine Worthies appointed by the 'Antients' in 1792 (see Plate XXXI); it will be seen that the arches are one within the other, so lending colour to the legendary story of the three separate discoveries made in the course of the successive removal of three arch stones.

A triple arch of quite different character appears in a certificate issued by a chapter of "the Royal Arch, York Rite," at Paris in the Phœnix Lodge in 1817—an attractive drawing of three arches probably of a completely impracticable character (see Plate II); two arches side by side have resting on their central arch stones a third arch. In another certificate issued by the same lodge there is the image of a semicircular arch divided by internal masonry to form three arches (see second · illustration, Plate II).

In an added degree whose ritual is closely suggested by that of the Royal Arch the essentials of the Royal Arch discovery were traditionally preserved through the centuries by certain means, including the construction of a secret vault which led through nine arches from Solomon's innermost apartment to a spot immediately under the Sanctum Sanctorum.

There is no doubt that some old chapters and Royal Arch lodges, particularly Irish and American, found some use in their ceremonial for miniature arches made of wood; one known to exist was semicircular, about eighteen inches wide and built of mahogany. A 'real' arch was used in the North of England ceremonial given in an earlier section.

The Double-cubical Stone

The most helpful inquiry into the evidence for the existence in ancient Jewish times of a double-cubical stone was made by the Rev. W. W. Covey Crump, and in publishing its result in *Miscellanea Latomorum*, vol. xxix, he admits that he does not know how the double-cube came into freemasonry, and feels that no precedent can be seriously claimed for it in ancient symbolism. (It is regretted that the learned author did not widen his search to include alchemical writings, for the basic idea of the double-cubical stone might possibly be found there.) The V.S.L., says Covey Crump, does not provide any authority for the idea that the Hebrews attached any significance to a cube or to a double cube, except that it can be inferred that the Sanctum Sanctorum of the *Mishkan* (or 'Tabernacle,' as distinct from the *Ohel*, or 'Tent') was a cubical apartment—10 cubits in length, breadth, and elevation. The Ark of the Covenant—by far the most sacred and important appurtenance of the Tabernacle and of the subsequent Temple—was 2½ by 1½ by 1½ cubits, thus neither a cube nor double cube. The Altar of Burnt Offering in the Tabernacle was 5 by 5 by 3 cubits, a hollow bronze enclosure intended to be filled with earth and stones. In the Temple of Solomon those dimensions were much greater, 20 by 20 by 10 cubits, but still did not constitute a double cube.

Finally, says Covey Crump, in the description of the Tabernacle (Exodus xxx, 2; xxxvii, 25) the dimensions of the Golden Altar of Incense are given as 1 by 1 by 2 cubits, thus a double cube (see Josephus iii, 6, 8). Modern scholars question whether there really was an Altar of Incense in the Mosaic Tabernacle, for at that period manual censers were used—that is, ladles of bronze with stems and handles of gold, such as are frequently shown on Egyptian monuments and referred to in Numbers xvi, 6, 39; Leviticus xvi, 12; and elsewhere. Not until the time of King Uzziah (roughly 759 B.C.) can we be certain that there was an Altar of Incense in the Temple (2 Chronicles xxvi, 16); after which time such altars became numerous in Jerusalem (2 Chronicles xxx, 14), but apparently no significance was attached to their proportions. In Zerubbabel's Temple there was a similar altar, which was carried away when the Temple was plundered in the second century B.C.

With the foundation-stone of King Solomon's Temple the mythical "Stone of Foundation" is often confused. Still quoting Covey Crump, the stone *Shethiyah* mentioned in the Talmud is said to have been taken from His throne in heaven by God, Who cast it into the primeval Abyss to form a foundation for the world. A Talmudic legend relates that it (or a fragment of it) became a base for the Ark of the Covenant in Solomon's Temple; there it stood "three fingers above the ground"—that is, not touching the ground, but poised in mid-air to preserve the sacred Ark from contact with the earth.

A remarkable allusion to Solomon's principal foundation-stone of the Temple occurs in Samuel Lee's *Orbis Miraculum*, freely quoted from earlier in this section:

> The Mysteries laid up in the foundation of the Temple .. some assert that God placed this [foundation] stone ... in the Centre of the World, for a firme basis and settled consistency for the Earth to rest upon. Others held this stone to be the first matter, only which all the beautiful visible beings of the World have bin hewn forth, and produced to light. Others relate that this was the very same stone laid by *Jacob* for a pillar near his head, in that night when he dreamed of an Angelical vision at *Bethel*, and afterward annointed and consecrated it unto God. Which when *Solomon* had found ... he durst not but lay it sure, as the Principal Foundation stone of the Temple. Nay (they say further) he caused to be engraven upon it, the Tetragrammaton or the ineffable name of Jehovah. All which stories are but so many idle and absurd conceits.

The characters borne by the double cube in our chapters are referred to at p. 246; meanwhile such an early and significant allusion as Samuel Lee's to a stone bearing the Tetragrammaton in engraved characters—it is of the year 1659—will not escape the reader's attention.

Section Twelve

TRADITIONAL HISTORY:
THE BIBLICAL BACKGROUND

The magnificent Temple built and furnished by King Solomon at stupendous cost of thought, labour, and of treasure was not blessed with long life. Solomon was surrounded by pagan peoples, and the Jews themselves tended from time to time to fall away into idolatry; indeed, ten of the twelve tribes broke away soon after Solomon's death to form an independent kingdom, which later made the fortified city of Samaria its capital. The two faithful tribes, Judah and Benjamin, held the mountain stronghold of Jerusalem, which, commanding the great trade route between Syria and Egypt, had brought Solomon both wealth and power; but for some hundreds of years to come the position was a difficult one, for in the long wars between the Assyrians and the Egyptians Palestine was often ravaged from many different points. In the fifth year of Rehoboam's reign the Egyptians sacked Jerusalem and carried away the gold from the Temple. Then, in the year 722 B.C., the Kingdom of Samaria fell, Israel became an Assyrian province, and the Ten Tribes were taken captive. But in Jerusalem itself Hezekiah paid tribute to his conquerors, and was able, to some extent, to restore the Temple worship. Eighty years later Josiah repaired the Temple, refurnished it, and it was at this time that Hilkiah found the Book of the Law in the House of the Lord, an event which will be dealt with when discussing the Irish ritual. (Our narrative embodies an account, probably by Lionel Vibert, in *Miscellanea Latomorum*, vol. xvi.)

What appeared to be the end both of Jerusalem and of its Temple came in 586 B.C., when, under the orders of Nebuchadnezzar, who was founding his Babylonian empire, Jerusalem was sacked, the Temple treasures were stolen, and the two faithful tribes, Judah and Benjamin, were carried off to Babylon, the only people left in the country of Judea being peasants and others whose enforced duty was to till the land.

In Babylon the Jewish exiles lived in small colonies, and, although they had no temples, they were able to form worshipping congregations which served to keep alive in at least a section of the people their love of Judea and their faith in their God. Their lament is set forth in emotional language in Psalm 137:

By the rivers of Babylon, there we sat down, yea, we wept when we remembered Zion. We hanged our harps upon the willows in the midst thereof. For there they that carried us away captive required of us a song; and they that wasted us required of us mirth, saying, Sing us one of the songs of Zion. How shall we sing the LORD's song in a strange land? If I forget thee, O Jerusalem, let my right hand forget her cunning. If I do not remember thee, let my tongue cleave to the roof of my mouth; if I prefer not Jerusalem above my chief joy.

The empire that Nebuchadnezzar had brought together had short shrift when the Medes and Persians came against it. About seventy years after the Jews went into exile Cyrus the Persian conquered Babylon and extended an empire which covered the countries of West Asia for the next two centuries. Only a few months after Cyrus had reached Babylon he issued an edict permitting the Jewish exiles to return to Palestine and inviting the two faithful tribes to rebuild the city and the Temple of Jerusalem. His motives in doing so are unknown, but what matters is that he gave the two tribes his protection, supplied them with treasure and materials for carrying out their work, and promised to restore the riches carried off from the Temple some seventy years before.

The invitation was not at first warmly or widely accepted, for most of the Jews, having been born in exile, had never seen Palestine, and it was only a small group that at first availed itself of the permission and made the journey to Palestine. A band of Jewish pioneers under Sheshbazzar returned to Jerusalem in 537 B.C. and started the work. Seventeen years later came a much stronger contingent under Zerubbabel, but the returned exiles were mortified to find that they could occupy only the ruins and immediate vicinity of Jerusalem, for tribes of mixed blood had moved into Judea during the years of exile.

Under Zerubbabel the Governor, Joshua the High Priest, and the Prophets Haggai and Zechariah the Second Temple was built, and dedicated, in 516 B.C., to the worship of God. Priests among the returned exiles regulated the ritual of the new Temple in accordance with the Book of the Law discovered by Hilkiah rather more than a century before. Cyrus had been succeeded by Cambyses, who, influenced by the hostility of the tribes dwelling near Jerusalem, stopped the work, but he in turn was succeeded by Darius Hystaspes, who gave the Jews badly needed assistance, for all through the period of the rebuilding they were harassed by the neighbouring tribes, in whom was more than a tinge of Jewish blood. The Samaritans, appealing to Darius, tried again to hinder the work, which, however, continued under the encouragement of Haggai the Prophet.

Darius permitted the stolen treasures to be returned to Jerusalem under armed escort, and it is this difficult and dangerous journey which is thought by some writers (and only some) to be symbolized by the early Royal Arch ceremony known as the 'passing of the veils' (see Section 17).

Haggai the Prophet deserves a great place in the narrative of the returned exiles. He had been born in Babylon, and is believed to have travelled to Judea with Zerubbabel, and to him fell the immediate task of exhorting the Jews to finish the rebuilding of the Temple, work in which there had been a break of about fourteen years owing to the hostile action of the neighbouring tribes. He assured the Jews that "the glory of this latter house shall be greater than of the former"—a difficult prophecy, inasmuch as the second Temple could not compare in its richness with the first one, but a prophecy claimed to have been fulfilled many years later when Christ entered it. The history of the period is to be found in the Book of Ezra, part of which book some scholars believe to have been written by Haggai. Not only with the Jews does the memory of Haggai stand in great regard, for both the Greeks and the Latins keep his festival, the former on December 16 and the latter on July 4.

As the years passed the Jewish priests, becoming careless and corrupt, neglected the Temple services. Fifty-eight years after the completion of the Temple Ezra arrived in Jerusalem, and at once set about reforming and purifying the priesthood; fourteen years later still Artaxerxes of Persia allowed Nehemiah (his aristocratic Jewish courtier and cup-bearer) to go to Jerusalem with the status of Governor. Under Nehemiah the Jews rebuilt the broken walls of the city, in face of the fierce hostility of the Samaritans, who were suffering under a grievance, for they had professed themselves as willing to assist the returned exiles to rebuild the Temple, but had been spurned by the two faithful tribes, who regarded them, in spite of their (largely) Jewish blood, as foreigners. All through the rebuilding of the Temple and of the walls of the city the Jews had to reckon with the hostile Samaritans, but they rebuilt the city walls in fifty-two days in spite of opposition. Their valour is recorded in the Book of Nehemiah iv, 17–18:

> They which builded on the wall, and they that bare burdens, with those that laded, every one with one of his hands wrought in the work, and with the other hand held a weapon. For the builders, every one had his sword girded by his side, and so builded.

It is this text that the ritual renders "with trowel in hand and sword at side."

Here, for a moment, we digress from the main narrative to remark that freemasons are not alone in having adopted as a symbol the sword and trowel. They were anticipated by the Order of the Templars, the aristocratic, rich Crusading order that arose in the year 1119, and which is said to have made of the trowel a fourfold device taking the form of the Cross of the East, the Temple Cross, known to us as the Maltese Cross or Cross of the Knights of St John. In this device, it is claimed, four trowels meet at their points. We learn from A. E. Waite that this same cross was an Assyrian emblem before Christian times, a curious coincidence. It is possibly a matter for slight wonder that Royal Arch masonry did not adopt the four-trowel cross as its symbol instead of the tau cross, which, although of great philosophical significance, has no obvious relation to the traditional history of the Order. But it is well worth noting that in the hexalpha jewel worn by the First Principal of the First Grand Chapter, as depicted in the margin of the Charter of Compact, the internal delta is actually a triangular trowel.

Among quite a number of books containing religious symbols and emblems published in the sixteenth and seventeenth centuries is the well-known *Choice of Emblemes* (reprinted in facsimile in 1866), by Geoffrey Whitney, who died in 1603–4. As in most of such works, there is a succession of engravings, each with descriptive verses, and one of these engravings (reproduced in Plate II of the present volume) depicts two hands extending from a cloud, the right one holding a sword, and the left a delta-shaped trowel. Here is the first of the verses accompanying the engraving:

> When Sanabal Hierusalem distrest,
> With sharp assaultes, in Nehemias tyme,
> To warre, and worke, the Jews them selves addrest
> And did repaire theire walls, with stone, and lime:
> One hand the sworde, against the foe did shake,
> The other hand, the trowell up did take.

During much of the time occupied by the rebuilding at Jerusalem a group of priests who had remained in the land of exile were putting into writing the ritual laws which had regulated the Temple worship in earlier days. Greville Lewis's excellent book[1] tells the story in simple terms. The priests were compiling something more elaborate than the Deuteronomy laws, for they were providing instruction on Temple services, Sabbath-keeping, and such like, and the result of their work is the priestly code given in parts of Exodus, Numbers, and especially Leviticus. Ezra, with fellow-priests, took the priestly code to Jerusalem and set out to create a Jewish nation. This was a turning-point in Jewish history, for the Jews accepted the code, and henceforth became known as "the People of the Book." In this we see the birth of Judaism—that is, the religion of the Jews when it became a religion of obedience to the Law, so elaborate and

[1] *An Approach to the New Testament* (Epworth Press, 1954).

complicated that it required the skill of specialists to teach it to the people. These teachers were the Scribes, mostly priests, of whom we hear so much in the Gospels of the New Testament.

The history of the Second Temple was as troublous as that of the First. Again plundered and again profaned, the Temple was dedicated to Jupiter but a few years later, in 168 B.C., Judas Maccabeus, the deliverer, rededicated it, an event which the Jews commemorate to this day, but on the death of the deliverer the Romans under Pompey entered the Temple and the Holy of Holies, and in 54 B.C. a successor, Crassus, finally carried off everything of value. But again the Temple was dedicated, some sort of worship maintained, and High Priests continued to be appointed. Herod the Great besieged Jerusalem, and eventually pulled down the Temple, although he allowed the priests to rebuild the Holy of Holies, while he himself built the great Court of the Gentiles. So, ultimately, every vestige of the Temple of Zerubbabel disappeared, and Herod erected on its site a temple with which he associated his own name.

That is a reasonable but highly condensed story of the Temple history, and provides much of the background for the Royal Arch ritual, but a few inconsistencies—anachronisms—may be mentioned. In the ritual story three great men—Zerubbabel, Joshua, and Haggai—are closely associated with the rebuilding of the Temple during the reign of Cyrus, but actually it was Zerubbabel who travelled from Babylon to Jerusalem, and when the three did collaborate it must have been in a later day, that of Darius. With Haggai was Zachariah, who is not mentioned in the ritual, but these two were co-workers with Zerubbabel. Then, in the ritual, Ezra and Nehemiah are associated, but this is quite a serious anachronism, for, although Ezra came to Jerusalem probably seventy years later than Zerubbabel, Nehemiah did not arrive in the city for yet thirteen more years. A period of roughly eighty years, therefore, separated Zerubbabel on the one hand and Ezra and Nehemiah on the other, and their work was the rebuilding of the walls of the *city*, not the walls of the *Temple*—although this last point is of small moment, because, from the masonic point of view, the Temple and city of Jerusalem are one. The Sojourners, who travelled by permission of Cyrus, apparently did not arrive until Darius was on the throne, and in the ritual they make their report to the Sanhedrin, which is unlikely to have been in existence in Zerubbabel's day.

Other inconsistencies in the Royal Arch ritual have been pointed out from time to time, and we may instance those mentioned in Lionel Vibert's address to the Essex First Principal's Chapter, reprinted in the 1934–35 *Transactions* of that chapter, and in the address by A. G. Duncan in the 1938–46 *Transactions* of the same chapter. Vibert holds that in the Royal Arch the sojourners make an independent discovery of the sacred word already known to the Principals and to E. and N.; they report it and their discovery is acknowledged to be correct. . . . We appear here to have a reminiscence of some other philosophy . . . the lesson that the truly humble workman, though engaged on unskilled and uninteresting work, may nevertheless find in it or by it a great reward . . . entitling him to a place among the wisest of men and in the council of rulers.

A. G. Duncan says that by no stretch of imagination could the names and symbols revealed in the vault be the secret which enabled Hiram to function as a Master Mason, but that the Royal Arch mason "realises that below the surface aspect of our rites and ceremonies is the substance . . . which each must grasp for himself." W. W. Covey Crump says that to us the Temple of Zerubbabel is a prototype and its erection is a parable of our own masonic work.

The dimensions of the Temple have many times been investigated. Roderick H. Baxter, having studied the comparative dimensions of the various temples built by the Jews at Jerusalem, concludes that Zerubbabel's Temple was more or less the same size as Solomon's, except that the total width was one-third more, the chambers and gallery roughly half again as wide, and the outer courts more than three times as long. He gives the total length of Solomon's Temple as ninety cubits, and its total width as forty-five cubits, and its height (which is subject to question) as sixty cubits.

Between the women's court and the men's, says a seventeenth-century work, *Moses and Aaron*, written by a divine, Thomas Godwyn, "there was an ascent of fifteen steps or stairs . . . upon these steps the Levites sung those fifteen Psalms immediately following the one hundredth-and-nineteenth, upon every step one Psalm, whence those Psalms are entitled *Psalmi Graduales*, Songs of Degrees." (Many of the Psalms are described in the Bible as "Songs of Degrees." It will be noted that a flight of three, five, and seven steps gives a total of fifteen.)

The Sanhedrin or Sanhedrim

The supreme judicial council of the Jews was the Sanhedrin (a word commonly spelled 'Sanhedrim'). The word comes from the Greek through the Hebrew and means 'a council,' 'a sitting together.' Traditionally the Sanhedrin existed from the time of Moses, but historically, especially in view of the derivation of the word, it is safer to regard the great Sanhedrin as having existed from the days of Judas Maccabeus (second century B.C.) till somewhere about A.D. 425. It was the supreme place of judgment, and was sometimes called Beth Din, the House of

Judgment. Constituted of chief priests and other learned men engaged in sacred duties, it had as its chief officer a prince (*nasi* or president), who is believed in the later days to have enjoyed a hereditary office. The Sanhedrin was a State council, a legislature that interpreted tradition and religious laws and regulations, a parliament with responsibility for military decisions, a high court of justice, and it met daily except on sabbaths and feast-days.

The New Testament calls the members of the Sanhedrin "elders"—obviously they were men of acknowledged position and standing—and there were seventy of them, in accordance with Numbers xi, 16: "And the Lord said unto Moses, Gather unto me seventy men of the elders of Israel, whom thou knowest to be the elders of the people, and officers over them; and bring them unto the tabernacle of the congregation, that they may stand there with thee." The President was in addition to this number. (When Napoleon attempted by edict to erect a Jewish Sanhedrin in France in 1806 he fixed the number at seventy-one.) The assembly sat usually in a hall near the great gate of the Temple, and in the form of a semicircle, the President's raised seat being in the centre. In a two-volume Latin book by Jehan Faure (Toulouse, France, 1517) is a full-page wood engraving entitled "Arbor Judaica," representing three judges occupying the presidential raised seat, the whole bearing a strong resemblance to the principal officers of a Royal Arch chapter. (Reference has already been made to the frontispiece of Samuel Lee's *Orbis Miraculum* and to alchemical illustrations depicting a somewhat similar arrangement.)

How the Royal Arch ritual came to emphasize that the august Sanhedrin had *seventy-two* members and to use the phrase "unless *seventy-two* of the elders be present" has been much debated. It is barely possible that it is merely a literal mistake, but quite definitely the number seventy-two is everywhere accepted in Royal Arch practice.

It is very difficult to believe that, in arriving at this number, its cabbalistic significance was any consideration, but a French author has shown that the equilateral triangle containing the Tetragrammaton could be calculated to give the mystical number of seventy-two. The present writer, however, is sceptical of any 'evidence' founded on the mystical value of alphabetical letters.

It is impossible to rule out, nevertheless, the influence of the number seventy-two. For example, the name Jehovah is said to comprehend the seventy-two names of God; then, too, the Greek translation of the Old Testament scriptures, the oldest translation known, was alleged at one time to have been made by six translators from each Jewish tribe, seventy-two in all, who completed their work in seventy-two days, thus giving the name "Septuagint" to the translation!

PLATE XVI

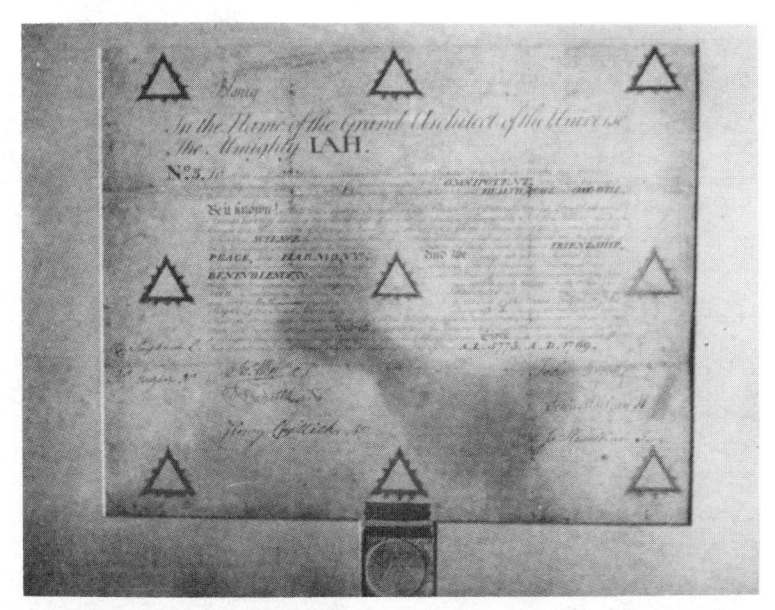

CHARTER OF THE CANA CHAPTER, COLNE, NO. 116
Dated 1769, one of the earliest granted; the seal shows the jewel of the First
Grand Principal.
(See Plate IV, with which this charter should be compared.)

BANNER OF AN OLD LODGE, NO. 208, AT WIGTON, CUMBERLAND
It displays emblems of the Royal Arch and other degrees.
Both illustrations are from Beesley's *Record of Antiquities*.
By courtesy of the Manchester Association for Masonic Research

PLATE XVII

One of the chairs of Duke of Athol Lodge, No. 210, then of Denton, Lancs; 7 feet 10 inches high, of walnut.

One of the chairs of Lodge of Charity, No. 350, Farnworth, Lancs; 7 feet high, displaying many painted symbols. In cipher are the words " Establish " and " In this sign I conquer."

TWO HANDSOME CHAIRS, COMBINED CRAFT AND ROYAL ARCH
From Beesley's *Record of Antiquities*.
By courtesy of the Manchester Association for Masonic Research

The number of Companions additional to the Principals and Scribes in a Royal Arch chapter is in theory limited to seventy-two, and if in practice this number is exceeded the Companions in excess of the number may not bear the staff of office. As one version of the ritual says: "this staff you will be always entitled to bear, unless seventy-two of your elders be present"; in that case, the full number of the Sanhedrin being completed, the younger members must be excluded," the "exclusion" being from office.

We know that the limitation of the number to seventy-two goes back at least as far as 1778, when in the 'Antients' chapters there were the Three Principals, Two Scribes, Three Sojourners, and Seventy-two others as council; we know also that the premier Grand Chapter observed that same number. J. Heron Lepper has suggested that the number cannot now be taken literally, but is to be regarded as a relic of the past, bearing in mind, for example, that at Grand Chapter meetings far more than seventy-two Companions are always present, each with a right to speak and vote.

The Irish Tradition: Repairing the Temple

Much is made of the difference between the English and the Irish traditional histories. They appear to be so different, but in *essentials* the two ceremonies are much the same. Although the details do not agree and in the Irish ceremony the Candidates themselves take a more active part in the working out of the drama, in both the English and the Irish versions a part of the whole of the early Sacred Law is among the traditional discoveries, and it is not too much to say that the two rituals are identical in philosophy and teaching. The qualifications of the Candidates are not the same, and it is impossible for the Royal Arch mason of one jurisdiction to effect an entrance into a chapter held under the other unless supported by independent credentials. As already made quite clear, the English legend refers to the *rebuilding* of the Second Temple by Zerubbabel and the Irish to the *repairing* of Solomon's Temple by Josiah.

The Biblical history upon which the Irish narrative is partly based is to be found in 2 Kings xxii. Josiah, a good King, but only eight years old when he began his reign, was on the throne in Jerusalem for thirty-one years. He sent Shaphan (a Scribe and of a family of Scribes), son of Azaliah, to the House of the Lord, and there he ordered Hilkiah, the High Priest, to make over the silver contributed by the people to those engaged in the repairing of the Temple—"unto carpenters, and builders, and masons, and to buy timber and hewn stone to repair the house." Hilkiah, probably acting as overseer, brought back to Shaphan the report: "I have found the book of the law in the house of the Lord. And Hilkiah gave the

Book to Shaphan, and he read it." Further, Shaphan read it before King Josiah, who greatly feared when he heard of the wrath of God. Huldah, a prophetess, "a wise woman," reassured the King, and told him that because of his tenderness and humility, he would be gathered to his fathers in peace and would not see all the evil that would come. The people having been called to the Temple, the King read to them the Book of the Covenant that had been found during the repairing of the Temple, and he made a new covenant—namely, to keep the commandments and to perform the words of the Covenant that were written in the Book. (In Carpenters' Hall, London, are to be seen paintings of Henry VIII's day, discovered only in 1845, illustrating Josiah's repairing of the Temple.)

The discovery of what are known as the Dead Sea Scrolls within a few miles of the site of Solomon's Temple is a remarkable parallel in modern times to the finding of the scroll of the Book of the Law. Very ancient Hebrew scrolls were discovered that had been preserved in quite natural conditions certainly for many hundreds and possibly for a few thousands of years. Seven scrolls came to light in 1947, and later the fragments of four hundred others. They are chiefly of papyrus and leather preserved by the natural action of the very hot, dry climate at a depth of many hundreds of feet below sea-level. (The surface of the Dead Sea itself is more than twelve hundred feet below sea-level.) Scholars have already spent years in the task of deciphering the scrolls, and say that some contain variations of stories told in the Book of Genesis, while others are copies of the Book of Isaiah and about a thousand years older than any comparable Hebrew writings in the Old Testament.

An impression commonly prevailing at one time was that the Book of the Law mentioned in both Irish and English ceremonies was the Bible. A moment's thought will show that to be impossible. The discovery was made at a time when even the history of King Solomon's reign had not been committed to writing. It has been traditionally thought that the book was the Torah, now known as the Pentateuch, literally "five tools" or "five books" comprising the first five books of the Old Testament (Genesis, Exodus, Leviticus, Numbers, and Deuteronomy, and perhaps part of Joshua), known as the Law of Moses or the Book of Moses. *A Pictorial History of the Jewish People* suggests that this traditional belief is at fault, and that the discovery is nothing more than the Book of Deuteronomy, and that until its discovery there had been no written Torah or law for the guidance and teaching of the people, who therefore relied on oral tradition, into which it was easy for heathen beliefs to creep. The authority quoted says that "the discovery of the Fifth Book of Moses, therefore, was epoch-making in its effect on the future course of the Jewish religion and on the development of the Jews as a people." This view is supported by Dr A. G. Aglen, who says that the book discovered was either Deuteronomy or the central part of that book, this book codifying what both prophets and priests had always taught.

Josiah's work of reformation included the uprooting of pagan worship. A great religious movement was concluded by the observance of "such a passover" as had not been kept "from the days of the judges . . . nor in all the days of the kings of Israel, nor of the kings of Judah."

Learned archæologists who have studied the discovery made under Hilkiah believe that the writings in the foundation chamber were etched not in Hebrew (which was not the original or universal language of mankind, and, indeed, at that date was little more than an obscure dialect), but in cuneiform script that in those days was current through all the land between the River of the East and the River of the South.

The Irish legend superimposes upon the Biblical story the discovery of certain "foundation deposits," including the squares of the three Grand Masters, ancient coins, an engraved golden plate, and a cubic stone on which had been sculptured certain initial letters.

There has been argument as to whether, at one time, in the early days of the Royal Arch, there were two distinct traditional histories in use in the Irish lodges or chapters. W. J. Chetwode Crawley speaks of an ill-advised and unsuccessful attempt, lasting intermittently from 1829 to early in the 1860's, to introduce the English version into the Irish chapters. He is referring to the Irish Grand Chapter at its constitution in 1829, when it attempted to follow the Zerubbabel story, but, owing apparently to the custom of conferring certain step degrees to qualify the Candidate, met formidable difficulties. Thus, at times in the nineteenth century, in some parts of Ireland, one version was worked, and in another the other version. A special committee appointed in 1856 to inquire into the confusion completed its labours in 1863, and as a result it was decided to insist upon the story of the *repair* of the Temple as the *motif* of the traditional history, the principal officers being designated J., H., and S. instead of, as in England and elsewhere, Z., H., and J.

Section Thirteen

THE INEFFABLE NAME

The Ineffable Name, the name that may not be uttered, is a subject of such great magnitude that the most that can here be done is to give some idea of the meanings attached to the Ineffable Name by the early peoples, by the Jews, to whom it meant so much, and by the Royal Arch mason, in whose traditional history and ritual it has so eminent a place.

Among the ancient peoples what we should regard as the mere name of an individual carried with it the idea of a separate entity, but let it not be thought that this idea is entirely pre-Christian; "Hallowed be thy *Name*," says the Lord's Prayer, a prayer which a Jewish writer, Nathan Ausubel, has hailed as the "supreme expression of Christian faith," a prayer "obviously derived from Jewish religious writings, even using some of the same figures of speech."

The Scriptures record that it was to Moses that God first revealed His Holy Name, and that to a descendant of David was given the divine command to "build an house for my name." The Royal Arch mason is reminded in the ritual that only in the Holy of Holies within the Temple was that sacred name pronounced, and then but once a year and by the High Priest.

The teaching of the Old Testament is that the "name" is itself the quintessence of God, the essential part, the purest and most perfect form. From the beginnings of Royal Arch masonry the Ineffable Name has been set in its high place and ever associated with the Word. In 1778 the first Grand Chapter has this to say in its laws concerning it:

> The Word . . . is not to be understood as a watch-word only, after the manner of those annexed to the several degrees of the Craft, but also Theologically, as a term, thereby to convey to the mind some idea of the great *Being* who is the sole author of our existence.

The early peoples, including the Hebrews, regarded the name of a deity as his manifestation, but far from all of the names so regarded were of beneficent powers. There were many that were evil. Milton, in *Paradise Lost*, speaks of "the dreaded name of Demogorgon," the infernal power, the mere mention of whose name the ancient peoples believed brought death and disaster.

Lucan's *Pharsalia* (Nicholas Rowe's translation) asks:

> Must I call your master to my aid,
> At whose dread name the trembling furies quake,
> Hell stands abashed, and earth's foundations shake?

The Jews in the period following their return from Babylonian exile had such a strong belief in the power of a name that they adopted two family names, says an enlightening article in the *Jewish Encyclopædia*, one civil or for civic affairs, the other a more sacred name, for use in the synagogue and in Hebrew documents. Much later the name equations became doublets—that is, the two names were used together as one. At one time, says the above authority, it was not thought that Jews of the same name should live in the same town or permit their children to marry into each other's families, difficulty being sometimes avoided by changing a name!

Among elementary peoples there was often a fear of disclosing a man's name, the idea behind this fear being identified with the practice of disguising an uncomplimentary name, as, for example, among the Greeks, who altered their early name of Axeinos ("inhospitable") for the Black Sea to Euxine, which has the opposite meaning. The Greeks, on second thoughts, decided to call the Furies not Erinyes, their apt name, but Eumenides, the good-tempered ones.

Plutarch, the Greek philosopher, of the first century of the Christian era, asks:

> What is the reason that it is forbidden to mention, inquire after, or name the chief tutelary and guardian deity of Rome, whether male or female, which prohibition they confirm with a superstitious tradition, reporting that Valerius Suranus perished miserably for expressing that name? . . .

Plutarch added that the "Romans reckoned they had their God in most safe and secure custody, he being inexpressible and unknown."

Then, coming again to the Jews, we may well quote the twelfth-century Jewish philosopher Maimonides, *The Guide for the Perplexed* (Friedländer's translation of 1881):

> This sacred name [the name of God] . . . which was not pronounced except in the sanctuary by the appointed priests, when they gave the sacerdotal blessing, and by the high priest on the Day of Atonement, undoubtedly denotes something which is peculiar to God. . . . It is possible that in the Hebrew language, of which we have now but a slight knowledge, the Tetragrammaton, in the way in which it was pronounced, conveyed the meaning of 'absolute existence.' . . . The majesty of the name and the great dread of uttering it, are connected with the fact that it denotes God Himself, without including in its meaning any names of the things created by Him.

In some ancient religions the idea of power was commonly associated with certain names—power, in some cases, over a person arising from the fact that his name was known. A power, awful and tremendous, is associated with the dread name of the Deity. Hebrew legend is full of instances where the mysterious and Ineffable Name is used either by itself or with other names to invoke magical powers against adversaries and evil spirits and for healing purposes.

The knowledge of the pronunciation of the Ineffable Name was confined, among the Jews, to certain wise men, and in medieval days a "Master of the Name" among the Jews was one who knew the sacred vowels of the word Jehovah, which knowledge was thought to invest him with magical powers.

Two texts, one from the Old and the other from the New Testament, give considerable support to the idea of power and importance being represented by names: "The Name of the Lord is a strong tower; the righteous runneth into it, and is safe" (Proverbs xviii, 10); "At the Name of Jesus every knee should bow" (Philippians ii, 10).

The Jews had many opportunities in their early history of imbibing from the pagan nations around them ideas which, when developed and idealized, played a serious part in their religion and philosophy. The forefathers of the Hebrew tribes are believed to have come from Ur Casdim (Ur of the Chaldees), in Mesopotamia, and to have brought with them religious ideas and customs borrowed from the surrounding peoples. Preserved in the Louvre, Paris, is an inscription (dating back to, very roughly, 2000 years B.C.) putting into the mouth of a Babylonian sovereign these words: "The god Enzu [Moon God and Lord of Knowledge], whose name man uttereth not." Israel, in the course of becoming a nation, learned in its Egyptian bondage beliefs which became grafted into its culture, for Egypt had many, many divinities and many names for them. The modern Jewish writer Nathan Ausubel has said that the influence of the Hittite and Babylonian-Assyrian religions and civilizations (to which the Jews were subject in their later exiles) was perhaps even greater than that of the Egyptian, owing to the kinship of the Hebrew and Assyrian languages. The peculiar genius of the Jewish people allowed of their adapting these external ideas in such a way as finally to weave them into the very texture of their faith in the one true God. We quote from what the Jew regards as the most holy portion of his Liturgy of the Day of Atonement:

> And when the priests and the people that stood in the court [of the Temple] heard the glorious and awful Name pronounced out of the mouth of the High Priest, in holiness and purity, they knelt and prostrated themselves and made acknowledgement, falling on their faces and saying, "Blessed be his glorious, sovereign Name for ever and ever."

Definition and Meaning

'Ineffable' is from the Latin, and means something that is unutterable, that cannot or may not be spoken out, this definition well illustrating the Jewish attitude to the Divine Name. Milton refers to the Son of God as "ineffable, serene." The "Incommunicable Name" is a frequent term for the Name of the Deity (as in the Apocrypha)—that is, a name that cannot be communicated to or shared with another, and it is usual to go back to Exodus vi, 2 and 3, for the earliest light upon its proper meaning:

> And God spake unto Moses, and said unto him, I *am* the LORD: And I appeared unto Abraham, unto Isaac, and unto Jacob, by *the name of* God Almighty, but by my name JEHOVAH was I not known to them.

In Judges xiii, 18, the Angel of the Lord puts this question to Manoah: "Why askest thou thus after my name, seeing it is secret?" And in Amos vi, 10, we have this direct injunction: "Hold thy tongue: for we may not make mention of the name of the Lord." Other significant passages are to be found in the New Testament and in the Apocryphal books as well as in Josephus. The Talmud, answering the question "Who of the Israelites shall have future life and who shall not?" says, "Even he who thinks the Name of God with its true letters forfeits his future life."

The Royal Arch ritual gives the impression that the pronunciation of the Sacred Name had been prohibited back into the farthest days, but actually it does not seem to be known when that prohibition first took effect, and there are scholars who believe that it is not earlier than the building of the Second Temple. Support is lent to this belief by a masonic writer, Bertram B. Benas, himself a learned Jew, who contributed to the *Transactions of the Merseyside Association for Masonic Research*, vol. xxii, a remarkable paper under the title of "The Divine Appellation," one of the sources of information to which the present writer has freely gone and which he gratefully acknowledges. Benas says that "since the destruction of the Temple, the Ineffable Name is never pronounced by an observant son of Israel, awaiting until time or circumstance should restore the true Temple established by King Solomon."

The Tetragrammaton

The early nations had many names by which to describe the Deity. The Jews used a variety of names, some expressing His attributes in terms comprehensible to all people, as, for example, the Rock, the Merciful, the Just, and the Mighty. Other Jewish names attempted to describe the more extraordinary qualities of the Deity—the Almighty, the Eternal, the Most High; supreme over them all was and is the Ineffable Name of four letters known to the Greeks as the Tetragrammaton (*tetra*, four; *grammatos*, letter), which in the Hebrew takes the form, יהוה or יְהֹוָה.

In the second form points have been added to give the pronounciation 'Adonai'. The letters are read from *right to left*; in English, in the order given they read Y H V H, Yod (J or Y); He; Vau; He. The Name itself is understood to be a composite form of the Hebrew verb *hayah*, meaning 'to be'. The meaning of the Tetragrammaton, says Bertram B. Benas,

> is evident, instinct, and implicit. It denotes the Divine eternity, and is the synthesis of the past, the present, and the future of the verb *Hayah* 'to be.' ... It is aptly expressed in the phrase:
>
> > He is what He was,
> > Was what He is and
> > Ever shall remain both what He was and what He is
> > From everlasting to everlasting.

The marginal references to the Revised Version of the Bible give five related meanings:

> I am that I am.
> I am because I am.
> I am who I am.
> I will be that I will be.
> I will be.

The Tetragrammaton is an attempt to signify God in His immutable and eternal existence, the Being Who is self-existent and gives existence to others. It associates all three tenses—past, future, and present—and is the name to which allusion is made in Exodus iii, 13–15:

> And Moses said unto God, Behold, *when* I come unto the children of Israel, and shall say unto them, The God of your fathers hath sent me unto you; and they shall say to me, What *is* his name? what shall I say unto them? And God said unto Moses, I AM THAT I AM: and he said, Thus shalt thou say unto the children of Israel, I AM hath sent me unto you. And God said moreover unto Moses, Thus shalt thou say unto the children of Israel, The LORD God of your fathers, the God of Abraham, the God of Isaac, and the God of Jacob, hath sent me unto you: this *is* my name for ever, and this *is* my memorial unto all generations.

The Hebrew words *Ehyeh asher ehyeh* translated in the above as I AM THAT I AM are also forms of the same root word from which Y H V H is derived.

The ban against the utterance of the Ineffable Name applies not merely in ordinary conversation but also when the Name appears in Sacred Writ or in the Liturgy. When the Name appears by itself, the Jews use a substitute word *Adonai* (the Lord). When Y H V H appears in conjunction with the actual word *Adonai* the word *Elohim* (God) is read in place of the Tetragrammaton. Thus there are two substitute words used in place of the Ineffable Name. In reading the Liturgy or Holy Writ the Jews may pronounce *these substitute words* without any sense of sin, but—elsewhere the words are never uttered lightly or unnecessarily. Indeed, if the name of God is to be spoken or invoked in ordinary conversation the word *Hashem* (the Name) is used.

In earlier days the omission of vowel points led to frequent doubts as to the proper pronunciation of certain words, especially where the meanings may seriously vary with the vowel sounds.

Certain Jewish scholars, the Massoretes, for the particular purpose of keeping inviolate the interpretation of parts of the Scripture, introduced a system of vowels and accents at a somewhat late date; their marks are known as the Massoretic points and consist of a system of dots, dashes, and other symbols which perform the function of vowels and indicate how words should be pronounced and which syllables should be stressed. Thus against the letters of the Tetragrammaton they inserted the *vowels* of the substituted word 'Adonai,' so producing the word YE-HO-VAH, and this, in the course of time, was transliterated by Luther, who, being German, substituted a J for the Hebrew Y (in German the J has the sound of the English Y). The English translators of the Bible adopted Luther's spelling except for the final I, thus giving a word closely resembling 'Jehovah.' For the pronunciation *Adonai*, the Vau of the Tetragrammaton is pointed as in the second example on opposite page.

Non-Jews derive the pronunciation JE-HO-VAH from the 'vowel-points' that are usually appended to the four Hebrew YHVH, a comparatively modern introduction, say of the period between the fourth and the ninth century A.D.

The exact pronunciation of JHVH is not known. It appears that the actual word 'Jehovah' was introduced in 1520 by Galatinus, but scholars regard it as incorrect; however, it is the Biblical word, although it occurs in the Bible but a few times. One of the most significant texts containing the name is Psalm lxxxiii, ·18: "That men may know that thou, whose name alone is JEHOVAH, art the most high over all the earth."

An abbreviation, 'Jah,' is used frequently, especially as part of proper names and in the phrase-word, song, or exclamation "Hallelujah' or 'Alleluia,' meaning "Praise ye the Lord." Warrants and certificates issued by the First Grand Chapter in the pre-1813 period often bore the words: "In the name of the Grand Architect of the Universe, THE ALMIGHTY JAH."

Among the titles or descriptions of the Deity are some which "are not fenced around with bars of prohibition, protective of the real Name itself," remarks Bertram B. Benas, although they are not to be used carelessly or lightly; among them is the word 'Lord,' which has been generally adopted in English translations and may itself be translated fairly accurately as 'the Eternal.'

The fathers of all the tribes akin to the Hebrews had from time immemorial used the word *Elohim* as meaning 'God,' says Dr A. S. Aglen, and he offers the explanation that the nomad Semites had originally, no doubt, imagined the word to be surrounded, penetrated, governed, by myriads of active beings, each of whom was an *Eloh*, but had no distinct name. In the Bible *Elohim*, a plural word, is treated as a singular. *Elohim* came to mean 'God,' the supreme Master of the Universe; throughout the Old Testament it is the word generally rendered as 'God,' but other designations were in use, including *El* (meaning 'strong') and *Shaddai* (meaning 'almighty') and *Elyon* (meaning 'most high'). When the two names of God appear together in O.T. as ADONAI JHVH, the JHVH is 'pointed' with the *vowels* of *Elohim* and it is pronounced *Elohim*.

In some forms of the appellation for God, such as *El*, the plural form *Elim* can be applied to pagan deities, whereas by the Tetragrammaton is meant only the G.A.O.T.U.

An appellation of particular interest to the freemason is the word 'Shaddai,' already mentioned, which carries with it a great sense of reverence and which the Jews may pronounce freely. It has the significance of the 'All Sufficient,' He Whose being is in and from Himself and Who gives to others their being.

Still another omnific (all-creating) word is familiar to the Royal Arch mason. It has been stated that this word was originally of two syllables, but as from the revision of the ritual in 1835 it has been of three syllables and embraces three languages, in which connexion J. Heron Lepper states that in the year 1595 "the name of God in three languages was held to have not only a deep religious significance, but was also used as a means of recognition between men of the same way of thought."

It has already been pointed out that there is considerable doubt as to whether 'Jehovah' is the true pronunciation of the intended appellation, and at one time it was thought that the recovery of the true word awaited the coming of the Jewish Messiah. Obviously, in attempting the difficult task of deciding upon the spelling, interpretation, etc., of ancient words and phrases of Hebrew and related origin it is extremely easy to fall into error, however slight, and it is not therefore surprising to learn that scholars advance the possibility that the accuracy of certain words imparted to the Royal Arch mason is not beyond criticism.

The Christian Significance of the Tetragrammaton

It is impossible to concede that the Tetragrammaton could *originally* have had Christian significance, but we know that the name 'Jehovah,' borrowed from the Old Testament, is commonly used as an appellation for Christ, and that Jesus, the personal name of Christ and a common name in His day, included, as did many other Hebrew names, a form of the name of God (Jah). Fanatical Jews of the Middle Ages attributed the wonderful works of Christ to the potency of the Incommunicable Name, which He was accused of abstracting from the Temple and wearing about Him. It is well known, of course, that the Ineffable Name early acquired Christian import, and we may well suppose that in many early Royal Arch ceremonies this was the one insisted upon. The Tetragrammaton contained within a triangle is often displayed in chapters (the Church used this device in the sixteenth century) and is not unknown as an apron ornament.

Thomas Godwyn's book (see an earlier reference) attempts, none too convincingly, to show that the Tetragrammaton, although containing four letters, had but three *sorts* of letters; in it J (*Jod* or *Yod*) represented the Father, V (*Vau*) the Third Person in the Trinity Which proceedeth from the Father and the Son, and H (*He*) the Son of God.

"*Four Hieroglyphics*"

A ritual of the eighteenth century asks how the Sacred Name should "be depicted in our Lodges," and supplies the answer:

By four different Hieroglyphics—
   the first an equilateral triangle;
   the second a circle;
   the third a geometrical square;
   the fourth a double cube.

Section Fourteen

THE RITUAL AND ITS DEVELOPMENT

> Our rite presents drama as distinguished from mere spectacle; induces reflection on the meaning of life and its purpose; illustrates the most besetting passion of mankind, the desire for complete knowledge . . . in short, its phrasing and symbolism are designed to appeal to the spirit and intellect of each one of us.
>
> J. HERON LEPPER

EARLIER sections have shown how an ancient legend has been interwoven with familiar Biblical stories and given dramatic form, but it is very obvious that, in arriving at the present ritual, there has been considerable natural evolution and, finally, quite serious intentional revision. Our knowledge of the exact course of evolution and development must necessarily be somewhat hazy. The R.A. ceremony in, say, the 1750–60 period presented a legend and a Biblical background much as they are to-day, but the precise form, the symbolism, and much of the philosophic teaching of to-day's ritual—these were absent, and came at first gradually and over a period of years whose history is uncertain. It is known, of course, that revisions following the union of the Grand Chapter, in 1817 and, much more especially, those approved in November 1834, were drastic and brought about a considerable alteration in the form of the ritual. We do not doubt that a great many divergent and conflicting rituals had to be considered, the best elements retained, much omitted, including any manifest Christian allusions, and considerable new matter added, and that in the process some old, curious, and picturesque details were lost for ever.

The fact that the R.A. story was first unfolded in Craft lodges must have meant that during the formative period the Craft influence made itself felt in the building up of the ritual by the adoption of ideas, in the moulding of the ritual phrases, in the choice of officers' names, in the forms of the early opening and closing ceremonies, and even—and, indeed, especially so—in the nature of the esoteric communications made to Candidates. In spite of the coming of the senior Grand Chapter in 1766, and that of the 'Antients' five years later, chapters in the early days tended to please themselves in matters of ritual, and this was especially so where the chapter was actually a fourth degree in lodge working, as it must have been under the 'Antients' system for quite a considerable time. The 'Antients,' acting under their lodge warrants, had no doubt that they could work almost any rite and any version of it, and must have introduced, in the course of half a century, many variations into the ritual. And there were 'Moderns' lodges, also, that must have felt they were a law unto themselves, as to which we may cite Anchor and Hope Lodge, Bolton (constituted in 1732), which delayed applying to the premier Grand Chapter for a chapter warrant until 1785, holding that they were entitled to work what ceremonies they liked!

It has been remarked more than once that the R.A. bears marks of a twofold origin, but it would be just as truthful to say that streams from a number of sources have united to feed its tide of strength. There is the legendary story coming down from a Father of the Church in the fourth century after Christ. There are the Old Testament stories. There is the inspiration some time early in the eighteenth century which led fertile minds, either French or English and probably both, to seize upon and build together this excellent component material. There is the stream of influence, English in its character, that helped to mould the rite in its early days, and there is almost certainly imagination and colour brought in from Ireland, where the R.A. was worked at an early date. The certain borrowings from Craft and perhaps other degrees during the eighteenth century must be remembered, as also the by no means negligible fact that some of the R.A. symbolism has come not only from ecclesiastical sources, but from alchemy, many of whose adepts, men of great learning and culture, entered masonry in the formative period. No *printed* ritual, not even an irregular one, is known earlier than some time in the 1820's (there are earlier ones in manuscript), and it is obvious that, as the R.A. as a working degree was at least sixty years old by the year mentioned, many variations and curious additions had come about as a result of the handing down of the by no means simple ritual mostly by word of mouth. It is known that the rite practised by the Grand and Royal Chapter in 1766 resembled the present ceremonial in little more than essentials. Undoubtedly it had a distinctly Christian character: consider for a moment the inclusion of the veils ceremonial, which, supposedly reminiscent of the troublous journeys of the Jews returning from exile, is even more likely to have been derived from the imagery of the veil of separation "rent in twain" by the death of Christ.

All the materials are not available for an orderly discussion of the development of the ritual from its earliest form, but fortunately we are able to give a fair idea of the ceremonial commonly worked preceding the drastic revisions and alterations of the 1830's.

The Earliest R.A. Ritual known: Date 1760

The earliest R.A. ritual yet discovered dates from about 1760, and is contained in a French illuminated manuscript included in the Heaton-Card collection housed in the library at Freemasons' Hall, London. The manuscript, which is not by any means an exposure and which, according to J. Heron Lepper, shows signs of direct translation from the English, is a collection of short and fragmentary synopses of some thirty-five degrees current at the period. The manuscript is entitled *Précis des huits premier Grades, ornés de discours et d'Histoires allegoriques, relatifs au respectable Ordre de la Franc-Maconnerie*. The manuscript is written in the French language. In that part of the manuscript relating to a primitive R.A. ceremonial we learn of an underground chamber upheld by nine arches and having nine steps to descend into it and opened and closed by nine knocks. A light shows the way to a subterranean room. In the explaining of the tracing-board the sun is said to be the true light which served to lead the nine Brethren who discovered great secrets; on the board are depicted nine arches, the vault of an underground chamber, and the nine steps that "served to descend it"; a stone with a ring closing the chamber; a torch which was extinguished by the brilliance of the sun, a feature in R.A. symbolism new to J. Heron Lepper; a triangular plate of gold, bearing the Sacred Name. The ritual represents a date only sixteen years after the first definite mention of the R.A. (1744) and bears a close analogy to the R.A. Degree as it would be if shorn of legend and lectures. J. Heron Lepper believed the ritual to be a discovery of the first importance, as "proving the genuine antiquity" of the rite. The manuscript refers, in explaining a sign, to a "priest when he says Mass," a sign formerly given, says J. Heron Lepper, to all R.A. masons. The reference to the stone with a ring rather suggests that the manuscript was originally Irish, for such a stone is even to-day a feature of that ritual.

A Form of Prayer in 1766

Next, in a ceremonial of the year 1766 referred to by Lionel Vibert, are found two mottoes associated with the degree: "We have found" and "In the beginning was the Word." This last, the opening words of St John's Gospel, constituted in the early days the words on the scroll found by the Candidate in the vault, as in the case of some old rituals preserved at Taunton and as in a tracing-board figured by Dr Oliver; they appear also on seals of three early lodges of Exeter, No. 39, founded 1732; Bath, No. 41, and Bury, No. 42, both of 1733, the last two lodges being associated with early chapters. All Souls' Lodge, Tiverton (founded 1767, lapsed 1798), had attached to it for many years a chapter, and there has come down to us a form of prayer used in it, of no particular interest in itself except to indicate that late in the eighteenth century the ritual had a distinctly Devotional atmosphere. Here is the prayer:

> Almighty, Wise and Eternal God; we pray thee to bestow thy Favor and Blessing upon us who are now assembled with earnest and zealous Hearts to labor under thy most sublime and sacred Name in thy Divine Works. Give us Grace, we beseech Thee, that we and all our works may be acceptable to thy good Pleasure and endue us with wisdom and Knowledge in thy sacred, Holy and Sublime Truths, that we may instruct Each other therein and at the last obtain admittance into thy Heavenly Kingdom of Everlasting Rest.

Some Yorkshire "Toasts or Sentiments," 1769

A most unusual minute of a Royal Arch lodge, dated February 22, 1769 (given below in full), affords some hints on the nature of the ceremony worked in Wakefield, Yorkshire, at a date coming close on the heels of the founding of the first Grand Chapter. Our information is derived from John R. Rylands's "Early Freemasonry in Wakefield," an important and entertaining paper printed in *A.Q.C.*, vol. lvi, in which many excerpts are reproduced from the records of two Royal Arch lodges or chapters—Unanimity and Wakefield respectively—whose affairs are chronicled in two *Royal Arch Journals*, one covering the period 1766–93 and the other 1766–1844, two chapters which appear to have held joint meetings and over a long period entered their minutes in the same book (or books). The early minutes relate for the most part to the Lodge of Unanimity, a 'Moderns' lodge, meeting at the George and Crown Inn, Wakefield, in which lodge the Royal Arch was practised on special "nights," the first recorded one being on August 30, 1766. At a meeting of February 22, 1769, seven members were present, including Richard Linnecar; their names are set forth, and then follows:

> *Toasts or Sentiments*
> All tha's gone thro' y ͤ seven
> To him that grop'd in y ͤ Dark
> The first Man that enter'd y ͤ Arch
> To him that first shak'd his Cable
> May the Crown of Glory, y ͤ Scepter of
>   Righteousness & the Staff of
>   Comfort attend true Masons
> To the Memory of him that first move
>   his stones in the Dark
> Harmony among all those who have
>   rec'd the Cord of Love

> To the happy Messengers that carried the News
>   to King Cyrus
> The Roy Arch—Word—
> May the true beam of inteligence
>   Enlighten Ever Royal Arch Mason
> May we be all adorn'd with a
>   true internal robe at the last Day
> May we live to see our posterity to follow this Example
> As the Jewish High Priests put off
>   their shoes when they enter'd the
>   Sanctum Sanctorum, so
>   may every Mason divest
>   himself of every vice when he
>   enters this Lodge

Many of these Wakefield toasts are more or less self-explanatory, but some of them appear to apply only to the Irish R.A. mason. In the early Irish rituals emphasis was laid on the Cord of Amity and the Cord of Love, and one of the toasts above given suggests either a borrowing from the Irish or some natural affinity with the Irish working. Regardinn the toast ".to him that first shak'd his Cable," it should be said that, ig the Irish ceremony, which is much more realistic in some ways than the English, a cord acts as a lifeline and is a means of signalling from an underground chamber to the Craftsmen above, on whose attention and care the well-being of their companion within the vault depends. A letter written by the Rev. Jo: Armitage to Richard Linnecar on Christmas Day 1776 contains this passage:

> I must content myself with wishing you & the Lodge all the Happiness you can possibly enjoy, & treat myself with a Glass extraordinary to all your Healths, which I shall drink with peculiar Pleasure to all those Wanderers in the Wilderness who have had the honour of sitting in the Chair of Amity & of being presented with the Cord of Love.

Phrases in this letter rather suggest that, in the course of Exaltation, the Candidate was seated in a particular chair and had placed in his hands a cord or something emblematic of the cord of love, this inference being supported by the fact that at a chapter meeting in 1809, over thirty years later, Companion Wice presented to the First Principal for the use of the Wakefield Chapter "a very handsome silken Cord of Amity which was received most thankfully as a token of friendship."

A Ceremonial Arch, 1810

The Minerva R.A. Chapter, No. 35, Hull, has a curious minute under date January 5, 1810:

APRONS OF THE 1790 PERIOD

Left: Hand-drawn and coloured; red and blue ribboned border; gold fringe. *Right*: Leather, hand-drawn and coloured, with Craft and R.A. symbols.

By courtesy of United Grand Lodge

PLATE XIX

TODDY RUMMER, EARLY 1820'S

Once part of King George VI's private collection, it is now on permanent loan to the Museum, Freemasons' Hall, London, from Her Majesty the Queen.
By courtesy of United Grand Lodge

A material change and alteration took place in the Chapter this evening, namely the introduction of the Arch with Holiness to the Lord painted in gold letters thereon, in front of the three M.E.'s Grands. The Pedestal and Master's Level, with appropriate inscriptions in Brass letters thereon, and the Burning Bush within and under the said Arch, being the first introduction of these essential requisites in any Lodge in this part of the United Kingdom from time immemorial.

It will be noted that the minute regards as essential a number of things, including the burning bush, which, in the old days, were not always found in a 'Moderns' chapter, but it is possible that some ideas were being borrowed from a travelling military lodge or were introduced by an Irish visitor.

A Late Eighteenth-century Ritual

A little manuscript book measuring roughly 4 inches wide by 6 inches deep, and containing 90 pages, of which 79 are filled with faded writing, has been very kindly placed at the author's disposal by Bruce W. Oliver, of Barnstaple, into whose hands it came in 1949, but it was, at some time in its career, in the possession of Alexander Dalziel, who lived in the North of England. The manuscript appears to have been written towards the close of the eighteenth century, but bears on an early page the words "revised 1830," and there are, in fact, many alterations, additions, and deletions throughout. The meaning or intention is not everywhere clear, and a few words and initials are difficult to decipher. Many phrases are strongly reminiscent of Craft practice. The ritual is said to be of the North of England, but actually can be regarded as representing one known before 1817 in other, probably many, parts of England. Indeed, it should be said that in essentials it corresponds to some manuscript rituals preserved in the library at Freemasons' Hall, London, in particular that associated with the name of Captain Thomas Lincolne Barker, R.N. (deposited by G. S. Shepherd-Jones and believed to relate to the then Chapter of Prudence, No. 41, Ipswich), and that of William Banks, Master of the Free School, Butt Lane, Deptford. Both of these manuscripts give what are undoubtedly pre-1817 rituals, and so closely do these agree with the North-country ritual about to be dealt with that it is apparent that they all have come from one original source. So, although the following is taken actually from the North of England manuscript, it may perhaps be regarded as representing in general, and subject to small differences, the ritual common to those pre-Union chapters more 'Modern' than 'Antient' in their systems of working.

The forming and opening of the chapter have many points of difference from those of to-day. To form the chapter the Three Grand Chiefs or

Principals are placed in the East, representing the three Keystones of the Arch; the Three Sojourners are in the West; the Scribes E. and N. in the *South* and *North*[1] respectively. An arch of a square or triangular form is placed in the centre, and under it is the Grand Pedestal. In the East is another Pedestal with the Three Great Lights upon it. All things being duly prepared in the chapter-room, the Most Excellent Grand Chiefs or Principals, now wearing their respective robes and carrying their sceptres, etc., withdraw with the Companions into an adjoining chamber, where the two Scribes immediately take their places on "each side" of the open door, "which is now tyled." The Companions range themselves into a double line, two by two, and they then open to the right and left to allow of the Principals' advancing between the lines and passing into the chapter-room, where they work a short threefold ceremony, and ceremoniously take their places in front of their respective chairs. On a signal from the First Principal the organist, "being ready in his robes," enters. Then "the Companions enter in due form," the organ playing a solemn march. The First Principal then invites them to assist him in opening this Grand and Royal Arch chapter, and in an address says, "This degree is of so sublime a nature that none can be admitted but men of the best character and first respectability; open, liberal, and generous in their sentiments; totally devoid of all heresy, bigotry and false persuasion."

The opening in chapter is largely a series of questions asked by the First Principal and answered by the Principal Sojourner and other officers. It is the Principal Sojourner's duty to see that the chapter is properly tiled. He proves it by five knocks. Asked how many officers compose an R.A. chapter, he answers, "nine . . . three Grand Chiefs, two Scribes, three Sojourners, and a Janitor." The Principal Sojourner says that his situation is in the West and his duty to introduce all Sojourners from the Babylonish captivity and such as areable to do the Lord's work at this grand offering of peace; to report all discoveries that may come to his present knowledge. Companion N. says that his place is in the North and his duty to receive all those Western reports from the Principal Sojourner; communicate them, and see that none approach from the West to disturb the symmetry and harmony of this sublime building. Companion E. says his place is in the South and his duty to receive all those Western reports from Companion N. and communicate the same to the Three Grand Chiefs; to register all records, acts, laws, and transactions for the general good of the chapter; and to see that none approach from the East to disturb the symmetry and harmony of this sublime building. The Three Grand Chiefs are said to be placed in the East to confer with each other, trace the outlines of their work, and to complete the intended building.

[1] Italics are the present author's.

J. says his duty is to assist in carrying on the Lord's work; H. says his duty is to assist in completing that work. J. says he comes from Babylon; H. that he is going to Jerusalem; their purpose is to assist in rebuilding the Temple and endeavouring to obtain the Sacred Word. H. says that the hour is that of a perfect mason. "Then, Companions," says the First Principal, "it is time for us to commence our labours by endeavouring to celebrate this grand design." The Three Principals again work a threefold rite. The Principal Sojourner says that the next duty is to respect the decrees of the Most High, render homage to the Great Architect of the Universe, and bend the knee to Him from Whom we received our existence. The First Principal, in a prayer which follows, addresses the Great and Grand Architect of the Universe . . . at Whose words the Pillars of the Sky were raised and its beauteous arches formed, Whose breath kindled the stars, adorned the moon with its silver rays, and gave the sun its resplendent lustre. . . .

Chapter having been opened by the Principals, the minutes "are read for confirmation," and the Junior Sojourner is sent to prepare and introduce the Candidate. In response to the Principal Sojourner's challenge the Junior Sojourner or the Janitor announces the Candidate as "Brother A.B., a Geometric Master Mason who has regularly gone through all the degrees of Craft Masonry, passed the chair in due course and now wishes to complete his knowledge in masonry by being exalted to the Sublime Degree of a R.A. Mason." He is admitted on the Word of a Past Master of Arts and Sciences. Three Sojourners from the Babylonish Captivity who had heard the proclamation of Cyrus, King of Persia, offer their services in the rebuilding of the Holy Temple. They claim to be of their own kindred and people and descended from Abraham, Isaac, and Jacob.

> We are not of the lineage of that race of traitors who fell away during the siege, who went over to the enemy and basely betrayed their country when their city and country had most need of their assistance, nor of the lower class of people left behind to cultivate the soil . . . but the offspring of those Princes and Nobles carried into captivity with King Zedekiah.

The narrative continues on in the way now familiar; the Sojourners are duly provided with the necessary tools to carry out their work of assisting in the rebuilding of the Temple and are instructed in their use.

The drama of making the discoveries is acted in the chapter in full view of the Companions. (Work on the keystones centres at the arch.) The rubbish is cleared away, to reveal a keystone, which is removed by the help of the crow. The suspicion that there is a hollow space below is confirmed, and the Principal Sojourner reports accordingly. The First Principal directs that the Sojourners be "well bound" and provided with lifelines and supplied "with proper refreshment to assist them in their labours." (The Sojourners each have a glass of wine, and are instructed in the use of the life-lines.) They now proceed "to pass the Arches which have been formed in the usual way." On drawing the second keystone they find a roll of parchment containing part of the Holy Law, and on drawing the third they find the pedestal on whose top is a plate of gold in the figure of a 'G,' and within that, contained in a triangle, are characters beyond their comprehension. The Sojourners make their report "to the Three Grand Chiefs," and the truth of their great discovery is confirmed by Companion N. (apparently by him alone). The Sojourners, restored to their personal comforts, again report; the Z. then gives an emblematical explanation of the work done and discoveries made by them. To prepare them for the revelation of things yet hidden from them the Z. now offers prayers phrased very much as is the prayer in to-day's ritual on the Candidate's behalf. The Candidate affirms his trust "in God," the Sojourners advance to the altar, and the Candidate takes his Obligation, referred to "as drawing forth the keystone," the Obligation having a strong likeness to the Craft Obligation and embodying a penalty clause. Then follows an oration which alludes to the sprig of cassia which bloomed over the grave of him who was truly the most Excellent of all Super-excellent masons, and who parted with his life because he would not part with his honour. There are references to the Rose of Sharon and the Lily of the Valley, and to

> death, the grand leveller of all human greatness, drawing his sable curtain round us. And when the last arrow of this, our mortal enemy, hath been despatched and the bow of this mighty conqueror broken by the iron arm of time; and the Angel of the Lord declares that time shall be no more . . . then shall we receive the reward of our virtue. . . .

Following comes a recital of Biblical history relating to the return of the Jews from exile.

The Candidate, now restored to the light, is next invited to attend to a "description of the pedestal and its glorious contents." It was of white marble in the form of the altar of incense, a double cube, and from its figure and colour a most perfect emblem of innocence and purity. On the base of this pedestal was the letter 'G,' signifying a common name for all masons that are Masters of their business. This double cube was said to be most highly finished, and the work of the great Hiram himself. On the front were inscribed the names of the three M.E. Grand Masters, and below these was the "compound character 吐 " (which character is explained as *Templum Hierosolymae*; see Section 22).

Hence we find that what was there concealed was the Sacred Name or Word itself. On the top was a covering of white satin, the emblem of innocence and purity, fringed with crimson, denoting virtue, constancy, and power; tasselled with gold . . . the most perfect of all metals as it resists the chemist's art and the power of fire, being the more pure the more it is tried, and therefore the highest emblem of truth, stability and perfection. . . . On the top was likewise a plate of Gold wherein was inscribed [etc., etc.]

There follows an explanation of tripartite name; the initials of the Three Grand Masters, S.K.I., H.K.T., and H.A.B., the W.I.; and a reference to the compound character 㧞 . Then follows a long charge leading up to a closing reference to the lost word and the circumstances under which it was found—a word "now reserved for those only who profess themselves students of this Sublime Degree and may we my Brothers Companions preserve its margins pure and undefiled till time shall be no more."

The chapter is closed in a manner obviously based on the Craft ritual and largely repeating the opening ceremony.

The Ceremonial immediately preceding the 1835 Revisions

Fortunately we are reasonably well informed with regard to later rituals preceding the 1835 revisions.

The following relates in particular to the ceremonial followed in chapters of an 'Antients' persuasion, in which, of course, the Candidate must have qualified by 'passing the chair' and in so doing would have had his attention particularly directed to the symbolism of the plumb-line and been taught to regard that line as the criterion of moral rectitude, that he should avoid dissimulation in conversation and action and seek the path that leads to immortality. The Candidate may have passed the chair long previously in his Craft lodge or, if on the evening of his Exaltation, either in his Craft lodge or in a lodge especially opened by the members of the chapter.

The ceremony as outlined below included the passing of the veils, which, however, was not an invariable part of the ceremonial.

Ruling the chapter were three Principal Officers, Z. as Prince, Haggai as Prophet, and Jeshua or Joshua as High Priest, these forming the keystones of the arch; at the base were the three Sojourners, known in some chapters as the Principal, Senior, and Junior Sojourners; Scribe Ezra was at the North side and Scribe Nehemiah on the South side. The Companions, seated as to form (in plan) the sides of an arch, represented the pillars of Solomon's Temple. In front of the Principals was an altar carrying certain characters. Outside the door was the Janitor, often still called the Tiler.

The opening of the chapter was very different from to-day's ceremony and more obviously based upon the opening of a Craft lodge. The various officers subjected to catechism answered for themselves and explained their duties.[1] The Junior Sojourner said that his duties were to guard the first veil and allow none to enter but those who were properly qualified; the Senior Sojourner that his duty was to guard the second veil; and the Principal Sojourner that his was to guard the third. (Such duties in many chapters were carried out by officers known as Captains of the Host or Captains of the Veils, as they often still are in chapters where the veils ceremony is worked.) Essentially, the opening by the Principals was much as it is to-day, but in many chapters the esoteric portion was worked in a separate room by the three Principal Officers, who then entered the chapter and, in all likelihood, worked a short completion of the ceremony there.

The Exaltation now proceeded. The choice of officer to announce the Candidate differed somewhat from chapter to chapter. The Candidate was announced much in the same form as he is to-day, with the significant addition that he had been duly elected Master of a Lodge of Master Masons, installed in the chair, and entrusted with the grip and word, and with the sign and salutation of a P.M. On admission there was a prayer by the High Priest, Jeshua, in which were many phrases familiar to-day. Following a long Scripture reading, the Candidate took an Obligation including a peculiar penalty not now present in the R.A. but not unknown in some other degrees. The Candidate received an exhortation from the First Principal in terms obviously based on Craft masonry, and which, as in the other old ceremony already described, contained references to the "the sprig of cassia found on the grave of the *most excellent* of Masons," "the beautiful rose of Sharon," "the lily of the valley," and ending with a reference to "death, the grand leveller of all human greatness," as in the ritual already given.

Then began the ceremony of passing the veils, treated at some length in a later section (see pp. 195 *et seq.*), but here briefly summarized so as not unduly to interrupt the story of the Candidate's progress. The Candidate, prepared much as he is to-day, was conducted by Scribe Nehemiah with all suitable ceremony to the First Veil, which was guarded by the Junior Sojourner. Here he was made acquainted with the miracle of the burning bush; the Second Veil was suitably guarded, and beyond it he learned of Aaron's rod that became a serpent; again, with Bible readings and ceremonial, he passed the Third Veil, where there was exemplified the miracle of the leprous hand. Each of these veils had its password. Beyond the Third Veil he learned of the passwords admitting him to the Sanctum Sanctorum. He saw the emblems of the Ark of the Covenant, the tables of stone, the pot of manna, the table of shew bread, the burning incense, and the candlestick with seven branches, and he was now qualified to take his

[1] Many R.A. chapters do the same to-day.

part as a Sojourner in the final drama of discovery, which was much as it now is, although the phrasing was somewhat commonplace by comparison with to-day's ritual. In reward for his industry and zeal he was given certain esoteric explanations. (In many chapters, at some later date, he was closely examined or catechized on the details of the ceremony; the catechism was a 'lecture,' which in its five sections would take about half an hour to work, but it is likely that, on any one occasion, only a part of the lecture was given.)

The closing of the chapter would often be reminiscent of the closing of a Craft lodge, or in some chapters would much resemble that at present in use.

When we compare this old ceremonial with the one following the revisions of the 1830's we realize that in its newer form it has been most drastically rearranged and edited, imperfections of phrasing have been removed and the veils ceremonial abandoned. The long addresses from the Three Principals have been added, and it may be said that in the earlier ceremonial there was, in general, not much material upon which the present lectures could have been based, although their phrasing echoes here and there many things that were found in the earlier rituals.

The Bristol Working

Bristol chapters appear to have worked since their earliest days a most impressive ceremony for which the old manuscript ritual above drawn upon serves as an excellent introduction.

At the opening of chapter the two Scribes act as Outer Guards and test Companions on entering. The D.C. leads in the Principals, and the Scribes then enter and take their places. Following a catechism between the Z. and his fellow-Principals, the Word is completed, questions are put to the officers and answered by them, and the chapter is declared open. The ballot having proved favourable, the P.S., accompanied by any Companions who so wish, retires to prepare the Candidate in an anteroom—the chapel—where the ceremony is directed by the P.S., who is seated at a desk or pedestal near to the door of the chapter. The Candidate, having proved his Craft qualifications, then 'passes the veils'—four veils in the Beaufort and some other chapters, but three in others, as in the Royal Clarence Chapter, the white (fourth) veil being there omitted. The Companions return to the chapter, passing through the veils and giving the passwords necessary at each veil and on re-entering the chapter. Before the Candidate enters the Principals put on their headgear, Z. a crown, H. a smaller crown, and J. a mitre; in addition, J. wears the traditional breastplate studded with gems.

It should be noted that the full-size vertical pillars familiar in the old Craft lodges are retained in chapter and that much of the work with the Candidate is framed within those pillars, so adding greatly to the dramatic effectiveness of the ceremony, a feature common to all Bristol working, both Craft and Royal Arch. In its essentials the Exaltation ceremony is the same as elsewhere, but the story is unfolded rather differently, and the ceremony retains many of the features common to Royal Arch masonry prior to the revision of 1835, being more devotional and laying far less emphasis on the geometric aspect of the symbolism. Some of the phrasing of the ritual echoes that known to us in the eighteenth-century manuscript rituals; thus we are told, for instance, of death, the grand leveller of all human greatness, drawing around us his sable curtains; of the dispatch of the last arrow of our mortal enemy; of the breaking of the bow of the mighty conqueror by the iron arm of Time. The Principals' lectures introduced at the revision of 1835 and which elsewhere in England commonly conclude the Exaltation ceremony are unknown. The altar stone is east of the arrangement of candles, while west of it and more or less between the pillars is a set-up of three arch-stones of massive appearance. The Candidate, still in darkness but in full view of all the Companions, dislodges these stones one by one at a critical point in the development of the story, the Janitor entering the chapter and having a duty in connexion with them. Although the ceremonial details are peculiar in many respects to the Bristol working, it is, of course, the essential and familiar Royal Arch story that is demonstrated and the same well-tried emblematical secrets that are brought to light.

Opening and Closing

It has now been shown that the opening and closing of an R.A. chapter was largely in early days a catechism—that is, questions and answers—on lines already made familiar in the old Craft working and surviving in a modified form in the Craft ritual of to-day. As already made clear, each officer answered for himself and explained the duty of his office, a practice still in use in Irish, American and some English chapters, inherited from lodges and chapters of the eighteenth century. In the 1820's the opening ceremony was often a lengthy catechism in the course of which reference might be made to the coming of Haggai from Babylon and the going of Jeshua to Jerusalem to assist in the rebuilding of the Second Temple and also to endeavour to obtain the Sacred Word, this constituting the "Grand Design."

It was common practice for only the Principals and the Past Principals to be present at the opening, and in an old West-country record is found the direction that "Agreeable to the new regulations of the Grand Royal Arch Chapter the three Principals only should be present at the opening; the Chapter door secured, the Janitor without." Again, this particular direction comes from an old Craft custom, and, apart from any conclusion that the chief officers of lodge or chapter were working a ceremony at which ordinary members could not be present, there seems support for the idea that the custom of conducting a higher ceremony in a side-room may possibly have been dictated by lack of space, the lodge or chapter generally having to make the best use it could of the often limited accommodation offered by an inn.

It is accepted that up to some time in the nineteenth century there was a fairly common custom of opening the chapter in a side-room, but the propriety of this proceeding was a subject for frequent discussion. Grand Chapter debated resolutions relating to it in 1880, 1893, and 1896, and finally, on May 7, 1902, resolved that "It is expedient that all R.A. Masons be permitted to be present at the Opening Ceremony in Private Chapters."

Much of what has just been said applied equally to the Closing Ceremony, which frequently took the form of a catechism, even as late as the 1820's, when, however, there was an alternative form of closing almost identical with that now followed. Over a long period there was the custom (now in a great many chapters tending to fall into disuse) of offering the V.S.L. open to Principals and closed to Companions. Probably this has been given many different symbolical explanations, but the simplest is that to the experienced and more enlightened Principal the V.S.L. is an 'open book.'

Here we may recall the great reverence in which the Bible was held in those days preceding our first knowledge of any masonic ritual. Thomas Heywood's *If You Know Not Me, You Know Nobody*, a play dealing with the troubles of Queen Elizabeth I before her accession, was printed in 1605, two years after her death, and in its last scene the Queen is shown entering London and being given a Bible by the Lord Mayor. The way in which she thanks him tells us a great deal:

> We thank you all; but first this book I kiss;
> Thou art the way to honour; thou to bliss—
> An English Bible! Thanks, my good Lord Mayor,
> You of our body and our soul have care;
> This is the jewel that we still love best;
> This was our solace when we were distressed.
> This book, that hath so long concealed itself,
> So long shut up, so long hid, now, lords, see,
> We here unclasp [open]: for ever it is free.

It is worthy of note, suggests J. Heron Lepper, that the reference to the Bible's having long laid buried and concealed has supplied imagery to the Irish ritual.

The Revision of 1834-35

Many rituals divergent in their details were in use until the 1830's, when the very-necessary revision required to co-ordinate them and provide a uniform working was carried out and approved. The revision and considerable additions are believed to have been the work chiefly of the Rev. George Adam Browne, a Fellow of Trinity College, Cambridge, who held and had held important offices in Grand Chapter. Back in May 1832 he acted as First Grand Principal in an emergency, and at that meeting the Marquis of Salisbury, the Marquis of Abercorn, and Lord Monson were exalted by him. At the time he was Provincial Grand Superintendent for Suffolk and Cambridge, a post which, so far as Cambridge was concerned, he had occupied for twenty-two years. In 1810 he was the First Principal of the Chapter of Plato, and in May 1813 was appointed Grand Orator, an office which has long been obsolete. In 1815 he was Grand Chaplain to the United G.L., and an ode written by him was sung by Mr Bellamy in January 1817 at a masonic celebration in Freemasons' Hall, London, on the birthday of the Duke of Sussex, Grand Master, to whom he was at some time chaplain. If the work of recasting and revising the ritual did fall upon him, as seems extremely likely, it fell upon a scholar possessing all the attainments for such a heavy and difficult task.

A committee was appointed by Grand Chapter in February 1834 to take into consideration the ceremonies for the Installation of Principals as well as the various other ceremonies of the Order. Its nine members were the three Grand Principals (the Duke of Sussex, Lord Dundas, and John Ramsbottom) and six distinguished companions, including the Rev. George A. Browne.

This committee reported to Grand Chapter in November 1834 the result of their labours, and it was then resolved "that members of the Grand Chapter be summoned in classes to consider separately such portions of the ceremonies as their qualifications and advancement in the Order and Craft entitle them to participate." The first of the classes met in a special convocation on November 21, 1834, consisting of highly experienced Companions, and, having had read to it the report duly approved and signed by the Grand First Principal and having received the necessary explanations, then gave its entire and unanimous approval to the revised ceremonies. At this meeting the Rev. G. A. Browne had acted as H., and at a special convocation four days later he presided as J., and the report was submitted to the Excellent Companions present in portions according to their several and respective ranks. It was fully explained, some few amendments made, and the Grand Chapter then unanimously approved and confirmed the arrangements of the several ceremonies as submitted by the special committee to the various classes. It is to be particularly noted that the Companions present at this meeting "then expressed their thanks to the M.E. Companion the Rev. George Adam Browne for his attention to the welfare and interest of the Order."

About six weeks later, on February 4, 1835, a special Chapter of Promulgation was warranted for six months only; it consisted of the existing committee but increased to twenty-seven members, its duty in general being to work as a chapter of instruction and promulgation and, in particular, to ensure uniformity of practice throughout the Order. The Exaltation ceremony was worked on some Tuesday evenings and the Installation ceremony on other Tuesdays from May to August of that year (1835), and so seriously did Grand Chapter regard the necessity for this instruction that the Grand Principals were prepared to suggest suspension of any chapter failing in its duty of teaching its members the accepted ritual. In addition, Grand Chapter resolved in November of that year as follows:

> Some misconception having arisen as to what are the ceremonies of our Order it is hereby resolved and declared that the ceremonies adopted and promulgated by special Grand Chapter on the 21st and 25th Nov., 1834, are the ceremonies of our Order which it is the duty of every Chapter to adopt and obey.

The standardized (and recommended but not compulsory) ritual is often referred to as the Sussex ritual, obviously because it had been prepared under the auspices of H.R.H. the Duke of Sussex, First Grand Principal and, for thirty years from 1813, Grand Master in the Craft.

Comparison of to-day's ritual with the earliest printed ritual available embodying the 1835 revisions does not disclose important differences, any small changes being a matter of a few insignificant words.

The Sussex ritual is believed to represent what is to-day called the "Perfect" ritual, versions of which are known as the "Complete," "Aldersgate," "Standard," "Domatic," etc. As already made clear, the revision eliminated the ceremony of passing the veils, and it is known that this ceremony almost went out of use so far as English chapters are concerned, although it is curious to note that the 1881 edition of *The Text Book of Freemasonry* (Reeves and Turner, London) still carried the description of the ceremony but not a ritual of it, and remarked that this ceremony is sometimes dispensed with. It will be explained in a later section how the full veils ceremony came to be revived in Bristol about the year 1900. It is known, too, that the standardized ritual represents a revision of passwords, etc., a matter which cannot be pursued in these pages.

The Christian elements included in most of the early divergent rituals were eliminated in the revision of the 1830's, and eliminated, we must suppose, for the sake of harmony and uniformity with long-established Craft practice. The scroll carrying the first verses of St John, "In the Beginning was the Word . . . ," became a scroll on which were words taken from the first and third verses of Genesis: "In the beginning God created the heaven and the earth. . . . And God said, Let there be light: and there was light."

The Chapter of Promulgation seems to have been successful so far as London chapters were concerned, but had difficulty in meeting the needs of the country chapters, which often could only bring themselves into line by delegating one or more of their members to travel to London to receive instruction. Thus we know that from the Chapter of Concord, Bolton, now No. 37, an Excellent Companion went to London in August 1835 to learn and obtain the ritual promulgated, the cost of his journey being met by his own and other local chapters. It is known, also, that the Rev. G. A. Browne himself, at the time Grand Superintendent for the County of Suffolk, held a chapter of Principals for instruction in Bury St Edmunds and, the next day, a chapter for the instruction of Companions in general, and it is to be expected that what he did in one centre he and other informed Companions did in others.

In general, though, many country chapters were soon in trouble. The Grand Chapter Regulations of 1823 had made every office open to any R.A. mason; those of 1826 had restricted the chairs to Master Masons who were Installed Masters, a rule often disregarded until the coming of the revised ritual in 1835. The revised ritual confirmed the restriction, with the result that in some country chapters it was impossible to find enough qualified Companions to occupy the Principal chairs; further, as yet there was no printed ritual to which Companions could go for help.

In the years following the revision there was urgent need of a printed edition of the new laws and of the more general and more complete promulgation of the revised ceremonies. A correspondent said in 1839 that there were Taunton chapters where the chairs had never been conferred in an esoteric manner; a few zealous Principals in Somerset obtained the necessary instruction in the Chapter of Promulgation, and from it chapters in Bath, Tiverton, Yeovil, and Taunton had benefited, but in the year 1835 they still had not a single duly Installed Principal. These instances were typical of many.

The Principals' Lectures

Quite distinct from the early catechisms, then termed lectures, are the addresses or lectures delivered by the Three Principals following an Exaltation. It has already been noted that these lectures are not older than 1835, and this would account for their being unknown in the Irish and American systems, nor are they present in the Bristol ritual, which is credited with preserving a pre-Union system and an affinity with the Irish working. The lectures as such, although not known until the 1830's, echo phrases and ideas in the *Abstract of Laws*, printed in 1778 and addressed "To all Companions of that Society but more particularly to Initiates."

The Table Ritual or Catechism

The ritual at table, taking the form of question and answer, is either a survival or the revival of an old Craft custom. That the early R.A. ritual contained many catechisms is beyond question, and it is supposed that some of these crystallized into the present table ritual in the 1830's, being worked now not in the chapter itself, but after refreshment. The method of teaching by means of question and answer goes back into antiquity. The Jews, Greeks, and other peoples used it, and it is from a Greek word that the term comes down to us through the Latin. The method of catechism was employed in English literature in the Middle Ages and even earlier, for about the year 1000 Ælfric, Abbot of Evesham, a religious writer and grammarian, wrote his *Dialogue*, a catechism for imparting religious knowledge. The word was familiar to Shakespeare, whose contemporary, Richard Hooker, said that "for the first introduction of youth to the knowledge of God, the Jews even till this day have their catechisms." Since Shakespeare's time a great many books have taken this form, among them being Izaak Walton's famous *Compleat Angler* written about 1650. Indeed, in Walton's day, the very period when the Craft ceremonies were in the course of formulation, the method of imparting religious instruction by the catechism was a subject of keen public interest.

It has been generally held that ritual in the early Craft lodges could not have been much more than a long series of questions and answers, the so-called lectures, exchanged between the Brethren seated round a table. As the eighteenth century advanced the Craft ceremonies became more colourful and the lectures tended to fall into disuse, but there is no doubt that all through the first three-quarters of a century of Royal Arch history catechisms were the rule; known as lectures, they recapitulated the ceremonies through which the exaltee had passed, and in a sense tested his knowledge of the symbolic explanations that had been vouchsafed him.

It has been said that the table ritual continues an old Craft custom. It certainly appears that the "pious memory" toast owes something to Craft working, for Browne's *Master-Key* in cipher (1798) gives a First Degree toast in these words: "To the pious memory of the two Saint Johns, those two great parallels in Masonry."

Section Fifteen

THE PRINCIPALS AND THEIR INSTALLATION

It will already have been realized that the Installation ceremonies are not of ancient date, being much later than the corresponding Craft ceremonies and, *in their present form*, not earlier than 1835.

Until the Union there was much diversity of custom with regard to the Installation of the Principals; in many chapters the elected Principals just 'assumed the chair' without ceremony, and when, in later years, the time arrived when they were expected to be esoterically installed it became necessary for them to attend other chapters where experienced Companions could properly install them and, in addition, teach them how to install their successors.

In the first Grand Chapter in 1776 Captain Bottomley "installed" the M.E.Z., and other officers were "appointed"; the J. and H. were "invested" and received their charges from the M.E.Z., but the word "installed" did not carry all the significance it carries to-day. In that same year Companions Heseltine, Brookes, and Allen are distinguished as P.Z. in a list of Companions present. In Wakefield, where the designations Z., H., and J. began to appear after 1790, there are no records of Installations about that time.

It was quite usual for only the First Principal to be installed and for him then to *invest* the other officers. (Bear in mind that "to install" is to put a Companion into his chair of honour; "to invest" him is merely to clothe him with the insignia of his office, although it must be admitted that, in Scottish phraseology, all officers are "installed," nominally if not actually.) Thus, in the Chapter of Knowledge, No. 92, Middleton, Lancs, constituted Sunday, May 10, 1807, the First Principal only was placed in his chair with certain rites. In a relatively few cases in the old chapters all Three Principals were separately installed, and it is possible that here and there the ceremonies were of a (probably slight) esoteric character. As an example, in the Chapter of St James in 1800 all Three Principals were separately installed; then Past Principals of the different chapters were severally introduced, after which the M.E.Z. requested that the Steward (then a more important officer than he is to-day) be informed that chapter was opened, the Steward then duly introducing the Companions. It is on record that in the first Grand Chapter, in May 1810, on the occasion of the Installation of the Duke of Sussex as M.E.Z., each of the Three Principals was installed by means of an esoteric ceremony.

The ecclesiastical word "inducted" will be noted in some old by-laws and minutes. The literal meaning of "to induct" is "to lead." The South Australian Chapter, Adelaide, had a by-law in the year 1854 directing that officers "so elected and appointed shall be duly installed, invested, and inducted in ancient form." Many similar by-laws are known.

Installation following the Union

Obviously, following the Union, much thought had to be given to the ceremonies of Royal Arch masonry and to the qualification of Companions for office. It must not be assumed, though, that the ceremony of Installation *necessarily* in the years immediately following the Union included the conferment of special secrets. Serious students are convinced that, at the Royal Arch Union of 1817, the 'Antients' in general had no particular secrets restricted to the principal chairs and that in Ireland the Principals had no esoteric ceremony until as late as 1895. What was true of the 'Antients' in general must have been equally true of the 'Moderns,' although it has been shown that a few chapters, one of them as early as 1807, another in 1810, had a definitely esoteric ceremony.

Supreme Grand Chapter appointed in May 1818 a special committee to install with proper ceremony such Present and Past Principals as had not been already so installed, and in 1822 this committee was enlarged to include all the installed P.Z.'s of London chapters. A similar committee was functioning in 1824, and its duties were not confined merely to London.

That at the time of the Union there had come a more general recognition of the importance of a true Installation ceremony may be presumed from the fact that in the Chapter of Friendship, London, which had just been founded, a Companion was in the year 1824, "in ancient form and with the accustomed rites, duly installed in the Chair of the Third Principal."

In St George's Chapter, No. 140, esoteric Installation was adopted apparently no earlier than 1838 (working a drastically revised ceremony as compared with that of 1824), which is extraordinary in view of the fact that this chapter had long observed the custom by which the Principals alone opened the chapter, the Companions being afterwards admitted "and placed in their respective station"; this practice held good until 1902.

The alteration in the Installation ceremonies following the Union and, later, the revisions of 1835 led to a general practice of installing Companions "out of their Chapters." W. H. Rylands's history of St James's Chapter explains that in 1839 the Principal Officers of the Cheltenham

PLATE XX

PLATE JEWELS AND HEAVY CAST JEWELS, LATE EIGHTEENTH CENTURY

Top left : A popular type engraved with many symbols; Irish. *Top right :* Very unusual jewel; on reverse is engraved many symbols. *Bottom left :* Another unusual type, heavily cast in brass gilt. *Bottom right :* First Grand Principal's jewel, silver gilt (approved 1802), made by Thomas Harper.

By courtesy of United Grand Lodge and Quatuor Coronati Lodge

PLATE XXI

Old Prints Emblematic of Traditional History

Left: French, from *Précis du Respectable Ordre de L'Art Royal et Maçonique*; date about 1760. In the foreground is shown a triangular metal plate. *Right*: Believed to be a Scottish print, but its precise origin is doubtful. A pedestal triangular in plan appears to be intended.

Chapter and of the Oxford Chapter were installed in the St James's Chapter. An unusual case is that of March 1858, when Robert Hamilton, M.D., the J. of Chapter 299, Jamaica, who had left the island before his Installation, was introduced into the St James's Chapter and installed "Joshua of the Order." In April 1870 a dispensation to install James Percy Leith into the First Chair of the Chapter of St George, No. 549, Bombay, was read in St James's Chapter, and the Companion was "then duly installed into the Third, Second and First Principals' Chairs." The Chapter of Fortitude, No. 102, Leicester, met in October 1821 for the special purpose of installing Companions of other chapters; at this meeting the First Principal of the Royal Brunswick Chapter of Paradise, Sheffield, was installed as J., H., and Z.; the Second Principal as J. and H.; and the Third as J. The chapter from which the Three Principals came is still attached to the lodge, No. 296, that bears its old name, but the chapter itself is now known as the Chapter of Loyalty.

The sequence of Installations above given should be noted—J., H., and Z. It is, by the way, the one that alone is recognized in Scotland, but in England is commonly reversed, with, it is feared, some loss of continuity and sense of progression.

After the Installation of the Three Principals comes first the investiture of the Scribe E. Still, as in the eighteenth-century Craft lodges where the custom arose, he takes precedence of the Treasurer, although in the Craft itself the Secretary became junior to the Treasurer quite early in the nineteenth century. Another reminder of Craft practice is the placing of the Scribe N. in the South to control admissions, just as the Junior Warden in the South is responsible for all admissions.

Following the heavy revision of the ritual in the 1830's recourse was had to the earlier method of bringing into existence special Chapters of Promulgation and Instruction in which the Principals could be installed and the new ceremonies taught. Thus, when a chapter of this kind was held by the Provincial Grand Chapter in July 1837, at Plymouth, several Prominent Royal Arch masons of the city were installed. This Especial Chapter must have been one of many.

To-day's Grand Chapter Regulations permit a Principal to be installed out of his chapter at the written request of the chapter and on producing proof of election.

Installation in the Bristol Chapters

In the Bristol chapters the actual chairing of the Principals, who have first been obligated, invested, and entrusted in a separate chapel or anteroom, is in full view of the Companions. The ceremony, which retains much of the atmosphere of early nineteenth-century working, opens with the Three Principals Elect standing between the pillars (these are full-size, as in the old Craft lodges) and being addressed by the installing Z. They are then obligated "as regards the government of the Chapter," and all First Principals then withdraw to the chapel, where the Z. Elect, who has accompanied them, takes his second obligation, is anointed, invested, a crown is placed upon him, and he is given his sceptre and then entrusted. The Second Principal Elect is then admitted, obligated, invested, crowned, and entrusted. Next the Third Principal Elect is admitted and invested, a rite based upon Leviticus viii, 5–9, is then performed, this including particularly his investiture with the jewelled breastplate and mitre and crown, following which he is entrusted. For the actual Installation all now return to the chapter, where the other Companions await them, and the Three Principals are duly placed in their chairs by the installing Z., the appointment and investiture of officers then following.

The Office of Principal

The Three Principals when in chapter are to be regarded conjointly and each severally as the Master (see p. 125). As to their qualifications, the Regulations of Grand Chapter require the Third Principal to have been installed as Master of a Craft lodge (this dates back to May 1826) and to have served one year as a Scribe or as a Principal or Assistant Sojourner (overseas such service in office is not insisted on). The Second Principal (as from August 1826) must be an Installed Third Principal, and the First Principal an Installed Second, and in each case there must be a full period of one year since his election to the junior chair. A First Principal may not serve for more than three years in succession; a Second and Third not more than two years in succession, other than by dispensation. A companion may not serve as First Principal in two separate chapters at the same time, except by dispensation.

On the death of any Principal, either before or after an Installation, another is to be elected by ballot and then installed. In the absence of the First Principal, the Immediate Past or Senior Past First Principal of the chapter may, in that order, act in his stead; failing either, then a Senior Past First Principal among the subscribing members may serve, failing whom any qualified Companion may be invited by the First (or acting) Principal to do his work. Principals temporarily absent may, in some circumstances, request qualified Companions to occupy chairs and exalt Companions "as if they were themselves present."

The First Principal of a chapter has the prefix "Most Excellent" attached to the title of his office, but not to his name, but all Principals, present and past, are "Excellent Companions," a matter more particularly dealt with at p. 125.

Passing the Z. Chairs

Just as on occasion a Brother was 'passed through the chair' of a Craft lodge (as explained in a later section), so, too, there were occasions when a Companion would be given the dignity or status of a Principal by being 'passed through a chair,' in which regard the minutes of the first Grand Chapter contain many surprising instances. At the festival meeting, January 9, 1778, Brother Ross was elected Principal, "and was invested accordingly; but offering many satisfactory reasons for not continuing in that high office the Companions proceeded to a second ballot," at which the Z. of the preceding year was re-elected. It was then moved "that the honours of P.Z. be given to Companion Ross for his Zeal and Attachment to this sublime Order and that a Medal be . . . presented." At the next meeting "a gold medal of the Order in the rank of P.Z." was presented to two dukes, one Italian and the other English, who had been exalted that very evening, without apparently even the semblance of an Installation. In the following January the rank of P.Z. was conferred by the same subterfuge on another Companion. In January 1783 there was exalted in Grand Chapter the Rev. Waring Willett of Oxford, who was immediately invested Chaplain, the first holder of the office; at this same meeting the rank of P.Z. was again conferred, but the "Brother" so honoured declined the P.Z. jewel "as the Chapter had not benefited by his passing the Chair so suddenly."

Now all these Brethren had been dignified with a title, but had not passed, even temporarily, through the actual chair of a chapter, but we come to a rather different and even diverting incident in June 1801, when, in St James's Chapter, two members who had been appointed Provincial Superintendents but were not Past Principals were passed through the Z. chair at a special Chapter of Emergency "in order to qualify them for discharging the functions of their exalted situations." Companion A. was elected to the H. chair and Companion W. to the J. chair (and we presume installed). Then Companion A. was proposed as Z. and Companion W. as H. They were installed, whereupon Companion A. resigned "his new situation," and Companion W. was elected Z. to succeed him and installed. This was not the end of the proceedings, for at this same meeting Companion H. passed "the several chairs by regular election and installation," and, on his resignation as Z., the former M.E.Z. (Companion Wright, the real M.E.Z.) was re-elected as Z. Other Installations and resignations took place, altogether eleven Installations on the one occasion, as fully described by W. Harry Rylands in his history of the St James's Chapter, more properly the Chapter of St James.

A hint as to the possibility of there having existed at one time something in the nature of a "P.Z. Degree" comes from the knowledge that one or two chapters had a custom of making an esoteric communication to the First Principal on his leaving the chair at the end of his period of office, as, according to J. R. Rylands, was the case in the Wakefield Chapter.

Section Sixteen

AN EARLY QUALIFYING CEREMONY: PASSING THE CHAIR[1]

OVER a long period bridging the eighteenth and nineteenth centuries, as the reader is now well aware, none but Installed Masters were acceptable as Candidates for the Royal Arch. 'Passing the chair' was a device, a subterfuge, an evasion, originally designed for the one purpose of giving the Master Mason who had not ruled a lodge the status qualifying him as a Candidate. Originally, it is believed, it was introduced by the 'Antients,' but was soon adopted by the 'Moderns.' It took the form of installing the Third Degree Mason in the Master's Chair by means of the customary ceremony or one closely resembling it, and then facilitating his leaving the chair in the course of a very few minutes.

The 'Antients' believed the Installation ceremony to be time-immemorial, to which belief a great many authors have lent support, and have even asserted that between the two systems was one chief distinction—the abandonment by the 'Moderns' of the Installation ceremony. A statement to this effect has been repeated over and over again, but the present author has found no evidence of its truth.

Although the Lodge of Promulgation decided in 1809 that the ceremony of Installation was one of "two" (thought to be a literal error for "true") landmarks that ought to be preserved, it does not follow that the 'Moderns' had ever abandoned it. They did not have it to abandon! The 'Antients' branded the 'Moderns' as innovators, but, in fact, the amount of innovation introduced by them was small compared with that of their opponents. The 'Moderns' were, in general, a more conservatively minded body, on the whole better educated and more sophisticated than their opponents. It was the 'Antients' who found no particular difficulty in accepting any colourful and attractive ceremonial so long as it came dusty with the cobwebs of what Shakespeare has called "antique time."

A fair inference is that the Craft Installation ceremony was introduced some time early in the 1740's, which would allow of the 'Antients' (who were forming from late in the 1730's) adopting a ceremony which they must be credited with believing to have been a time-immemorial rite

[1] This section is largely based upon the present author's paper read to Quatuor Coronati Lodge in February 1957.

heartlessly abandoned by the Premier Grand Lodge and its adherents. Many wholly independent lodges must have been meeting in various parts of the country at that time, each believing that it had the right to work any ceremonies it pleased. Growing from the bare practice of merely leading the Master to the chair, the Installation ceremony had apparently become, by a period not earlier than about 1740, a rounded-off and established ceremony clearly associated with the Hiramic story and possibly or probably already complete with an Obligation and penalty of its own.

Gould believed that the Installation ceremony "was neither known nor practised in England during the early stages of the Grand Lodge era."

It is impossible or at least extremely difficult to believe that the Installation ceremony, which would be nothing if robbed of its allusions to the Hiramic story, could ever have preceded the coming of the Third Degree. Now that degree, it will be remembered, did not reach the few lodges until late in the 1720's or the generality of lodges until many years after then—not till the 1740's probably. The suggestion that such a significant ceremony as one reflecting the Hiramic tradition could have been abandoned by the 'Moderns' is quite untenable, although a claim to that effect was commonly made by their opponents and by masonic writers on their behalf—and frequently taken for granted by some masonic historians.

Some of the 'Moderns' must have met the ceremony in its early days, but they were working under the discipline of a Grand Lodge and could not so easily please themselves in such a matter; later they adopted a version of it—not, at first, for the installing of Masters, but as a means of conferring upon their Royal Arch candidates a qualification whose real significance must have escaped them, and would continue to escape the great majority of them for half a century or so.

The 'Antients' insist that Royal Arch Candidates be Installed Masters

It is difficult to put into precise words the 'Antients' attitude to the Installation ceremony. It was much more than approbation and esteem, more than regard; it had something in it of reverence and veneration. A Master was not only a chairman or past chairman of the lodge, superior to junior Brethren, but one who, having passed through an esoteric ceremony of distinction, was now of a definitely higher grade. This is recognized in their refusal to confer the Royal Arch Degree upon a Brother who had not passed through the chair; he was simply not good enough to be a Royal Arch Master.

There is a remarkable minute of the 'Antients' Grand Committee as early as June 24, 1752, upon the occasion of Laurence Dermott's being "installed" as Grand Secretary and being proclaim'd and saluted accordingly.—After which he repeated the whole Ceremony of Instaling Grand & in the manner which he had learn'd from Brother Edward Spratt Esq: the Celebrated Grand Secretary of Ireland. The long Recital of this solemn Ceremony gave great satisfaction to the Audience, many of which never had an Opportunity of hearing the like before.

The 'Antients' insisted that their Masters of Lodges should not only be correctly installed, but be able to install their successors. Take, for example, this further minute of the 'Antients' Grand Lodge (June 2, 1756):

> The Grand Secretary was Order'd to Examine several Masters in the Ceremony of Installing their Successors, and declared that many of them were incapable of performance. Order'd that the Grand Secretary shall attend such difficient lodges and having obtain'd the consent of members of the said Lodges he shall solemnly Install and invest the Several Officers according to the Ancient Custom of the Craft.

Warrants of the 1761 period help us to understand the insistence placed by the 'Antients' on the Installation ceremony:

> We do hereby further authorise and impower our said Trusty and wellbelov'd Bro. to nominate chuse and install their successors to whom they shall deliver this Warrant . . . and such successors shall in like manner nominate chuse and install their successors.

It must be apparent that the 'Antients' were definitely teaching, and insisting upon, an Installation ceremony at a time when, in the 'Moderns' lodges in general, an Installation was little more than the incoming Master taking the chair. It is extremely likely that the Installation ceremony became embellished in the course of time, and ultimately developed into what is now called the Extended Ceremony of Installation (the ceremony which, after some discussion, was permitted by Grand Lodge as recently as 1926 to be worked under certain safeguards, the most important of which is that the Installing Master must declare precisely that no further degree in masonry is being conferred).

The Royal Arch is referred to as "an organised body of men who have passed the chair" by Dr Fifield Dassigny, in his much quoted book, dated 1744 (see p. 45). Further, Laurence Dermott, in *Ahiman Rezon* of 1756, scornfully alludes to those "who think themselves R.A. masons without passing the chair in regular form." (The word "passing" in this sentence must mean "going through" in the ordinary way, becoming a 'past' Master; in the light of Dermott's hostility to subterfuge 'passing,' no other interpretation is possible.)

It is hardly open to doubt that by the time we hear of the 'Antients' working the Royal Arch ceremony they were already observing (and doubtless had always observed) the rule that Candidates must be Installed

Masters. With the rise of the Royal Arch to popularity this rule proved unworkable. It was too restrictive, for while, on the one hand, there was a growing demand for Exaltation, there was, on the other, the bottleneck created by the rule, an embarrassing condition quickly but unofficially remedied by the subterfuge of passing a Brother through the chair for the sole purpose of qualifying him as a Candidate for Exaltation. He went through a 'constructive' ceremony, soon to be known as the Past Master Degree, and became a 'virtual' Past Master.

The word 'virtual' has many definitions, the one best suiting our purpose being "in essence or effect, not in fact; although not real or actual, equivalent or nearly so."

The device of 'passing the chair' was invented by the 'Antients' lodges themselves, and not by their Grand Lodge, as becomes clear from a minute of the 'Antients' Grand Lodge for December 4, 1771, a minute, by the way, which lights up the relative dependence of the 'Antients' Grand Chapter:

> The Rt. Worship! Deputy Grand Master informed the Grand Lodge of the Proceedings of the *Royal Arch* meetings, Vis. on the 2nd October and 6th of November last and expatiated a long time on the scandalous method pursued by most of the Lodges (on S? John's Days) in passing a Number of Brethren through the chair on purpose to obtain the sacred Mystery's of the *Royal Arch*, and proved in a concise manner that those proceedings were unjustifiable; therefore Moved for a Regulation to be made in order to Suppress them for the future. The Deputy was answered by several Brethren, that there were many Members of Lodges who from their Proffesions in Life (the Sea for Example) that could never regularly attain that part of Masonry, tho' very able deserving Men, and humbly Moved that might be Considered in the new Regulations. The Grand Lodge in General thought such a Clause necessary and therefore the Question being put for the Regulation, it was unanimously Resolved
>
> > That no person for the future shall be made a *Royal Arch Mason* but the legal Representative of the Lodge, except a Brother (that is going abroad) who hath been twelve months a Register'd Mason; and must have the Unanimous Voice of his Lodge to receive such Qualification—and in order to render this Regulation more Expedient it is further Order'd that all Certificates granted to Brethren from their respective Lodges shall have inserted the Day the Brother or Brethren joined or was made in said Lodge and that this Regulation take place on St. Johns Day the 27th Dec! 1771.
>
> The Deputy Grand Master . . . informed them that there was several Brethren of Different Lodges that had been Admitted amongst the *Royal Arch Masons* Illegally and that it would be necessary to take their case into consideration but as it was concerning the *Royal Arch* presumed they would leave it to the next Grand Chapter and they might depend that every thing

should be pursued for the real honor of the Fraternity. The Grand Lodge having duly weighed the forgoing proposition and considering that several of the Members of the Grand Lodge were not *Royal Arch Masons* It was agreed by the Majority That the R: A: Chapter were the properest persons to adjust and determine this matter and therefore it was agreed that the case should be reffered to the Royal Chapter, with full Authority to hear, determine and finally adjust the same.

On St John's Day in December, twenty-three days later, the Grand Lodge confirmed the 'New Regulations,' the D.G.M. giving the Brethren present to understand that these were "to be strictly observed in their respective Lodges." It is doubtful whether this protest and resolution had much effect; indeed, the 'Antients' Grand Lodge itself was hardly consistent in the matter, for it seemed to have no objection on principle to 'constructive' or 'virtual' ceremonies when, for instance, on December 2, 1789, Sir Watkin Lewis, Knight, City of London's Alderman and M.P., having been elected Junior Grand Warden, it smoothed the way for his Obligation and Installation by resolving "that his private lodge be directed to pass him through the Chair in the Morning of St. John's day next, if he should not before that time be installed Master of a Lodge." Actually he was "obligated and installed" at a meeting of Grand Lodge at the Crown and Anchor Tavern in the Strand, on St John's Day, December 28.

Although the qualifying ceremony through which the Royal Arch Candidate passed was essentially identical with the Installation ceremony, it did not confer upon him in the early days (and only occasionally in the later ones) any privilege other, it is supposed, than a higher status; it seldom availed him when he came to be elected Master of his lodge, for then he generally had to be regularly installed.

The 'Moderns' adopt the Qualification

It is well known that the 'Moderns' were working the Royal Arch Degree at an early date. Now they knew nothing (officially) of an esoteric Installation ceremony, and originally could not have demanded that Candidates should have the Master's qualification. The Grand Master did not sanction the ceremony of Installation until 1828, many years after the Union, although there is plenty of evidence that the Installation ceremony was being worked in a great many lodges long before that year.

Unexpectedly, the earliest surviving minute recording a passing through the chair is that of a 'Moderns' lodge—Anchor and Hope, Bolton, Lancs. At a Lodge of Emergency, November 30, 1769, "Bro. John Aspinwall, Bro. James Lever and Bro. Rich[d] Guests were installed Masters and afterwards Bro. James Livesay Sen: was re-installed." Livesay, it should be said, had already been installed on June 24 of the same year, and James Lever had served as the Master of the lodge. This minute antedates by rather more than two years the first mention in the 'Antients' records (see p. 184) of this practice, but all the circumstances are against the 'Moderns' having been the first to use it.

Undoubtedly, as the eighteenth century progressed, some 'Moderns' worked an Installation ceremony as they worked others borrowed from the 'Antients,' but not to the 'knowledge' and with the approbation of their Grand Lodge. But, in preparation for the Union, the Lodge of Promulgation (1811) was teaching the Installation ceremony, and the instructed lodges were teaching others.

Whatever the practice became in the course of a few years, it is quite clear that under the rules of the first Grand Chapter (1766) it was not necessary for the Candidate to be of higher rank than Master Mason. Neither these rules nor those given in the Charter of Compact (the authorizing document) required or could require the Candidate to be a Past Master; obviously so, inasmuch as the Installation ceremony was unknown officially to the 'Moderns,' although individually and irregularly they may have been aware of it. It is not unreasonable to assume that had a 'virtual' P.M. degree for exaltees been *common* practice among the 'Antients' as early as 1766, both the Charter of Compact and the rules of the Grand and Royal Chapter might have made a glancing or oblique reference to the fact, but they did not. The wording in the Charter of Compact is quite simple: "That none but discreet and Experienced Master Masons shall receive Exaltation to this Sublime Degree." There is not here the slightest hint that any higher qualification than Master Mason was required. Nevertheless, the eighth 'clause' of the Charter says "that none calling themselves Royal Arch Masons shall be deemed any other than Masters in operative Masonry." (The last term must be taken as meaning 'Craft masonry.') This statement appears to echo the claim to superior status made years before by the 'Scotch Masons' (see p. 39) and thus strengthens any supposition that the earlier rite was indeed a prototype of the later one; but does it also help us to understand how it came about that Grand Chapter, with no certain experience of esoteric installation but regarding itself as an association of Masters, was so soon to insist on the Past Master qualification in its candidates?

While it is accepted that the 'Moderns' were quick upon the heels of their opponents in adopting the custom of 'passing the chair,' it is safe to say that in the year of the Charter of Compact (1766) they knew but little about it and that the 'Antients' were only beginning to work it. In March 1766 of four new Master Masons who took the Royal Arch Degree in the Mourning Bush Lodge, Bristol (founded 1740), not one had been in the chair, and not a suspicion of a hint is given in the lodge records that they had passed through any 'constructive' ceremony.

However, within a very few years, the 'Moderns' were in general requiring prospective exaltees to be Past Masters, which mostly meant actually that they should have taken a constructive degree learned from their opponents, a degree whose significance must have been largely lost on the 'Moderns' and one that embodied a ceremony not recognized by their Grand Lodge. We find the Regulations of the premier Grand Chapter in 1778, twelve years after its founding, laying down that none should be admitted to this exalted degree but those who were proved to have "been regularly apprenticed and presided as Masters, to be justly intitled to, and have received the Past Master's token and pass word." Three years later (May 1782) this was altered to those "who have passed through the three probationary degrees of Craft masonry; and have presided as Masters." The wording might appear to convey the impression that Grand Chapter was well aware that Candidates were evading the Regulation. The reference to "Past Master's token and pass word" appears to indicate that by 1778 some 'Moderns' lodges may have been sufficiently 'Antient' in sympathy (adoption of the Royal Arch Degree was in itself fair evidence of such a condition) to have adopted an Installation ceremony.

Many times between 1771 and 1813 did the 'Antients' officially denounce the subterfuge 'passing' and try to insist that Candidates for the Royal Arch be Masters of twelve months' standing or *bona-fide* Past Masters—but without much success until the end of the period. It is very doubtful, also, whether the 'Moderns' could do much to prevent Candidates taking the 'virtual' P.M. Degree. Obviously the 'Antients' had set the fashion in this matter, and as they started so they continued. The rules of a great many chapters about this time provide that Candidates must have been Master Masons for at least twelve calendar months, and that none ought to be admitted except "men of the best character and education; open, generous, of liberal sentiment, and real philanthropists; who have passed through the probationary degrees of Masonry, have presided as Master. . . . The Brother to be not less than twentythree years of age at the time of exaltation."

Apparently, the matter can be summed up in this way. All 'Antients' Royal Arch lodges and chapters required Candidates to have passed the chair, actually or virtually, and a number of 'Moderns' chapters did the same, but certainly not all of them; as one example, the Chapter at Wakefield did not regard the P.M. Degree as a necessary prerequisite, J. R. Rylands tells us, and he records that of five Candidates in 1816, all Master Masons, two had passed the chair and three did not appear to have done so.

It is curious to learn that some Candidates were passed through the 'virtual' ceremony *after* they had been exalted, and this in spite of the Royal Arch ritual (catechism) then demanding from each Candidate answers to such questions as "How were you prepared as a P.M. of Arts and Sciences?" and "How were you prepared as an Excellent Mason?" In the 'Antients' Neptune Lodge, No. 22, in the month of October 1808, three Brethren were exalted, not one of whom had passed the chair; they went through that ceremony in the following July. But probably this may have been nothing more than an attempt to remedy an accidental omission!

Lodge Permission to be exalted

A Brother wishing to be exalted had customarily to get the consent of his lodge, firstly to pass the chair, and commonly he had to be elected to the honour. He might be proposed by a Brother, or often he would propose himself, just as in some early Craft lodges a Fellow Craft might propose himself to be raised to the Third Degree. The result was generally, but not always, a foregone conclusion; in the Mount Moriah Lodge, then No. 31, 'Antients,' in the year 1801, permission was refused because, apparently, the prospective exaltee was going abroad and was Senior Warden; the lodge would "not approve . . . without leave from the Deputy Grand Master."

It is quite usual to find the proposal taking the form of the Candidate's asking for a certificate as a Geometric Master Mason to allow of his being made a Royal Arch mason. Neptune Lodge, No. 22, 'Antients,' at Rotherhithe, London, August 8, 1809, opened in the Third Degree when Brother Peter Rokes moved for his Private Lodge Certificate as a Geometric Master Mason, for the purpose of passing the Holy Royal Arch. The certificate, duly signed by the officers, was handed to him in open lodge. This was not quite a simple case, though, for Brother Peter Rokes was actually the Master of the Lodge and as Senior Warden had been "passed to the chair" the previous February; in June he had become Master, having, however, already served in the meantime as Acting Master for about six weeks—on the strength, it is supposed, of his 'virtual' qualification! But he still needed a certificate as a Geometric Master Mason to get him through the door of the chapter.

Conferring the P.M. Degree—making a 'Virtual' Master

As the 'virtual' ceremony developed in the course of a few years into what was in effect a distinct degree, the practice arose in some places of conferring it in chapter instead of lodge, a likely indication that it was coming to be regarded as one of a sequence of Royal Arch Degrees (as in effect it is still so regarded in some American states) and that its original significance was in danger of becoming dimmed. The practice met with opposition (echoes of which remain in American masonry to this day), and we note one instance, recorded by H. Hiram Hallett, in which a West of England chapter expressed the opinion that chapter should not be adjourned to allow Candidates to pass the chair, but that the ceremony should be performed at a regular lodge or at a lodge held prior to the opening of the chapter. From this it appears that the custom had been to adjourn the chapter, open a lodge for the conferring of the P.M. Degree, and then change back to chapter for the Exaltation. Thus, in 1811, the by-laws of the Chapter of St James directed that the "first assistant Sojourner should take the Chair as Master of the Previous Lodge and open the same in due form, in the Third Degree... and then prepare the Candidate for the Ceremony of Exaltation according to ancient usage." In this "Previous Lodge" the Candidate occupied a Warden's chair, was proposed as Master and elected. He took an Obligation at the Pedestal, was raised, placed in the chair, and "exercised the duties of W.M." He was then again taken to the Pedestal, and the Principal Sojourner as Worshipful Master then explained the purpose of the qualifying ceremony, following which the Candidate was told that he was not entitled to consider himself a Past Master or to wear the badge of a Master of a Lodge. He was next entrusted with the secrets of a Master of Arts and Sciences, and was finally introduced into chapter and exalted. (But often elsewhere a 'virtual' Master was entitled to wear the Master's badge.)

Care was generally taken to impress upon the 'virtual' Master that he was not being qualified to rule over the lodge for more than a very brief time, but there was considerable variation in the form of words. Occasionally he was empowered to preside over a lodge *pro tem.* and also to conduct a ceremony (as, for example, at Wakefield). In an American ceremony, obviously stemming off from early English practice, the 'virtual' Master is told that "no test of his proficiency is at this time required of him." In the Mount Moriah Lodge, No. 34, Wapping, in the year 1785, he was installed "to be Master until next stated lodge night, if in his power to be so long in the place."

A MS. in the possession of Bruce Oliver (see p. 161) gives a ritual which in its broad lines must represent the 'virtual' chair ceremony of the 1790–1835 period. The ceremony is assumed to take place in a lodge opened by members of a chapter preceding an Exaltation. The lodge is opened in the "P.M. Degree" and is declared by the W.M. to be dedicated to the noble Prince Adoniram. In general the working suggests the Craft Installation, and many present-day familiar phrases are found in it. The Obligation is on customary lines. The W.M. gives the Candidate the distinguishing mark or signature used by the Brothers of this degree—namely, $\frac{A}{S}$, in which the first letter stands for Adoniram and the second for the Sidonians, the famous class of workmen who distinguished themselves in finishing the Porphyre (Porphyry). The Candidate is now entrusted with the signs, etc., of the degree, these resembling those of the Extended Ceremony, emphasis being laid on the symbolism of the plumb-line. Next he is invested with a Master's jewel, warned to exercise his new authority with discretion, and having enjoyed a moment of authority, is delicately relieved of the semblance of the Master's honours and invited to regale his Brethren "with a suitable refreshment." On leaving the chair he is invested with the P.M. jewel.

Following the Craft and Royal Arch Unions, we find a remarkable instance of the 'Moderns' adapting or applying a ceremony to what was to many of them an unfamiliar purpose—a ceremony long known to many of them, but one whose true significance they had in general only dimly understood. The instance (it may have been one of many about that time) is related by J. R. Rylands in *A.Q.C.*, vol. lxv. After 1823 the Master of Unanimity Lodge, Wakefield, had to be installed "according to ancient usage," but no "ancient usage" was known, so apparently the 'passing' ceremony—involving a formal opening and closing with esoteric matter appropriate to a separate degree—was adopted to meet the new rules!

Late Instances of Passing the Chair

In spite of many attempts to bring the practice to an end, the ceremony of passing the chair was worked in many lodges until long past the middle of the nineteenth century. Thus, in 1822 or 1823, the Howard Lodge of Brotherly Love, an old Sussex lodge, opened "into the fourth degree," and a Brother was "rewarded with the degree of a P.M. of Arts and Sciences"; five Brethren in this same lodge in the year 1833 "passed the chair in ancient form." In the Chapter of Sincerity, No. 261, Taunton, ten Brethren were so "passed" in 1832. In the old Bury Lodge, now Prince Edward's Lodge, No. 128, the ceremony continued to be worked until 1840; in the Durham Faithful Lodge, No. 297, Gibraltar, in 1837, six Brethren "received the fourth... degree which they withstood manfully," four more underwent the degree "with fortitude and courage."

In Bolton's old lodge, originally Hand and Banner, now St John's, No. 221, several Brethren passed the chair in 1846; one of them, the Master of the Lodge three years later, recorded that these several Candidates "were the last persons in Bolton permitted to go through this Ceremony, the New Authorities having prohibited the practice." In the Lodge of St

John and St Paul, Malta, five Brethren passed the chair in 1852, and apparently, about four years earlier, any Brethren wishing to take the degree had it "conferred upon them." In an old 'Antients' lodge, Commerce, No. 215, Haslingden, Lancs, when ordinary masonic business was not pressing, it was customary in the 1862 period to confer the chair degree on Master Masons! Even later instances could be quoted to show that the custom was "an unconscionable time a'dying," although it is obvious that the P.M. Degree had long been in decline and by the middle of the century was, in the great majority of places in England, quite obsolete; it should have disappeared as from May 20, 1817, when the Past Master qualification was modified and all that was required was that of twelve months' standing as a Master Mason. But none of the principal chairs is open to a Companion below the rank of Installed Master.

Twelve months had been the general qualification for some time. It was replaced by one month in the Regulations of 1893.

The suppression of the P.M. Degree met with resentment in some quarters, a few Candidates tending to be disappointed at failing to receive what had come to be regarded as one of a proper sequence of degrees. The Lodge of Probity, No. 61, West Yorkshire, raised the legality of the degree with the Deputy Provincial Grand Master, who replied that the practice was "altogether illegal," and he "was not aware that one lodge could be found in the Province of West Yorkshire pursuing such a practice." In 1859 Grand Scribe E. wrote to the British Chapter, No. 334, Cape Town, saying that no such degree as the P.M. Degree was "known to or acknowledged by either the Grand Lodge or the Supreme Grand Chapter . . . the Companions who feel aggrieved at not receiving an irregular degree ought rather to congratulate themselves, and the Chapter, that the orthodox working has been restored."

Not All Passings were for Qualifying Candidates

Andrew Hope, in his history of St John the Baptist Lodge, No. 39, Exeter (dating back to 1732), says that officers of that lodge, in cases of emergency, had the degree of P.M. conferred upon them; he cites a minute of an Installation meeting of January 27, 1823, at which four Brethren "were (in order to assist at ye installation) admitted to ye degree of Past Master." In the minutes of St John Lodge, No. 348, Bolton, appear numerous references to "passing the chair" in the 1816–40 period, with no accompanying indication that the Brethren concerned were proposing to be exalted; a chapter warrant was not obtained until 1840. J. R. Rylands has made it clear that in Unanimity Lodge, for a period ending in 1826, the 'virtual' P.M. Degree was worked without reference to or association with the Royal Arch. The British Union Lodge, No. 114, Ipswich, passed twelve Brethren through the chair on the one occasion in 1790 to qualify them to attend an Installation.

Passing the Chair in Ireland and Scotland

Ireland. In the later part of the eighteenth century Irish lodges were in close accord with the 'Antients' in regarding the rank and status of a Past Master with marked respect, and they commonly conferred the "P.M. Degree"; instance the Banagher Lodge, No. 306, which in 1794 opened and closed a P.M.'s Lodge; a Royal Arch chapter then opened; the proceedings of the P.M.'s Lodge were read and approved; and the Brethren who had been advanced to the Chair Degree were then made Royal Arch masons. The funds of the chapter were combined with those of the lodge. The 'virtual' degree was widely worked in the nineteenth century, but in 1864 the Irish Grand Chapter brought the custom to an end.

Scotland. There was no (official) ceremonial Installation of the Master of a Lodge in Scotland until 1858. In that year, George S. Draffen tells us, "a ceremonial for the Installation of a chairman of a Lodge" was adopted. This was followed in 1872 by the introduction of the English Installation ceremony now in use, the "only Craft Degree for which there is an authorised Grand Lodge ritual" (a 'degree,' the reader will note). The Scots Grand Lodge resolved that this ceremonial or degree should not be conferred on any one except the Master of the Lodge or one who produces a certificate that he has occupied the chair as duly elected Master.

However, in Scotland, as elsewhere, the lack of official recognition did not prevent the 'virtual' P.M. Degree from being worked, but not, it is thought, before the early nineteenth century. George S. Draffen's valuable little book *The Triple Tau* states that the Supreme Grand Chapter of Scotland (not the Grand Lodge) authorized charters in 1842 to what were called "Chair Master Lodges," and in these lodges was worked the degree called in Scotland "Master Passed the Chair." There was some anomaly here because these lodges were Craft lodges, and "the R.A. Chapters were already empowered to work the [P.M.] degree by virtue of their existing charters and required no further authority." Not more than three of these 'Chair Master' charters were issued: (*a*) Kinross, 1842, recalled four years later; (*b*) Edinburgh, 1842, recalled four years later, although the degree was worked until 1856, when the lodge became dormant; the lodge was revived without sanction in 1867 and finally dissolved in 1899, when it took out a charter as a Royal Arch chapter; (*c*) St John's, Manchester, England, 1845, recalled in the following year.

The degree of Master Passed the Chair was removed in 1846 from the

PLATE XXII

FIVE SMALL JEWELS, 1780–1825 PERIOD

Top: Two pierced jewels, respectively of 1814 and 1827, showing development of Triple Tau. *Centre:* Irish plate jewel, covered with engraved symbols. *Bottom left:* Jewel of Temple Chapter, New York, with Mark emblem on reverse of medallion. *Bottom right:* Pierced jewel of most unusual design.

Four of the jewels by courtesy of United Grand Lodge

PLATE XXIII

A Set of Principals' Robes, Aprons, and Headdresses
Formerly used in the Cana Chapter, Colne, No. 116, chartered in 1769.
Reproduced by permission of Sir Edward Rhodes, Grand Superintendent, Lancashire (Eastern Division)

Royal Arch rite in the chapters of Scotland, and they were forbidden to work it, but Scottish chapters overseas continued to work it until 1872, when it was finally abolished.

Passing the Chair in the United States of America

The fact that only about one in three of the American jurisdictions works a Craft esoteric Installation ceremony inevitably affects the question of the qualifications of Royal Arch Candidates in the United States of America, although, contradictory as it may seem, it does not always follow that in jurisdictions where there is no Craft Installation, as the English mason understands the term, there is necessarily any waiving of the ancient requirement that the Candidate should have passed the chair.

Fortunately for the present purpose, a manuscript entitled *The Degree of Past Master: a Degree of the Chapter*, by Ward K. St Clair, Chairman of the Library and Museum Committee of the Grand Lodge of New York, has been very kindly placed at the author's disposal in response to a request for information, and from it is learned that, of the U.S.A.'s forty-nine masonic jurisdictions existing in the year 1943, only fifteen required the Master-elect to be installed in an esoteric ceremony, and even then the custom was not always observed. In twenty-two jurisdictions the Master is not so installed, as, for example, in Minnesota (since 1918), in Nebraska (since 1930), and in Montana (since 1941); in these jurisdictions the lodge pleases itself in the matter. The Installation ceremony is only sometimes termed a 'degree,' but the ceremony in which a 'virtual' Past Master is made is commonly known as the 'Past Master Degree,' although the rituals of the two ceremonials are said to be practically identical.

The 'virtual' Past Master Degree is conferred under the jurisdiction of chapters of R.A. masons to qualify a Mark Master Mason to receive the R.A. or, more correctly, the Degree of Most Excellent Master. The last-named is a prerequisite to the R.A. in every jurisdiction except that of Pennsylvania, where the Candidate automatically receives in lodge the qualification of Installed Master (P.M. Degree) that he may need as a prospective exaltee. In Northern and North-eastern States, the oldest of the United States jurisdictions, the P.M. Degree goes back to before 1800, when only twelve American Grand Lodges were in existence; it was worked in Pennsylvania in 1783, and was regarded as "a fully-fledged Degree" when the Grand Chapter for the Northern States was founded in 1797. But in one of these old jurisdictions, where Installation is regarded as obligatory, a Past Grand Officer has stated that he did not receive the degree until some time after he went into the chair. Old minute-books of chapters in the Northern States prior to 1797 mention the Degree of

Excellent Master and indicate that this was really that of Past Master. An old Connecticut chapter, now Washington Chapter, No. 6, recorded in 1783 that a Candidate "was raised an Excellent Mason passing the chair in due form," and this is believed to be the earliest American minute of its kind.

Apparently, all through the nineteenth century there was discussion, often pointed and forthright, on whether the Installation ceremony and the P.M. Degree should be under the jurisdiction of Grand Lodges or Grand Chapters. Seldom did the Grand Lodges assume rights over what may here be called the Chapter P.M. Degree, but very frequently Grand Chapters sought to justify their claim that both the Craft Installation ceremony and the P.M. Degree were their concern alone. But in 1853 the General Grand Chapter (the highest Royal Arch authority in the U.S.A.) resolved that it did "not claim jurisdiction over the P.M. degree when about to be conferred on the Master-elect of a Symbolic [Craft] Lodge." Three years later, in 1856, the suggestion of some Grand Chapters that the P.M. Degree should be omitted from the degrees controlled by the General Grand Chapter aroused much argument, which reflected the controversy in the English Craft back in the eighteenth century when only the 'Antients,' in general, installed their Masters in an esoteric ceremony.

A recommendation by the General Grand Chapter that the Grand Chapters and chapters should "abridge the ceremonies of the P.M. Degree" met with some approval, but the many jurisdictions had each their own point of view with regard to the desirability of retaining the degree itself. Many, including New York, insisted on the importance of the degree, and the Grand Chapter of Michigan claimed the exclusive right to confer it within its territory. In Indiana the Candidate was qualified if he had received the degree in lodge or in chapter, whereas in Maine, even the Past Master of a lodge had to take the 'virtual' degree to qualify him for the Royal Arch. In Kentucky and Columbia, a 'virtual' P.M. could preside over a Craft lodge. The Grand Chapter of Delaware claimed the power to warrant a Lodge of Past Masters. The P.M. Degree was not regarded as a true degree in Kansas, West Virginia, Georgia, and some other states, including Louisiana, the last-named not objecting to the Craft Installation being performed in public. In West Virginia and Virginia the degree was customarily conferred on Wardens of a Craft lodge. Pennsylvania, as already stated, insisted on the P.M. qualification, but gave it automatically to every Master Mason. In the jurisdiction of Indian Territory and Oklahoma the Craft Installation was optional, and in the 1890's a Grand Master who had already served three years stated that he had not been esoterically installed.

Section Seventeen

PASSING THE VEILS

The ceremony known as 'passing the veils,' forming part of the Royal Arch rite from some time rather late in the eighteenth century, probably had a Christian origin, and was customary only during the period when the Royal Arch itself was largely a Christian degree. With the de-Christianizing of the degree following, firstly, the 'union' of the Grand Chapters in 1817 and, secondly, the drastic revision in 1835, the ceremony of the veils rapidly disappeared from English masonry. Where we still find it worked—for instance, in Bristol—it offers itself more as a revival than as a survival, as explained more fully later in this section. How the ceremonial came to be adopted is quite unknown, but its inspiration may well have been a decidedly Christian Craft working in one or more of the early lodges. The passing of the veils symbolizes the enlightenment that comes with masonic progression, but originally, it might well be, the veils were the emblem of the mysterious veil that was rent in twain when the crucified Saviour passed through it. In an old Lancashire Craft lecture of the possible date of about 1800 the Veil of the Temple "signified the Son of God, Jesus Christ, hanging upon the Altar of the Cross, as the true veil between God and us, shadowing with His wounds and precious blood, the multitude of our offences, that so we might be made acceptable to the Father." A catechism on these lines was probably worked in a lodge or lodges in which the Craft and the Royal Arch ceremonials had become curiously interwoven and both of them marked by strong local influences. We should not care to rule out the possibility that the veils also had an alchemical interpretation. The Rev. Dr J. R. Cleland, a Provincial Grand Chaplain, has said that the entire object of the alchemic art "is the uncovering of the inner faculty of insight and wisdom and the removal of the veils intervening between the mind and dividing it from its hidden, divine root." We know also that the veils have been thought to be a symbol of the sufferings of the Jews in returning from exile.

The veils, in the early ceremonials, were generally three in number, but at an early date a fourth was added in some localities, and we know that the American chapters of to-day largely work a four-veil ceremony. The Bristol Chapter uses four veils. Josephus, the first-century Jewish historian, unduly forced the symbolism of the veils in saying that they were composed of four things which declared the four elements: the fine linen signified the earth because the flax grows out of the earth; the purple signified the sea because the colour is dyed by the blood of a sea shellfish; the blue is fit to signify the air; and the scarlet will naturally signify fire.

It has been assumed at times that the ceremony of passing the veils goes back to possibly the earliest period of the Royal Arch. Curiously, however, the records do not support the assumption, unless, however, the ceremony was known over quite a period as the Excellent Master or the High Excellent Degree, a possibility which some masonic authors appear to admit and which is lent support by George S. Draffen's statement that the Scottish Excellent Master Degree "is frequently known as the passing of the veils." If in some lodges either the Excellent or the Super Excellent Degree was actually the passing of the veils, then, of course, it was worked at quite an early date. There is an impression (known to have been shared by J. Heron Lepper) that the veils ceremony was originally an entirely separate ritual, and this impression, if well founded, would strengthen the inference that the veils ceremony in early days was a separate degree with its own name. In Scotland it is, in fact, the Excellent Master's degree, the official title of the ceremony.

Most, however, of the particular references to the passing the veils come towards the end of the eighteenth century or the beginning of the nineteenth. Thus we know that the Union Waterloo Chapter, No. 13, at Gravesend had three Grand Masters of the Veils in 1819 and also, about that date, had Captains of the Third, Second, and First Veils respectively, as had many other chapters. There are certainly more references in the early nineteenth century than there are in the late eighteenth. In 1841 George Claret, who was thoroughly acquainted with the masonry of the early years of the century, said that the ceremony of passing the veils took place soon after the Obligation, but was not much known or practised in London, although, he adds, it was always given in the 'Antients' chapters before the Craft Union in 1813.

The veils ceremonial continued well into the nineteenth century, and in Lancashire, for example, it was often conferred in Prince Edwin Chapter, No. 128, Bury, until 1867; a letter to the Grand Scribe E., asking if they were in order in giving the veils, said that they had worked the ceremony "from 1803." In an earlier page we mention that a ritual printed as late as 1881 includes notes on the ceremony; earlier printed rituals referred to it, but generally in such a way as to suggest that the ceremony was losing its vogue. In 1833 in the Chapter of Concord, Bolton, a Candidate paid 11s. 10d. for "Vails" and 5s. 6d. for "Rods," the latter, we believe, having reference to a feature of the veils ceremony.

The ceremonial as worked in the 1820 period was much as follows, subject to variation in details: The Candidate was prepared with a blindfold, his knees bared, his feet slipshod, with a cable-tow round his waist. Three Sojourners acted as the guardians of the veils. The Junior Scribe conducted the Candidate, and gave four knocks at the door of the First Veil. The Candidate was admitted by giving the Past Master's word and sign. Scripture reading was from Exodus iii, 1–6, referring to the burning bush, following which the thirteenth and fourteenth verses of the same chapter were read, including the words "I am that I am." At the second veil the Candidate gave a password already received and met the emblems of the Serpent and Aaron's Rod, and the relevant Scripture (Exodus iv) was read. Suitably entrusted, he was now enabled to pass the Guard of the Third Veil; here the Scripture reading, from Exodus iv, told of the miracles of the leprous hand and of the water poured upon the dry land and turning into blood. He now heard the words "Holiness to the Lord," and was shown the Ark of the Covenant containing the tables of stone, the pot of manna, the table of shew-bread, the burning incense, and the candlestick with seven branches, and was now qualified to enter as a Sojourner and Candidate for Exaltation. During the veils ceremonies he received passwords and signs enabling him to pass the successive veils and finally to present himself as a Sojourner.

It is accepted that the ceremonial, while retaining its main features, varied considerably in its details from district to district and even from chapter to chapter.

The Veils Ceremony in Bristol

The Royal Arch was worked in Bristol at an early date not only by the 'Antients,' but by the 'Moderns,' the latter in a Craft lodge meeting at the Crown Inn, Christmas Street, Bristol, which, as already said, is thought to provide the earliest minute relating to the Royal Arch Degree in England, for on Sunday evening, August 13, 1758, two Brethren were "raised to the degree of Royal Arch Masons," further minutes revealing that four other meetings of the same kind took place, always on Sunday evenings, during the next twelve months. In another Bristol 'Moderns' lodge four Brethren took the degree in 1766. The Lodge of Hospitality was founded in Bristol in 1769, and almost immediately its members obtained a charter for a new chapter, the Chapter of Charity, No. 9, upon the register of the Grand Chapter and for many years the only chapter in the province. When the two Grand Chapters united, No. 9 became formally attached to the Royal Sussex Lodge of Hospitality, with which it had been and still is closely associated. It is now No. 187.

While it is well known that the veils ceremonial is worked in the Bristol chapters, the reader must understand that the claim (not made by Bristol) that it is a true and uninterrupted survival of an eighteenth-century custom needs to be regarded with care. The facts were thoroughly investigated by Sir Ernest Cook, Grand Superintendent, who subsequently published a pamphlet, from which it appears that in the later years of the nineteenth century the Beaufort Chapter of Bristol, which had been founded not earlier than 1846, worked the *verbal* part of the veils ceremony, but did not use the veils themselves, and nobody could give information about them. Their introduction or reintroduction early in the years of the present century was due to Sir Ernest Cook and other enthusiasts. Up to about 1902 the Candidate was told that the ceremony should be performed in a room in which the veils were suspended, but following that date real veils were brought into use and have added remarkable interest and colour to the ceremony. While in Ireland, Scotland, and some parts of America the veils are customarily suspended in the chapter-room itself, in Bristol they hang in an adjoining chapel. Sir Ernest discovered that there were no references to the veils in minutes of any of the older Bristol chapters, but in 1890, when he himself was exalted, it was the practice in the Beaufort Chapter, No. 103, for the M.E.Z. to direct the Principal Sojourner to withdraw "and put the Candidate through the Ceremony of Passing the Veils." The work "was done almost exactly as at present, but there were no Veils." Sir Edward Letchworth, the Grand Scribe E. (in office from 1892 to 1917), confessed that he knew nothing about them, and could not say whether they were in use in any English chapter. Sir Ernest and a friend visited Ireland, and, although they could not during their stay find a chapter using them, they were able to get some vague information, as a result of which they had three veils made and hung in the anteroom of the Beaufort Chapter, their example being quickly copied by other Bristol chapters. In 1929 they became convinced that there ought to be a fourth veil, and this they added. From this account, on the authority of a careful investigator, it must be concluded that the ceremony as now worked in Bristol is not an uninterrupted survival of an eighteenth-century practice. It is understood that in Bristol, the chapter having been opened and the Candidate elected, the Principal Sojourner, his assistants, and the Director of Ceremonies retire with some members and there work the veils ceremonial—always before and separate from the actual Exaltation, the point being made that passing the veils is not really part of the Exaltation ceremony. There is no truth in the idea held in some quarters that Bristol has been given special permission to retain the veils ceremony.

The Irish Ceremony of the Veils

In the Irish ceremony as customarily observed the chapter-room is divided by curtains or veils, beyond which the Companions sit together in the East. There are four veils: the first is blue, denoting friendship; the second purple, denoting unity and concord, the symbolism being based on the union of blue and scarlet, producing purple; the third scarlet, denoting fervency and zeal, truly typical of Royal Arch masonry; the fourth white, denoting purity, and beyond which sit the three Principal Officers of the chapter. In front of the white veil is the Royal Arch Captain, whose duty is to prevent anyone from entering the council chamber without permission. Before each of the other veils is a Captain of the Veil, whose duty is to allow none to pass except those duly qualified by a password. Particular Scripture readings apply to each veil ceremony, as explained in the account of the old English ceremony, the three parts of the ceremonial being based upon episodes in the life of the great Lawgiver, Moses. The Candidate is one of three, the number being made up by Companions.

The Scottish Ceremony of the Veils

The Veils, or to give the ceremony its official title, the Excellent Master's degree, and the Royal Arch may be conferred at the same meeting, but the candidate must be a Mark Mason. If he has received the Mark in a Scottish Lodge or is an English Mark Mason, he is 'affiliated', in a short ceremony, in the Mark Lodge within the chapter; but if he is not so qualified then that degree is first conferred. The normal practice is to open the Chapter in the R.A., to adjourn to the Mark degree, to close in the Mark degree, and to open a lodge of Excellent Masters for the passing of the veils.

It is to be noted that, whereas in Ireland an English visitor is permitted to be present throughout the ceremony of the Veils, he may not attend a Scottish Chapter during the ceremony of the Excellent Master's degree (the Veils) which is the second of the three degrees in the R.A. Series (the first being the Mark; see further p. 221). An English Mark Mason (not being a R.A. Mason) would not be allowed to witness the opening and closing of a Scottish Chapter but only that part in which the Mark is conferred. An English R.A. Mason (not being a Mark Mason) may not witness the conferment of the Mark or Excellent Master degrees; he would also be required to withdraw when a R.A. candidate is asked for the signs of recognition of an Excellent Master. In short, an English R.A. Mason or Mark Mason may witness only those parts for which he is qualified.

The Veils Ceremonial in America and other Countries

In such a large country as the United States, where the affairs of Royal Arch masonry are administered by nearly fifty separate Grand Chapters, it is inevitable that some diversities in custom and practice must occur, but in general the Royal Arch ceremony includes a highly elaborated passing of the veils, which seems to be based on an old Irish ceremony. There are four veils, as in the Irish system, and the episodes are as already described, although towards the end of the ceremonial the Candidate may be given the signet of truth, a finger ring bearing a circle enclosing a triangle. The officers guarding the veils may wear a robe and cap of the colour of their veil and may be armed with a drawn sword.

The veils ceremonial is still worked in parts of Canada (Quebec, Montreal, and other places) and in certain of the Australian chapters. In some of the chapters in Victoria, Australia, it is regarded as a desirable preliminary to the Royal Arch ceremony, but is of a permissive character. Apparently the ceremony is sometimes worked not as part of the Exaltation ceremony, but for the purpose of exemplifying the symbolic lessons which grew up around the ceremony of the veils in the early days. Where accommodation permits the veils are suspended in an anteroom.

Section Eighteen

SEQUENCE AND STEP DEGREES

DEGREES to which attention will be devoted in this section are chiefly those that served as steps to the R.A. in the early days. The subject cannot be pursued at length, there being space for little more than an explanation of the relationship of these degrees both to the Craft and to the R.A. Many of the added degrees not only contain R.A. elements, but include the word 'Arch' in their titles, as, for example, Royal Arch of Enoch and Royal Arch of Solomon. It is a question whether certain degrees have borrowed from the R.A. or whether, as some students have thought possible, they have all evolved more or less from the same source.

The nomenclature of the added degrees historically associated with the R.A. is perplexing. We have already seen that the P.M. Degree was originally the 'Antient,' esoteric Installation of the Master of a Craft lodge. Similarly, what in Ireland was called the High Priest Degree was in England the esoteric Installation of the First Principal. The R.A. of old had at times some curious relationships with some of the added degrees, and we find a startling example in Cape Town, where, early in the 1800's, two lodges, the Union and the British, were each working the R.A. In due course the latter regularized the position by applying to the Supreme Grand Chapter for a warrant and founded the existing British Chapter, No. 334, in 1829. T. N. Cranstoun-Day, in his history of that chapter, says that the local custom was for the members of the Rose Croix to attend the Craft Lodges in their red robes and also to attend the chapter, even though they had never been exalted to the R.A. Degree, a custom which endured until 1866.

Excellent and Most Excellent Degrees

There is no doubt that the 'Antients' lodges worked a number of degrees under their Craft warrants, not, as has already been said, that these warrants mentioned any such degrees, but that the 'Antient' mason took a very comprehensive view as to what constituted the ceremonies of the Order. The 'Antients,' and later the 'Moderns' too, worked in addition to the Craft degrees a Past Master Degree derived from the

Installation ceremony, an Excellent Mason or Excellent Master Degree, Super Excellent Mason, Super Excellent Master or High Excellent Master Degree, the R.A., Mark, and occasionally such further degrees as Knight Templar, Red Cross, and possibly others. A common sequence of step degrees was P.M., Excellent Master and Super Excellent Master, the R.A. and other degrees then following.

How old these Excellent and Super Excellent degrees are it is difficult to say, but they certainly were known in 1770, and were worked in that year in the Chapter of Friendship. (W. Redfern Kelly says that the Super Excellent Degree was conferred in 1756 in an 'Antients' lodge, and that in 1763 both Excellent and Super Excellent were worked in a 'Moderns' lodge, but he does not state the authority.)

In the early 1800's one form of the Excellent Master's Degree worked in England celebrated the completion of an arch. Pillars were erected and bridged with an incomplete arch, one still needing its arch stone or copestone, which in the course of the ceremony was put in place. In another form this degree included historical incidents to be found in the first part of the R.A.

The Excellent Mason Degree as worked in England in the 1820's period was conferred only on P.M.'s, and seemed to be only a step to another degree. Regarded from any other point of view, it was very inconclusive. It led to the Super Excellent Mason Degree, in which the Candidate wore the habit of a High Priest, but apparently this degree introduced very little new matter, but harped back to the Craft ritual and included a reference to the point within a circle.

Some old lodges and chapters refer not to the Super Excellent, but to the High Excellent Degree, and possibly the two were identical. The term 'High Excellent' appears a few times in the minutes of St Paul's Lodge, No. 194, in the 1812-13 period.

In recording that of fifty chapters and 'Antients' lodges working the R.A. in Lancashire up to 1825 almost all of them, as from at least 1780, worked the Excellent, Most Excellent, and High Excellent degrees, S. L. Coulthurst says that these degrees were generally known as passing the veils. The statement or suggestion that these degrees were related to the ceremony of passing the veils crops up from time to time, but the present author is unable to confirm it from available evidence. However, George S. Draffen, an authority on Scottish masonry, states that the Scottish Excellent Master Degree is actually the passing of the veils, and other students say the same about a Scottish Super Excellent Degree. Neither the Super Excellent Degree given in a well-known English irregular print of about 1825 nor that now included in the American system is a 'veils' ceremony.

A minute of the Neptune Lodge, now No. 22, of the year 1808 is a typical 'Antients' record of a raising and Exaltation:

> Proceeded to raise Br. Gibbs to that sublime degree of a Master Mason. Returned thanks in due form. Then adjourned the Master Masons Lodge & opened in the Excellent and High Excellent Masons Degree, then proceeded to exalt[1] ... to that Sublime degree of an Ex^t & High Ex^t Master Masons. Returned thanks in due form, then Closed the Business and ReOpened a Master Masons Lodge.

A sequence of degrees brought to light by Norman Rogers as having been worked in an 'Antients' lodge in Liverpool, founded in 1792 and erased in 1822, has some special points of interest. Here is a revealing minute of the lodge:

> This being regular Royal Arch night, the Lodge was opened on the 111 of Masonry by Bro. L. Samuel, W.M. in the Chair. When Bros. A.B. and C.D. were duly proposed, and seconded as advocates for Holy Royal Arch, the ballot was in their favour and they were Past the Chair, and a Lodge of Past Masters was formed and they were entrusted with the P.M. degree. The Lodge was then closed on the 111 of Masonry and the Chapter was opened on the Excellent Super Excellent degree of masons, when the above Brothers were balloted for and approved; they were then passed through the three veils of the temple and into the Holy of Holies; the Chapter was then closed on the Excellent degree and opened on the H.R.A. Chapter, when the above Brothers with amazing skill and courage received the Order of R.A.M. Nothing further for R.A., the Chapter was closed.

The Knight Templar Degree in Relation to the R.A.

The most important of the chivalric masonic orders, the Knights Templar, is probably younger by twenty years or so than *recorded R.A.* masonry, but it is well proven that the two degrees were closely related in their early days and that in the 1780's the R.A. was just as essential a preliminary to the Knights Templar as it is to-day. Members of the K.T. are eligible for the Knights of Malta, one other degree of which we find mention late in the eighteenth century. It has been stated that the Scottish Lodge of St Andrews, of Boston, Massachusetts, had in 1769 an R.A. meeting at which the degree of K.T. was conferred; possibly the degree had been introduced by an Irish lodge in the 29th Regiment stationed at Boston in that year. A well-known minute of the Chapter of Friendship, Portsmouth, of October 21, 1778, quotes a letter from Dunckerley stating that "we might make Knight Templers if we wanted and it was resolved to" (see p. 206).

---

[1] Sometimes "pass" is used.

and Super Excellent masons. In this same chapter a minute (already given) of October 21, 1778, records that the Z. "read a letter from Com. DUNCKERLEY, that we might make KNIGHT TEMPLERS if we wanted and it was resolved to . . ." (Two Brethren "took the MARK," and each chose his mark; one of the two was "made ARCH next time.")

There is a clear indication in the 1820 period that the R.A. and the Mark Degrees were still intermingled with the Craft, and we find repeated references to these degrees being conferred on Brethren in both regular and emergency meetings. (It is worth noting, by the way, that R.A. certificates of the period often include the phrase "Given under our Hands and Masonic Mark in Chapter this —— day of ——." Certificates issued by the old Albion Chapter, No. 9, 'Antients,' exemplify this.)

In Benevolence Lodge, now No. 226, five Brethren were made Mark masons on October 16, 1825. At one meeting in 1827 "the Brothers met on the Master's Mark." Nothing could be clearer than a minute of August 30, 1829: "Bro. Thos. Taylor took the degree of Pass [Past] Master and afterwards took the degree of Mark Mason and also the degree of Arch Mason"—and all these in an 'Antients' lodge going back no further than 1797, the year in which it was founded in Blackburn, Lancs.

In a much older 'Antients' lodge, the Mount Moriah, No. 34, founded at the Ship and Anchor Inn, Gun Dock, Wapping, in 1775, there are references in 1788 and onward to the Excellent, High Excellent, and Mark Mason Degrees, the first two being prerequisites for the Mark. Similar entries are to be found in the minutes of other 'Antients' lodges of the period. As showing the very close connexion between the Mark and the R.A. even as late as the 1866–87 period, there is a minute of the Serendib Chapter, Ceylon, showing that the chapter had been opened "by virtue," and was then "lowered to the Mark Degree"; if necessary, the chapter would afterwards be "opened in due form."

Much has been said and written on the subject of the Harodim Degree (there are various spellings, such as Herodim, Herodium, Heredim, and Heredom), a degree which may have come between the Fellow Craft and the Master Mason, was possibly an early form of Mark, and may have included "Marked Masons." It is not within the province of this book to deal at length with the Harodim Degree, but it should be said that one version of it embodied the idea of the Hiramic Degree; the loss and finding of the word; and even a Mark idea, the rejection of the stone! In the Restoration Lodge, Darlington, in the 1780's, and perhaps even earlier, the Harodim Degree was a prerequisite for the Royal Arch, and is thought to have included the Old Mark, Ark, and Link. It should be stated, however, that *Harodim*, a plural word, is derived from 1 Kings v, 16; the chiefs or princes over the work of building the Temple at Jerusalem were so named, and Anderson in his *Constitutions* uses the word in this sense. It has been said that from a rite (worked chiefly in the North of England) known by this name came part of the Royal Arch and other ceremonies, but the 'facts' are few and confusing, and, indeed, the later Harodim ceremonies may well have been influenced by the Royal Arch. However, some students hold very definite opinions in this matter, as, for example, William Waples, who has told the present author that a perusal of the minute-books of the Lodge of Industry, No. 48 (founded in Durham in 1735), Phœnix Lodge, No. 94 (founded in Sunderland in 1755), and Sea Captains' Lodge, now Palatine Lodge, No. 97 (also of Sunderland, founded 1757), shows clearly how the old Harodim system was divided into what are now separate Orders of masonry, and, further, that "the Royal Arch and its subsequent development were originally part of the Harodim." (The Grand Chapter of Harodim, founded by William Preston in London in 1787, was an organization with an instructional purpose, and has no bearing on the argument.)

In England nowadays the Master Mason is qualified to become either a Mark mason or a R.A. mason and in the order that he prefers, but in Scotland, Ireland, and the U.S.A. the Mark, as in the eighteenth century, is still a preliminary to the R.A.

Crossing the Bridge

In some early R.A. and Mark rituals, and even in to-day's American R.A. ritual, the Candidate is made to cross a bridge, generally of a shaky and decrepit condition. We are reminded in L. C. Wimber's *Folk Lore in the English and Scottish Ballads* that the symbolism of crossing the bridge goes back into the ancient mysteries. The Mohammedans held that the road to Paradise included a bridge laid over the midst of Hell, a bridge finer than a hair and sharper than the edge of a sword and beset with briars and hooked thorns which would offer no impediment to the good but would entangle the wicked, who, missing their footing, would fall headlong into Hell. The Magi, a priestly caste of the Medes and Persians, taught that, on the last day, all mankind will be obliged to pass a straight bridge in the midst of which will be angels who will require of every one a strict account of his actions, while the Jews speak of the Bridge of Hell, no broader than a thread, from which the idolaters will fall into perdition. Folklore contains many references to such bridges.

Section Nineteen

THE IRISH ROYAL ARCH

THE Royal Arch in Ireland has a long history. The Youghal reference to the "Royall Arch" in 1743, the Youghal minute of 1759, Fifield Dassigny's book of 1744—all these have already been cited in this book as indicating the early acquaintance of the Irish freemason with the Royal Arch ceremony. Ireland took its Craft freemasonry from England in the 1723 period, probably *via* Bristol. The Irish freemasons were far from appreciating the condescension of the English Grand Lodge, whose *Constitutions* of 1738 announced that the lodges of Scotland, Ireland, France, and Italy were "affecting independency"; behind this curious phrase there lay the implication that there was one Grand Lodge, the English, and that all others owed allegiance to it. The alterations made by the premier Grand Lodge in its effort to fight clandestine masonry alienated masons in England and many other countries, particularly Ireland, and it inevitably followed that as soon as the 'Antients' Grand Lodge of England found itself established it entered into close association with the Irish Grand Lodge, which body, early in 1758, wrote stating that it "mutually" concurred in a strict union with the 'Antients' Grand Lodge, and promised to keep in constant correspondence with it. In 1772 there came about a reciprocal arrangement by which Irish masons in England and the 'Antient' masons in Ireland received "all the honours due to a faithful Brother of the same Household with us." In the following year the Grand Master of Scotland wrote expressing the wish to establish "Brotherly Intercourse and Correspondence" and repeating the phraseology of the Irish Grand Lodge's letter.

Thus we find the 'Antients' recognizing fully and completely the sister Grand Lodges of Ireland and Scotland, but in this mutual recognition there was a remarkable anomaly: in English masonry a great, and perhaps the greatest, difficulty as the eighteenth century developed was the 'Antients' love of the Royal Arch and the 'Moderns' hostility to it. Yet the Grand Lodges of Ireland and Scotland officially regarded the Royal Arch more or less as the 'Moderns' did! In England the 'Moderns' did not officially cease their hostility until 1813, but in Ireland, whose Grand Lodge was, also officially, just as hostile to the Royal Arch, there

PLATE XXIV

THE UNIQUE JEWELS OF UNANIMITY CHAPTER, WAKEFIELD
Top: Principals' jewels and breastplate. *Bottom:* Sojourners' jewels. (See pp. 261 and 269.)
By courtesy of John R. Rylands and Quatuor Coronati Lodge

PLATE XXV

HEADDRESSES, ANCIENT AND TRADITIONAL

Top : Headdresses formerly worn in Melchesedec Chapter, attached to Lodge of Antiquity, Bolton (No. 146), the present owners.
From Beesley's *Record of Antiquities*
By courtesy of the Manchester Association of Research

Bottom : Mitre, Crown, Turban, and Breastplate as made by Messrs Spencer, London, in 1856.

was no Grand Chapter until 1829, and in Scotland none until 1817, in which latter year some, but far from all, of the Scottish chapters came into one jurisdiction.

The good understanding between the 'Antients' and the Irish Grand Lodge is best exemplified in the fraternization of their military lodges abroad. Here is a revealing example: The Irish military lodges stationed at Gibraltar in the 1790's supported the 'Antients' Provincial Grand Lodge of Andalusia (a division of Southern Spain), paid contributions to the 'Antients' Grand Lodge in London, although retaining their Irish allegiance, and were ordered by their own Grand Lodge to submit to the ruling of the Provincial Grand Lodge of Andalusia!

In the decades immediately before the end of the century the official Irish attitude to the Royal Arch was frankly hostile. In 1786 the Grand Lodge banned Royal Arch entries in lodge minute-books, although in the following year, and again in 1805, it tried, but failed, to gain control of the Royal Arch and other degrees. On June 11, 1829, fifty-three chapters constituted themselves into a Supreme Grand Royal Arch Chapter (following the pattern of Supreme Grand Chapter of England that had been founded about twelve years before). It has been said that the new Grand Chapter was given the "blessing and approval" of the Irish Grand Lodge, but at the beginning it had very little power, although it could issue warrants. Its officers were three Grand Principals, three Sojourners, First and Second Scribes, with a High Priest as Chaplain. When, in December 1829, the regulations were formally adopted 158 chapters had already applied for warrants. In the following year it resolved that recognition be refused to chapters that were without warrants and that the presiding officers of subordinate chapters be styled Grand Masters, and not High Priests.

Many Dublin lodges quite early in the 1800's were working the Royal Arch, two of them being known as "Royal Arch Lodges," but an agreement which was bound, in the long run, to kill the old custom of conferring the degree in lodge was arrived at in 1834, by which time the Grand Master and his deputy (Craft) had automatically become Grand Principals. This agreement, to be found in print in the Irish *Ahiman Rezon* of 1839, provides that Companions excluded or suspended or restored by Grand Chapter should suffer the like treatment by Grand Lodge and *vice versa*; no lodge could hold a chapter unless it had previously obtained a warrant for it, but in practice this law was often disregarded.

Although the Grand Chapter came into existence in 1829 with the Irish Grand Lodge's "blessing and approval," not until 1931, 102 years later, did the Grand Lodge, in response to a memorial supplicating it to recognize the Royal Arch degrees, add this new law (No. 2A):

Pure Ancient Masonry consists of the following Degrees and no others, viz:—The Entered Apprentice, the Fellow Craft, the Master Mason and the Installed Master, but the degrees of R.A. and Mark Master Mason shall also be recognized so long as the Supreme Grand Royal Arch Chapter of Ireland shall only work those two degrees in the form in which they are worked at the passing of this Law.

The Irish Grand Lodge based its custom of issuing warrants upon that of the 'Antients.' Over a long period the ordinary lodge warrant was regarded—at any rate by the lodges themselves—as conferring the right to work the Royal Arch and such other unspecified degrees as were customary at the time, and it is known, for example, that Belfast lodges and chapters in 1842 were conferring the degree of Knights Templar under their ordinary warrants.

As from the establishment of the Grand Chapter in 1829 the Craft lodge warrant was commonly called a "Blue Warrant" (American practice perpetuates this), and the chapter warrant a "Red Warrant." The term "Craft Warrant" was not used officially of an Irish warrant until 1875.

Step and other Degrees in Ireland

The Royal Arch became in quite early days popular in Ireland in spite of the lack of official recognition, and in the course of time, and probably as a reflection of English practice, it gathered to itself a small collection of added degrees, some of them step degrees leading up from the Craft, while others were Christian degrees to which the Royal Arch itself acted as an introduction. That no secret was made of the existence of these degrees is obvious from the following advertisement in Dublin journals of 1774:

> The Knights Templars of Ireland, Royal Arch, Excellent and Super-Excellent Free and Accepted Masons, Lodge No. 506, intend dining together at their Lodge-room, at the Thatched Cabin, Castle St., on Friday, 24th instant to celebrate the Festival of St. John; Such of the Fraternity as chuse to Dine with them are requested to leave their Names at the Bar two days before, Signed by Order, J.O. E.G.S. Dinner to be on the Table at Four o'Clock.

(E.G.S. would represent Excellent Grand Scribe.)

The Rose Croix is believed to have been introduced into Dublin in 1782—"years before any trace of the Degree, or the Rite to which it belongs, is found in any other English-speaking Jurisdiction," says Chetwode Crawley.

There was the customary sequence of degrees at the making of a Royal Arch mason in a Craft lodge in Lifford, County Donegal, in 1785, when a Brother was made Excellent and Super Excellent before he was exalted in a Craft lodge. In 1786 the title-page of the by-laws of Irish lodge No. 620 mentioned the above degrees, and followed them with the Knights Templar; then, bearing date 1789, a parchment certificate is impressed with the Craft, Royal Arch, and Knights Templar seals of the Lodge. The Knight Templar Degree was commonly conferred in Irish Royal Arch chapters; indeed, in 1836 it was "irregular" to attach a Knight Templar encampment to a lodge that had no Royal Arch chapter connected with it.

Banagher Lodge, No. 306, opened and closed a Past Master's Lodge in June 1794; then it opened a Royal Arch chapter and confirmed the proceedings of the last chapter and of the P.M.'s Lodge; Brethren who had been advanced to the Chair Degree were then made R.A. masons, the fee being two pounds. The chapter funds were combined with those of the lodge, "both being held for the common good," and chapter and lodge were subject to the same laws so far as they were consistent.

The minutes of a lodge or chapter at Castle Bar in the year 1816 appear to be typical. Two Brethren were exalted to the Degree of "Royal Arch Super Excellent Mason." The High Priest gave a lecture and the chapter was closed, "after which the Lodge was transferred to the Third or Master's Degree of Masonry." The chief officer was the High Priest, and assisting him were the First, Second, and Third Grand Masters. Other minutes of this lodge are on similar lines.

There was a tendency for the Excellent and Super Excellent Degrees to disappear as such from the Irish R.A. They are not mentioned in the Irish *Ahiman Rezon* of 1839, and it was at one time presumed that officially they were extinct in the 1840's, but lodge minutes still show them as being worked. In Lodge 1012 in 1843 a Brother passed the chair, was made Excellent and Super Excellent, passed the First, Second, and Third Veils of the Temple, was made an R.A. mason and subsequently a Knight Templar; two years later, in this lodge, a Brother passed through the same sequence and paid as fees £1 11s. 4d.

The High Priest's Position

The principal officer of an Irish chapter was the High Priest, and this was so for a long period, but the Irish Grand Lodge (founded in 1829) brought about an alteration and ordered that the presiding officers of subordinate chapters should be known as Grand Masters, with the result that the High Priest sank to the bottom of the list of the nine officers then "ordained." At the same time the names of the Principals in an English chapter began to be heard in the Irish chapters, but this introduction was not popular and not everywhere adopted. The High Priest, who had been the chief officer of the assembly, chapter, or lodge (all three terms were in vogue) had in some cases now become simply the Chaplain, but it was difficult for the Scribe E. always to remember the alteration, and his minutes were subject to vagaries in this particular matter. By 1858 the presiding officers in quite a number of chapters were still known as the First, Second, and Third Principals, the High Priest taking a minor place, but, following the work of a special committee, an additional officer—the King—became in 1861–62 the First Principal, while the Chief Scribe, who since 1839 had been seventh in the list, advanced to third place. The Sojourners, so called, now disappeared, and as such have no place in Irish ritual to-day, the Brethren assisting the Candidate in the repairing of the Temple being known as Craftsmen.

There was a period early in the nineteenth century when many Installed Masters found themselves, as a result of lack of facilities for obtaining instruction, incapable of conferring degrees, and had to resort to the services of some expert Brother, in which connexion J. Heron Lepper has explained that the Master continued to preside over the lodge, but there was a "Degree Giver," who remained close to the Candidate all through the ceremony, an arrangement favoured by the form of an Irish lodge. The following brief extracts from Irish minutes illustrate the point: "Worshipful A.B. in the Chair. C.D. and E.F. was Initiated by Jas. Quinn" (1834); "a night of emergency. Bro. A.B. in the Chair. . . . Bro. C.D. was made a Royal Arch Mason and consequently Made a Knight Templar mason. Received the instructions from Bro. G.H." (1840); "Bro. C.D. was made a Master Mason. . . . Bro G.H. done the business that was required" (1842); three Brethren were made "pass masters in the Chair, etc. . . . paid Bro. G.H. 5^s for giving instructions this night" (1843); " gave Bro. G.H. 11/4½d. for his trouble to come to instruct the Lodge" (1803). (All these minutes are more fully quoted in *A.Q.C.*, vol. xxxv, p. 183.) It goes without saying that the custom is now obsolete. (There are still some aspects of masonry in the relatively large American lodges which apparently reflect but do not quite reproduce the old Irish custom.)

The Three Principals

The First Principal of an Irish chapter has always, right back to the earliest days, been a Past Master in the Craft, actual or virtual, and the secret instructions relating to all three chairs are essentially the same, irrespective of names and designations, as in Irish, English, and Scottish constitutions. However (by special permission of the Irish Grand Chapter) neither the Second nor the Third Principal is necessarily a Past Master, but, if he is not, he must so inform any chapter under *another* jurisdiction which he may happen to visit. All three must be Mark Master Masons and have been registered as Master Masons for five years at least. The Excellent King elect must also have served the office of High Priest or Chief Scribe and have been installed as Master in a Mark lodge.

There is a general impression that esoteric ceremonies associated with the Principals' chairs are, in general, not older than fairly late in the nineteenth century; a ritual of 1864 includes a ceremony for the "Installation of a King, within a Royal Arch Chapter," and it is known that somewhere about the 1890's all Principal Officers of subordinate Irish chapters had to be re-obligated in order to conform to an arrangement arrived at between the Grand Chapters of Ireland and England; prior to that period it is likely that only the King and not the other Principals was obligated.

The chief officers of an Irish chapter nowadays are the King, High Priest, and Chief Scribe. Other officers are the Captain of the Host, Superintendent of the Tabernacle, R.A. Captain, three Captains of the Veils, the Registrar, and the Janitor; there may also be a Treasurer and a Chaplain. Up to 1922 the Three Principals collectively were addressed as "Your Excellencies" and the First Principal as Most Excellent King, but nowadays the term "Most Excellent" is reserved for the Three Grand Principals, "Very Excellent" for Grand Officers, and "Excellent" for Principals of subordinate chapters.

Grand Officers

The chief officers of the Grand Chapter are the Most Excellent Grand King, High Priest, and Chief Scribe. The most important of the Grand Officers are the Grand King, his Deputy, Grand First Principals of District Grand Chapters, Provincial Grand Superintendents, the Grand High Priest, the Grand Chief Scribe (all "Most Excellents"); the Grand Treasurer, the Grand Registrar, the Grand Director of Ceremonies, the Grand Chaplain (all "Right Excellents"); the Grand Captain of the Host, the Grand Superintendent of the Tabernacle, the Grand Royal Arch Captain, the Grand Captain of the Scarlet Veil, and the Grand Captain of the Purple Veil and the Grand Captain of the Blue Veil (all "Very Excellents"); then the Grand Standard-bearers, the Grand Janitor, the Grand Very Excellent Registrar of the Grand Chapter of Instruction, District Grand Officers, Officers of the Grand Master's Chapter, and the Excellent King, High Priest, and Chief Scribe of every subordinate chapter. Grand Officers are nominated at the July convocation of Supreme Grand Chapter every year, elected at the November convocation, and installed and inducted in February. (The remaining "Stated Convocation" of Grand Chapter is in May.)

Chapter officers are elected annually, and their names must be approved by Supreme Grand Chapter before Installation (if overseas, then by the Provincial Grand Superintendent). Each of them must be a subscribing member of a Craft lodge, in good standing, and not in arrears in any lodge or chapter. A Principal Officer cannot resign office until the termination of the year for which he has been elected; in his absence a Past King shall rule the chapter.

Clothing

The *full-dress apron* of the Order is of white lambskin, 12 inches to 14 inches deep and from 14 inches to 16 inches wide, bordered with scarlet ribbon 2 inches broad, having in the centre half-inch gold lace; the flap has a border 1½ inches broad and carries a triangle of silk or satin, edged with a gold border, and within the triangle, the triple tau, of gold-spangled embroidery. The silk or satin ground is scarlet for Kings and Past Kings and white for all other Companions.

The *sash*, of plain scarlet ribbon 4 inches broad, is worn under the coat from right shoulder to left hip, and has a triple tau at the tie. The sashes of Grand Officers, etc., including those of Kings, have their ends trimmed with gold fringe 2 inches deep; the sashes of all other Companions have a silk fringe.

Collars carry either three or two bands of half-inch gold lace according to the importance of office; chains of office and gauntlets are worn by the more important Grand Officers.

Jewels of office are suspended from collars of scarlet-ribbed silk, trimmed with half-inch gold lace and, in the case of Grand Officers, etc., gold fringe 2 inches deep.

The jewel of the Order is worn on the left breast—on Companions it is pendant from a white ribbon; on the Principal Officers, etc., from a scarlet ribbon. (Grand Chapter specifies the apron and jewels of office to be worn by Mark Masters.)

The Candidate and his Qualifications

A Candidate for the Royal Arch must have been registered as a Master Mason for twelve months (one month for Naval, Military, or Air Force Brethren), and must be a Mark Master Mason and a subscribing member of a Craft lodge. The Mark Master Mason Degree must be worked under the jurisdiction of Grand Chapter and conferred only on Brethren who are Master Masons and who actually have been proposed and balloted for Exaltation in chapter; Brethren either residing in Dublin or proposed for Exaltation in a Dublin chapter must be approved by the Committee of

Inspection, consisting of the Grand Officers and the King of every subordinate chapter meeting in the Dublin district. It meets monthly and does not consider a Candidate until after he has been balloted for and approved by the chapter which he proposes to join.

The chapter ballot takes place in the presence of either the proposer or the seconder; every member present must ballot; the Candidate fails to be elected if there are more than two negatives in the ballot.

The degree is not conferred upon more than three Candidates at one time, and neither the Mark nor the R.A. Degree may be divided or curtailed.

A memorial for a warrant to constitute a new chapter must be signed by at least nine R.A. masons, who must also be Mark masons and Master Masons of at least five years' standing and be subscribing members of a lodge under the Irish Constitution.

Ceremonial, Exaltation Ceremony, etc.

The Irish Grand Chapter prescribes approved ceremonies for constituting new chapters and for installing officers and prescribes the prayers and charges and the Scriptural readings used in chapters. Indeed, every chapter is required to conform with the established ritual, failure involving a fine or even the cancelling or suspension of the warrant. Further, all matters of ritual or ceremony are subject to the approval of the Grand Chapter of Instruction, which consists of the most important of the Grand Chapter Officers together with other experienced Brethren of rank and standing elected for the purpose.

The quorum for a chapter is six Companions, including the Three Principal Officers, but for conferring a degree nine must be present during the entire ceremony.

An Outline of the Exaltation Ceremony

The Opening Ceremony includes reference to the Captains of the Veils and their places, one outside the blue, one outside the purple, and one outside the scarlet veils, their duties being to guard their veils. The colours of the veils are symbolic. The place of the Royal Arch Captain is outside the white veil (purity) at the entrance to the council chamber, and his duty is to guard that veil. The Captain of the Host has a place in front of the Three Principal Officers. The Chief Scribe is in the East, at the left hand of the Excellent King, the High Priest being at his right hand. The exaltee wears the Mark Master Mason's apron. An officer of considerable importance is the Conductor, whose duty is to announce and instruct the exaltee, to lead him in a devious way and introduce him to the veils which he duly passes. The exaltee is encouraged to persevere in his desire to recover that which was lost and to engage in the search for truth. Though there are no 'Sojourners' so called, Companions act with the exaltee to bring the number of Craftsmen to three. The Craftsmen, having begged permission to assist in the work of repairing the Temple, are given implements as in the English rite, but the explanations are different. Symbolically, the pick roots out from our minds all evil thoughts; the shovel clears away from our minds the rubbish of passion and prejudice; and the crowbar raises our desires above the interests of this life, the better to prepare for the search after knowledge and the reception of truth and religion.

The discoveries are dramatized more or less in view of the chapter. The Craftsmen, standing on what is represented to be part of the foundations of the Temple, clear away the rubbish and raise a stone slab which gives entrance to an arched vault. The exaltee is actually lowered into the vault, and there he makes certain discoveries, among them being the squares of the three Grand Masters; ancient coins of Israel and Tyre; a medal bearing the interlaced triangles and the triple tau; a plate of gold on which is engraved the sacred Tetragrammaton; a cubical stone on which has been sculptured certain initial letters; and, lastly, a copy of the Sacred Law. The later development of the ceremony is on familiar lines. The sash, as explained, is worn from the right shoulder so that the triple tau comes at the left hip.

Royal Arch Certificates

The earliest-known masonic certificates are Irish, and all the Irish R.A. certificates have a style of their own. Here is one dated 1795, issued in Cookstown, County Tyrone:

> We the High Priest & & & of the Royal Arch Super Ex: Encampment of No. 553 On the Registry of Ireland Do Certify that ——— past Master of said Lodge & Was by us Installed and Initiated Into that Most Noble & Sublime Degree of Royal Arch Super Ex: Masonry he having suported the Amazing tryal attending his Admittion With courage fortitude And Valiour & as such We Recommend him to all Worthy Royal Arch Super Ex: Masons Round the Globe; Given Under Our Hands & Seal of Our Grand Charter Held In the house of B: Ja: Gray In Cookstown In the County of tyrone In Ireland, this 11th Day of May 1795 & of Royal Arch Super Ex: Masonry 3795.

This is signed by officers describing themselves as High Priest, Grand Master, Senior Warden, Junior Warden, and Secretary.

A second example, dated 1801, is a certificate preserved at Freemasons'

Hall, London; it is printed (except for names and date) on a large sheet of paper bearing more than fifty symbolic illustrations:

> In the name of the Most Holy and Undivided Trinity, Father, Son and Holy Ghost. We, the High Priest, Captain General, and Grand Masters of a Royal Arch Super-excellent Masons Encampment and Grand Assembly of Knight Templars under the sanction of the Carrickfergus, the Blue [Craft] Lodge, No. 253, on the Registry of the Grand Lodge of Ireland, do hereby certify that our beloved Brother the Worshipful Sir Peter Mathews having duly passed the chair of the aforesaid Lodge was arched a Royal Arch Super-excellent Mason, and was subsequently dubbed a Knight of the Most Noble and Worshipful Order of Knights Templars, after having withstood with skill, fortitude, and valour, the amazing trials attending his admission. Given under our hands and the seals of our Grand Encampment and Assembly aforesaid this 21st day of August, 1801. A.L. 5801

This is signed by officers describing themselves as High Priest, Captain General, and two Grand Masters.

A third example, a certificate issued by a chapter in Wexford in 1850, well maintains the hyperbolical language:

> WE the HIGH PRIEST, etc, etc, of the Grand Chapter of ROYAL ARCH super-excellent MASONS, of Lodge 837, in the Town of Wexford and on the Registry of IRELAND, DO hereby certify the Bearer hereof, our trusty and well-beloved Brother —— —— Past Master of said Lodge, was by us INSTALLED, and INITIATED in that most noble and sublime Degree; he having with due Honour and Justice to the Royal Community, truly supported the amazing Tryals of Skill and Valour attending his admission; and as such we him recommend to all true and faithful ROYAL ARCH SUPER-EXCELLENT BROTHERS around the Globe.

Although the above certificate is of comparatively late date, it is signed by the High Priest, the Royal Arch Captain, the Grand Master, and Senior and Junior Grand Wardens, all of them officers of the lodge.

A certificate issued by Ballina Lodge, No. 548, in 1820, includes a recommendation of the Brother "to all the Sublime Lodges and brethren who understand the angles and squares of 3 × 3."

An Irish Masonic Funeral

Funerals of prominent and well-beloved Brethren and Companions were frequently of an imposing order. The *Limerick Herald*, in two issues of the year 1820 recording the death and funeral of Francis Wheeler, described at length the elaborate funeral procession, with its three bands, that accompanied the coffin to its resting-place, and particularly mentioned the inclusion of the "Royal Arch, with the Lodge within, borne by two

Brethren and covered with crape." Apparently there was a printed order of procession, and this included a monody (an ode expressing grief), in which occurs a reminder of an ancient funeral custom:

> The wands there brok'n for the dead
> Form'd Royal Arches o'er his head.

During some hundreds of years there was a custom by which a chief mourner—perhaps one whose authority passed with the death of the individual then being buried—broke his wand of office and threw the fragments into the grave. Other instances are given in the present author's earlier book.

Section Twenty

THE SCOTTISH ROYAL ARCH

SUBJECT to some elements of doubt explained in earlier pages, it is known that there was an R.A. lodge in Scotland in 1743—the lodge at Stirling, which might therefore claim to be the oldest-known Royal Arch body in the world. Even admitting the doubt, Scotland's place in R.A. history remains a high and honoured one, although, truth to tell, the facts of that history have been difficult to come by, and it is therefore all the more necessary to make quite clear, as we do most gratefully, that much of the information in this present section is due to a manuscript entitled *The Triple Tau: An Outline of the History of the Supreme Grand Royal Arch Chapter of Scotland*, generously placed at the present writer's disposal by its author, G. S. Draffen, then Grand Librarian of the Grand Lodge of Scotland, and since published in printed form under the authority of the Scottish Grand Chapter. Many other sources have been referred to, but the Draffen information has been the mainstay.

The Scottish Royal Arch is not designated "Holy," nor is it described as an "Order." Scotland has, of course, an ancient and honourable masonic Order—the Royal Order of Scotland—which "in respect to the preservation of records" (quoting D. Murray Lyon) appears to be senior to any degree other than the three Craft degrees.

The oldest of the Scottish chapters are given here in the order of their official numbers, but not, unfortunately, in the order of the dates of their founding. As from the early nineteenth century, however, Scottish chapters, with but few exceptions, are numbered in accordance with their priority of date. No. 1 is Edinburgh, founded in 1779 (F); No. 2, Stirling Rock, Stirling, 1743 (F); No. 3, Enoch, Montrose, 1765 (F); No. 4, Operative, Banff, 1766 (F); No. 5, Linlithgow, 1768 (F); No. 6, Union, Dundee, 1773 (F); No. 7, Noah, Brechin, 1774 (F); No. 8, Haran, Laurencekirk, 1774 (F); No. 9, Hope, Arbroath, 1779 (F); No. 10, Josiah, St Andrews, 1780 (F); *St Luke*, Aberdeen, 1782 (F); No. 12, Elijah, Forfar, 1783 (F); No. 13, Macduff, Macduff, Banffshire, 1784 (F); No. 14, St Andrew, Banff (now Buckie), 1787 (F); No. 15, Land of Cakes, Eyemouth, 1787 (F); *Old Aberdeen*, 1788 (F); No. 17, Greenock, Greenock, 1789 (F); No. 18, Ayr St Paul, Ayr, 1789 (F); No. 19, Strathmore, Glamis,

1789 (F); *St James'*, Aberdeen, 1789 (F); No. 21, St George, Aberdeen, 1795 (F); *Royal Caledonian*, Annan, 1796; No. 22, Banks of Douglas Water, Douglas, 1797 (F); *Loyal Scots*, Langholm, 1797; St Albans, Lanark, 1797 (F); No. 23, Horeb, Stonehaven, 1799 (F); *Military*, Ayrshire Militia, 1799 (F); *Grand Assembly*, Kilmarnock, 1798; No. 41, Operative, Aberdeen, 1792. (Names in *italics* are of chapters no longer in existence. 'F' indicates founding chapters of the Grand Chapter.)

The R.A. ceremonial is believed to have been introduced from England, and in the case of one chapter, the Union, No. 6, Dundee, is known definitely to have been brought by a military lodge warranted by the 'Antients' Grand Lodge of England. An early chapter, Land of Cakes, of Eyemouth, a coast town less than ten miles north of Berwick, has two charters, an English one of 1787 and a Scottish one of 1817, and was, of course, working on the English charter when Robert Burns was exalted in that chapter on May 19, 1787.

The Scots Grand Chapter

The Supreme Grand Royal Arch Chapter of Scotland is entirely independent of any Craft connexion. Its chapters are not attached to Craft lodges. Its chief officials ('office-bearers') are not necessarily officials of the Scots Grand Lodge, although, by coincidence, they may well be so. English writers generally give the date of its founding as 1817, but it is now accepted that 1816 is the truer date. It came into existence in spite of the opposition of the Scots Grand Lodge, and the reader is already well aware in this connexion that the Grand Lodges of England, Ireland, and Scotland were for long very cold in their regard of the Royal Arch, and the only Grand Lodge in whose favour it held a warm place was that of the 'Antients' in England. (During the remainder of this chapter the terms 'Grand Lodge' and 'Grand Chapter' must be taken to mean the Scottish bodies.)

In 1800 the Grand Lodge "expressly prohibited and discharged all Lodges having charters from the Grand Lodge from holding any other meetings than those of *The Three Orders*" (the Craft degrees). In the year following the founding of Grand Chapter, Grand Lodge resolved that "no person holding an official position in any Masonic Body, which sanctions higher Degrees than those of St John's Masonry, shall be entitled to sit, act or vote in the Grand Lodge of Scotland"; this resolution was directly aimed at the new Grand Chapter (two of whose Three Principals were Past Grand Masters), which promptly issued a protest, of which little notice was taken.

The Grand Chapter was formed by chapters of two classes: (*a*) those that had long been working in connexion with Craft lodges and (*b*) those working under charters issued by the Royal Grand Conclave of Scotland. As a consequence the coming of the Grand Chapter did not, unfortunately, bring together all the Scottish chapters into one fold. Remaining outside were any chapters holding charters from the English Grand Chapter (with the exception of Land of Cakes, already mentioned and still at work); the last of the chapters remaining under the English jurisdiction was that at Kirkcudbright (Royal Gallovidian), which dissolved by mutual consent of its members in 1861. Also there were some unchartered chapters, such as Ayr St Paul, dating back to 1789, which must have been regarded as irregular. In addition, there were some chapters working under Irish warrants, all of whom regarded the new Grand Chapter as irregular; four or five of them became in 1822 "the early Grand Encampment of Scotland," which lingered until 1877, when it received a new lease of life; it was divided shortly afterwards into three bodies. The first of these was the Early Grand Royal Arch Chapter of Scotland, which had twenty-one chapters when, in 1895, it amalgamated with or was absorbed by Grand Chapter. (The two other bodies do not concern us in this book.)

Until the coming of Grand Chapter the R.A. Degree, with many others, was worked in the Templar encampments and, in spite of the Grand Lodge ban in 1800, in a number of country lodges. It was agreed that the new Grand Chapter should supervise (in addition to seven Templar degrees with which we are not here concerned) twelve degrees as follow: (1) Master passed the Chair (already particularly referred to in an earlier section); (2) Excellent Master; (3) Super Excellent Master (one of the degrees believed to have been brought to Scotland from America in 1877); (4) the Arch Degree (of which nothing appears to be known); (5) and (6) R.A. and Mark Mason (early versions of the degrees now worked); (7) Ark Mason (just possibly the present Royal Ark Mariner Degree); (8) Link and Wrestle (one of the 'Wrestle' degrees worked early in the nineteenth century, possibly based on the story of Jacob wrestling with the angel); (9) Babylonian Pass, or Red Cross of Daniel; (10) Jordan Pass (possibly still being worked); (11) Royal Order or Prussian Blue (of which little is known); (12) High Priest (possibly an Installation or Chair degree).

The degrees which the Supreme Grand Chapter of Scotland recognizes and controls today are (i) *The Royal Arch Series:* Mark, Excellent Master, Royal Arch, Installed 3rd, 2nd, 1st Principals and Installed Mark Master. (ii) *The Lodge and Council Series:* Royal Ark Mariner, Commander Noah, Babylonish Pass or Red Cross, Chief and President. (iii) *The Cryptic Rite Series:* Royal Master, Select Master, Super Excellent Master, Thrice Illustrious Master.

Six West of Scotland chapters set themselves up in 1863 as the General

Grand Chapter for Scotland and the Colonies as the sequel to a quarrel centring upon Dr George Arnott Walker Arnott; this body issued charters to at least eight chapters, but faded out about 1870.

Grand Office-bearers

Officers are known as 'office-bearers,' and in the Grand Chapter are as follow: First Grand Principal; Past First Grand Principal; Depute First Grand Principal; Second and Third Grand Principals; Grand Scribes E. and N.; Grand Treasurer; Grand Recorder; Grand Chancellor; First, Second, and Third Grand Sojourners; Grand Sword-bearer; G.D.C. and Depute G.D.C.; Grand Superintendent of Works; First, Second, Third, and Fourth Grand Standard-Bearers; Grand Organist; eight Grand Stewards; Grand Janitor. Members eligible for these offices above rank of Organist must have received all the seven degrees included in the Scots R.A. series, but Grand Principals elect, if not in possession of any of them, receive them upon election and before Installation.

The jewel worn by the Third Grand Principal is a breastplate corresponding to that worn by the High Priest of Israel with the names of the twelve tribes engraved upon it.

A subordinate chapter consists of at least Three Principals, two Scribes, a Treasurer, and three Sojourners. The Three Principals and all Past Principals are styled M.E.[1] In the absence of the First Principal his immediate predecessor or another present or past Installed First Principal may act for him; the rule is similar in the absence of the Second and Third Principals. The period for which any office-bearer holds the same office is not limited except by any limitation in the by-laws. Chapter by-laws may provide for separate office-bearers for the several associated degrees, with the consent of the Three Principals, failing which, the First Principal of the chapter has the right to the chair in the Mark and Excellent Master's Degrees, the Second Principal to that of Senior Warden and the Third to that of Junior Warden.

The office-bearers are 'installed,' a word which in English lodges and chapters means 'chaired,' but which in Scotland covers both 'chairing' and 'investing.'

Petition for a new chapter is made by no fewer than nine Companions in good standing. A Royal Arch chapter or a lodge of Excellent Masters cannot hold a meeting unless seven regular Royal Arch masons be present; nor a lodge of Mark Masters unless three Mark Masters be present.

Robes when worn by the Principals agree in colour with those worn in English chapters.

[1] The Scribes and Sojourners are styled E.C.

Scots Ritual

The ritual tells substantially the same story as that in England, but very little is known of what it was in the early days, particularly at the beginning of the nineteenth century. Following on the ritual revision in England in 1834–5 the Scots ritual was standardized in 1840. But there is in existence a manuscript ritual which George S. Draffen supposes might have been used in an unknown Glasgow chapter in the 1820 period; it has a definite Christian complexion, and recites the story of some pilgrims removing the keystone of an arch and discovering the books of the Gospel. The Candidate is led between two columns (lines) of Brethren, who form an arch with batons and, when the Candidate is 'passing the arch,' beat him with the batons. (This is almost certainly a survival from an Irish ceremony in which the beating used to give rise to horse-play.) The Candidate passes the first and second arches and raises a third keystone, actually a large Bible. In the course of the ceremony, which includes references to the burning bush and the casting off of the shoes, he is conducted to twelve candlesticks standing on the floor, one of which, proving a Judas, he extinguishes. (Commonly in medieval churches a little candle was made to appear a big one by being mounted on a candle-like pillar, the arrangement, because of its falsity, being known as a Judas.) The ceremony is quite short, including Scripture readings, and apparently in the lodge was a canvas representation of the burning bush, around which some amount of symbolism centred.

Some little information on the ritual observed in a Scots chapter warranted by the English Grand Chapter emerges from the minutes of the Royal Gallovidian Chapter, Kirkcudbright, South-west Scotland, chartered in 1809 and dissolved in 1861. A valuable paper by Fred L. Pick in *A.Q.C.*, vol. lx, indicates that the Principals were placed in their chairs without any form of esoteric Installation, and apparently at every meeting the whole or part of the R.A. lecture (catechism) was worked. A minute of November 11, 1812, refers to a procession to church, and says that the members "having gone through part of the Lecture, no other business having come before them, the Chapter was shut in Common form—(M.Z. pronouncing the Blessing)—until the second Wednesday of next month." There was no reference to the Mark Degree, but it is apparent that a ceremony of the veils was worked, and the Scripture readings for 'passing the arches' are noted, these being: Isaiah xii; Psalm cxlix; Psalm xcix; Psalm lxxvii; and the first four verses of Psalm lxviii. For 'shutting the chapter' the readings are: "2nd Thessalonians 3^d Chapter from the 6th verse to the end, leaving out the 17th verse."

Coming to the ritual ceremonies and regulations of to-day, it should be said that Candidates for Exaltation must be Master Masons, not less than twenty-one years of age, and of proved good standing. They are balloted for in the R.A. Degree, and three black balls exclude, or a smaller number if so provided in the by-laws. The Candidate must have received the Mark Master and Excellent Master Degrees, the former of which must have been conferred in a lodge or chapter whose right to do so is recognized by Grand Chapter. Candidates who have already been made Mark Masons elsewhere must be affiliated in the Mark Degree (must become members of) in a lodge held within the chapter before they can proceed further. The conferment of the Excellent Master and R. A. Degrees at the same meeting is allowed, but, whatever the degree to be worked, the R.A. chapter is opened before and closed after it. Neither the Mark nor the Excellent Master Degree is conferred upon honorary members. Candidates are not required to be P.M.'s, in regard to which there is a long past history which is briefly related in an earlier section of this book.

The J., H., and Z. Installations are regarded in Scotland as separate degrees, as is also the Installation of the Mark Master, and although these must be conferred in regular sequence they may, if necessary, be conferred on the one individual on the one occasion and at a meeting of the R.A. chapter held in ordinary form.

A particular form of ceremonial for constituting and dedicating a chapter and installing its officers is approved and provided by Grand Chapter; contrary to the English practice, these ceremonies include some small amount of choral sanction and Psalm singing. The Exaltation ceremony follows an approved form.

The Supreme Committee, constituted and elected by Grand Chapter, exercises a general control over R.A. masonry, acts as a judicial tribunal, visits the Metropolitan chapters and sees that their working conforms with the authorized working, all chapters being obliged to observe *The Book of Instruction* issued by Grand Chapter.

Scottish Mark Masonry

The Mark Degree is indigenous to Scotland and of particular importance to Scots masons, who hold it in high regard as the Fourth Degree in freemasonry. Most Candidates for the R.A. will have already taken the Mark Degree in their Craft lodge, and it almost follows that nine out of ten Scots Craft masons are also Mark masons.

It is only in two countries, Scotland and Germany, that we know operative Masons' Marks (marks of identity on stones shaped or laid by the masons concerned) to have been registered or organized, and it is

PLATE XXVI

RICHLY ORNAMENTED APRONS OF THE 1800 PERIOD

Left: Apron once belonging to Irish Lodge No. 898. *Right:* Possibly a Scottish apron.
By courtesy of United Grand Lodge

PLATE XXVII

JUGS DECORATED WITH MASONIC TRANSFERS

Left: The transfer ornament is A. Slade's well-known effigy *A Free Mason, Form'd out of the Materials of his Lodge* (1754).
Right: Cream ware jug (probably Wedgwood), transfer printed, showing Arms of the 'Antients.' (See Plate III.)

By courtesy of United Grand Lodge

to Scotland that we naturally turn for the early history of Mark masonry, both operative and speculative. The Mark Degree is an essential preliminary to the R.A. in Scotland and in all jurisdictions not deriving directly from the English Grand Chapter.

Following keen controversy in 1858 it was agreed that the Grand Lodge and the Grand Chapter should jointly control the Mark Degree; nowadays, and dating from 1865, the Craft lodges work the Mark Degree by virtue of their ordinary charters, while the chapters work it under their charters and for the purpose of qualifying their Candidates. Obviously, then, if a Candidate has received the degree in his Craft lodge, he need not take it from the chapter, whereas an exaltee who has not yet received it takes it from the chapter.

There is a particular point that needs to be understood. The Grand Lodge holds the Mark Degree to be a second part of the Fellow Craft Degree; notwithstanding this, it is conferred only on Master Masons and in the presence of those who have taken it from a lodge or chapter entitled to grant it, the object being to obviate confusion to Mark masons under other jurisdictions.

When a chapter meets solely for the purpose of working in the Mark Degree its minutes are treated as chapter minutes, and the only Mark masons admitted, except as Candidates, are those who are also Royal Arch masons; this restriction does not apply when a Mark meeting is held without opening or closing the chapter.

Section Twenty-one

SYMBOLS: INTRODUCTORY REMARKS; THE CIRCLE

"In antiquity," says Voltaire, "everything is symbol or emblem ... the whole of nature is represented and disguised." For our purposes symbol and emblem are the same. There was once upon a time a distinction between them, but to-day one means much the same as the other. The ancient peoples imparted religious instruction by means of symbols, the method being used not only by the early Christians but by the Egyptians, Assyrians, Greeks, and others. When we say that freemasonry is a peculiar system of morality, veiled in allegory and illustrated by symbols, we need to remember that an allegory is closely related to the parable and has both a literal and a spiritual meaning.

Whence came symbolism into freemasonry, and when and how? The old MS. Charges, the more important of which cover the period of roughly 1390 to 1700 and in whose possession freemasonry is peculiarly fortunate, throw light on the traditions and customs of the medieval operative mason, but contain nothing recognizably of an esoteric nature and little or nothing of allegory and symbolism. This absence of symbolism is surprising in the light of two facts: first, during the latter half of the period mentioned it was common to interpret the Scriptures in an allegorical and symbolical way; second, freemasonry has always tended to draw its ideas and methods of presentment from the religious and learned writers of late medieval days.

Perhaps the most nearly correct answer to "*When* came symbolism into masonry?" is, "Some time in the late seventeenth and any time in the eighteenth centuries." The question of *whence* came symbolism is closely allied to the question of *how* it came. It is well known, of course, that the early editions of the Bible are a source of much masonic symbolism. The present author has come to believe, however, that much of the more important symbolism was provided by high-principled, classically educated men who discovered in the course of a life-absorbing study of alchemy the rich store of symbolism that had been gathered together by their learned predecessors. To any keen reader new to the subject a perusal of that great classic Robert Fludd's Latin work *Clavis Philosophiæ et Alchymiæ Fluddianæ*, published in the 1630's, would be a revelation, for, even if he were not familiar with Latin, he could at any rate revel in many of the old engravings, which in themselves are prototypes of familiar masonic devices.

Of modern easily read books on alchemy there are two to be especially recommended to the student of symbolism: F. Sherwood Taylor's *The Alchemists*[1] and John Read's *Prelude to Chemistry; An Outline of Alchemy, Its Literature and Relationships*.[2] A remarkable collection of provocative illustrations is brought together in *Psychology and Alchemy*,[3] by the famous Swiss psychologist C. G. Jung, and it is for these illustrations, and not for its text, that this book is particularly recommended to the student of symbolism.

Let it not be thought that the present author is suggesting or even hinting that speculative masonry was invented by the alchemists. He is far from doing anything of the sort, but he knows full well that the alchemic idea is represented in freemasonry's ideas, allusions, symbols, and illustrations and that in the two philosophies are to be found certain coincidences—for example, the stress laid on the regeneration of the initiate—the idea of being 'born again' runs throughout alchemy; the secrecy taught by freemasonry and not only insisted on by alchemy, but so closely guarded by it as to make spiritual or "esoteric alchemy . . . a close body of knowledge, sacred to the elect"; and the extent to which both freemasonry and alchemy have resorted to pictorial expression as a means of imparting knowledge.

To anyone who has lightly concluded that the alchemist had but one idea, a fixed one—the transmutation of base metals into gold—it must be said that this was undoubtedly the purpose of most 'operative' alchemists, but not of all, and that there was in the late medieval days a body of spiritually minded 'speculative' alchemists to whom the principle of transmutation was in itself little or nothing more than an allegory. As Sherwood Taylor puts it, the leading idea was the "need for such a transformation to take place by the corruption of the material to be transformed and the generation of a new form therein." Says another writer, alchemy was "in its primary intention and office the philosophic and exact science of the regeneration of the human soul."

The secrecy inculcated in the old MS. Charges was a slight thing compared with the "deliberate and avowed concealment of parts of their work" which the alchemists consistently practised, and "no literature," says Sherwood Taylor, "is so maddeningly and deliberately obscure." Alchemic treatises, their authors freely confessed, were intentionally "written in

[1] Heinemann (1952).   [2] Bell (1936).   [3] Routledge (1953).

such a way as to conceal the practice from all who had not been initiated into a certain secret which enabled them to understand."

"Alchemy was pictorial in its expression to a degree which is not realized in this age." Alchemic symbols express truths in allegorical pictures, which for the most part were beautifully conceived and skilfully executed. A reader looking for reflections of some of them should study the eighteenth-century masonic pierced jewels, tracing-boards, and engravings. One old alchemical book pictures a group of three individuals—a Crowned King as the Sun on one side, a Crowned Prince on the other, and in the centre Hermes (Mercury); the strong resemblance of this triple group to the Three Principals of an early chapter, or even of to-day's American chapter, is startling. Hermes provides the adjective 'hermetic' or 'hermetical,' a word alluding to a state in which secrets are so sealed as to be inviolable and, as readers may know, the word actually gives its name to certain rites related to masonry.

It was the close concealment of alchemic teachings that necessitated the use of a multitude of emblems and of a highly developed secret language in which 'facts' and 'truths' were veiled.

No reference to alchemy must omit mention of the Philosopher's Stone. This stone was, of course, not an actual stone, for even with the materialist type of alchemist the 'Stone' was often a powder or a liquid. The idea of the Philosopher's Stone, says one of the authors above quoted, "seems to have arisen in the early centuries of the Christian era and is in keeping with the early mystical beliefs concerning the regeneration of man." The Stone points to perfection, and many of the ancient alchemists believed that they derived the Stone direct from God. The Stone had many names and was subject to many different interpretations. One old writer likened it to the Biblical stone which the builders rejected, the stone which the builders of Solomon's Temple disallowed, but believed that "if it be prepared in the right way, it is a pearl without price, and, indeed, the earthly antitype [representation] of Christ, the heavenly Corner Stone." And here we have an idea of which much is made in some early Royal Arch rituals.

So many, so very many, were the names given to the Stone that it was worth the while of an author in 1652 to produce a book in which they were listed! Among its better-known names were the "Elixir of Life," or the "Grand Elixir," the Stone being depicted as a panacea for all human ills and capable of restoring youthfulness and prolonging life (John Read). This idea was familiar through the then known world, including China, much earlier than the thirteenth century.

A meaning of peculiar interest to freemasons was the one depicted by the image of a serpent eating its own tail, an emblem of eternity and immortality, the serpent being regarded by the alchemists as symbolical of divine wisdom, of power and creative energy, of life and regeneration.

From many an alchemic illustration there jumps to the eye the stylized sun and moon, which might have been the veritable patterns of the old metallic cut-outs surmounting the chairs of the Senior and Junior Wardens in the eighteenth-century lodges. Alchemic illustrations in profusion show the compasses, square, balance, rule and plumb-line, perfect ashlar, pillars, the point within a circle, the sacred delta (triangle), the five-pointed and six-pointed stars (the second of these an outstanding symbol of alchemy), the double-headed eagle, the oblong square, and the image of Hermes or Mercury, this last a very potent symbol and used throughout the eighteenth century as the Deacon's jewel or emblem. Mercury (Hermes) himself is one of the most significant but variously interpreted figures in alchemical lore and is given a place in hundreds of illustrations. We find, too, in these illustrations the ladder which in the ancient Egyptian mysteries had an enormous significance and as Jacob's ladder is well known as a masonic emblem; it symbolizes the ladder of salvation leading from earth (or hell) to heaven, and one revealing instance of its use in ecclesiastic decoration, dating back to the twelfth century, is to be found on the interior walls of Chaldon Church, Surrey.

The signs of the zodiac, conventional symbols dating back to about the tenth century, adorn the ceilings of many a lodge and chapter. The constellations have been known for thousands of years. Six of them ascend north of the equator and six descend south of it. The first six are Aries, the Ram; Taurus, the Bull; Gemini, the Twins; Cancer, the Crab; Leo, the Lion; Virgo, the Virgin. The six southern signs are Libra, the Balance; Scorpio, the Scorpion; Sagittarius, the Archer; Capricornus, the Goat; Aquarius, the Water-bearer; and Pisces, the Fishes.

Zodiac, a Greek word, conveys the meaning of a series of imaginary animals:

> Our vernal signs the RAM begins,
> Then comes the BULL, in May the TWINS;
> The CRAB in June, next LEO shines,
> And VIRGO ends the northern signs.
>
> The BALANCE brings autumnal fruits,
> The SCORPION stings, the ARCHER shoots;
> December's GOAT brings wintry blast,
> AQUARIUS rain, the FISH come last.[1]

Astronomically the zodiac is the zone or belt of constellations which is apparently traversed by the sun in the course of the year and in which the moon and major planets also appear to move. The symbols are frequently

---

[1] Verses by "E.C.B.," quoted in Brewer's *Dictionary of Phrase and Fable*.

seen in alchemic literature, which is the most likely source from which freemasonry could have taken them, but it is most unfortunate that no point can be given to their masonic association and that an attempt made to associate the signs of the zodiac, the images on the R.A. banners, and the four "beasts full of eyes before and behind" in St John's celestial vision (Revelation iv, 6–8) is fanciful and has no worth-while basis.

Of the classical allusions apparently due to alchemy, probably the most obvious are those of Jason and his Golden Fleece, which occupied a considerable place in alchemic symbolism; it has been held that the Golden Fleece of the Argonauts was a papyrus containing the secrets of gold-making! Even Tubal Cain gets a place, although a small one, in the literature of alchemy.

The Circle

Of all the symbols met in Royal Arch masonry comes first the circle, the emblem of eternity, having neither end nor beginning and justly deemed a type of God without beginning of days or end of years. In folklore it was given magical properties, and was believed to protect from external evil everything which it contained or surrounded; thus a child placed within a circle was thought to be protected from outside malevolent influences. So, too, the finger-ring, the bracelet, the anklet, and the necklace, all of which came to be worn as ornaments, were originally regarded as means of protection from evil. The circle is the image of the sun, which led to its becoming the symbol of pure gold, in which respect, John Read reminds us, there was understood to be a mystical relationship with the Tetragrammaton, the Ineffable Name. The circle as symbolizing eternity was frequently represented by the serpent eating its own tail, as already mentioned. The serpent itself is the emblem of life, but right back into Biblical days must also have been the emblem of wisdom. "Be ye therefore wise as serpents" (Matthew x, 16). The fastener of the belt of the masonic apron retains the form of a serpent, but the idea of the serpent devouring itself and the many variations of the serpent *motif* are less seen to-day than formerly. The whole device was an emblem of eternity and immortality, the serpent being symbolical of divine wisdom, of power and creative energy, of time and eternity, of life and regeneration. Readers may remember that this device was the *motif* of a jewel with which in May 1811 the Grand Master, the Duke of Sussex, Master of the Lodge of Antiquity, No. 2, invested William Preston, a great character in eighteenth-century masonry, one whose name is linked with the Prestonian Lecture; the jewel, which is still in use in the Lodge of Antiquity, is of gold, and takes the form of a complete circle, the eye for the ribbon coming just where the snake's head is beginning to eat the tail.

SYMBOLS: INTRODUCTORY REMARKS; THE CIRCLE

Ancient philosophers were much concerned with the problem of squaring the circle—that is, in effect, finding the exact ratio of the circumference of the circle to its radius. Some bold illustrations relating to the problem in alchemic works are almost uncanny in their suggestion of the sequence of certain geometrical figures known to the Royal Arch mason. For example, in an early seventeenth-century book by a notable Rosicrucian and alchemist, Michael Maier, is a forceful drawing of a

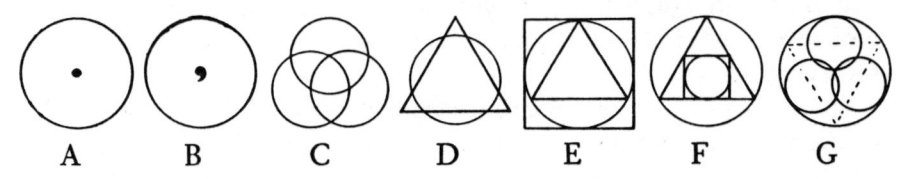

Symbolic Circles

A. Point within circle. *B.* Yod within circle. *C* and *G.* Interlaced circles. *D*, *E*, and *F*. Triangles, squares, and circles in familiar arrangements, in general suggestive of the Trinity.

student holding mighty compasses in the act of squaring the circle, a wall serving as his drawing-board on which circle and triangle are shown in conjunction. In another drawing of the same period, this time by Stolcius, is a complete collection of geometrical figures or symbols, including the square, triangle, and circle, and also, be it noted, the cubic stone—and all this in the 1620's, a period of fundamental importance in relation to the emergence of freemasonry. The geometrical representations of the Trinity —interlaced circles, circle, and triangle, and the interlaced triangles, so closely suggestive of Royal Arch devices and ideas—are all to be found in such books as those above referred to.

The Point within a Circle

The circle, itself a symbol of extraordinary significance, acquires even more importance when it includes a central point—that is, when the symbol becomes the well-known point within a circle. This symbol was known to pagan rites thousands of years ago, and, while in its very early history it had a phallic interpretation and represented the male and the female principle, it took upon itself in the course of time other meanings. It was at one time the wheel symbol and the subject of religious rites universally observed. A Greek writer many centuries before Christ represented God as a circle whose centre was everywhere and the circumference nowhere, a conception that needs much thought to begin to grasp and one with which Plato, only two or three centuries later, associated himself. A modern philosopher, C. G. Jung, says that the way to the goal "is not straight but appears to go round in circles . . . the whole process revolves round about a central point." Long ago the point within a circle was adopted as a device in Christian churches, and still later it became a masonic emblem.

The symbol has been given a number of masonic meanings. The point has been regarded as the Supreme Being and the circle either as the circuit of the sun or as eternity. In yet another interpretation the point is the initiate and the circle is the boundary line of his duty to God—not a very satisfying definition.

In one old version of the Craft Installation ceremony the Master Elect is made to represent the point within a circle of Installed Masters, and is taught to regard himself as the centre of his lodge and an emblem of justice and morality.

The Yod within a Circle or Triangle

What appears to be a comma placed at the centre of a circle, thus ⊙, is closely associated with the point within a circle, for the 'comma' is the Hebrew letter *Yod* corresponding to the English letter 'J' or 'Y', the initial of the Sacred Name. The Yod within a triangle represents the power and efficiency of the Almighty; this symbol, according to G. S. Shepherd-Jones, may have had its place in the centre of the plate of gold, within the circle, on top of the altar, and, although it is not now seen there, he suggests that the actions in the Royal Arch "fire" indicate the various symbols on the altar—the point, the triangle, the circle, and the square.

Section Twenty-two

SYMBOLS: THE TAU AND THE TRIPLE TAU

THE tau itself, one of the two most important symbols in Royal Arch masonry, is the Greek letter T, the nineteenth letter in the Greek alphabet, a letter which takes the same form in many different alphabets, including the English. It was in ancient days regarded as the mark or symbol of life, whereas another Greek letter, 'theta' Θ or Θ, the eighth letter in the Greek alphabet and corresponding to the English sound 'th,' was regarded as the symbol of death. Three taus came together to form the triple tau, but they did not do this in ancient days—not earlier, as a matter of fact, than somewhere about 1820.

An Early Form of Cross

The tau is an extremely early form of cross. In shape it is the simple T. It is often called St Anthony's Cross because the saint was martyred on a cross of that simple form, but long before then it had been the anticipatory cross or type cross of the pre-Christian Scriptures. It is not known

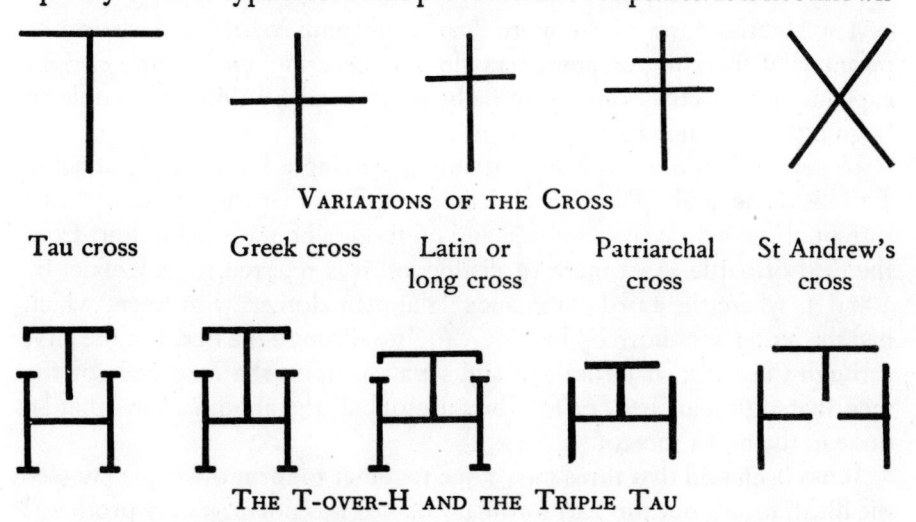

VARIATIONS OF THE CROSS

Tau cross   Greek cross   Latin or   Patriarchal   St Andrew's
                                     long cross   cross   cross

THE T-OVER-H AND THE TRIPLE TAU

The first four figures suggest how the T-over-H sign became the triple tau. The fifth figure shows the three taus apart.

as a simple cross in Craft, Royal Arch, or Mark masonry, but is so recognized in certain of the additional degrees. It is understandable that, as the cross has been adored as a sacred symbol from the earliest of pagan times, it has assumed many different forms, and it is even said that more than three hundred variations are known. The illustrations herewith show a few of the chief forms; one of them is the swastika which originally may have been an emblem of the Deity and is so ancient that it is found in Chaldean bricks many thousands of years old and in the ruins of Troy dating back to, say, 2500 years B.C.

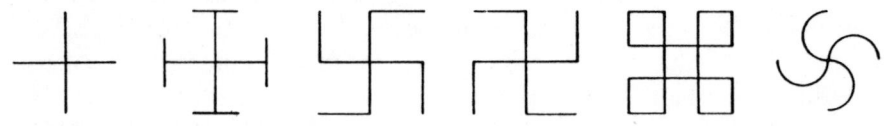

HOW THE PLAIN CROSS DEVELOPED INTO FORMS OF THE SWASTIKA OR FYLFOT

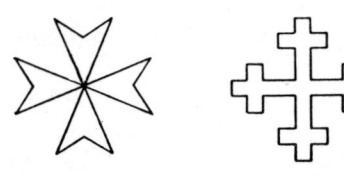

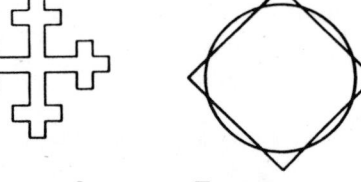

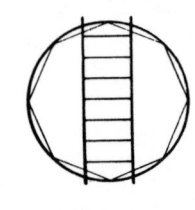

SYMBOLIC FIGURES

| Maltese or 8-pointed cross | Crosslet | Square and circle interlaced | Circle, octagon, and Jacob's Ladder |

The Hebrew form of the word 'tau' is pronounced *tov* and carries the meaning of marking, etching, scrawling, delineating, etc., which *perhaps* explains how a cross came originally to be used by illiterate people in 'signing' their name to a document.

In pagan days a warrior honourably surviving a battle could attach a T to his name, and a Royal Arch lecture explains that the tau was set as a sign on those who were acquitted and on those who returned unhurt from the field of battle. As a mark of distinction it is referred to in Ezekiel ix, 3 and 4, where the Lord commands "the man clothed with linen, which had the writer's inkhorn by his side," to "go through the midst of the city, through the midst of Jerusalem, and set a tau upon the foreheads of the men that sigh and that cry for [because of] all the abominations that be done in the midst thereof."

It has been said that three taus come together to form the triple tau (see the illustration), but this extraordinary device was not *originally* produced by the conjunction of the three T's; rather it developed from T over H as suggested by the sequence of figures given on p. 233. There is no doubt that the triple tau was originally ⛿ meaning *Templum Hierosolymæ*, the Temple of Jerusalem. It was so alluded to in a letter from Dunckerley given later in this section.

The early symbol has been given other meanings. For example, it signified *thesaurus*, a treasure or treasury, usually given as *clavis ad thesaurum*, a key to the treasure. It was also known as *res ipsa pretiosa*, the precious thing itself, which may have referred to the Sacred Name; in a sense this idea is supported by another of its descriptions, *theca ubi res pretiosa deponitur*, reasonably translated as "the depository in which the sacred thing is placed or hidden," this again suggesting the preservation of the Sacred Name.

The simple tau was the Egyptian's nilometer, a gauge by which was measured the rise of the Nile in flood. The instrument was a solidly constructed giant T which might be as much as 32 feet high, its crossbar at the top being about 10 feet or 12 feet wide. In its permanent form, standing in a well that communicated with the Nile, the height of the rising water was read from the graduated pillar, and that height might be anything from 12 cubits (meaning famine to the population) to 22 (meaning an abundant supply). A height of 24 cubits of water might mean the destruction of people, their stores and their houses. It is easy, indeed, to see that, as the life and health of the Egyptian people depended upon the rise and fall of the Nile as recorded by the nilometre, the instrument itself became a symbol and later grew into a talisman which was believed to avert evil and charm away sickness. The Egyptian logos or god-incarnate, Thoth, carried it as his emblem.

Of the meaning of the triple tau the ritual provides explanation, but it must be remembered that the geometrical interpretations have come since the complete joining up of the T and the H and probably were unknown much earlier than 1835. The Scottish ritual knew nothing of the triple tau for a great many years, but it well knew the T-over-H emblem, and the official Irish ritual is not concerned with that symbol, although there were many Irish lodges in which it had a place.

The Christian Interpretation or Significance of ⛿

The old sign sometimes had a Christian interpretation. It has even been defined, but doubtfully, as "Holiness supporting Trinity." More definite is a device at the head of a Trinity College, Dublin, MS. dated 1711. taking the form of a Christian cross over the H (see over page); there is reason for assuming that this exemplifies the cross upon the name Jehovah—that is, the mystical union between the Son and His Father. The Jesuit church of Il Gèsu at Rome, built late in the 1700's, has a ceiling representing the worship of the holy name of Jesus, its centrepiece being a glory containing a distinctly Christian version of the ⏉ . It takes this form: I ⏉ S.

Its meaning is *Jesus Hominum Salvator*, or possibly and less commonly *in hac salus*, to be translated in this case as "safety in this cross." (The first of the translations is the conventional one, but in itself contains an error, for the middle letter H is actually one form of the Greek E.) The same symbol minus the S is found in a Swansea chapter warrant of 1771 and a London one of 1784, a possible interpretation being "Jesus, His Cross and His Father." Readers particularly interested in the subject should consult *A.Q.C.*, vol. lvii, in which Ivor Grantham advances a theory founded on verses 11–13 of Chapter 8 of the General Epistle of Barnabas (an apocryphal book possibly dating to the second century and not accepted as a part of the regular Gospel). Ivor Grantham suggests that if, as some students feel, the triple tau is Christian in its origin, then the verses referred to might well show that the symbol could be "traced back to the 4th century A.D. when the canonical nature of the New Testament writings was determined—or possibly even to the lifetime of the twelve Apostles, if the attribution of this Epistle to St Barnabas could be sustained."

Some Variations of the Triple Tau

In some Irish certificates appears the T-over-H sign where, apparently, the letters refer to the second of the Three Grand Masters. In an Irish ritual used in the middle of the nineteenth century the symbol is referred to as "The Initials of the Architect"; this, says J. Heron Lepper, refers not to the Monarch, but to the Craftsman, as in Mark masonry, and he adds the comment that in those days the anachronism of the lettering would have caused qualms to few, either in England or in Ireland. In the minute-books of Concord Chapter, No. 37, Bolton, whose records go back to 1768, we find the emblem superimposed on H. AB., these last being carefully drawn capital letters.

On a silver Mark jewel, dated 1819, the symbol has an E added to it (thus: ⏉E), and, whatever its significance was in the Mark, it was not regarded as acceptable in the Royal Arch by so good an authority as Thomas Dunckerley, who, in a letter written in 1792, asks that it be amended "on the Patent under my name. It is the signature of our order *Templum Hierosolyma Eques*. For the Royal Arch it is ⏉ *Templum*

Hierosolyma." To this may be added the necessary explanation that *eques* means 'horseman,' and, by implication, a knight gave the ⛬ sign a Knights Templar connotation. In the museum at Freemasons' Hall, London, is an apron bearing the ⛬ symbol.

The T-over-H sign was, of course, known before the Charter of Compact, 1766, and even in that charter some examples of it have taken on a midway form. The earliest Grand Chapter regulations directed that aprons should bear on their bibs a T and H of gold. The symbol appears in the Wakefield Royal Arch records of 1767. On Dunckerley's Royal Arch certificate issued in 1768 we find it again, the T touching the bar of the H, but both letters retaining their serifs, these being the tiny crossbars at the ends of the limbs of the letters. Instructions issued by Grand Chapter in 1803 specify that the curved bib or flap of the apron is to have the ⛬ "embroidered in spangles on a piece of purple satin." In a United Grand Chapter illustration of 1817 the letters are on their way to becoming the triple tau, but the serifs are still retained; so it appears that the changeover to the geometric symbol—the three taus—took place in the interval between May 1822 (to which date the 1817 regulations had been extended) and 1834–35, when the revised ritual was promulgated. Although we find the true triple tau following 1820, it does not appear to have an official character until the issue of the revised regulations in the 1830's. The distinction between the ⛬ where these two letters have been brought into contact and the true triple tau is that in the latter device the serifs have disappeared, and what were letters have now become right angles. And it is this difference that often provides a touchstone when judging the dates of early documents, jewels etc.

No authority for the change can be advanced. A very unconvincing explanation is to the effect that the alteration was made to accord with the symbolic explanation that the squares are repeated three times on the Installed Master's apron. It may be that the true triple tau took on imperceptibly, particularly by the dropping of the serifs of the letters, a neater and conventionalized form which offers itself as the basis of geometrical symbolism. The Harper family, jewellers, made many distinctive masonic jewels, and among them is one dated 1823 carrying the true triple tau. A noted member of the family was Edwards Harper, Deputy Grand Secretary of the 'Antients' before the Union and later Joint Grand Secretary of the United Grand Lodge.

Section Twenty-three

SYMBOLS:
THE TRIANGLE AND INTERLACED TRIANGLES

THE triangle, especially the equilateral triangle (see illustration), is one of the most ancient symbols in the world. To the Christian it symbolizes the Trinity, all its three sides being equal. So sacred has the emblem always been regarded that, says the ritual, an oath given on it has never been known to be violated. The three lines in conjunction represent the Sacred Word, the essence of the Deity. In early days such a triangle was conspicuous in Craft lodges, and within it was the V.S.L., an arrangement still

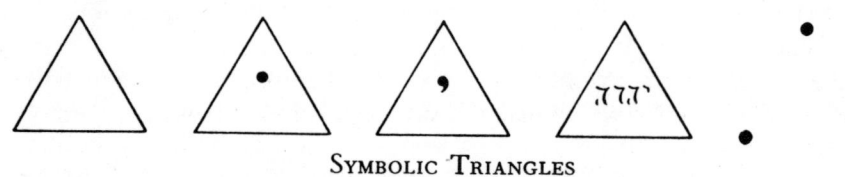

SYMBOLIC TRIANGLES

Triangle   Point within triangle   Yod within triangle   Tetragrammaton within triangle   Triple trine

to be seen, it is thought, in the Bristol working. It has already been explained that the triangle containing the Yod (the first letter of the sacred name) represents the power and efficiency of the Almighty. The point within a triangle or the point within a circle represents the Supreme Being, the infinite yet unknowable, the all-pervading yet unknown. Similar emblems were familiar to the old alchemists. A German work (1718) on elementary chemistry (and alchemy was the forerunner of true chemistry) illustrates a triangle with a human head or skull occupying its lower part, a device peculiarly sacred to the alchemist and carrying with it the idea of the Supreme Being. Sometimes there was an "all-seeing eye" within the triangle, the meaning being much the same but including the idea of an omnipresent God.

The Chaplain of a Craft lodge has the triangle in his jewel. The Grand Master's jewel, the open compasses, includes a gold plate on which is the "all-seeing eye" within the triangle. The circle within a triangle or trine compass (Chaucer's term) is one of the most venerable of symbols ("that of trine compass Lord and gide is"), and carried with it the meaning of the coequality and coeternity of the Three Persons in the Trinity.

The triangle is often called the delta, a name derived from the shape of an island formed by alluvial deposits between the two mouths of the Nile and now a common name for a triangular piece of land formed by the diverging mouths of any river. In some additional degrees the delta is the luminous triangle or brilliant delta and encloses the Tetragrammaton.

To the alchemist the triangle was a symbol having many meanings. Standing on its point it meant water; on its base it meant fire; standing on its point and divided horizontally it meant earth; on its base and divided horizontally it meant air. To many alchemists the Philosopher's Stone was "triangular in essence," and the statement is made that in one or more old masonic rituals the stone is given as being of triangular form. Dunckerley, writing to the Grand Secretary, William White, says, "I greet you with the Triple Trine," and then follow three dots in triangular form —so .·. In French and American literature this trine is very commonly used, and in the French writings frequently means 'lodge.' When six triangles of this kind are assembled together to bring their apex to one common centre, as in the illustration on p. 243, we arrive at the symbol of universal creation, bearing close relationship to the point within a circle.

The circle and triangle are part of a distinctive engraving by Matheus Gruter, made in 1595. It is interpreted as the Father holding an equilateral triangle with its apex pointing downward, this representing "the human nature of the logos"—the Son of God.

In medieval architecture the circle, square, and equilateral triangle were occasionally introduced to represent wisdom, strength, and beauty.

Interlaced Triangles

Interlaced triangles are of many forms, those with which the English mason is concerned being two: the hexalpha, or six-pointed star, a prominent emblem in Royal Arch masonry, and the pentalpha, or five-pointed star, more used in the eighteenth century than now. 'Alpha' comes into each name because the devices are formed with alphas—that is, 'A's'—suitably arranged. Eighteenth-century masonry knew both of these devices, the 'Antients' preferring the five-pointed star and the 'Moderns,' chiefly, the six-pointed star. We expect that masonry took the devices from alchemy, which, in its turn, found them awaiting it in that great body of traditional lore that always attributed magical properties to the triangle and particularly to triangles interlaced. They were symbols of the everlasting truth of the Deity, and became, in Christian days, emblems of Christ.

The Hexalpha

The six-pointed star, the Shield of David, sometimes known also as Solomon's Seal, had a host of meanings. It is the hexalpha because it includes six triangles, whereas the pentalpha includes only five, but there is much confusion between the two, largely brought about by the fact that the old books on astrology and medieval magic tended to call any device made up of angles a 'pentacle,' regardless of its number of angles or its shape. The Royal Arch to-day knows chiefly the hexalpha. Sometimes the device is known as the hexagram, but that name truly applies to any six-line or six-sided figure. Occasionally it is called the hexagon, but this is an error, the true hexagon being the six-sided figure formed by the internal lines of the figure.

Everybody knows that the hexalpha has strong Jewish associations. It is said to have been used as a wall ornament incised in the stonework of the fortress of Meggido in Canaan, built 800–1050 years before Christ and, judging from the many references to it in the early books of the Bible, a place of great importance. To the medieval Jew the hexalpha was a talisman guarding him against fire and disease, for which reason it was commonly used on amulets, was placed as a distinguishing mark on the outsides of Jewish houses, and has been found on a Jewish tomb of the third century, although, in general, the Jews did not make much use of it until a thousand years later than that. To-day it is everywhere accepted as the symbol of Judaism, is commonly seen on synagogues and on orthodox Jewish restaurants, and has a strong national and racial association rather than a religious one.

It is to be supposed that the likeness of the flower known as Solomon's Seal has given that name to the hexalpha, but there is, of course, an extremely well-known magical story describing how King Solomon was able to confine a genie in a bottle by means of this seal. The story is well told in E. W. Lane's *Arabian Society in the Middle Ages*, published in 1883:

> No man ever attained such absolute power over the Jinn as Suleyman Ibn Daood [Solomon, the son of David]. This he did by virtue of a most wonderful talisman, which is said to have come down to him from heaven. It was a seal-ring, upon which was engraved 'the most great name' of God, and was partly composed of brass and partly of iron. With the brass he stamped his written commands to the good Jinn; with the iron, those to the evil Jinn or Devils. Over both orders he had unlimited power; as well as over the birds and the winds, and, as is generally said, over the wild beasts. His Wezeer, Asaf the son of Barkhiya, is also said to have been acquainted with 'the most great name,' by uttering which, the greatest miracles may be performed . . . even that of raising the dead. By virtue of this name engraved on his ring,

THE BELZONI AND OTHER RARE JEWELS, SET IN BRILLIANTS

Left: The Belzoni Jewel worn by the First Principal of Chapter of St James, No. 2. (See p. 260.) *Centre top:* Oval jewel, glass-fronted, with gilt centre; date, 1856. *Centre bottom:* Triangular jewel, glass-fronted, of Continental, possibly French, origin. *Right:* Jewel of Lodge of Virtue, Reading—gilt centre on opal glass (1809).

By courtesy of the Chapter of St James and the United Grand Lodge

PLATE XXIX

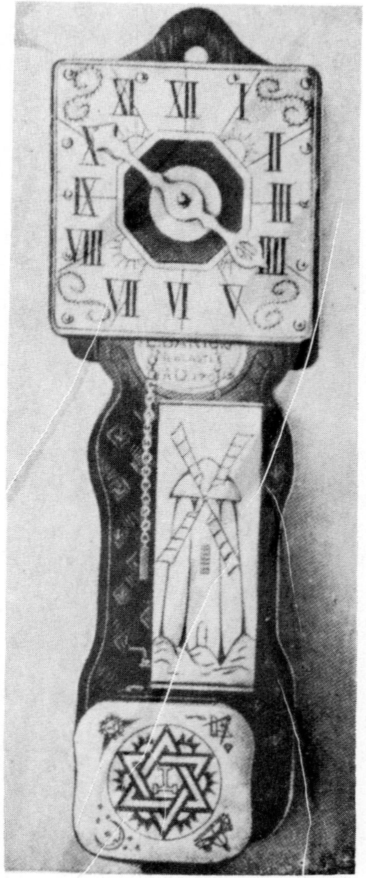

THE NEWCASTLE WATER-CLOCK

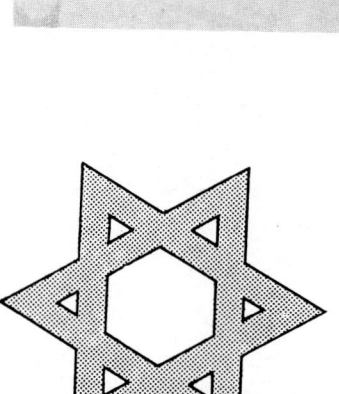

Left: Pedestal, 9 inches high, formerly in use in the Swalwell Chapter, Durham; of its copper plate (shown above) the sides of the triangles are 4½ inches long.

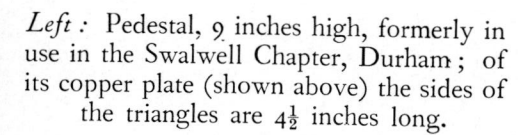

Right: This water-clock was made in 1701 by L. Barton, and is now in Durham's Masonic Museum. As the water drips from a tank into a reservoir in the base a float falls and actuates by chain a pulley whose spindle carries the clock hand. Brass face, 8 inches by 8 inches. Black oak support, 27 inches high. The clock is possibly about seventy years older than its Royal Arch decoration, but this is subject to argument.

A MINIATURE PEDESTAL

SYMBOLS: THE TRIANGLE AND INTERLACED TRIANGLES

Suleyman compelled the Jinn to assist in building the Temple of Jerusalem, and in various other works. Many of the evil Jinns he converted to the true faith, and many others of this class, who remained obstinate in infidelity, he confined in prisons.

As to when and why the hexalpha was adopted by Royal Arch masons in the eighteenth century very little can be said. As it was definitely a part of alchemical symbolism and from that source may have entered freemasonry, it is possible that it was adopted as a Christian symbol, however incongruous the association of a definitely Jewish device with the Christian idea might appear to be. It is, of course, the *motif* of the Royal Arch jewel of England, Ireland, and Scotland, but was not known in the Irish and Scottish Orders by any means as early as in the English.

THE HEXALPHA (SIX-POINTED STAR) AND A FEW OF ITS VARIATIONS

A remarkable scroll, known as the Kirkwall Scroll, in the possession of the Scots lodge Kirkwall Kilwinning, No. 38[2] (known to have been working from 1736), is described and illustrated in *A.Q.C.*, vol. x. Its history is not recorded. The scroll is of strong linen, 18 feet 6 inches long, 5 feet 6 inches wide, and, so far as height is concerned, more than occupying the West wall of the lodge room. It is roughly painted on both sides in oil, and it would be difficult to enumerate all the things that are shown on it; they include trees, rivers, houses, fishes, beasts, altars, masonic emblems in profusion, and a few geometric devices, among them being two examples of interlaced triangles, one of which is an elaborate hexalpha. The scroll may have been designed for use as a floor-cloth somewhere in the 1736–50 period, and it certainly would repay the study of anyone particularly interested (see Plate VII).

Quite a different scroll or roll, Roman Catholic and German in origin, dating back to the late seventeenth century is described by W. J. Hughan in *A.Q.C.*, vol. xvi. Here again is an ancient document well worthy of study, even though it does not appear to have an obviously masonic source. It is composed of six strips, 4 inches wide, of the finest vellum, making a continuous roll 10 feet long. Its beautiful illumination provides a wealth of detail, among which can be seen the Tetragrammaton and, among the seals, some bold interlaced triangles. The scroll, its seals and devices are literally covered with religious and 'magical' signs, and the purpose of the scroll appears to be that of a charm bought at a high price by a rich man to avert evil of all kinds from him. In German the scroll gives a list of well over fifty evils and misfortunes against which it will protect its owner—including thunder, envy, poisoning, sudden death, the evil spirit, sorcery, leprosy, despair, poverty, and snake-bite, while some of the positive advantages it is supposed to confer are that it will ensure the love of men, bring treasure, honour, and riches, and the friendship of great men, and finally that when a person is imprisoned and he carry this about him, he will be set at liberty.

A VARIETY OF INTERLACED TRIANGLES FOUND IN MASONIC ILLUSTRATION

An early example of the use of interlaced triangles having a definite masonic connexion is the engraved portrait (date 1761), of Dr Francis Drake, the Grand Master of the Grand Lodge of ALL England. As illustrated in *A.Q.C.*, vol. xiii, the portrait carries under it both the hexalpha and the pentalpha. The Charter of Compact (1766) carries in a margin clear representations of the hexalpha, but not of the pentalpha.

A white marble block, dating back to 1772, formerly owned by Tyrian Lodge, No. 5, but now owned by its successor, the Westminster and Keystone, No. 10, includes the hexalpha among its emblems.

Many officially approved jewels incorporate the interlaced triangles. There is the pentalpha in the jewels of the Deputy Grand Master and of the Provincial and District Grand Masters of England and many other officers; in Ireland members of the Grand Chapter of Instruction wear the hexalpha jewel, while in Scotland it is the jewel of Past Grand Principals and Grand Representatives.

Some less Usual Forms of the Hexalpha

The groups of illustrations in these pages include some only of the various forms which interlaced triangles have taken.

Occasionally the lines of the hexalpha are curved, and of this a somewhat remarkable example is afforded by one of the illustrations on Plate IX, this being based on a discovery made in Northern India, a fact in itself suggesting that early peoples, especially in the East, closely guarded

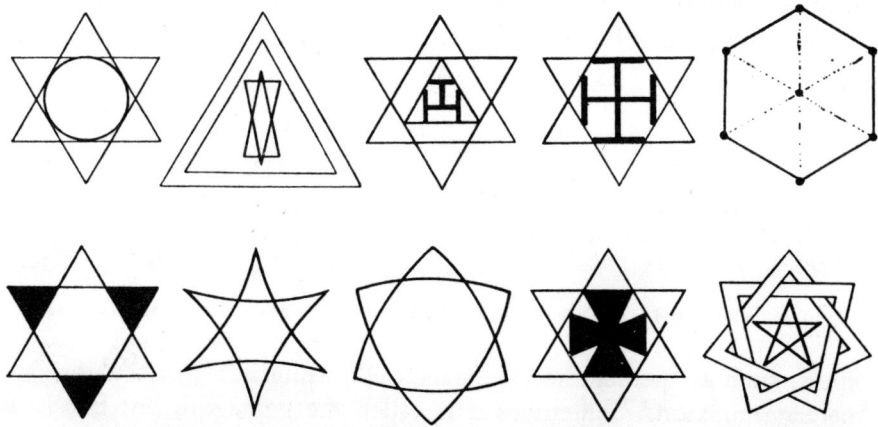

MANY MASONIC DEVICES BUILT UP WITH AND WITHIN INTERLACED TRIANGLES. END FIGURE OF TOP ROW SHOWS SIX TRIPLE TRINES IN UNION.

the names of their god. Norman Hackney has kindly provided the photograph from which the illustration was made. While he was staying at Udaipur, in Rajputana, Northern India, the plough brought up two little metal plates, slightly convex, with sun-baked clay tightly adhering to them. The ages of the plates, probably great, are unknown. The particular plate represented by the illustration measures about 3 inches by 3 inches. It should be explained that in each of the twelve lobes of the outer lotus flower and in each of the eight lobes of the inner one there is in the original a word in Sanskrit expressing a name or attribute of God. In the central delta or triangle is the word 'Om'—it is repeated in the tip of each petal—a word seeking to express the very essence of the Deity. The use of the plate cannot be stated with any certainty; it might be a temple ornament, it might be an ornament carried by the plough ox, but what is significant to the Royal Arch mason is the nature of its internal device and the presence of words representing the Ineffable Name.

A distinctly different type of interlaced triangles is the one adopted as the emblem of the Ancient and Accepted Rite (bottom second figure p. 242).

One of the most elaborate of the many variations is illustrated in Zimmer's *Myths and Symbols*. It is the *Shri-Yantra*, a form of the magic circle which is regarded as an aid to contemplation and as a type of the oldest religious symbols known.

The Pentalpha, the Five-pointed Star

The pentalpha was the 'Antients' Royal Arch emblem. It is commonly confused with its companion device and often called the Seal of Solomon and the Shield of David. Probably, more accurately, it is the talisman or morning star, but it has a great many names in which the prefix 'penta'

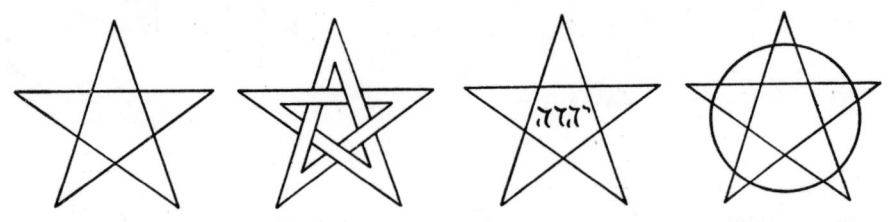

THE PENTALPHA (FIVE-POINTED STAR) IN SOME OF ITS VARIATIONS

enters, such as 'pentagram,' 'pentageron,' 'pentacle,' 'pentaculum,' and 'pentagrammaton.' Sometimes it is called the pentagon, but this is an error; its inner lines constitute that figure. It has been generally adopted as the basis of ornament, and one example, we are told, is to be seen in the eastern window of the south aisle of Westminster Abbey. A church in Hanover built in the fourteenth century contains a device consisting of a circle, double triangles, and a pentagon. A deed of 1276–77 conveying land from a mason (*cementarius*) to his son carries a seal which includes a hammer, a half-moon, and a five-pointed star.

William Hutchinson says in his *Spirit of Masonry* (1775) that the pentalpha was a Christian emblem referring to the Trinity. Elsewhere we are told it was a reminder of the five wounds of Christ, and these are typified in the five lights of the east window of many Gothic churches. To the Pythagoreans and some other schools it was the symbol of health and salutation. It entered into alchemic illustration. Pentalphas in mosaic adorn the thresholds of Freemasons' Hall, London. Laurence Dermott's original design for the 'Antients' certificate found a place for the pentalpha just above the altar.

Section Twenty-four

THE ALTAR STONE, LIGHTS, BANNERS

THE idea of a central altar originated in early Craft lodges, for in these the Royal Arch was nurtured. To the speculative Brethren of those days the Royal Arch ceremony was undoubtedly a religious ceremony, and, quite naturally, it centred spiritually upon an altar. In the minds of the Brethren would be many Biblical texts to inspire and guide them.

The Jews, as from the days of Noah, used an altar not only for sacrificial purposes, but as a memorial, the sacrificial altar being outside and in front of the Temple, while the altars of incense were within. Directions were given on Mount Sinai (Exodus xx, 24–26) for the erection of altars of earth or of unhewn stone to which the ascent should not be by steps. Later the altar was of wood covered with beautiful metals, and on this the incense was burned; the altar had horns, one at each corner, as found in the altars of American chapters to-day. Altars in the early Christian centuries were of wood, and later of stone, but following the Reformation they gave way in English churches to what the Prayer Book calls "the Holy Table."

The early eighteenth-century lodges did not invariably have pedestals. The first pedestal was a central one, either an altar or a pedestal having the associations of an altar, and even to-day the Master's pedestal is, in a sense, a combination of altar and table. It must always be remembered that the early chapters—held in lodge rooms—were necessarily considerably influenced by the common lodge arrangement, and there naturally grew up in them the idea that the central pedestal was an altar around which gathered strongly religious and probably always Christian conceptions. The central altar survives not only in the chapter but in the St John's lodges—the ordinary Craft lodges—of Scotland. It is obvious, also, that at the time when America took its speculative masonry from England there must have been a central altar in the English lodges, for to-day it is a feature of the American lodges, although, in addition, the Master and his Wardens often have pedestals.

The altar in a chapter takes the form of a double cube (briefly, two cubes joined together), a form that has come to have a ceremonial significance, although the historic basis is unknown (see p. 136). The stone carries certain initial letters, and references to these occur in lodge minutes back to the early days. For example, it is known that the St James's Chapter paid £1 10s. in 1803 for the gilding of fifteen letters; eleven years later the chapter resolved to make an alteration to the "Mystical Parts of the Pedestal."

As to the letters themselves, there is not much that can be said in the printed page. It must be admitted that there is no uniformity in regard to the language or languages represented by the initials. In an Edinburgh chapter the letters are in Hebrew. English initials are felt by many scholars to be meaningless. The usual language, we suppose, is Latin, equally illogical and anachronistic, where the three letters 'S.R.I.' stand for 'Solomon King of Israel.' the 'R' being the Latin for 'Rex.' The matter is one that is subject to much and, we fear, fruitless argument.

Three, Five, and Seven

The ceremony associated with the altar makes much of the numbers 3, 5, and 7. It may be noted that in King's College, Cambridge, there are three steps in the south porch, five at the west door, and seven at the north porch. Says a writer in 1769: "These are numbers, with the *mystery* or, at least, the *sound*, of which Freemasons are said to be particularly well acquainted"—a telling piece of evidence that the Royal Arch ceremonial of that early day included a feature of which much is now made.

Each of these numbers has been credited with "mystic" properties, and many particular Biblical references to them will rise to the mind: three branches to the candlestick; the altar three cubits high; three witnesses; windows in threes; three that "bear witness"; the three of the Trinity; "these three agree" (1 John v, 8); five years; five curtains; five rams; five goats; five smooth stones; "at the rebuke of five"; five loaves; seven kine; seven sabbaths; seven pillars; seven churches; seven candlesticks; seven golden vials; seven times; seven years; and so on.

Three was a 'perfect number,' the symbol of the Deity. Some pre-Christian religions had three gods or had gods with three heads. There were three Fates and three Furies, three Christian graces and three kingdoms of nature. There are said to be five wits or senses; five books constitute the Torah (Pentateuch); five days multiplied by ten was the length of the original Pentecost. There were seven sacred planets; creation was complete in seven days; there were seven ages in the life of man; the Jewish jubilee was seven times seven; man was thought to have seven natures and to be composed of seven substances; there were seven churches, seven cities, seven dials, seven joys, seven sages, seven sisters, and as often seen in masonic symbolism, seven stars.

The six lights around the altar owe much to the spiritual significance long since associated with candles, and, further, exemplify by their disposition the mystical importance given to the triangle, both plain and interlaced. In the quite early Craft lodges, certainly as far back as the 1730's, candles were placed to form simple triangles, and from them developed ultimately the present chapter arrangements of lights whose symbolism is so fully dealt with in the ritual and therefore need not be here explained. It is true that the arrangement of the candles is older than the final elaboration of the related symbolism.

The Principal Banners

Entering a chapter, we see the altar with its twelve small banners or ensigns around it, and beyond, in the East, four principal banners carrying ancient emblems; generally, also, we see in the East a fifth banner, centrally placed, displaying the Royal Arch device—the triple tau within a triangle within a circle. We may, in some chapters, see in the West three banners beyond the Sojourners. Let us deal first with the principal banners, secondly with the ensigns, and lastly with the banners sometimes seen in the West, and in doing so attempt to avoid any undue repetition of information to be found in the printed ritual.

The banner comes into freemasonry from ecclesiastical and high civic custom. Great significance attends its display in the chapels of certain orders of knighthood—of the Garter, St George's Chapel, Windsor; of the Bath, Henry VII's Chapel, Westminster, are examples—where each knight's personal banner is suspended above his stall on special occasions. It is thought that from the establishment of Grand Chapter in 1766 banners have been in use—probably, to begin with, no more than four in number. If they were what are now the principal banners carrying the symbols of the ox, man, lion, and eagle they must have been borrowed from the 'Antients,' who had themselves recently discovered the four emblems in a coat of arms associated with a model of Solomon's Temple originally exhibited in London in 1675 by a Spanish Jew, Jacob Jehudah Leon. The 'Antients' adopted the coat of arms complete with its symbolic devices just as they found it.

With regard to the arrangement of the four banners, there is no definite rule; Ezekiel in its tenth chapter gives the arrangement as cherub, man, lion, eagle, but in its first chapter as man, lion, ox, eagle. The lion represents the tribe of Judah, the man that of Reuben, the ox Ephraim, the eagle Dan. These tribes were encamped respectively east, south, west, and north of the Tabernacle. The order last given (lion, man, ox, eagle) is the sun-wise direction. In the present armorial bearings of Grand Lodge, which, of course, incorporated those of the 'Antients' Grand Lodge at the Craft Union, the order is lion, ox (calf), man, eagle, agreeing with that given in Revelation iv, 7. Taking this order and remembering that the lion represents strength and power, the ox, or calf, patience and assiduity, the man intelligence and understanding, and the eagle promptness and celerity in doing the will and pleasure of the great *I am*, then the progression in meaning and significance is appropriate.

The Book of Revelation represents the emblems of four distinct *beings*: the Old Testament represents them as four *faces*. The oldest emblazonment known in the records of Freemasons' Hall, London (date about 1776), shows a golden lion on a red ground, a black ox on a blue ground, a red man on a white or yellow ground, and a golden eagle on a green ground, but it is obvious that banners have been produced to suit the different tastes and whims of many individuals.

The derivation of these four emblems has been learnedly dealt with by G. S. Shepherd-Jones. He recalls that the very ancient peoples regarded fire, light, and air as direct manifestations of the Deity, and symbolized them by the bull, the lion, and the eagle: the rage of the bull to denote fire; the piercing eyes of the lion to denote light; and the soaring flight of the eagle to denote air. Later they gave the Deity these three attributes, and depicted a human body with three heads—those of the bull, the lion, and the eagle. To other ancient gods they gave several heads, and to some several arms, all in an attempt to signify their god and his attributes. Then, in the course of time, the Egyptians and possibly still earlier peoples transformed their three-headed god into four separate figures which, after some elaboration, became the bull, the lion, the eagle, and the man. The Hebrews, after their exodus from Egypt, adopted the symbols, and thus we find the ox and the lion upon the bases of the lavers (brazen vessels in which the priests washed) of the Temple at Jerusalem.

These four sacred symbols, to which there are many references in the Jewish Talmud, were ascribed in a book by St Irenæus (second century) to the four Evangelists, Matthew, Mark, Luke, and John, so obviously they had acquired a Christian significance at a very early date. The eagle became a prominent church symbol, and in some old parish churches there was an eagle desk at which certain processions halted and the Gospel was sung. The Old Masonic Charges well knew the eagle symbol. The presence in an old lodge of a carved eagle may possibly mean either that the lodge was dedicated to St John the Evangelist, as lodges commonly were, or is evidence of a Royal Arch association. In the Chapter of St James, No. 2, is an eagle carved and gilded.

In their Christian application a winged man represented the incarnation of Christ; a winged ox His passion; a winged lion His resurrection; and the eagle His ascension (and in the order thus given are respectively associated with SS. Matthew, Luke, Mark, and John). All the four emblems appear on a notable crucifix, that in the cathedral of Minden, Germany. At the foot of the cross is the man, and at the head the eagle. At the end of the arm on the figure's right is the lion, on his left the ox.

The arms of the Grand Lodge of England consist essentially of two cherubim (plural of cherub), one on each side of a shield. Above the shield is the Ark of the Covenant, over which is Hebrew lettering, *Kodes la Adonai*, meaning 'Holiness to the Lord.' We learn much of the genesis of the whole device when we read Exodus xxv, describing the cherubim spreading out their wings on high and covering the mercy seat with their wings. Cherubim in the coat of arms are obviously symbolic figures, probably derived from an Assyrian representation in a sacred figure of the wings of an eagle, the body partly of an ox and partly of a lion and the face of a man. These figures have a close affinity with the symbolic figures represented by the four principal banners.

The Twelve Ensigns

The ensigns arranged around the altar commemorate the Children of Israel during their forty years' travel in the wilderness, in the course of which banners were regularly set up and the tribes assembled and pitched their tents around their own individual banner.

Each ensign carries an emblematic device, the choice of emblem being governed by Jacob's prophecy relating to the posterity of the different tribes. These tribes had been scattered throughout the length, but not much of the breadth, of Palestine. In the extreme North, near Lake Meron, were Asher and Naphtali, south of them Zebulun, and to the east of the Sea of Galilee Manasseh. Much farther south, below Manasseh, came Gad, and at the extreme south, to the east of the Dead Sea, Reuben. The six other tribes were all west of the river Jordan: starting from the North, they were Issachar, next a branch of the tribe of Manasseh, then Ephraim, Dan, Benjamin (close to Jerusalem), and finally, on the west shore of the Dead Sea, Judah and Simeon.

Jacob had twelve sons, each the head of a tribe, but on his deathbed he adopted Ephraim and Manasseh, the sons of Joseph, although on the distribution of land by Joshua the tribes counted but as twelve. Levi had no land, but some cities and many privileges. Rather more than 700 years B.C. ten of the tribes revolted from the House of Israel and took Jeroboam as their king, leaving Judah and Benjamin still faithful to the government of the line of David. Vast numbers of the revolted tribes under Jeroboam were carried into captivity beyond the Euphrates, and it is unlikely that many of them ever returned. Ultimately the tribes of Judah and Benjamin were taken into exile by Nebuchadnezzar, this exile leading up to the epoch in Jewish history with which the story of the English Royal Arch is concerned.

Each ensign carries the name of a tribe and a distinguishing emblem, as here shown:

Judah	lion couchant and sceptre.
Benjamin	wolf.
Dan	horse and rider, a serpent biting the heels of the horse; sometimes an eagle in the background.
Asher	tree or cup.
Naphtali	hind.
Manasseh (took the place of Levi)	vine on a wall.
Issachar	ass couched between two burdens.
Zebulun	ship in haven.
Reuben	man on red ensign.
Simeon	sword or crossed swords, sometimes with tower.
Gad	troop of horsemen.
Ephraim	ox.

Originally these ensigns were arranged to form a square, a most inconvenient arrangement, so it has come about that in most chapters the ensigns are in two lines, six in each, generally facing inward towards the altar, although sometimes all the ensigns face west. Some chapters have compromised by placing the ensigns in a slightly slanting position so that they can be clearly seen by anyone in the west.

Other Banners

Behind the Sojourners' chairs in some chapters are three banners, and apparently their original emblems were respectively lion, sceptre, and crown. J. Heron Lepper thought that these banners were at an early date behind the chairs of the Three Principals, but at some time or another, possibly following the 1835 revision of ceremonies and ritual, they were moved over. In the process of time the crown emblem has been dropped or forgotten.

Some chapters early in the nineteenth century are believed to have displayed banners carrying the signs of the zodiac.

Tracing-boards

Some of the old chapters had, and probably may still have, tracing-boards, the idea of which came straight from Craft usage. In the old Irish chapters were boards depicting the symbols not only of the Royal Arch,

THE ALTAR STONE, LIGHTS, BANNERS

but of the Craft and a number of additional degrees. It is thought that the oldest Irish floor-cloth (and the floor-cloth was in effect a tracing-board) is owned by Lurgan Lodge, then No. 394, Irish Constitution, and its chief feature is an arch.

An engraved plate dated 1755 represents a very early instance of a tracing-board displaying a Royal Arch idea. It is a curious illustration showing an arch in three stages and an indented border on a tracing-board which is in course of use by the architect. In the Chapter of Fortitude, Edgbaston, No. 43, is a painted floor-cloth, not thought to be older than 1840, showing the signs of the zodiac, while in the Chapter of Sincerity, Taunton, No. 261, is a tracing-board, originally a cloth, dating back to the early 1800's, and displaying as one of its emblems the mariner's compass. This last board, illustrated in a full-page plate in the author's earlier volume, is quite outstanding; within an indented border it includes a main arch supported by two great pillars, and inside that is seen a succession of three arches, with the Sojourners at work.

A Third-degree tracing-board belonging to the Britannia Lodge, No. 139, Sheffield (started as an 'Antients' Lodge in 1761), presumably dating back to not earlier than the 1840's, displays the clearest possible evidence of association with the Royal Arch. Within an outline of a coffin (surmounted by a sprig of acacia) are a few bold Craft emblems and three pent-alphas, those last probably an indication of the survival of the 'Antients' feeling originally in the lodge.

On old Craft tracing-boards, banners, jewels, etc., a hand holding a plumb-line is a symbol often indicating a Royal Arch connexion. It comes from the 'Antients' ceremony of Installation, and dates back to the time when the Past Master's 'Degree' was considered an essential step to the Royal Arch. It is a matter for conjecture whether anything was contributed to this particular symbolism as a result of Galileo Galilei's investigation of the properties of the pendulum, but it is impossible to contemplate the well-known statue of the great physicist holding a line with pendulum bob without instantly calling to mind the hand-and-plumb-line symbol to be seen on numberless tracing-boards and jewels of other days. An excellent example of a design in which the same symbol occurs is on a Royal Arch banner (1780–1800) in the masonic museum at Canterbury, reproduced in this book as Plate XIV.

The anchor, a device common on old tracing-boards and jewels, was (and still is) a Christian emblem of eternal life, particularly so when combined with the cross.

The group of seven stars so commonly seen on old tracing-boards, jewels, and the like is inspired by the texts in Revelations i, 16; ii, 1; and iii, 1, these speaking of the seven stars in the hand of Christ.

Section Twenty-five

ROYAL ARCH CLOTHING

The Royal Arch mason's clothing (the word comes down from guild custom) includes robes, aprons, sashes, collars, chains, jewels, and, exceptionally, headdresses.

The by-laws of the Excellent Grand and Royal Chapter, 1766, lay down "that the Excellent Grands be clothed in proper Robes, Caps on their Heads, and adorned with proper jewells.—No Aprons. . . . That all the Companions wear Aprons (except those appointed to wear robes) and the Aprons shall be all of one sort of fashion." (For the completion of this by-law see p. 71.)

The Charter of Compact, 1766, specifies "an apron indented with Crimson, and the Badge ⊞ properly displayed thereon, and also the indented Ribbon or Sash of this Order."

The robes worn by the Three Principals are traditional, not of any definite period, and descend from the ancient and world-wide custom of persons in authority and having ceremonial duties wearing a loose, flowing outer-dress. Judges, priests, scholastics, etc., have commonly worn such clothing of dignity. It is known that robes were worn in the early chapters, for in May 1777 the minutes of the Grand and Royal Chapter mention a proposal to have a new robe for the Principal (if the fund would admit of it), and in December of the same year Chevalier Ruspini showed drawings of proposed new robes which, with some alterations, were approved.

The colours of Royal Arch clothing take their significance from Biblical texts—"blue, and purple, and scarlet" (Exodus xxv, 4, and xxvi, 1)—but there has been some variation since the earliest Royal Arch days. Before the union of the Grand Chapters the Three Principals wore respectively robes of scarlet, mazarine blue (a deep sky-blue), and light grey, but nowadays the First Principal wears a robe of scarlet, the emblem of imperial dignity, the Second a robe of purple, the emblem of union (purple being a combination of blue and scarlet), and the Third a robe of blue, indicating universal friendship and benevolence. In Ireland the Principals do not wear robes. In Scotland robes are optional and, when worn, agree with those worn in an English chapter, although, to be precise, the First

Principal's "scarlet" is there called "crimson." In some American chapters the chief officer wears all four colours of the Jewish High Priest—blue, purple, scarlet, and white linen—the King wears scarlet, and the Scribe purple.

Many theories have been advanced to explain the choice of colours, but nothing more definite can be said than that, in general, the colours agree with those given in the Book of Exodus.

The surplices or vestments of white linen worn by the Sojourners date back at least to 1778, when their use was authorized by the first Grand Chapter; the reference in the printed rules of 1782 is "For the sojourners, surplices." The Scribe's surplice may go back to about the same period or rather later and be developed from the alb, a longer linen vestment originating in Greek and Latin days and worn by priests of the Christian Church since, say, the third century. It has been said to be emblematical of the renewal of man in justice and in the holiness of truth.

The Headdress

The headdress was once part of the regular clothing of the Grand Principals. The laws of Grand Chapter, 1796, for example, say that the Z. will wear a turban with a triple crown, the H. an ornamental turban or a plain crown, and the J. a purple Hiera cap with a silver plate in front bearing "Holiness to the Lord" in Hebrew characters engraved thereon. This custom survives in many chapters of the United States of America, in which the High Priest wears a mitre and breastplate, the King a crown and carries a sceptre, the Scribe a turban, the Captain of the Host a cap, and the Principal Sojourner, Royal Arch Captain, and the Captains or Grand Masters of the Veils wear hats or caps.

Many ordinary chapters also used headdresses, for we are told that the Chapter of Hope "for some years was not wealthy enough to indulge in such ornate adornment," and in 1818 was reported to Grand Chapter for not wearing proper regalia. To-day the headdress is seldom seen in English chapters. True, St Stephen's Chapter, Retford, Notts, possesses headdresses and they have now come into use again since the 1950's. However, headdresses are still worn in the Chapter of St James, No. 2, and in the Bristol chapters and include both crowns and mitres or turbans.

The headdress was not originally a mitre, it is thought, although so shown in some old illustrations. Plate XXV shows mitre-like headdresses worn by the Principals of the Chapter of Melchizedec (1801–60) (attached to the Lodge of Antiquity, No. 146, Bolton), and doubtless in a number of chapters the headdress came to be regarded as a mitre after the style of the bishop's headdress, actually his coronet. Curiously, the word 'mitre' appears to have been associated in the first place with the idea of a thread, and to have signified something tied on or bound on, probably derived from the two wide 'strings' always attached to the mitre. In the Middle Ages mitres were of costly material and covered with gems and precious metals, though sometimes they were of simple damask silk or white linen. There is good reason for the opinion that the High Priest's headdress should be, not a mitre, but a turban mounted on an encircling plate of gold on which is inscribed "Holiness to the Lord."

The Royal Arch Apron

The original Royal Arch apron could have been nothing more than the Craft apron (as it was for 150 years or so in American masonry) with or without the addition of symbolic decoration, many examples of these elaborate old aprons being on view in masonic museums. This would apply chiefly to 'Antients' practice, however, for we have seen that the 'Moderns' were prescribing in 1766 an apron closely resembling that of to-day. 'Antient' masons were proud to wear their aprons displaying Royal Arch symbols in any and every masonic meeting, but the premier Grand Lodge raised objection early in the 1770's to the wearing of the special Royal Arch apron in the Craft lodges, with the result that in 1773 Grand Chapter decided to "disuse" the Royal Arch apron until Grand Lodge should permit Companions to wear it in the Grand Lodge and in private lodges. But Grand Lodge recognition was not forthcoming (and never has been, to the extent of permitting Royal Arch clothing to be worn in a Craft lodge), and the Royal Arch masons were not long in resuming the Royal Arch apron in their own chapters.

A Companion writing to one living in the country in the year 1795 said that, "the R.A. Masons in London wore no Aprons when assembled in such a Chapter," but little credence should be given to this inasmuch as we have many recorded references to Royal Arch aprons about that period, and as an example may quote a minute of the St James's Chapter of 1798, proposing "that the Indented Apron to be worn by the Companions of the Chapter should be Red Indent on a Royal Blue Ground, and lined with White Silk," and, apparently, about the end of the century some change in the Royal Arch apron was officially made, J. Harry Rylands, for example, believing that the original crimson gave way to blue about 1798.

Much could be written about the 'Antients' curious old aprons showing Royal Arch symbolic devices. Aprons printed from engraved plates, common in the 1800 period, are far from lacking in beauty, and some of them have been coloured after printing. One or two particular aprons will be noted as examples of the highly ornamental style affected in those days.

An apron worn in an Irish lodge, No. 837, held in His Majesty's 22nd or Sligo Regiment of Militia, has a semicircular bib or flap trimmed with ribbon, the inside ribbon light blue and the outside red, and on the outside is a narrow black fringe. The flap carries a square and compass in light blue, and on the square is a red-ribbon rosette. The top of the apron is bound with blue ribbon. The centre ornament of the apron is an arch of red ribbon resting on three strips of black, red, and blue ribbon. Within the arch is worked in red silk a key, and below that a serpent on a rod. Above the key is the letter G. Accompanying the apron was a sash of black silk with a narrow border of red and a short fringe of blue, there being a rosette of blue and red on the shoulder; at the breast was a seven-pointed star in black sequins, and beneath that the emblems of mortality. The owner was a Knight Templar, and the ornamentation of the apron includes the seven stars and other emblems.

A most elaborately silk-embroidered apron, also Irish, is of linen worked with silks of many colours by a process known as tambouring, the approximate date being 1820. It possibly belonged to a member of the Lodge of Truth, Belfast, founded in 1817. Included in its emblems are: the arch, from whose keystone hangs the letter 'G'; a figure within the arch; many emblems of the Craft, the veils, etc., of the Royal Arch, and devices of some additional degrees. Figures of a Master and his Wardens form a triangle, and the central figure has on his right the Tetragrammaton.

Many old and distinctive aprons are shown in a number of the plates accompanying this present volume.

A Companion's apron in the English Royal Arch to-day is of white lambskin, from 14 inches to 16 inches wide and from 12 inches to 14 inches deep. Together with its triangular overlap, it has an indented crimson and purple (dark blue) border not more than 2 inches wide except along the top. In the centre of the overlap is a triangle of white silk within a gilt border, and within the triangle the emblem—three taus united in gilt embroidery; two gold or metal gilt tassels are suspended from beneath the overlap by ribbons. In the aprons of Principals, Present and Past, the silk triangle on the overlap and the backing on ribbons are crimson. The aprons of Provincial and District Grand Officers, etc., have the gilt emblems of office or rank in the centre, within a double circle, in which is inserted the name of the Province or District, or, in the case of London Grand Chapter rank, the word 'London,' and in the case of overseas Grand Chapter rank the word 'Overseas'; backing and ribbons are of dark blue.

The aprons of Grand Officers and Grand Superintendents have a double indented crimson and purple border 4 inches wide, with the emblem of office embroidered in gilt in the centre within two branches of laurel; the backing and ribbons in this case also are dark blue.

The Sash

English Grand Chapter regulations require all Companions to wear a sash over the left shoulder passing obliquely to the right side, but there is ample evidence of the sash having been worn over the *right* shoulder in some of the early chapters. Worn over the right shoulder, the sash may possibly hark back to the sword-belt, but worn over the left to the decorative badge of honour such as would be worn by a court official. From this difference in the method of wearing has arisen a keen controversy on the true origin and meaning of the sash.

Those who believe that the sash was originally a sword-belt and should, therefore, be hung from the right shoulder so that the sword is conveniently grasped by the right hand have in their mind the ancient craftsmen who rebuilt the walls of the Holy City with sword at side and trowel in hand. They feel that the sash so worn implies a sword, and are inclined to associate it with a knightly degree that may have had a French origin.

A famous masonic portrait, that of Richard Linnecar, Right Worshipful Master of the Lodge of Unanimity, No. 202, Wakefield, and one of His Majesty's Coroners for the West Riding of the County of Yorkshire, depicts a notable R.A. mason with his sash worn over the right shoulder. This portrait dates back to the 1770 period. Linnecar was a mason of outstanding quality and a most versatile person—linen draper, wine merchant, postmaster, playwright, coroner, and many other things as well.

In a painting about forty years later of another Royal Arch worthy, this one belonging to an old Whitby lodge, the sash again is shown on the right shoulder, but both of these companions were 'Modern' masons, and the possibility must therefore be faced that some 'Antients' wore the sash in the reverse position. In some Yorkshire chapters towards the end of the eighteenth century the sash was worn on the right shoulder, and in Ireland today the sash is worn under the coat from the right shoulder to the left hip.

There is an equally strong case for wearing the sash over the left shoulder. The Charter of Compact (1766) says, "every Companion shall wear . . . the indented Ribbon or Sash of this Order," but does not explain how it should be worn, but the Grand Chapter's printed laws of 1778 ordered the "Ribbon to be worn over the left shoulder." Some students have emphasized that a ribbon (in the Gates MS. of about 1790 it becomes a "large" ribbon) was not a sword support, but rather a sash corresponding to the decoration of a court official of the chamberlain type or to the stole of the church priest and deacon which, right back to ancient days, was worn over the left shoulder, and "in its mystical signification,

PLATE XXX

FOUR APRONS, PAST AND PRESENT

Top left: "Antients" silk apron, hand-painted, with Craft and Knight Templar emblems. *Top right:* Unidentified apron, hand-painted and ornamented in gold; date 1785. *Bottom left:* Hand-painted apron, including emblems of many degrees; date about 1785. *Bottom right:* Apron as now worn by the First Grand Principal of Supreme Grand Chapter.

Three by courtesy of United Grand Lodge.

256

PLATE XXXI

FIVE NOTEWORTHY AND CONTRASTING JEWELS

Top left: An "Antients" Jewel in Battersea enamel. (See p. 260.) *Top right:* Pierced silver jewel of very unusual design. *Centre:* Irish Past King's Jewel formerly worn by F.M. Viscount Wolseley. *Bottom right:* Jewel of "the Nine Worthies." (See p. 260.) *Bottom left:* Jewel of Lodge of Faith, now No. 141; date about 1800.

By courtesy of United Grand Lodge and Quatuor Coronati Lodge

257

represented the yoke of Christ." A Royal Arch MS. of about 1795 says that we wear the Ribbon "as Badges of Honour and Ensigns of our Order." That is greatly at variance with the sword-belt idea. It is worth bearing in mind, too, that from time immemorial it has been understood that English masons should assemble without carrying any offensive or defensive weapon and that up to 1813 notices for the Grand Festival (of the English Grand Lodge) invariably contained an injunction that the Brethren appear unarmed. J. Heron Lepper has said that the sword and trowel are displayed in chapter as an incentive to diligence, labour, and patriotism in defending our country, but, as Royal Arch masons, we do not carry either of them in celebrating our mysteries.

English Grand Chapter regulations to-day require all Companions to wear a crimson-and-purple indented sash over the left shoulder, passing obliquely to the right side, with silk fringe at the end, the emblem to be embroidered on a white background. In the aprons of Principals Present and Past the fringe is of gold or metal gilt, and the emblem is on a crimson background. Grand Officers and Grand Superintendents and all other Companions of senior rank wear the same apron as the Principals of chapters, save that the emblem is on a dark blue background.

Collars and Chains

Certain officers—Grand Officers, for example—have had the privilege of wearing collars or chains over quite a long period. During the last century the Grand Superintendents wore chains or collars similar to those of officers of Grand Chapter, and to-day many more officers share the privilege. The Royal Arch jewel may be worn in a Craft lodge, but not a R.A. collar or chain.

Collars, sashes, and aprons belonging to Royal Arch masonry may not be worn on public occasions, and permission is therefore never given. A dispensation to wear 'masonic clothing' on public occasions does not include permission to wear Royal Arch clothing.

Masonic clothing includes jewels, and these are treated separately in the next section.

Section Twenty-six

ROYAL ARCH JEWELS

MASONIC jewels are more accurately medals, badges of distinction and honour, although many of the early examples were pieces of real jewellery, a few of them, indeed, being elaborate articles of virtu, heavily set with brilliants and other stones. Many of the early Royal Arch jewels are beautiful in their simplicity, especially those formed by fret-cutting, piercing, and engraving, and jewels of this kind were made by famous silversmiths, notable among them being the Thomas Harper family of Fleet Street, London, many of whose jewels, now rare and valuable, are distinguished by the letters 'TH,' not to be confused with the well-known T-over-H device that ultimately became the triple tau.

The masonic practice of displaying medals or 'jewels' probably owes something to a sixteenth-century Church custom of wearing medals, each bearing a religious emblem, or picture, incidentally a custom encouraged by various Popes during the nineteenth century.

Craft jewels were known as far back as 1727, when Masters and Wardens of private lodges were ordered by Grand Lodge to wear "the jewels of Masonry hanging to a white ribbon." The approved Royal Arch jewel, the badge of the Order, incorporates the interlaced triangles and triple tau, and its early form is illustrated in the margin of the Charter of Compact, 1766. This official jewel will be considered later in this section.

Early Royal Arch jewels of the 'Antients' depict an altar under a broken arch, and are known from about 1781, and include the sun in splendour on a triangular plate. The illuminated MS. of a French ritual of 1760 also shows this device, with the addition of the Ineffable Name, the triangle now including a torch extinguished by the light of the sun—a most unusual idea.

The Royal Arch jewels of the 'Moderns' generally are based on the Craft Master's jewel—the open compasses and segment—to which are added the arch and columns. It is known that the jewels of the Three Principals were changed between the year 1796 and 1802 to bring them more closely in accord with the jewel of the old Craft Master. Thus the Principals' jewels illustrated in a circular of Grand Chapter in 1803 and in an *Abstract of Laws*, 1807, have an arch with keystone supported by two columns which stand upon the lowest of three steps. As a reminder of the holder's Craft qualification, a bold pair of compasses, with square, rests on a segment of a circle, both points of the compasses being visible. These are the jewels of the Second and Third Principals, that of the First Principal having, in addition, a sun in splendour between the compasses and the square.

Above: A PIERCED JEWEL SHOWING TRIPLE ARCHES AND FIGURE OF SOJOURNER
Right: A JEWEL OF THE THREE CROWNED STARS LODGE, PRAGUE

The earliest-known P.Z. jewels were those voted by the new Grand Chapter to John Maclean, the first Z., and to James Galloway, the outgoing Z., at the anniversary feast in December 1766, these Companions having probably played a big although unknown part in forming the Chapter and gaining Lord Blayney's indispensable help; Maclean's jewel was in token of his being "Father and Promoter" of the Chapter.

Readers will realize that there is such a mass of material relating to Royal Arch jewels that the subject cannot be more than introduced in these pages; certainly any comprehensive treatment is out of the question. All that can be done is to mention a few of the more outstanding examples.

A First Principal's jewel in the Wallace Heaton collection, illustrated in Plate XV, is based on the old Craft Master's jewel, the open compasses with square and segment, one of the boldest designs known, and into it have been introduced columns, the arch with prominent keystone, and over the top of the arch the hexalpha. The sun in splendour is shown within the arch.

A fine example of a jewel inset with gems (date early eighteenth century) is that of the European traveller, Egyptologist, and 'character' Giovanni Battista Belzoni, born in Padua, North Italy, in 1778. He twice paid long visits to England, and in the Chapter of St James (in which the First Principal wears this identical jewel) he wore the jewel shown in Plate XXVIII, and which is now to be seen at the Freemasons' Hall Museum, London. It was made by the Harper family in 1820, and its fine-quality stones, 'white' and red, are mounted in silver. On each side of the keystone are six red stones. The interlaced triangles also are red. Belzoni on his first visit to England in 1803 was obliged by poverty to earn a living by acrobatic performances in the public street, but he was a student of mechanics, inventor of mechanical methods and appliances, and developed into a well-known discoverer of Egyptian archæological remains. He died in the course of an expedition near Benin, North Africa, in 1823.

A pierced silver jewel (date about 1780) in the custody of Leicester Masonic Hall has the triple arches and the quaint figure of a man engaged in wrenching forth the keystone of the smallest of these arches (see illustration on p. 259).

A jewel of unusual shape—rectangular, with a curved top—is shown on the opposite page. It is crowded with emblems—among them Noah's Ark, beehive, Jacob's ladder, hand holding the serpent by its head, the plummet. It is believed to be a Royal Arch jewel, and is included as an example of the manner in which the old craftsman took joy in crowding in the emblems.

A jewel of striking design—a circle interlaced with a square—belonged to the eighteenth-century Three Crowned Stars Lodge of Prague, capital of Bohemia, then part of the Austrian Empire. The square and triangle may have been of silver, the crowns of silver or gold, and the background red, the ribbon probably being blue. It is illustrated on p. 259.

The collar jewel of bold design, date about 1780, shown in Plate XXXI is unusual in that it is finished in Battersea enamel to give the effect of porcelain.

The Chapter of St George, No. 140 (founded in 1787), has a set of five jewels with red ribbons, intended to be used as collar jewels. They are identical, the device being a plain brass circle enclosing two triangles, one within the other.

Jewels of the Nine Worthies, supervising officers appointed by the 'Antients' Grand Chapter, were of a strongly individual design. Earlier sections explain that these Nine Excellent Masters were given a medal emblematic of their office, the medal to be given up when the Masters left office. Alas! it was often difficult to get these medals returned, but eight of the nine are now in the Grand Lodge (7) and Worcester (1) Museums. In this jewel, again, is the device of the man levering up the keystone of the smallest of the three arches. In the ancient Greek and Roman illustrations showing building work the masons were always shown unclothed, and apparently the designer of this jewel has based himself upon those classic examples (see Plate XXXI).

A late eighteenth-century Royal Arch jewel, pierced and engraved, a design based upon square and sector and containing familiar emblems, is shown on Plate XV.

Jewels of the Unanimity Chapter, Wakefield, as described by J. R. Rylands, were made by James Rule, a watchmaker and jeweller and an active mason in York; jewels made by him are still in the possession of the Unanimity Lodge and Chapter. The chapter jewels include two silver

TWO SIDES OF OLD JEWEL OF UNCOMMON SHAPE AND CROWDED WITH EMBLEMS

triangles and three Sojourners' jewels (see Plate XXIV) and were found years ago in a box after long concealment among accumulated rubbish. The triangles are of extreme simplicity, their sides measuring 5¼ inches, the width of the silver being just under seven-tenths of an inch; they are suspended from faded silk ribbons, 2 inches wide, originally perhaps of a deep purple. On one side they are inscribed "Omnipotent," etc., and on the other "In the beginning," etc. The Sojourners' jewels are beautifully made of silver. The crossed sword and trowel are suspended from red silk ribbons. The swords are nearly 5 inches long and the trowels 4½ inches. With the three silver triangles for the Principals these jewels cost a total of £5 15s. 6d. in March 1799. John R. Rylands draws a possible inference from the Sojourners' jewels that, in the Yorkshire Royal Arch in the latter half of the eighteenth century, there may have been some element similar to, if not derived from, the Scots degrees.

A handsomely engraved silver collar jewel made in Birmingham in 1812 was in the possession at the end of the century of Lodge St Peter, Malden, Essex, but, of course, was not made for that lodge. It is of the square-and-sector type and has a figure standing on an arch stone; other figures in the design are not easily explained in relation to the Craft or Royal Arch. The jewel is nearly 3½ inches wide and 4½ inches deep (see opposite page).

The Royal Arch Jewel, the Jewel of the Order

Earliest authority for the design of the Royal Arch jewel is the margin of the Charter of Compact, as already stated, the design there shown very closely resembling that now in use. The device is the two triangles interlaced, and its now highly developed symbolism is explained later. In the centre space the jewel of Grand Officers carried a delta or triangle, but in the ordinary Companion's jewel the centre was blank. This distinction appears to have disappeared somewhat quickly. A simple, attractive jewel of the year 1766, then belonging to Dr John James Rouby, of St Martin's Lane, London, agrees with the above (see Plate VIII); its owner "passed the arch" in April 1765, and only two months later was signing the by-laws of the Excellent Grand and Royal Chapter.

The Royal Arch jewel may be worn in a Craft lodge under the authority of Grand Lodge Regulation No. 241. It was not specifically referred to in the Craft *Constitutions* immediately following the Craft Union, but in 1841 the permission given in those *Constitutions* to wear certain jewels in lodge was extended to such "as shall appertain to or be consistent with those degrees which are recognized and acknowledged by and under the controul of the Grand Lodge." In 1853 came an addition to the above, the wording being "under the controul of Grand Lodge being part of Pure and Antient Masonry." In 1884 the word "controul" was omitted, possibly because its use may have been interpreted as prohibiting the wearing of a Royal Arch jewel in a Craft lodge. Instead there were substituted words which are still retained in Grand Lodge Rule No. 241, here given in full:

> No Masonic jewel, medal, device, or emblem shall be worn in the Grand Lodge, or any subordinate Lodge, unless it appertains to, or is consistent with, those degrees which are recognised and acknowledged by the Grand Lodge in the preliminary declaration to these Rules, as part of pure Antient Masonry, and has been approved or allowed by the Grand Master.

It will be seen that Grand Chapter Regulation No. 84, as follows, is closely modelled on the above:

> No Masonic jewel, medal, device or emblem shall be worn in the Grand Chapter or any private Chapter unless it appertains to, or is consistent with,

an order or degree recognised and acknowledged by the Grand Lodge or the Grand Chapter as part of pure Antient Masonry, and has been approved or allowed by the First Grand Principal.

The Symbolism of the Royal Arch Jewel

The symbolism of the interlaced triangles has been explained in a previous section, but there has developed in relation to the Royal Arch jewel embodying that device some highly specialized symbolism, and the

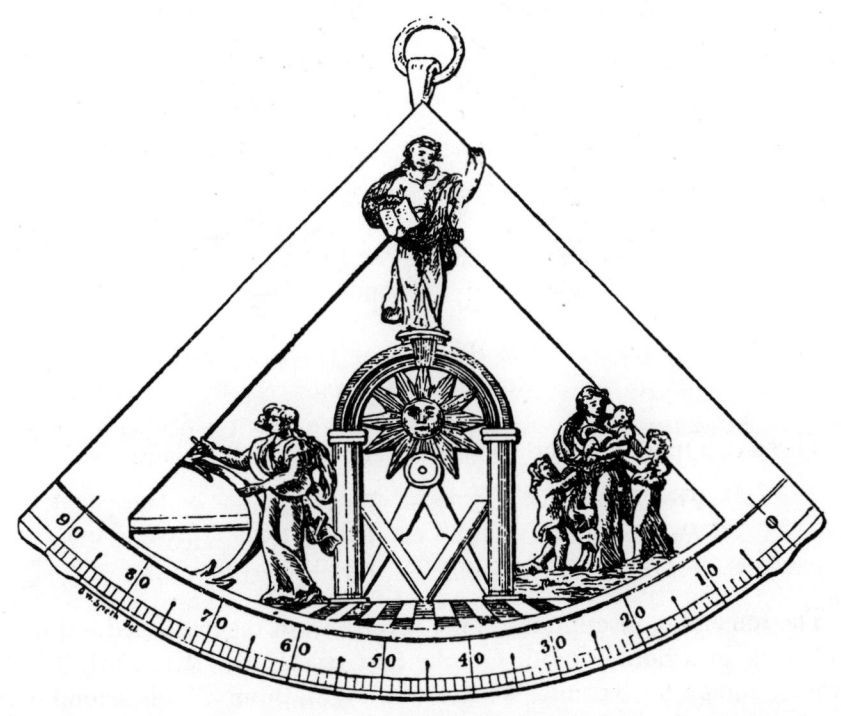

A SQUARE-AND-SECTOR COLLAR JEWEL OF BOLD AND ATTRACTIVE DESIGN, DATED 1812

author is particularly indebted to G. S. Shepherd-Jones, who has offered in an address (1951) a comprehensive explanation of it. The address cannot be quoted at length, but here following it is possible to give some of its author's salient points: The interlaced triangles portray the duality of masonry and its comprehensive teaching, covering the twofold nature of man, spiritual and material. On the jewel is a sun, but a sun within a triangle, representing an emblem of the Deity. Enclosing the interlaced triangles are two concentric circles, the inner one denoting the Deity and His Omnipresence, and the outer one eternity.

At the bottom of the jewel, outside the two concentric circles, is a small circle, again an emblem of eternity, and within that circle is the triple tau, the badge of a Royal Arch mason and representing the completion of a Candidate's spiritual journey in masonry. On the reverse of the jewel, between the two concentric circles, is a double triad in Latin: *Deo, Regi, Fratribus; Honor, Fidelitas, Benevolentia.*

OBVERSE AND REVERSE OF THE ENGLISH
ROYAL ARCH JEWEL

These two triads are read conjointly, and a literal translation is:

Deo Honor   = To God honour.
Regi Fidelitas   = To the King fidelity.
Fratribus Benevolentia = To the Brethren love.

The remaining inscription on the reverse is on the interlaced triangles, and is again a double triad. On the first triangle is "Concord, Truth, Peace," and on the second "Wisdom, Strength, Beauty," this second triad alluding, says the author quoted, not to the wisdom of K.S., the strength of K.H., and the beautifying hand of H.AB. but to the "Omniscience, Omnipotence and Omnipresence" of the Deity.

Turning now to the obverse of the jewel, the wording on the scroll is seen to be complete: *Nil nisi clavis deest* ("Nothing is wanting but the key"). There is a somewhat similar meaning in the inscription between the two concentric circles: *Si talia jungere possis sit tibi scire satis* ("If thou canst understand what follows thou knowest enough"). On the interlaced triangles of the obverse we again have a double triad, but the triad on the second triangle is not yet complete. The triangle with the apex pointing upward is the spiritual triangle, and the inscription on the base is "We have found," which is repeated in Greek and again in Latin on the sides of the triangle. On the triangle with the apex pointing downward the base is left blank, and on the two sides are *Cultor Dei; Civis Mundi.* When the Companion's name has been engraved in the blank space, then the triad on that triangle will be completed, and will read, "A.B.; *Cultor Dei; Civis Mundi.*" By this endorsement the holder of the jewel acknowledges that he is a "worshipper (or reverencer) of God, a citizen of the world"; at the same time he subscribes to the wording on the spiritual triangle, "We have found." The Companion who has found the Word should be able to appreciate the meaning of the inscription between the concentric circles, "If thou canst understand this thou knowest enough," for the WORD, the will of God, comprises all the tenets, precepts, and principles of freemasonry, everything that masonry teaches. It will be appreciated that this explanation owes much to the individual interpretation of its author, G. S. Shepherd-Jones.

OBVERSE AND REVERSE OF THE SCOTTISH ROYAL ARCH JEWEL

OBVERSE OF THE IRISH ROYAL ARCH JEWEL
Note the Mark emblem in the centre

The jewel of the Order is worn pendent from a narrow ribbon on the left breast—white for Companions, crimson for Principals, Present and Past, of private chapters, tricoloured (dark blue, crimson, and light blue) for all other Excellent Companions, including Grand Officers. (Purple is the true Royal Arch colour, but, by long-established usage, dark blue takes its place in regalia.)

The jewels of all the Three Grand Principals are the open compasses, their points touching interlaced triangles; a crown within the compasses distinguishes the jewel of the First, the all-seeing eye the Second, and the V.S.L. the Third Grand Principal.

Chains or collars are worn strictly in accordance with Grand Chapter *Regulations*, and must have appended to them in every case the jewel appropriate to the office or rank to which they relate.

For the official and closely detailed regulations relating to jewels the reader should consult the *Regulations* of Supreme Grand Chapter, these including engravings of the authorized jewels.

What might appear to be a prefigurement of the R.A. jewel was produced in 1630 (136 years earlier than the Charter of Compact) when Jacob (Jacques) Callot, a famous French etcher, engraved his portrait of a

A Design (date 1630) by the French Engraver Callot, a Possible Prefigurement of the Royal Arch Jewel (1766)

well-known physician and made it the centre-piece of an hexalpha. He inserted Greek letters on the arms of the geometrical device and surrounded it with a circle, actually the serpent devouring its own tail (see p. 230). The illustration herewith suggests the irresistible but superficial resemblance between Callot's design and the R.A. jewel.

Irish Jewels

Irish Royal Arch jewels include some of the most informative and pictorial of late eighteenth-century examples. Many of them are of a quite distinctive design and crowded with emblems, thirty or so of which may

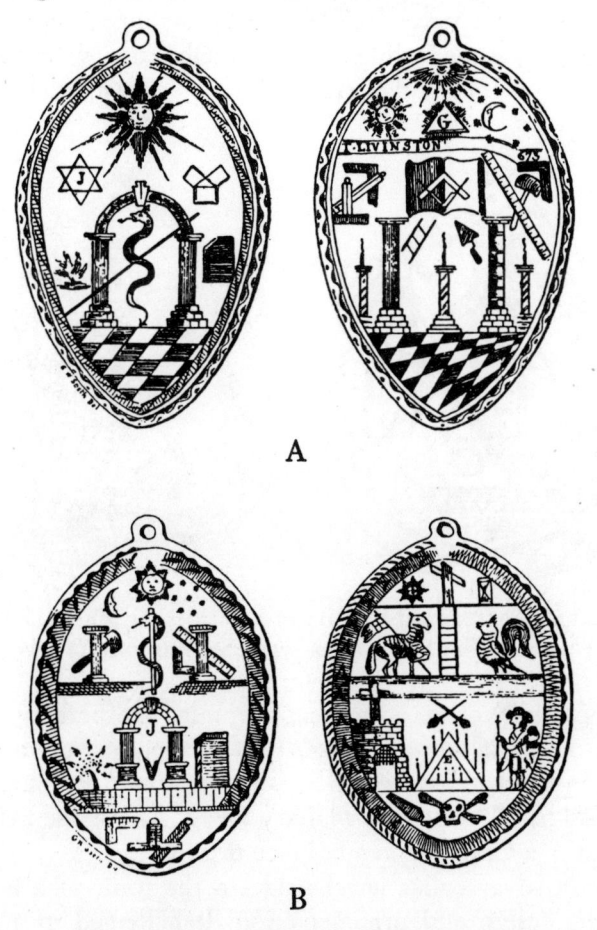

A

B

Two Irish Silver Jewels, Late Eighteenth Century

A: Reverse with Royal Arch and obverse with Craft emblems. *B*: With Craft, Royal Arch, and Templar emblems

sometimes be found on the two sides of a jewel measuring not more than 1½ inches by 2¼ inches. Very typical are the two jewels here shown; they are oval and of silver, carrying on the obverse Craft symbols and on the reverse Royal Arch symbols, these, most curiously, including the 47th Proposition of Euclid, an allusion to the owner's qualification as a Past Master. The first jewel is dated about 1800 and the second five years later. The two belonged to Thomas Livingston, who became a member of Lodge 673 in 1799. He took both Royal Arch and Templar Degrees, so he bought himself a second jewel, and although the approximate date of purchase is 1805, the jewel had been made about ten to twenty years earlier. We get the same feeling in a more elaborate jewel, which was the property of a member of Lodge 410 (see below). The military figure on the

AN EARLY IRISH JEWEL CARRYING EMBLEMS OF MANY DEGREES
AND SHOWING SOJOURNER WITH SWORD AND TROWEL

right-hand side may cause a moment's wonder and perhaps a moment's smile. He is the medallion-engraver's idea of a mason Sojourner working with trowel in hand and sword at side. The knight in armour, the helmet, and the armed fist all suggest a military lodge. Above the helmet will be noted "I.H.S.," a Christian symbol (see p. 236).

A Warden's silver collar jewel made in the form of a level is most unusual in its design and ornamentation. It belonged to a member of Lodge Ballygawley, Co. Tyrone, No. 679, Ireland, warranted in 1788, so the jewel is probably of the late eighteenth century. On the broken arch sit two Sojourners, who have lowered their companion into the vault, which contains a central cubical stone. On the left is an ark, an indication that degrees other than Craft and Royal Arch were practised.

The Breastplate

The High Priest of some old chapters, when he happened to be Third Principal, wore a breastplate. In a very few chapters to-day he still does so, and a breastplate is part of the official Scottish regalia, the Third Grand Principal wearing a breastplate closely resembling the description given in Exodus xxviii, 15–30, a description so precise that a craftsman has no difficulty in following it. Both the Old and New Testaments speak of "the breastplate of righteousness," and the New Testament refers to it also as "the breastplate of faith and love." The High Priest, in Biblical days, wore this rich piece of embroidery, the work of cunning workmen, about 10 inches square and "of gold, of blue, and of purple, and of scarlet, and of fine twined linen . . . four square . . . doubled," a span both in length and breadth. On it were mounted in gold settings four rows of precious stones, all different, twelve stones in all, and upon each stone was engraved the name of a tribe of Israel. Two chains of "wreathen work of pure gold" were attached by means of golden rings. For strength and to make it possible for it to receive the Urim and the Thummin the breastplate was of double thickness, actually a kind of bag or purse. It was called the badge of judgment inasmuch as Aaron was told to bear the names of the judgment of the children of Israel upon his heart "when he goeth in before the Lord." We are told that in those early days the High Priest had an oracular manner of consulting God. He wore his robes and the pectoral or breastplate containing the Urim and Thummin, of the nature of which oddly named things we know just nothing. Urim is believed to represent light and excellence, Thummin perfection and completion, and there are several Biblical references to them, but of their physical nature, if they had any, we know nothing whatever.

Evidence that the jewelled breastplate had a vogue in ancient religious observances is provided by an historical statement that Julius Cæsar dedicated to a goddess—the Mother of Living Creatures—a costly breastplate studded with pearls that had been obtained from British freshwater streams.

We know of many masonic breastplates. Minutes of Sanquhar Kilwinning Lodge, No. 194, Dumfriesshire, of January 1757, say that "The Breastplate or long Square Medell with all the Jewells belonging to a Lodge engraven upon a manteling engraven about it, and silverised was made a present of by James Boyle, sen., to the Lodge." It is thought that this breastplate of hammered copper, convex and measuring 4 inches by 6 inches, is still worn by the Master of the Lodge.

Made in 1777 is a breastplate forming part of the regalia of the Lodge of Unanimity, Wakefield, and illustrated in Plate XXIV. It is a small rectangular pad, about 4 inches deep, of dark blue velvet, on which are mounted twelve coloured bosses, the whole being suspended from a blue-and-white-striped ribbon. The jewels or bosses are oval, faceted, and on brass mountings, and are arranged in the following order:

White	Purple	Green
Red	Yellow	Red
Blue	Purple	Blue
Yellow	Green	White

In Sincerity Chapter, No. 600, Bradford, the Third Principal wears at Installation meetings a breastplate about 10 inches square containing twelve precious stones, on each of which is a Hebrew inscription. The stones are $1\frac{3}{8}$ inches by $\frac{7}{8}$ inch. The chapter possesses a set of crowns, and on that of the Third Principal (it might be called a mitre) there is, on the front, an appropriate inscription in Hebrew; that officer wears the breastplate suspended from the neck by a golden cord and tied round the body by a red ribbon from the lower corners. The stones are arranged in four rows of three each, and each stone is set in a gilt mounting which is engraved with a Hebrew word.

The British Chapter, Cape Town, owns a brass breastplate presented in 1830, the year following its consecration. In the Royal Cumberland Chapter, No. 41, Bath, dating back to 1782, the Third Principal wears at all meetings a breastplate measuring about 6 inches by 9 inches and containing three rows of four (imitation) gems. "An elegant Breastplate set in gold" was presented to the De Lambton Chapter, Sunderland, in 1825 "for the M.E.Z. to wear when in office"; in those days each of the three principal officers of that chapter wore a crown, the Z. having a breastplate in addition. The J. wears a breastplate in the Bristol chapters and in the Chapter of St James, No. 2, London.

The Shamir Legend

From the engraved jewels of the breastplate to one of the most extraordinary legends related in connexion with Solomon's Temple may seem a long journey. Every freemason knows of the tradition that in the building of that Temple no iron tool was used. Around this tradition grew up a very curious myth (possibly having an Egyptian or Babylonian origin) to the effect that the stones were shaped by the agency of an insect, a worm, commonly called *shamir*. A masonic ritual of the eighteenth century embodied questions and answers relating to "the wonderful properties of that noble insect" which cut and shaped Solomon's sacred utensils, holy vessels, etc. Readers wishing to look into the matter should see an article, "The Legend of the Shamir," by Dr W. Wynn Westcott, in *Miscellanea Latomorum*, vol. xxviii. Probably *shamir* or *schamir* is a corrupted form of the Greek word *smiris*, meaning "emery," and the word has been spelled in many ways—*thumare, thamir, shamur,* and so on. The superstition was that the worm, *shamir*, was placed on the stone where the cut was to be made and, lo and behold! the stone parted exactly as required. In the course of time the same legend was adopted to explain the engraving or cutting of the inscriptions on the breastplate stones, the method of engraving the hard gems being a mystery to the common people. Out of the myth arises by implication the idea that Solomon's masons may have used emery in working and surfacing their stones and that the ancient gem workers were also acquainted with its abrasive properties. In support it must be remembered that from time immemorial emery was exported from Cape Emery, in the island of Naxos, in the Ægean Sea, a short sailing distance from Palestine.

Appendix

THE CHARTER OF COMPACT

(Two omissions in earlier impressions are shown here as footnotes.)

THE MOST ENGLIGHTENED EAST
I ∴ TN ∴ OTGA ∴ OTU ∴ ∴ ∴ ∴

To all the Enlightened, Entered ∴ Passed ∴ ∴ Raised ∴ ∴ ∴ and Exalted ∴ ∴ ∴ ∴ And to all others whom it may concern under the Canopy of Heaven, HEALTH, PEACE and UNION.

We, the Right Honourable and Right Worshipful Cadwallader Lord Blayney, Baron Blayney of Monaghan in the Kingdom of Ireland, Lord Lieutenant and Custos Rotulorum of the same County, and Major General in His Majesty's Service (P) Grand Master of Free and accepted Masons, And also Most Excellent Grand Master of the Royal Arch of Jerusalem send Greeting.

WHEREAS We have it principally at Heart to do all in our Power to promote the Honour, Dignity, Preservation and Welfare of the Royal Craft in general as well as of every worthy Brother in particular; and also to extend the Benefits arising therefrom to every created Being, according to the original Design of this Heavenly Institution; first planned and founded in Ethicks, and including in its grand Scheme every Art, Science and Mystery that the Mind of Man in this sublunary State is capable of comprehending

AND WHEREAS We having duly passed the Royal Arch have found our dearly beloved and Most Excellent Bretheren, James Galloway, John McLean, Thomas Dunckerley, Francis Flower, John Allen, John Brooks, Thomas French and Charles Taylor and the Rest of our Excellent Companions of the respectable Chapter held at the Turk's Head Tavern in Gerrard Street, Soho, in the County of Middlesex, not only to be perfect Masters in every Degree of the Royal Craft in its operative, but likewise, by their Study and labour to have made considerable advances in the SPECULATIVE or truly sublime and most exalted Parts thereof

AND WHEREAS Our said Most Excellent Companions have requested Us to enter into Compact with and to grant to them Our Charter of Institution and Protection to which We have readily concurred NOW KNOW YE that in tender Consideration of the Premisses, and for the Purposes aforesaid

We HAVE Instituted and Erected And, by and with the advice, Consent, and Concurrence of Our said Most Excellent Companions, in full Chapter Assembled (testified by their severally signing and sealing hereof) DO by these Presents as much as in Us lyes Institute and Erect them Our said Most Excellent Bretheren and Companions, James Galloway, John McLean, Thomas Dunckerley, Francis Flower,[1] John Brooks, Thomas French and Charles Taylor, and their Successors Officers for the Time being of the Grand and Royal Chapter jointly with Ourself and Our Successors Most Excellent Grand Master for the Time being from Time to Time and at all Times hereafter to form and be, The Grand and Royal Chapter of the Royal Arch of Jerusalem Hereby Giving, Granting, Ratifying and Confirming unto them and their Successors All the Rights, Priviledges, Dignities, Ensigns and Prerogatives which from Time immemorial have belonged and do appertain to those exalted to this Most Sublime Degree; With full Power and absolute Authority from Time to Time as Occasion shall require and it shall be found expedient to hold and convene Chapters and other proper Assemblies for the carrying on, improving and promoting the said benevolent and useful Work. And also to admit, pass and exalt in due Form and according to the Rites and Ceremonies Time immemorial used and approved in and by that most exalted and sacred Degree, and as now by them practised, all such experienced and discreet Master Masons as they shall find worthy

AND WE DO FURTHERMORE hereby Give, Grant, Ratify and Confirm unto Our said Most Excellent Bretheren and Companions and their Successors, Officers of our said Grand and Royal Chapter for the Time being, full and absolute Power and Authority in Conjunction with Us or Our Most Excellent Deputy for the Time being to make and confirm Laws, Orders and Ordinances for the better conducting and regulating the said Most Excellent and Sublime Degree throughout the Globe, as well as of their said Grand and Royal Chapter and from Time to Time to alter and abrogate the same Laws, Orders and Ordinances as to them and their Successors shall seem meet: And also to constitute, superintend and regulate other Chapters wheresoever it shall be found convenient and as to Us or Our Deputy and the said Grand Officers, Our and their Successors for the Time being, shall seem fit AND it is also declared, concluded and agreed upon by and between Us and Our said Most Excellent Companions, James Galloway, John McLean, Thomas Dunckerley, Francis Flower, John Allen, John Brooks, Thomas French and Charles Taylor, the said Most Excellent Grand Officers,

AND THESE PRESENTS FURTHER WITNESS that We and the said Most Excellent Grand Officer Do hereby for Ourselves severally and respectively and for Our several and respective Successors, the Most Excellent Grand Master, and the Most Excellent Grand Officers of the said Grand and Royal Chapter of the Royal Arch of Jerusalem in manner and form following, that is to say

[1] Omission. The name John Allen should be inserted here.

FIRST that the Most Excellent Deputy Grand Master shall preside and have full Power and Authority in the Absence of the Most Excellent Grand Master.

SECONDLY That the Jewels worn or to be worn from Time to Time by the Most Excellent[1] Grand Master, Deputy Grand Master, and Grand Officers shall be of the Form and Figure, and bear the same inscription as delineated in the Margin hereof And that the like Jewels, only omitting the Sun, Compass and Globe, shall be worn by the two Scribes and three S:N:R:S; And also that the like Jewels shall be worn by the Rest of the Excellent Companions, except that in them shall be left out the Triangle &c. in the center thereof

THIRDLY That every Companion shall wear according to ancient Custom an Apron indented with Crimson, and the Badge ⌂ properly displayed thereon, And also the indented Ribbon or Sash of this Order

FOURTHLY That the Common Seal of this Grand and Royal Chapter shall bear the like Impression as the Jewels worn by the Most Excellent Grand Officers

FIFTHLY That for every Charter of Constitution to be granted by and from this Grand and Royal Chapter shall be paid into the Common Fund thereof at least the sum of Ten Guineas

SIXTHLY That none but discreet and experienced Master Masons shall receive Exaltation to this sublime Degree in this or any other Chapter that may hereafter be duly constituted; Nor until they shall have been duly proposed at least one Chapter Night preceding. Nor unless ballotted for and that on such Ballot there shall not appear one Negative or Black Ball.

SEVENTHLY That every such person so to be exalted shall pay at least the Sum of Five Guineas into the Common Fund of the Chapter wherein he shall receive Exaltation; towards enabling the Companions to carry on the Business and support the Dignity thereof.

EIGHTHLY That none calling themselves Royal Arch Masons shall be deemed any other than Masters in Operative Masonry; Nor shall be received into any regular Chapter of the Royal Arch or permitted to reap or enjoy any of the Benefits, Dignities, or Ensigns of that Most Excellent Degree, Save and except those who have received or shall or may hereafter receive Exaltation in this Grand and Royal Chapter, or in some Chapter to be chartered and constituted by Us, or Our Successors, Most Excellent Grand Officers as aforesaid, And Except those coming from beyond the Seas: Or such as shall obtain Certificates of Adoption from this Our Grand and Royal Chapter; For which Certificate shall be paid in to the Common Fund the Sum of One Guinea at the least

NINTHLY That there shall be a General Chapter of Communication of the excellent Companions of this Grand and Royal Chapter with all other

[1] Omission. The word 'the' should be inserted here.

Chapters that shall or may hereafter come under the Protection of and be chartered by the same as aforesaid on, or as near as conveniently may be to, the Feast of Saint John the Evangelist yearly, or oftener as Occasion shall require and it shall be found convenient, for the Purposes of conducting, promoting and well ordering of this sublime Degree, and the Business and Affairs thereof in such manner as shall from Time to Time be found most expedient

TENTHLY That at and upon the said Feast of Saint John the Evangelist, or the General Chapter of Communication held next to such Feast, the Most Excellent Grand Master, Most Excellent Deputy Grand Master and the other Most Excellent Grand Officers of the Grand and Royal Arch of Jerusalem shall be chosen and elected: Which Election shall be by a Majority of the Companions present at such General Chapter by Ballot

AND LASTLY That the Grand Officers so chosen and elected shall continue to serve and be in Office for the Year ensuing: unless some or one of them shall happen to decline, in which Case, or in Case of the Death of any of them or otherwise it shall be found necessary, a special General Chapter shall be called for an Election to supply his or their Place or Places IN WITNESS whereof We the said Most Excellent Grand Master, and the Most Excellent Grand Officers have hereunto severally signed our Names and affixed our Seals in full Chapter assembled for this Purpose at the Turk's Head Tavern in Gerrard Street, Soho, aforesaid this Twenty second Day of July in the Year of the Birth of Virtue 5 ∴ 3 ∴ 7 ∴ 9 ∴ A.L. 5770(1). A.D. 1766(7).[1]

IN TESTIMONY of our ready Acceptance of and perfect Compliance with this Charter of Institution and Protection above written, and the Laws and Ordinances thereby prescribed, We the Rest of the Excellent Companions of this Most Excellent Grand and Royal Chapter, have hereunto severally subscribed our Names the Day and Year above written.	Manchester Pignatelli	Blayney James Galloway John Maclean Tho˙. Dunckerley Fra˙. Flower E:S Jn. Allen N. John Brooks P.S. Tho. French S. Cha˙. Taylor S.

Henry Chittick	Anglesey
G. Borradale	Tho˙. Morgan
John Turner	Jas. Heseltine
W. Ross	William Guest
Robert Kellie	Ro: Simpkinson
John Derwas	Rowland Holt
Samuel Way	J. P. Pryse
R. Berkeley	Jn°. Hatch
John Bewley Rich	Lewis Masquerier
	David Hughes

[1] For comment on the date, see p. 74.

BIBLIOGRAPHY

SOME only of the authorities consulted and drawn upon by the author are given in this list; many others are mentioned in the text and included in the Index.

Ars Quatuor Coronatorum (referred to in the text and in this list as *A.Q.C.*)—the "Transactions" of the Quatuor Coronati Lodge, No. 2076, London, the world's premier lodge of research.
Miscellanea Latomorum, vols. i–xxxi.

BENAS, BERTRAM B.: "The Divine Appellation," in *Transactions of the Merseyside Association for Masonic Research*, vol. xxii.
CRAWLEY, W. J. CHETWODE: "Notes on Irish Freemasonry," in *A.Q.C.*, vol. xvi.
DASHWOOD, JOHN R.: "Notes on the First Minute Book of the Excellent Grand and Royal Chapter," in *A.Q.C.*, vol. lxii.
 "The Falsification of the Royal Arch Chapter of Compact," in *A.Q.C.*, vol. lxiv.
DRAFFEN, GEORGE S.: *The Triple Tau* (Edinburgh, 1955).
DUNCAN, A. G.: "Reality and Imagination in the Royal Arch Ritual," in *Transactions* of the Essex First Principals Chapter, 1938–46.
GOULD, ROBERT FREKE: *The History of Freemasonry* (1884–87). Also the new edition revised by the Rev. Herbert Poole (1951).
HAWKYARD, W. H., and WORTS, F. R.: "The Ceremony of Passing the Veils," in *A.Q.C.*, vol. lxii.
HEWITT, A. R.: "The Supreme Grand Chapter of England, a brief history from Lord Blayney to the Duke of Sussex," 1966.
HILLS, GORDON P. G.: "How came the Supreme Grand Chapter of England into Being?" in *Miscellanea Latomorum*, vol. xvii.
HORSLEY, CANON JOHN WILLIAM: "Solomon's Seal and the Shield of David traced to their Origin," in *A.Q.C.*, vol. xv.
HUGHAN, WILLIAM JAMES: *Origin of the English Rite of Freemasonry*, edited by John T. Thorp (Leicester, 1909).
 "An Historical Catechism," in *The Freemason*, November 21, 1874.
JOHNSON, GILBERT Y.: "The York Grand Chapter, or Grand Chapter of All England," in *A.Q.C.*, vols. lvii and lviii.
JONES, BERNARD E.: "Masters' Lodges and their Place in Pre-Union History," in *A.Q.C.*, vol. lxvii.

KELLY, W. REDFERN: "The Advent of Royal Arch Masonry," in *A.Q.C.*, vol. xxx.

LEPPER, J. HERON: "The Traditioners," in *A.Q.C.*, vol. lvi.

READ, JOHN: *Prelude to Chemistry* (London, 1936), referred to for its information and illustrations relating to symbols.

ROGERS, NORMAN: "200 Years of Freemasonry in Bury," in *A.Q.C.*, vol. lviii.
"200 Years of Freemasonry in Bolton," in *Transactions of the Manchester Association for Masonic Research*, vol. xxxi.

RYLANDS, JOHN R.: *The Wakefield Chapter of Royal Arch Freemasons*, No. 495 (Wakefield, 1949).
"Early Freemasonry in Wakefield," in *A.Q.C.*, vols. lvi and lxv.

RYLANDS, W. HARRY: *Records of the First Hundred Years of the Royal Arch Chapter of Saint James* (London, 1891).

ST CLAIR, WARD K.: "The Degree of a Past Master," a manuscript.

TAYLOR, SHERWOOD: *The Alchemists* (London, 1952), referred to for its information and illustrations relating to symbols.

TUCKETT, JAMES EDWARD SHUM: "The Origin of Additional Degrees," in *A.Q.C.*, vol. xxxii.

VIBERT, LIONEL: "The Interlaced Triangles of the Royal Arch," in *Miscellanea Latomorum*, vol. xxi.
"Royal Arch Degree," in *Transactions* of the Essex First Principals Chapter, 1934–35.

INDEX

AARON'S ROD, 166, 197
Aberdeen Chapter, 219
Acception, the, 19
Act of Union, 112-117
Adams, Cecil, quoted, 120
Adonai (the Lord), 153
Adoniram, Prince, 189
Advertisements, meetings called by, 81, 124, 135
Ælfric, Abbot of Evesham, 173
Aglen, Dr A. G., quoted, 147, 154
Ahiman Rezon: its frontispiece, Plate III; Irish, 209, 211; 'Moderns' Brother asks for, 65; referred to, 45, 62, 95, 100; Toast, 72
Alb, the priest's, 253
Albemarle and others "made chapters," 41
Albion Chapter, 206
Alchemists, The, F. Sherwood Taylor's, 227
Alchemy: debt to, 20, 31, 195, 238, 239, 241, 244; its illustrations suggestive of R.A. Principals, 127, 227-229; 'operative' and 'speculative,' 227; Philosopher's Stone under many names, 228; its secrecy, 227; its store of symbolism, 226-230
Alchemy, Outline of, John Read's, 227, 228
"Aldersgate" ritual, 171
Alfred Chapter, 90
All Souls' Lodge and Chapter: a prayer, 159
"All-seeing eye," 238; in Viennese ironwork, Plate IX
Allen, John, attorney, 75, 77, 175, 272, 273, 275
Altar: of Burnt Offering, 136; candles, 247; central, in lodges, 245; double-cube, 245; horns, 245; of incense, 136, 245; its initial letters, 245, 246; Jewish, 245; lights, 247; pedestal, 245; in old prints, Plate XXI; sacrificial, 245; symbols and the R.A. "fire," 232
America and U.S.A.: catechism, 168; first exaltee, 47-49; headdresses, 253; passing the chair (P.M. Degree), 189, 193, 194
American lodges: central altar, 245; veils ceremony, 198, 200
Amity, Cord of, 160; Chair of, 160
An Da Ri, Irish folk-song, 45
An Seann-Bhean, Irish folk-song, 44
Anacalypsis, Godfrey Higgins's, 127
Anchor and Hope Lodge, Bolton, 65, 86, 185
Anchor symbol on old tracing-boards, etc., 251
Ancient and Accepted Rite, 24, 243
Ancient Lodge, Scots, 46
Andalusia Provincial Grand Lodge, 209
Anderson, James and his *Constitutions*, 28, 29, 32, 53, 100
Anglesey, Marquis of, 275
Anno Lucis, converting A.D. to, 75, 116

"Antediluvian Masonry," 38
'Antients': aprons, 254, 255; certificates, 97, 244; claim to be "York Masons," 58, 100; five-pointed star, 239; how they differed from 'Moderns,' 53; the real innovators, 25; interest declines following Union, 119; lodges automatically empowered by their charters to work R.A., 58; in negotiations for R.A. union, 110, 111; their regard for and attitude to R.A., 23, 25, 27, 34, 35, 52, 61; R.A. said to have been 'concocted' by, 21; as "Schismatics," 42; warrant, oldest, 58; worked any rite, 157
'Antients' and 'Moderns,' the terms, 57
'Antients' Grand Chapter: "Book of the Royal Arch: Transactions," 95; Candidate's qualifications, 94, 96; early chapters, 83; "flagrant abuses" in R.A. masonry, 94; form of return (1794), 96; founded, 68, 69, 93; its part in preparing for Union, 99; laws and regulations (1807), 98; lodge consent to become R.A. mason, 96; not an independent organization, 93-95; register, 95, 96, 97; Royal Arch rules and regulations, 95
'Antients' Grand Lodge: arms, 57, Plates III, XXVII; early Grand Masters, 55, 56; early references to R.A., 50, 59; formation, 33, 34, 35, 52, 55; and Installation, 183; 'passing the chair,' 185, 187; relationship with Irish lodges, 59-61, 208; regulations, 59; sword, Plate XII; and two impostors, 59
Antiquity, Lodge of (No. 2), 230
Antiquity Lodge, Bolton, 253; inscription to Plate XXV
Antiquity Lodge, Leith, 204
Apocalypse of Adam-Oannes, The, 127
Apollo Lodge, York, 103
Apprentices, Royal Arch, 47
Approach to the New Testament, Greville Lewis's, 141
Apron, Royal Arch: Antients', 254, 255, Plates VI, XXX; Cana Chapter, Plate XXIII; in Charter of Compact, 274; colours, 252; decorated in *appliqué*, Plate XIII; early, 71, 72, Plate XVIII; First Grand Principal's, Plate XXX; Harlequin, 110; Irish, 214, 255, Plate XXVI; Knight-Templar, 255; 'Moderns', 254, Plate VI; original, 254; present-time, 255; printed, 254, 255, Plate VI; not to be worn in Grand Lodge, 80, 254; Scottish, Plate XXVI; serpent-shaped fastener, 230; T-over-H sign on, 237
Arabian Society in the Middle Ages, E. W. Lane's, 240

Arch—*see also* Royal Arch: in chapter, 135, 162; in ancient building, 131, 132; catenarian, 134, 135; ceremonial, 160, 161; "Dedicated," 91; degree celebrating completion of, 202; Gothic, 131, 133; keystone or arch stone, 133, 161, 163, 164; miniature, 136; its principle, 133–135; and the rainbow, 38, 59, 132
'Arch,' meaning 'chief,' 132
Arch Degree, Scots, 221
"Arch or Arches, passing the," 70, 164
"Arch, well built," 36
'Arche,' meaning 'beginning,' 132
"Arched and Knighted," 204
Arched vault, 126, 130, 131
Arches: five, 132; nine, 136; triple, 135, Plate II
"Arches, the," 67
'Arching' ('Exaltation'), 67
Ark of the Covenant, 136, 137, 197
Ark and Link Degrees, 206
Ark Mason, Scots, 221
Armistead, Robert, 48
Armitage, Rev. Jo., his letter, 160
Arms, 'Antients' Grand Lodge, 247, Plates III and XXVII; United Grand Lodge, 249
Arms, offensive, not permitted in masonic dress, 257
Ashmole, Elias, 19
Assyrians, early, and symbolic instruction, 226
Athelstan's, 'Charter,' 100
Atholl, Dukes of, 56
Atholl Grand Lodge, 56, 93
Atonement, Day of, 149
Australia, veils ceremony in, 200
Ausubel, Nathan, quoted, 150
Aynson, Bro., 72
Ayr St Paul Chapter, 219, 221
Ayrton composes ode, 81

BABYLONIAN PASS degree, 221
Babylonish Exile, 138–140
Badge—*see* Apron *and* Jewel
Badge of Honour, 257; of Judgment, 269
Badges, Harlequin, 110
Balance, 229
Ball and supper, Grand Chapter, 81
Ballina Lodge, 217
Ballygawley Lodge, Co. Tyrone, 268
Ballygowan Lodge, Bible used in, 30
Banagher Lodge and Chapter, 211
Banff Lodge, early R.A. in, 50
Banks of Douglas Water Chapter, 220
Banks, William: his ritual, 161
Banner: Canterbury, 251, Plate XIV; origin, 247; Wigton, Plate XVI; zodiac signs on, 250
Banners: principal, 247–249; 'Antients,' 247; Christian significance, 248; emblems or sacred symbols, 247–249; images, 149; lion, sceptre, and crown on old, 250; order and arrangement, 247, 248
Barker, Captain Thomas Lincolne: his ritual, 161
Barnett, Rev. Matthew, 110
Barton, L., inscription to Plate XXIX
Bath, Knights of the, 247
Bath Lodge seal, 158
Bathurst, Charles, 39
Battersea enamel, jewel in, 260, Plate XXXI

Baxter, Roderick H., quoted, 113, 143
Beating the Candidate, 223
Beaufort Chapter, Bristol, 198
Beaufort, Duke of, 77
Beauty Chapter, 119
Beavan, jewel made by, Plate XI
Beesley, Thomas, 85
Beesley's *Record of Antiquities*, Plates XVI, XXV
Bellamy, Mr, sings ode, 170
Belzoni, Giovanni Battista, and his jewel, 260, Plate XXVIII
Ben Jonson's Head, lodge at, 62, 63
Benas, Bertram B., quoted, 151–153
Benevolence Lodge (No. 226), 206
Berkeley, R., 275
Bethlehem Lodge, 78
Bezalliell and the "trible voice," 38–39
Bible—*see also* St John's Gospel: Book of the Law is not the Bible, 146; held in great reverence (1605), 169, 170; in Ballygowan Lodge, 30; in closing ceremony, 169
Biblical background to traditional history, 138–147
Bibliotheca, Photeus's, 127
Bishop's coronet, 253
Black Sea: its name, 148
Blair, Tho, 48
Blayney, Cadwallader, ninth Lord; his career, etc., 68, 69, 72–74; portrait, Plate V; references to, 47, 57, 58, 64, 124, 259, 272, 275
Blesington, Earl of, 55
Blood, water turning into, 197
Blue and its symbolism, 252, 253
Blue Lodge, 217
"Blue Warrants," 210
Bohn's Ecclesiastical Library, 126
Book of the Covenant, 146
Book of God: *The Apocalypse of Adam-Oannes*, 127
Book of the Law, 145–147
Book of Moses, 146
"Book of the Royal Arch: Transactions," 95
Books under the Key-stone, 30
Borradale, G., 275
Bottomley, Captain, 175
Bouillon, Godfrey de, and the *Rite*, 42
Boyle, James, sen., 269
Boyle, Mich. James, 87
Brasses, Stirling Lodge, 132
Breastplate: Badge of Judgment, 269; in banner, Plate XIX; copper, 269; dedicated by Julius Cæsar to a goddess, 269; form and wearing, 168, 253, 269, 270; High Priest's, 268, 269; jewelled, 269, 270; Scottish, 222, 269; Unanimity Chapter, Plate XXIV
Brewer's *Dictionary of Phrase and Fable*, 229
Bridge, crossing the, and its symbolism, 207
Bridge of Hell, 207
Bristol: Crown Inn, Lodge at, 63, 65; early exaltation, 50; lodge transferring its allegiance, 58
Bristol chapters: breastplate, 270; headdresses, 167, 253; Installation, 177, 178; quorum, 123; triangular plate, inscription to, Plate XXI; veils ceremony 172, 195, 197, 198
Bristol working, 48, 167, 168, 238
Bristow, Rev. Wm., 48, 49

INDEX

Britannia Chapter and Lodge, Sheffield, 85, 205, 251
Britannic Lodge, 44
British Chapter and Lodge, Cape Town, 191, 201, 270
British Lodge (founded 1752), 91
Brooks, John, 175, 272, 273, 275
'Brother' becomes 'Companion,' 79, 106, 107
Broughton, Mick, 41
Browne, Rev. George Adam, 170-172
Browne, John: his *Master Key*, 30, 174
Bull or ox emblem, 248
Bulls, papal, 28
Burlington Lodge (1756), 91
Burne, Robert E., quoted, 118
Burning bush, 161
Burns, Robert: exalted, 220; quoted, 133
Burnt Offering, Altar of, 136
Burton, R.A. candidate, 51
Bury Lodge, 158, 190
Butler, Hon. Brinsley, 73
Byron's Jacobite verse, 57

CABLE, "him that first shak'd his," 160
Cable Tow, 72
Cæsar, Julius, dedicates breastplate to a goddess, 269
Caledonian Lodge and Chapter, 69, 70, 71, 82, 117; jewel, Plate XI
Callendar, John, 46, 47
Callistus, Nicephorus: his *Ecclesiastical History*, 127
Callot, Jacob (Jacques), and his design, 267
Cambyses, successor to Cyrus, 139
Campell (or Campbell), Daniel, 49
Cana Lodge and Chapter, 78, 87, 88; Chapter Charter, Plate XVI; *Principia*, 87, 88
Canada, veils ceremony in, 200
Candidate (exaltee): admission in early ceremonies, 163; English, 123; Irish, 214; Scottish, 224; old-time custom of beating, 223
Candidate's qualifications; in early days, 186, 187, 274; Installed Master, done away with, 181; need to be proposed in lodge, 110, 118; qualifications to-day, 123; twelve months as Master Mason reduced to four weeks, 121
Candle, Judas, 223
Candlestick with seven branches, 197
Canterbury banner, 251, Plate XIV
Canterbury Chapter, 82
Cape-stone, 133
Caps and hats worn in chapter, 71, 91, 92, 252, 253
Captain General, 205
Captain of the Veils, 196, 199, 215
Captain, Royal Arch, 199
Carpenters' Hall paintings, 146
Carrall or Carrol, William, 63
Carrickfergus Lodge, 217
Cassia, sprig of, 166
Catechism: Exaltee's, 167; opening and closing, 168, 169; table, 173; teaching by, 173
Catenarian arch, 134-135
Catholics—*see* Roman Catholics
Centenary warrant, difficulties in obtaining, 117
Certificates: 'Antients,' 97, 244; Cork (1809), 30; as Geometric Master Masons, 188; Grand

Chapter of ALL England, 102; Irish, 216, 217; Phœnix Lodge, Paris, inscription to Plate II
Chains and collars, 257, 266
Chains strengthening St Paul's dome, 134
Chair degrees, Scottish, 221
Chair Master Lodges, Scottish, 192
Chair, passing the—*see* Passing the chair
'Chairing,' 222. *See also* Installation
Chairs, two, Plate XVII
Chaldean swastika, 234
Chaldon Church, Surrey, 229
Chaplain, Grand: first holder of the office, 179
Chapter—*see also* Grand Chapter: attached to lodge, 116-117, 122; by-laws, returns, etc., 123; chalk lines on floor, 135; complete, 122; convocations, 123; 'grafted' on lodge, 117; held in town distant from attached lodge, 118; independent of lodge in some places, 116; lodge has power to form (1807), 98; lodge transforming itself to, 106; lodge meeting in, 95; membership and the 'seventy-two' limitation, 122, 145; officers, 122-125; precedence, 122; Principals equal in status, 124, 125; its registered number, 118, 119; 'virtual Master made in, 189, 193; quorum, 123, 124
'Chapter,' the word: early uses and history, 37, 105, 106; in Ireland, 106; 'lodge' becomes, 79, 83, 105, 106
Chapter of Instruction or Improvement, 124, 172, 177, 215
Chapter of Promulgation, 171-173
Chapter-house, 105
Chapters: early warrants, 78, 79, 117; Scotland's oldest, 219, 220
Charges, Old MS., 27, 32, 36, 226
Charity, Chapter of (Bristol), 78, 79, 117, 197
Charity Lodge, Farnworth: its chair, Plate XVII
Charter—*see* Warrants and charters
Charter of Compact: date, etc., altered in, 68, 74, 75; the document, 75; how it came about, 69-75; illustrated, Plate IV; jewel of the Order shown in, 262; transcript, 272-275; referred to, 47, 58, 64, 87, 242, 252, 256
Chaucer's trine compass, 238, 239
Cherubim, 249
Cheshire, early R.A. masonry in, 120
Chetwode Crawley, W. J., quoted, 147, 210
Chittick, Henry, 275
Choice of Emblemes, Geoffrey Whitney's, 141
Christ—*see also* Jesus: His five wounds, 244; "the heavenly Corner Stone," 228; 'the foundation-stone,' 29; Jesus the personal name of, 155; "Three peculiar initials," 30; "the True Veil," 195
Christian: associations of the altar, 245; degrees, Irish, 210; elements in early rituals, 26-30, 32, 35, 156, 172, 223; prayer, 159
"Christian Order of Melchisedec," 204
Christian symbolism: anchor, 251; interlaced triangles, 241, 244; point within circle, 232; T-over-H, 235; Tetragrammaton, 154; triangle, 238; passing the veils ceremony, 195
Christians, early and symbolic instruction, 226
Churchill Lodge, its tracing-board, Plate XII
Cipher ritual, John Browne's, 30, 174

Circle: and Ineffable Name, 230; point within, 231, 232; squaring the, 231; as a symbol, 230–232; and triangle, etc., 231, 238; Yod within, 232
Circles, interlaced, 231
Claret, George, 196
Clavis Philosophiæ et Alchymiæ Fluddianæ, 226
Clavis ad thesaurum, key to the treasure, 235
Cleland, Rev. Dr J. R., 195
Clock, Water, Plate XXIX
Clothing, Royal Arch—*see also* Apron, Caps, Chains, Collars, Crowns, Garters, Hats, Headdress, Jewel, Robes, Sash; early, 71; regulations of 1766, 252; not to be worn in lodge or on public occasions, 257; offensive arms not permitted in, 257
Colchester Chapter, 82
Coleraine, Co. Derry, early R.A. in, 47, 48
Collars, 214, 257, 266
Colours, Royal Arch, 252, 253, 254, 265
Columns, real or symbolic, in Chapter, 135, 168
Commerce Lodge, 191
Committee of General Purposes, 121
Compact—*see* Charter of Compact
Compact, International, attempted, 115
'Companion,' the word, 106, 107
'Companions,' 'Brethren' become, 79, 106, 107
Compass, mariner's, on floor-cloth, 251
Compasses in alchemic illustration, 229
Compleat Angler, Izaak Walton's, 173
"Complete" ritual, 171
'Completion Degree,' 27
Concord Chapter, Bolton, 85, 86, 122, 117, 196, 236
Concord Chapter, Durham, 90
Constitutions: Anderson's early, 28, 32, 33, 36, 37, 85, 95; following Craft Union, 112, 262
Cook, Sir Ernest, 198
"Cope-stone of the Masonic Order," 133
Cord of Amity, 160; of Love, 160
Cork certificate (1809), 30
Corner-stone as symbolizing Christ, 29
Coronet, bishop's, 254
Coustos, John, his story and sworn evidence, 43, 45; references to, 22, 25, 30, 135
Covenant, Ark of the, 136, 137, 197
Covenant, Book of the, 146
Covey Crump, Rev. W. W., quoted, 131, 136, 143
Craft: emblems in R.A. jewels, Plates XI, XX, XXVIII; influences on R.A. ceremonial, 169; installation ceremony, 34; masonry, early, and the R.A., 22, 31, 44; warrants, 210
Cranstoun-Day, T. N., 201
Crawley, Dr W. J. Chetwode, quoted and referred to, 27
Crimson and its symbolism, 253
Cross—*see also* Tau: anticipatory, 233; crosslet, 234; crucifix, Minden, 249; of the East, 141; Greek, 233; Knights of St John, 141; Latin or long, 233; Maltese, 141, 234; Patriarchal, 233; St Andrew's, 233; St Anthony's, 233; swastika or fylfot, 234; Tau, 233; trowel and, 141; type, 233
Crossle, Phillip, 204
Crown and Anchor Tavern, chapter at, 81, 185

Crown Inn Lodge, Bristol, early Exaltation in, 63, 65, 197
Crowns, 92, 168, 250, 253, 270
Crucifix, Minden, symbols on, 249
Crump, W. W. Covey, quoted, 131, 136, 143
Crusaders' ritual, 40
Crusading Order of the Templars, 140, 141
Crypt: form of, 130, 131; legends in historical literature, 26, 126–130; symbolism, 131; York, and the meeting held there, 102; Plate X
Cumberland Chapter, 82
Cumberland, Duke of, patron, 78, 82
Cyrus Chapter: Janitors within and without, 108
Cyrus, King of Persia, 84, 139, 163

D'ALVIELLA, COUNT GOBLET, 19, 20
Dalziel, Alexander: his MS. ritual, 161
Darius Hystaspes, 84, 139, 140
Dashwood, John R., referred to, 69, 74
Dassigny (D'Assigny), Fifield, and his book, 26, 45, 46, 101, 183
David, King, 44
David, Shield of, 240, 244
Day of Atonement, Jewish, 149
De Lambton Chapter and its breastplate, 270
Deacon's jewel or emblem, 229
Dead Sea Scrolls, 146
"Death, the grand leveller," 164, 166, 168
Death, symbol of, 233
"Dedicated Arch," 91
Degree—*see also* Four, Fourth, *and* Fifth: Completion, 27; first reference to R.A. as a, 45
"Degree Giver," Irish, 212
Degree of Past Master: A Degree of the Chapter, Ward K. St Clair's MS., 193
'Degree.' R.A. masonry not constituting, in England, 114
Degrees, early Craft, 33
"Degrees, Songs of," 143
Delafaye, Charles, song attributed to, 85
Delta, sacred—*see* Triangle
"Demogorgon, Dreaded Name of," 148
Dermott, Laurence—*see also* Ahiman Rezon: career, 56, 57; his depiction of Royal Arch, Plate I; references to, 41, 46, 50, 56, 63, 73, 93, 95, 100, 132, 183, 244; said to have introduced R.A., 58
Derwas, John, 275
Desaguliers, John Theophilus, 32
Deuteronomy, Book of, 146
Devil Tavern, Scotch Lodge at, 39, 40
Dialogue, Ælfric's, 173
Dibdin, Charles, composer, 84
Dicky, 'Antients' Grand Secretary, 93
Dictionary of Phrase and Fable, Brewer's, 229
Dillon, Hon. Charles, 78
Disease, hexalpha as protection against, 240
Dispensation pending issue of warrant, 78
District Grand Chapters and their Officers, 122
Dodgson, R.A. Candidate, 51
"Domatic" ritual, 171
Double-cube altar stone, 244
Draffen, George S., quoted and referred to, 47, 196, 202, 223; his *Triple Tau*, 192, 219
Drake, Dr Francis, 242
Drury Lane pantomime, 84
Dublin: Dassigny's book, 45
Dublin, Lodge No. 26, 56

INDEX

Dublin lodges working R.A., 209
Dublin: Trinity College MS., 235
Duffy, James, tobacconist, 59
Duke of Athol Lodge: chair, Plate XVII
Dumfries, early Exaltation in, 49
Dumfries No. 4 MS., 30, 36
Duncan, A. G., quoted, 142, 143
Dunckerley, Thomas: his career, etc., 72, 73, 74, 75, 76, 77; confers R.A. in private lodges, 65; exalted, 50; his estate, 76; hymn written by, 77; at Portsmouth, 205; references to, 82, 90, 203, 235-237, 272, 273, 275
Dundas, Hon. Lawrence, later Earl of Zetland, 103, 115, 170
Dunfermline Lodge, R.A. worked in, 49
Durham Cathedral, 131
Durham, early chapters in, 90, 91
Durham Faithful Lodge, 190

EAGLE: desk, 248; double-headed, 229; its presence in old lodges, 92, 248, 249; ox, lion, and man, 57, 248, 249
Early Grand Encampment, 204
Early Grand R.A. Chapter of Scotland, 221
Ecclesiastical History, by Nicephorus Callistus, 127
"Ecclesiastical History of Sozoman," 126
Edinburgh: "Chair Master" Charter, 192; R.A. lodge at, 49
Edinburgh Chapter, 192
Edwin, Prince, 100
Effigy, Slade's, inscription to Plate XXVII
Egyptian nilometer, 235
Egyptians, early and symbolic instruction, 226, 229
Elijah Chapter, Forfar, 219
"Elixir of Life," 228
Elizabeth I and the Bible, 169
Elohim (God), 153
Emblems—*see* Symbols and emblems
Emblemes, Whitney's *Choice of*, Plate II
Emery, in relation to the Shamir Legend, 270, 271
"Eminent, By Order of the," 124
Emulation, Chapter of, erased, 82
Encampment, General, 87
Encampments: of R.A. masons, 205; Irish, 216, 217; Scottish, 221
Enoch Chapter, Montrose, 219
Enoch, Royal Arch of, 130, 201
Enoch's vision of nine vaults, 130
"Ensign of our Order" (sash), 257
Ensigns, the Twelve, and their emblems and arrangement, 249, 250
Enzu, the God, 150
Essex First Principals Chapter, 142
Eternity, symbols of, 228, 231, 232, 251
Euphrates Lodge, 78, 106
'Exalt,' the word, 107
Exaltation fees, 91, 97, 99, 274
Exaltee—*see* Candidate
'Exaltee' and 'Initiate,' the words, 107
"Excellency of excellencies," 38
'Excellent,' early use of term, 38, 49, 132
Excellent Degree—*see also* Super Excellent: 202, 203, 205, 206; in Ireland, 210, 211
Excellent Grand and Royal Chapter—*see* Grand Chapter, First
Excellent Mason Degree, 45, 46, 98, 194, 202

Excellent Master Degree: English, 202; Scots, 196, 199, 202, 221, 222
Excellent Super Excellent Degree, 203, 204
Exeter lodge seal, 158
'Exposures,' so-called, 34
Extended Ceremony of Installation, 183, 190
"Eye, all-seeing," in Viennese ironwork, 238; Plate IX
Ezra in history, 140, 142
Ezra, Scribe, his precedence, 123, 177

FAITH LODGE R.A. jewel, Plate XXXI
Faulkner's Dublin Journal, 45
Faure, Jehan; his picture of judges, 144
Fees, Exaltation, 91, 97, 99, 274
Fellow Craft, status of early, 33
Fellow Crafts resorting to Masters' Lodges, 39, 66
Fidelity Chapter, 119
Fifth Degree, Knight Templar as, 102
"Fifth Order," 41
Finch, William: his career, 92
Findel, J. G., referred to, 113
Fire, hexalpha as protection against, 240
"Fire," R.A., 232
First Miracle, Chapter of, 78, 87, 88
Fitz-George (Thomas Dunckerley), 76
Five as a "mystic" number, 246
Five Degree rite, York's, 102
Floor Cloth—*see also* Tracing-board: Irish, 251; mariner's compass on, 251; referred to, 72, 91, 92; zodiac signs on, 251
Flower, Francis, 69, 72, 272, 273, 275
Fludd, Robert: his *Clavis Philosophiæ et Alchymiæ Fluddianæ*, 226
Folklore, 45, 207
Fortitude Chapter, 82, 177, 251
"Foundation deposits," 147
Foundation-stone, Temple, 29, 136, 137
Four degrees and the Union, 111
"Four Degrees, Grand Lodge of the," 57
'Fourth' degree: early mention of R.A. as, 40, 51, 57, 58, 77, 98, 102
France, Grand Lodge of, 42. *See also* French
Frazier, Simon, 48
Frederick, Prince of Wales, initiated, 73
Fredericksburg, Virginia: early Exaltees, 48, 49
Freedom, Lodge of, 118
Freemasons' Coffee House, Grand Chapter at, 81
Freemasons' Hall (1775), 81
French: alleged 'fabrication' of R.A., 24, 25; Craft working, early, 22; degrees, early, 24; Jacobites, 40, 41; jewel, Plate XXVIII; rite, rainbow in, 38; ritual, earliest ritual known, 158; Royal Arch, 25; tracing-boards, 22
French, Thomas, 64, 75, 272, 273, 275
Friedländer, Michael, his translation from the Maimonides, 149
Friendship Lodge and Chapter, Portsmouth, 78, 85, 203, 205; of London, 176
Frodsham, Bridge, Yorkshire comedian, 101
Funeral, Irish, 217, 218
Fylfot or swastika, 234

'G' and its signification in early ceremonies, 164
Galilei, Galileo: his catenarian arch, 133, 134; and the pendulum, 251

Galloway, James, 72, 73, 80, 259, 272, 273, 275
Garden of Eden, Chapter of, 78, 106
Gardner, Samuell, 48
Garland, Richard, 103
Garter, Knights of, 247
Garters (1765-66), 71
General Grand Chapter, 96, 98, 274, 275
Geometric Master Mason, 96, 188
Gibbs, Bro., 203
Gibraltar, Lodge at, 190
Gihon Lodge, R.A. jewel, Plate XV
Glass goblet, Plate XIX
Gloucester, Duke of, initiated, 73
God, symbols or emblems of, 230, 232, 239, 264
"God and Religion," 32
Godwin, Thomas; his *Moses and Aaron*, 143, 155
Gogel, J. Peter, of Frankfort, 64
Gold, symbol of, 230
Golden Fleece of the Argonauts, 230
Goldsworthy, J. H., Lecture Master, 98
Gordon, William, 51
Gould, Robert Freke, quoted and referred to, 40, 52, 74, 113, 182
"Grafted on Lodge," 117
Graham MS., 36, 38
Grand Assembly Chapter, 220
Grand Chapter, early use of term, 37
Grand Chapter of ALL England, 69, 101, 102
Grand Chapter of Harodim, 207
Grand and Royal Chapter—the First Grand Chapter: alters its title twice, 83; aprons, 237; Chapter of Emulation erased, 82; as Chapter of Instruction, 111; Candidates' qualifications, 186, 187; chapters or lodges warranted by, 78, 79, 106; code of laws and regulations, 81; early warranted chapters, 65, 78, 79, 83, 106; erection by Charter of Compact, 68-76; its Grand Master, 77, 78, 106; meetings called by advertisements, 124; its many names, 106; passing the Z. chair, 179; patrons, 78; private chapter preceding, 69-72, 82, 83; references to, 36, 47, 252, 262; social activities, 81; stated Communications, 82; Sunday meetings banned, 84
Grand Chapters, *other than the above—see* 'Antients,' Ireland, Scotland, Wigan, York, Supreme
Grand Elixir, 228
Grand Lodge—the First, Premier, or 'Moderns': formation and early days, 32, 33, 34, 35; in negotiations for the Union, 111, 112; officially hostile to R.A., 39, 62-64, 80, 81, 208; refuses help to Irish petitioner, 63; seal, 39; its transposition of means of recognition, 34; its troubles, 52, 53; relationship with Irish and Scottish Grand Lodges, 60, 208
Grand Lodge of ALL England, 39, 51, 100
Grand Lodge of England, South of the River Trent, 100
"Grand Lodge of Four Degrees," 57
Grand Lodge of France, 42
Grand Lodge No. 1 MS., 36
Grand Lodge of Royal Arch Masons, 68, 106
Grand Lodge of York Masons, London, 100
Grand Lodges, *other—see* 'Antients,' Ireland, Scotland, York, Supreme, United, etc.
Grand Master, first Grand Chapter, 74

Grand Master of Fourth Degree, 77
Grand Master of Irish chapter, 209, 216, 217
Grand Master of R.A. Masons, 83, 106
Grand Master of the Veils, 196
Grand Master's Lodge and Chapter, 119
Grand Officers: appointment, etc., 121-123; aprons, 255; early, 82; prefixes, styles of address, etc., 124; rules in Charter of Compact, 274, 275
Grand Principals—*see* Principals
Grand R.A. Chapter of Scotland, Early, 221
Grand Superintendent, his powers (1780), 77
Grantham, Ivor, quoted, 236
Grave, broken wands thrown into, 218
Gray, Br. Jas., 216
Greeks, early and symbolic instruction, 226
Greenock Chapter, 219
Gruter Matheus, his engraving, 239
Guest, William, 275
Guide, for the Perplexed, The, 149
'Guildmen,' 101

HACKNEY, NORMAN, his Indian plates, 243; Plate IX
Haggai the Prophet in history, 139-142
Halkerston, Dr Robert, 49
Hallet, H. Hiram, quoted, 189
Hamilton, Robert, 177
Hampshire, early R.A. masonry, 120
Hand and Banner Lodge, 190
Hanover church, pentagon, etc., in, 244
Haran Chapter, Laurencekirk, 219
Harlequin aprons and badges, 110
Harodim, Grand Chapter of, 207
Harodim Degree, 206, 207
Harper, Edwards, 237
Harper, Thomas, and family, jewels made by, 237, 258, 260; Plates VIII and XX
Hatch, Jno., 275
Hats and caps, 71, 91, 92, 252, 253
Headdresses: banner showing, Plate XIV; Bristol, 167, 253; Cana Chapter's, Plate XXIII; Chapter of Hope, 253; Chapter of St James, 253; crowns, 92, 168, 250, 253, 270; early use of, 253, 254; hats and caps, 71, 91, 92, 252, 253; Melchesedec Chapter, Plate XXV; mitres and turbans, 253, 254
Heaton and Heaton-Card Collections, 158, 259
Henry VII; Chapel, 134
Henrys, John, 81
Hermes or Mercury, 228
Hermes Chapter, 118
'Hermetic,' the term, 228
Herod destroys the Second Temple, 142
Heseltine, James, 64, 80, 91, 175, 275
Hexagon, hexagram, etc., 240
Hexalpha (six-pointed star): in alchemic illustration, 229; illustrated and explained, 239-244; on Indian metal plates, 243; in jewels, 241; many patterns, 243, 244; its meanings, 240; in old scrolls, 241, 242; as possible Christian symbol, 241
Hey, John Vander: his petition, 82
Heywood, Thomas: his play, 169
Hickson's house, Stirling, 47
"Hierarchical" Lodge, 91
"Hieroglyphics, Four," 155
Higgin, Godfrey: his *Anacalypsis*, 127

INDEX

High Excellent Degree, 196, 202, 203, 206
High Priest: his breastplate, 268, 269; in Irish chapters, 201, 211-213; in Jewish ceremonial, 150
High Priest Degree, 201, 221
Hilkiah finds the Book of the Law, 126, 138, 145, 147
Hiram, 143
Hiramic Degree: did R.A. develop from?, 19-24, 33, 34; in early years, 19, 20; in Masters' Lodges, 66
Hiramic tradition and Installation ceremony, 182
Historical Catechism, 127
History of Freemasonry, Alexander Lawrie's, 27
Hollis, 41
Holmes, John, 48
Holt, Ralph, 86
Holt, Rowland, 78, 275
'Holy' Royal Arch—*see* author's Preface, p. 8
Holy R.A. Knight Templar Priest, 204
"Holy secret," 36
Hooker, Richard, quoted, 173
Hope, Chapter of, and its headdresses, 253
Hope Chapter, Arbroath, 219
Hope's history of St John the Baptist Lodge, 191
Hopkin, William, 204
Horeb Chapter, Stonehaven, 220
Horn Tavern, Lord Blayney's lodge at, 73
Horns of altar, 245
Hospitality, Lodge of, 78, 79, 117, 197
Howard Lodge of Brotherly Love, 190
Hughan, W. J., quoted and referred to, 22, 23, 25, 42, 45, 63, 74, 113, 241
Hughes, David, 275
Hughes, John, 72
Hutchinson, W., his *Spirit of Masonry*, 244
Hutchison's house, Stirling, 46
Hymn written by Dunckerley, 77

"IF YOU KNOW NOT ME, YOU KNOW NOBODY," 169
Il Gèsu Church, 235, 236
Immortality, symbol of, 228, 230
Imperial George Lodge, 38
Improvement and Instruction, Chapter of, 124, 172, 177, 215
In hac salus, 236
Incense and altar of incense, 136, 164, 197, 245
"Incommunicable Name," 151-154
Indian metal plate, Norman Hackney's, 243; Plate IX
'Inducted' officers, 176
Industry Lodge, Durham, 207
Ineffable Name: among the ancient peoples, 148-151; in Charter of Compact, 75; circle and the, 230; definition and meaning, 151; in early French degrees, 24; knowledge of it confined to certain wise men, 150; magical powers invoked by, 150; many names for the Deity, 151; Massoretic points, 153; original idea, 150; pronunciation of Sacred Name, 151; *Res ipsa pretiosa*, 235; on Temple foundation-stone, 137; Tetragrammaton—*see separate heading*
Ineffable Word, 40
Initiate: Christian prayer, 29
Initiates put through both 'Antients' and 'Moderns' ceremonies, 109
Innovation, the question of, 54, 60

Inquisition, Portuguese, and freemasons, 43
Inspectors-General (1778), 81
Installation ceremony, Craft: 'Antients', 181-183; early esoteric, 53; Extended Ceremony, 183, 190; its introduction, 182; its part in R.A. development, 77; a 'landmark,' 181; Masters required to install successors, 183; Installation in 'Moderns' Craft lodge, 183; 'Moderns' did not 'abandon' it, 181, 182; Scots attitude to, 61; in U.S.A., 193, 194; 'virtual' ceremony adopted for purposes of, 190
Installation ceremony, Royal Arch: early, 79; esoteric, 176; in Bristol chapters, 177, 178; High Priest Degree, 201; following the Union 176; 'out of chapter,' 176, 177; postponed, but Principal's status not affected, 104
Installation or Chair degree, 221
'Installing,' the word, 175, 222
Instruction, Chapter of: Grand Chapter as, 111
Instruction and Improvement, Chapters of, 124, 172, 177, 215
Intercourse, Lodge of, 78, 86
Interlaced geometrical figures, 231
Interlaced triangles, 239-244; hexalpha, six-pointed star, 239-244; pentalpha, five-pointed star, 239, 244; symbolism of, 239
International Compact attempted, 115
'Investing,' the word, 175
Ireland: chapter known as assembly or lodge, 106, 212; Dassigny's book, 45; early historical references, 208, 209; first exaltee, 47, 48; 'Grand Masters,' 209, 211; Knights Templar Degree, 204; Mark Degree, 205; memorial for warrant, 215; officers and forms of address, 213; passing the chair, 192; Red Cross Mason, 205
Ireland, Grand Chapter of: constituted (1829), 61, 69, 209; Grand Officers and forms of address, 213; recognized (1931), 209, 210; "Red Warrant," 210
Ireland, Grand Lodge of: association with 'Antients,' 59-61; bans R.A. entries in lodge books, 209; "Blue Warrant," 210; fails to gain control of R.A., 209; hostility to R.A., 60, 61, 113, 208, 209; some military lodges submit to 'Antients' Grand Lodge, 209; warrants conferred right to work many degrees, 210
Irish: *Ahiman Rezon*, 209, 211; aprons, 255, Plate XXVI; certificates, 216, 217, 236; Chapters of Instruction, 215; Christian degrees, 210, 211; clothing, 214, 216; funeral, 217, 218; hostility to R.A., 21, 22; jewels, 214, 265, Plates XV, XX, XXII, XXXI; Lodges, their relationship with English Grand Lodges, 208
Irish masons 'remade,' 55; Rose Croix, 210; sequence and step degrees, 210, 211
Irish working: beating the Candidate, 223; Candidate's qualifications, 214; catechism, 168; the cord, 160; "Degree Giver," 212; Exaltation ceremony, 215; no esoteric Installation until 1895, 176; Excellent King, 212, 213; "foundation deposits," 147; worked in early Dublin lodges, 209; High Priest's position, 201, 211-213; Principals, 147, 211-213; quorum, 215; ritual and traditional history:

repairing the Temple, 126, 145–147, 215; robes not worn, 252; style of wearing sash, 256; Sojourners replaced by Craftsmen, 212, 216; stone with ring, 158; T-over-H emblem, 235; triangular plate of metal, Plate XXI; veils ceremony, 198, 199
Irregular prints, 34

JACOB'S LADDER, 229, 234, 260
Jacobite masonry, 28, 40, 41
Jah; a name of the Deity, 153; "The Almighty Jah," 153
Janitor: expenses for, 97; his duty within the chapter, 168; Jager or Janitor, 108; Junior and Senior, 108; unregistered R.A. mason as, 118; within or without, 108
'Janitor,' the word, 108
Jason and his Golden Fleece, 230
Jehova or Jehovah, Jews' and Christians' use of the word, 23, 38
Jerusalem Chapter, 119
Jesus—see also Christ: the name, 154
Jesus Hominum Salvator, 236
Jesus of Nazareth, a possible reference in Charter of Compact, 75
Jesus, Sayings of, 45
Jewel, Royal Arch, the Jewel of the Order: Craft emblems on, Plates XI, XX, XXVIII; development of, Plates VIII, XI; earliest, 258, 262, 274, Plate VIII; Grand Principal's, 265; illustrated, 264, 265, Plates VIII, XI; Irish, 267; possible prefigurement of, 267; Principals', 258; regulations of 1766, 252; Rouby's, 262; Scottish, 267; symbolic explanation, 263–265; triangles as *motif* of, 241; variations of, Plate XI; wearing, 265; worn in Craft lodge, 257, 262, 263
Jewels: 'Antient,' 258; in Battersea enamel, 260, Plate XXXI; Belzoni's, 260; Plate XXVIII; Beavon-made, Plate XI; Caledonian Chapter, Plate XI; combined P.M. and P.Z., Plates XV, XX, Continental, Plate XXVIII; Craft, 258; Craft and R.A., 259; Deacon's, 229; early, 71, 258; emblems on, 22, 251, 260; enamelled, Plates XXVIII, XXXI; engraved plate, Plate XX; Faith Lodge R.A., Plate XXXI; French (?), Plate XXVIII; gem-mounted, 259, Plate XXVIII; Gihon Lodge R.A., Plate XV; glass-enclosed centres, Plate XXVIII; Harper family, 237, 258, 260, Plates VIII and XX; interlaced square and circle, 260; Irish, 242, 267, 268; Plates XV, XX, XXII, XXXI; as medals and badges of distinction, 258; Mark, 236; 'Moderns,' 258; "Nine Worthies," 135, 260, Plate XXXI; P.Z., 259; P.Z., presenting, to non-installed Companions, 179; parcel-gilt, Plate XV; priced, 238, Plates XXII, XXXI; Preston's, 230; Royal Preston Lodge, Plate XI; Royal York Lodge of Perseverance, Plate XV; Rule (made by), 229, Plate XXIV; Sojourners', 261; Plate XXIV; square and sector, 261, 262; sword and trowel, 261, Plate XXIV; torch and Ineffable Name on, 258; triangle, 238, 261, Plate XXIV; with triple arches, 260; trowel *motif* in, 141, Plate XXIV; Temple Chapter, N.Y., Plate XXII; Unanimity Chapter, 88, 89, 261, 269, 270, Plate XXIV;

Viscount Wolseley's, Plate XXXI; Virtue Lodge, Plate XXVIII
Jewish: code, 141, 142; Exile, story of, 131, 138–140; history following Solomon, 138–142; tombs and houses, hexalpha on, 240; tribes and their distribution, 249, 250
Jewish Encyclopædia, 149
Jews; their origin, 150
Johnson, Gilbert Y., quoted, 101, 104
Jordan Pass Degree, 221
Josephus quoted, 126, 195, 196
Joshua the High Priest in history, 139, 142
"Joshua of the Order," 177
Josiah in Biblical history, 39, 138, 145–147
Josiah Chapter, St Andrews, 219
Judas candle, 223
Judas Maccabeus, 142
Judgment, Breastplate the badge of, 269
Jugs, decorated, Plate XXVII
Julian the Apostate, Roman Emperor, 128, 129
Jung, C. G., his *Psychology and Alchemy*, 227, 232

KECK, BRO., 72
Kellie, Robert, 275
Kelly, W. Redfern, quoted, 21, 23, 24, 113, 202
Kelly's *Solomon's Temple Spiritualized*, 127
Kent, early R.A. masonry, 120
Kent, Edward, Duke of, 83
Kent Lodge, Spitalfields, 58
Keystone, 133: books under the, 30; drawing forth the, 164
Keystones of the Arch, 162, 163, 164
Kilwinning—*see also* Kirkwall and Stirling: Lodge minute, 135
King Solomon's Temple—*see* Temple
Kinnaird, Lord, exalted, 115
Kinross 'Chair Master' Charter, 192
Kirkcudbright Chapter, 221, 223
Kirkwall Kilwinning Lodge: R.A. worked in, 49; its scroll, 50, 241, Plate VII
"Knight of the Royal Arch," 130
Knight Templar Degree: 'Antients,' 202; apron, 255; encampments, 221; as Fifth Degree, 102, 237; in Irish certificate, 217; in Irish lodges, 210, 211; jewel, 268; in relation to the R.A., 203, 204; *Templum Hierosolyma Eques*, 237
Knighthood orders and the banner, 247
Knights of Malta, 203
Knoop, Douglas, quoted, 22, 54, 113, 114
Knowledge, Chapter of, 124, 175

LADDER, JACOB'S, 229, 234, 260
Lancashire, early R.A. masonry, 85–88, 119, 120
Land of Cakes Chapter and its two charters, 119, 219–221
Land, R.E.A., quoted, 28, 29
Lane, E.W., quoted, 240
Lane's *Masonic Records*, 67, 79
Lanesborough, Earl of, 73
Law of Moses, 146
Lawrie's *History of Freemasonry*, 27
Le Veau, Abraham, 104
Lecturers, Sojourners as, 92
Lectures (catechisms), 92, 167, 223
Lectures, Principals', 104, 173
Lee, Samuel, and his *Orbis Miraculum*, 127, 137, 144

INDEX

'Leg of mutton' masons, 50
Leicester Masonic Hall, 260
Leinster, Duke of, exalted, 115
Leith, James Percy, 177
Leon, Jacob Jehudah, 247
Lepper, John Heron, quoted and referred to, 26, 45, 46, 50, 66, 145, 154, 156, 158, 170, 196, 205, 236, 257
Leprous hand, 166, 197
Letchworth, Sir Edward, 198
Letters: brass, 72; movable, 38; "three pairs" of, 38
Lever, James, 186
Lewes Journal, 92
Lewis, Greville, on Jewish history, 141
Lewis, Sir Watkin, 'passed through the chair,' 185
Library, West Yorks Masonic, 45
Life, symbol of, 230, 233
Lifford Lodge, Co. Donegal, 211
Lights, Lodge of (Warrington) 85, 86
Lily of the Valley, 164, 166
Limerick Herald, 217
Link and Wrestle Degree, 221
Linlithgow Chapter, 219
Linnecar, Richard, his book, hymns, etc., 89, 160, 256
Lion, ox, man, and eagle, 57, 248-250
Liquor, ordering (1765-66), 71
Lisbon lodges, 43
Livesey, James, 186
Livingstone, Thomas, and his jewels, 267, 268
Lodge: applies for R.A. charter, 117; chapter attached to, 116-117, 222; chalk lines on floor, 135; chapter 'grafted' on, 117; chapter independent of lodge in some places, 116; chapter mason distinguished from lodge R.A. mason, 83; consent to become R.A. mason, 96; distant from attached chapter, 118; its power to form chapter (1807), 98; not entitled to work R.A. following Union, 117; transforms itself into chapter, 106
'Lodge' (the term) becomes 'chapter,' 79, 83, 105, 106
'Lodge' and lodge board, 72. See also Tracing-board
Lodge of Lights, Warrington, 85, 86
"Lodge of R.A. Masons" (Darlington), 90, 91
Lomax, Elijah, 86
London Company of Masons, 19, 20, 31
London Grand Chapter rank, 122, 255
London's first exaltee, 47
Lord Blakeney's Head, Bristol, Lodge at, 50
Louvre, inscription preserved in, 150
Love, Cord of, 160
Loyal and Prudent Lodge, 90
Loyal Scots Chapter, 119, 220
Loyalty Chapter (Sheffield), 89, 90, 177
Lurgan Lodge, 251
Lyon, D. Murray, quoted, 219

MACDUFF CHAPTER, 219
McEuen or McEwan, James, 46, 47
McKewn, John, 49
Mackey, Albert Gallatin, American writer, 20
Macky or Mackey, John; impostor, 50, 59
Maclean, John, 72, 73, 78, 259, 272, 273, 275
'*Maçon Écossois*' Degree, 41

'*Maçonnerie Écossois*' Degree, 41
Magi and the straight bridge, 207
Maier, Michael, his book, 231
Maimonides, Moses, quoted, 149
'*Maître Écossois*' Degree, 41
Man, lion, ox, and eagle, 57, 248-250
Manchester Association for Masonic Research, inscription to Plates XVI, XXV
Manchester, Duke of, 275
Manna, 197
Manningham, Dr, 62
Mariner's compass on floor-cloth, 251
Mark, Masonic, 97, 206
Mark Masonry: as a Fourth Degree, 224; jewel, 236; emblem on Irish jewel, 265; as qualification for R.A., 193, 199, 212, 214, 215; in relation to R.A., 205-207; references to, 40, 76, 202, 205, 233; Scottish, 199, 221, 222, 224, 225
Mark Master Degree, 205, 221
"Marked Masons," 206
Marks, Masons', 224
Martin, James, 49
"Mason of the World," 87
Mason word, transferred, 21
Masonic Mark, 97, 206
Masonic Year Book, 117
Masonry Dissected, Samuel Prichard's, 34, 52
'Masonry, Pure Antient,' the phrase, 112-114
Masquerier, Lewis, 275
Massoretic points, 153
Master Key, John Browne's, 29
Master Mason Degree—*see* Hiramic
"Master of the Name," 150
"Master Passed the Chair," 192, 193, 221
'Master' becomes 'Principal,' 83
Masters: corresponding rank in R.A., 102
Masters' Lodges and possible connexion with R.A., 39, 66, 67
Masters in Operative Masonry, 76, 274
Masters, Royal Arch, 76, 91
Matthews, Sir Peter, 217
Medal—*see* Jewel
Meggido, hexalpha on walls of, 240
Melchisedec Chapter, Bolton, 204, 253; its headdresses, Plate XXV
Melchisedec Orders, 204
Mercury or Hermes, 228
Merseyside Association for Masonic Research, 151
Military Chapter, Ayrshire Militia, 220
Military lodges, Irish, submit to 'Antients' Grand Lodge, 209
Milliken, Robert, 54
Milton's *Paradise Lost*, 148
Minden Crucifix, symbols on, 249
Minerva Chapter: its Arch, 160-161
Miniature arches, 135, 136
Minnesota Craft Installations, 193
Minutes, Craft, not to include R.A., 64, 116, 209
Mitre, Fleet Street, Grand Chapter at, 81
Mitres worn in chapter, 92, 168, 253, 254
'Moderns': accuse 'Antients' of mutilating Third Degree, 21; adopt 'passing through the chair,' 185-187; aprons, 254; attitude to R.A., 62-65, 110; early regard for R.A., 27, 50, 63, 186; how they differed from 'Antients,' 53; lodges working R.A. without warrants, 65; six-pointed star, 239; worked any ceremonies they liked, 157

'Moderns' and 'Antients,' the terms, 57
Mohammedans' road to Paradise, 207
Moira, Francis Rawdon-Hastings, second Earl of, 82, 110, 111
Monson, Lord, exalted, 170
Montague, Duke of, 41
Montana Craft Installations, 193
Moon God and Lord of Knowledge, 150
Moon outline on Warden's chair, 229
Moore, Samson, 48
Morgan, Thos., 275
Morning Advertiser, 124
Morning Post, 84
Morning star or pentalpha, 244
Moses, founder of Israelite nation, 44, 148
Moses and Aaron, Thomas Godwyn's, 143, 155
"Most Enlightened East," 81
Most Excellent Master Degree, 193
Most Sacred Lodge, 78
Mount Lebanon Chapter, 119
Mount Moriah Lodge, 188, 189, 206
Mount Sinai Chapter, 119
Mourning Bush Lodge, 187
Murray, William, 50
Myths and Symbols, Zimmer's, 244

NAME, Ineffable, Holy, Sacred, etc.—*see* Ineffable Name
Napoleon's Jewish Sanhedrin, 144
Nativity, Chapter of, 78
Nebraska Craft Installations, 193
Nebuchadnezzar's Empire, 138, 139
Nehemiah in history, 140
Neilson, John, 48
Neptune Lodge (No. 22), 188, 203
Newcastle Water Clock, Plate XXIX
Newman, John, 205
Newspaper advertisements, calling meetings by, 81, 124, 135
Nicol or Nicholl, Mungo, 46, 47
Nilometer, a tau, 235
"Nine Worthies" (Nine Excellent Masters) and their jewel, 97, 98, 135, 260; Plate XXXI
Noah Chapter, Brechin, 219
Norwich Cathedral, 131

OBLONG SQUARE, 229
Ode, Ayrton's, 81
Office-bearers, Scottish, and their Installation, 220
Officers, Grand, holding office in the R.A., 122
Officers: 'Antients' (1807), 99; appellations in early days, 72; chapter, their precedence, prefixes, etc., 122, 124; Grand Lodge, holding office in Grand Chapter, 122; lodge, as chapter officers, 88
O'Kelly, Charles, 43
Old Aberdeen Chapter, 219
Old King's Arms Lodge, 37
Old Testament Books, 146
Oliver, Bruce W.: his MS. ritual, 161, 189
Oliver, Dr George, quoted and referred to, 21, 29, 42, 62, 106, 107, 158
Operative Chapter, Aberdeen, 220
Operative Chapter, Banff, 219
Operative lodges, 31
Operative masonry, R.A. not developed from, 25, 101

Operative Masonry, Masters in, 274
Orbis Miraculum, Samuel Lee's, 127, 137, 144, Plate III
Ox, lion, man, and eagle, 57, 248, 249
Oxyrhynchus, ancient city, 45

PALATINE LODGE, 207
Palmes, R.A. candidate, 51
Pantomime at Drury Lane Theatre, 84
Paradise Chapter, Sheffield, 85, 87, 88, 205
Paradise Lost, Milton's, 148
Paris Convocation, 42
Passing the Arch, 70, 223
Passing the chair: adopted by 'Moderns,' 185-187; in Bolton, 86; as a chapter degree, 188, 189; *after* Exaltation, 188; banned as from year 1822, 191; in Chapter of St James, 91; it conferred status, not privileges, 185; denounced by 'Antients' Grand Lodge, 184, 185, 187; a device or subterfuge, 181, 184; early references, 46; in Ireland, 192; invented by the 'Antients' lodges, 184; late instances, 190, 191; not always for R.A. candidates, 191; resentment at its suppression, 191; in Scotland, 192, 193; in United States of America, 193, 194; the 'virtual' or 'constructive' ceremony, 184-190
Passing the chapter chairs, 179, 180
Passing the veils, 195-200; age of the ceremony, 196; alchemical interpretation, 195; in America, 200; in 'Antients' chapters, 196; in Australia, 200; in Bristol, 167, 195, 197, 198; in Canada, 200; Captains of the Veils, 196, 199; ceremonial described, 197; Christian origin possible, 195; colours of veils, 196, 199, 215; in Durham, 91; 'elimination' of the ceremony, 171, 172; Grand Masters of the Veils, 196; guarding the veils, 166; in Ireland, 199; not part of Exaltation ceremony, 198; as separate degree, 196, 199, 202; number of veils, 167, 195, 198; in Scotland, 199; symbolism, 140, 215; survival or revival? 195, 196, 198
Past Master Degree in U.S.A., 193
"Past rank of Z," 82
'Past Z Degree,' a possible, 180
Patrons of Grand Chapter, 78, 81
Patten, Johen, 49
Paul the Apostle writes to 'companions,' 107
Peace, Lodge of (Meltham), 88
Pedestal, 164, 245; illustrated, Plates X, XXI; miniature, Plate XXIX; "mystical Parts," 91; triangular, inscription to Plate XXI
Pendulum, Galilei and the, 251
Pentagon, pentagram, etc., 240, 244
Pentalpha, five-pointed star, 229, 239, 244; as Christian emblem, 244; on Freemasons' Hall thresholds, 244; on tracing-board, 251; its symbolism, 195, 196, 199, 244
Pentateuch, the, 146, 246
Perfection, rite of, 24
Peters, Rev. Prebendary, 110
Petitions for charters, 83, 122; delayed and rejected following Union, 120
Phealan, Thomas; impostor, 50, 59
Philanthropic Chapter, 82
Philosopher's stone, its forms and many names, 228, 239

INDEX

Philostorgius, his story of the crypt legend, 126–130
Phœnix Lodge, Paris: triple arch, 135
Phœnix Lodge, Sunderland, 207
Photeus, his works, 126
Pick, Fred L., 223
Pictorial History of the Jewish People, A, 146
Pignatelli, 275
Pillars: full-size, in Bristol chapters, 168; symbolic in all chapters, 135
Plate, Indian metal, Norman Hackney's, 243, Plate IX
Plates, triangular, inscription to Plate XXI
Plato referred to, 231
Plumb-line symbol on old tracing-boards, banners, etc., 229, 251, Plate XIV
Plummer, Benjamin, 109
Plutarch on a prohibited name, 149
Plymouth Dock Lodge and Dunckerley, 65
Point within a circle, 231, 232, 238
Point within a triangle, 238
Politics and religion, 23
"Poor Old Woman, The," folk-song, 44
Pope of Rome and Jacobite masonry, 28. See also Roman Catholics
Pope of Rome's Bulls against freemasonry, 29, 43
Porphyry, 190
Portugal's early lodges and the Inquisition, 43
Prayer, Christian, over Craft Initiate, 29
Prayer of year 1766, 158
Précis du Respectable Ordre de L'Art Royal et Maçonique, inscription, Plate XXI
Preston, William, and the Prestonian Lecture, 69, 70, 100, 207; his jewel, 230
Prichard's *Masonry Dissected*, 34, 52
Priest's stole, 256
Prince Edward's Lodge, 190
Prince Edwin Chapter, 196
Prince Eugene's Coffee House Lodge, 44
Principal, First Grand, his seal and apron, Plates XVI, XXX
'Principal' (the term) becomes 'Master,' 83
Principals: absence of, 178; clothing suggested in old prints, 144; conjointly and each severally as Master, 178; death of, 178; designations, 72, 175; early, as Master and Wardens, 124; equal in status, 124, 125; 'Induction,' 176; Installation, 175–178; Installing, "out of their Chapters," 176, 177; investing J. and H., 175; Irish, 147; lectures, 104, 173; Masters' corresponding rank in R.A., 102; passing the Z. chairs, 179, 180; possible P.Z. Degree, 180; prefixes, 178, 179; qualifications, 172, 178; restriction of chairs to Installed Masters, 172; Second and Third, in Ireland, not necessarily P.M.'s, 212; sequence of Installations, 177
"Principia," Cana Chapter, 87
Probity, Lodge (Sheffield), 80, 191
Promulgation, Chapters of, 171–173, 177
Promulgation, Lodge of, 114, 181, 186
Protection, symbol of, 230
Provincial Grand Chapters and their officers, 122
Prudence Chapter, early ritual, 161
Prussian Blue, Degree, 221
Pryse, J. P., 275
Psalms: *Psalmi Graduales*, 143
Psychology and Alchemy, C. G. Jung's, 227

Punch Bowl Craft and R.A. Lodges, 1, 101
'Pure Antient Masonry,' the phrase, 26 112–114, 210
Purple and its symbolism, 252, 253
Pythagoreans, 244

QUALIFICATION FOR R.A., 94, 96, 97, 98, 99, 182–187
Quorum, 123, 124

RAINBOW and the arch, 38, 59, 132
Rainbow Coffee House Lodge, 44
'Raised' (Exalted), 79
Ramsbottom, John, 170
Ramsay, Chevalier Andrew Michael, his address (1737), 24, 41–43, 62, 106
Read, John: his *Outline of Alchemy*, etc., 227, 228
Reconciliation, Lodge of, 55, 115
Red Cross of Daniel Degree, 221
Red Cross Degree, 202, 204, 205
"Red Warrants," 210
Regalia—*see also* Apron, Caps, Chains, Collars, Crowns, Garters, Hats, Headdresses, Jewel, Robes, Sash: chapter reported for not wearing, 253
Regeneration, symbol of, 230
Register of Excellent Masters, inscription to Plate I
Regularity Chapter (No. 339), 117, 118
"Religion" in *Constitutions*, 32
Re-makings, 55, 60, 62, 86, 109
Res ipsa pretiosa, possibly the Sacred Name, 235
Restauration Lodge and Chapter, 78, 79, 82, 83, 106, 115
Restoration Lodge (Darlington), 90, 91, 206
Revelations of a Square, 62
Rhodes, Sir Edward, inscription to Plate XXIII
Ribbon—*see* Sash
Rich, John Bewley, 275
Richmond, Duke of, 41
Rickard, Colonel F. M., 92
Ring, signet of truth, 200
Rite—*see* Ritual *and individual names of rites*
Rite Ancien de Bouillon, 42
Ritual, Craft: Browne's *Master Key*, 30; early, 31; no rigidly fixed, in eighteenth century, 54
Ritual, Royal Arch: All Companions to be present at opening, 169; 'Antients,' 165; Banks's, 161; Barker's, 161; borrowings, mutilations, etc., 20–23; Bristol, 167, 168; Candidate's admission, 163; ceremonial arch, 160, 161; ceremonies declared adopted (1835), 171; Christian, 26–30; Christian elements eliminated, 172; Craft and R.A. mingled, 23; Crusaders', 40; Dalziel's, 161; development early, 54; 'discoveries,' 163; Dr Oliver's (1740), 21, 29; Dublin, 29; earliest (1760), 158; earliest printed, 157; its early materials, 156, 157; early Temple, 39; early nineteenth-century, 161–167; first worked in Craft lodges, 156; French language, 158; in Heaton-Card collection, 158; late eighteenth-century, 161–165; North of England, 161–165; nourished from many sources, 157; officers' duties, 162, 166; opening and closing ceremonies, 71, 162, 165, 166, 168, 169; prayer in year 1766, 158, 159; Principals' lectures, 173; Prudence Chapter, 161; Revisions, 156, 170–173; Scottish, 222;

standardized, 171; Sussex, 171; table catechism, 173; Unanimity, Wakefield, 159, 160; various versions named, 171; veils ceremony, 196
Robes: Cana Chapter, Plate XXIII; colours and their symbolism, 252, 253; early, 71, 72; origin, 252; Ruspini's designs, 80; Scottish, 222
Robinson, landlord, 94
Rock Fountain Shilo, Chapter of, 78, 82, 106
Rogers, Norman, quoted and referred to, 84–87, 120, 203
Rokes, Peter, 188
Roman Catholic scroll, 241, 242
Roman Catholics, 28, 42, 43. *See also* Pope
Rose Croix Degree, 204; its members attending lodge and chapter, 201
Rose of Sharon, 164, 166
Rosicrucian art, 20. *See also* Alchemy
Ross, Brother, passed to Z. chair, 179
Ross, W., 275
Rosslyn, Earl of, exalted, 115
Rouby, Dr John James, and his early R.A. jewel, 71, 262, Plate VIII
Royal Arch Captain, 199, 205, 217
Royal Arch covered with crape, 217
Royal Arch of Enoch, 130, 201; Knight of the, 130
Royal Arch Lodge, Wakefield, 88
Royal Arch lodges, 209
Royal Arch of Solomon, 201
Royal Arch masonry: a completion degree, 27; comprehended by phrase 'pure antient masonry,' 113, 114; Dermott's depiction, Plate I; development and early history, 25, 26; its 'fabrication' a question, 24–26; as 'fourth degree,' 40, 51, 57, 58, 77, 98, 102; how it came to be accepted, 34' 35; not now a 'degree' in England, 114; its tradition a blend of two or more stories, 28; theories concerning its origin, 19
'Royal Arch' in Youghall procession, 45
Royal Ark Mariner Degree, 221
"Royal Art," 37
Royal Bruce Castle Chapter, 119
Royal Brunswick Chapter of Paradise, 177
Royal Brunswick Lodge, 89, 90
Royal Caledonian Chapter, 119, 220
Royal Cumberland Chapter: its breastplate, 270
Royal Cumberland Freemasons' School, 80
Royal Gallovidian Chapter, 119, 221, 223
Royal Grand Conclave of Scotland, 221
Royal Lancashire Lodge, 87
Royal Masonic Institution for Girls, 80
Royal Order of Scotland, 219, 221
Royal Preston Lodge jewel, Plate XI
Royal St John's Chapter, 119
"Royal secret," 36
Royal Sussex Lodge of Hospitality, 79, 197
Royal York Lodge of Perseverance jewel, Plate XV
Royall Arch King Solomon's Lodge, New York, 49
Royall Arch Lodge, Glasgow, 49
"Rule of Three," 37
Rule, James, jewels made by, 229, Plate XXIV
Rummer, engraved, Plate XIX
Ruspini, Chevalier Bartholomew, 80, 81, 252
Russell and others "made chapters," 41
Rylands, John R., quoted and referred to, 88, 159, 180, 187, 190, 191, 261
Rylands, W. Harry, quoted and referred to, 91, 176, 180, 254

SACRED BAND R.A., Knight Templars, 204
Sacred Name, 158, 165. *See also* Ineffable Name
Sacrificial altar, 245
Sadler, Henry, quoted, 64, 74
St Albans Chapter, Lanark, 220
St Andrew's Chapter, Scotland, 119
St Andrews Lodge, Boston, 203
St Clair, Ward, his MS., 193
St Clement's Church, London, 56
St George Chapter, Aberdeen, 220
St George, Chapter of (No. 140), 108, 176, 260
St George Chapter (No. 549), 177
St George's Chapter (No. 5), 119
St Irenæus, book by, 248
St James, Chapter of (No. 2), 91, 92; apron, 254; Belzoni's jewel, 260, Plate XXVIII; breastplate, 270; headdresses, 253; Installation, 175–177; notes on 83, 91, 92, 189; passing the Z. chairs, 179
St James' Chapter, Aberdeen, 220
St John the Baptist Lodge, 191
St John the Evangelist legend, 89
St John Chapter, Bury, 119
St John Lodge, Bolton, 191
St John, lodges dedicated to, 89
St John and St Paul, Lodge of, 190
St John's Chapter, Bolton, 119
St John's Days, held in high regard, 184, 185, 275
St John's Gospel, 29, 30, 36, 38, 39, 44, 158, 172
St John's Lodge, Bolton, 120, 190
St John's Lodge, eagle in, 248, 249
St John's Lodge (Manchester), 'Chair Master' Charter in, 192
St John's Lodges, central altar in, 245
St John's, the two, 174
St Luke Chapter, Aberdeen, 219
St Paul's dome strengthened by chains, 134
St Peter Lodge, Malden, 262
St Stephen's Chapter, Retford, 253
Salisbury, Marquis of, exalted, 170
Salvation, ladder of, 229
Sampson, Robert, a charlatan, 92
Samuel, L., 203
Sanctum Sanctorum, 130, 136
Sanhedrin or Sanhedrim and the number of its elders, 122, 143–145
Sanquhar Kilwinning Lodge, 269
Sanskrit plate, Plate IX
Sash, 252, 256, 257; as decoration of honour, 256, 257; early regulations, 256; possible French origin, 256; Irish and how worn, 214, 216; ribbon as, 256; as sword-belt, 256, 257; styles of wearing, 256
Sayings of Jesus, a papyrus, 45
Scannaden, Spencer, 48
Scarlet and its symbolism, 252, 253
Sceptre, 253; emblem on old banners, 250
'Scotch' or 'Scots' masonry, 25, 39, 40, 41, 76, 186, 261

INDEX

Scotland: early English chapters in, 120; early R.A. lodges, 219; English Craft Installation ceremony introduced, 192; first exaltee, 47, 49; Mark masonry (*see* Mark masonry); operative lodges, 31; passing the chair, 192, 193; T-over-H emblem, 235
Scotland, early Grand R.A. Chapter of, 221
Scotland, General Grand Chapter for, 221, 222
Scotland, Grand Chapter of, 220-222; degrees supervised by, 221; founded, 61, 220, 221; its independence, 220; "Chair Master Lodges," 192; office-bearers, 222; Supreme Committee, 224
Scotland, Grand Lodge of: 'Antients' association with, 60; founded, 31; hostility to R.A., 21, 22, 61, 113 208, 220; Installation ceremony, 61; and Lord Moira, 110; officers 'installed,' 175
Scotland, Royal Grand Conclave of, 221
Scotland, Royal Order of, 219
Scottish chapters: holding English or Irish charters, 119, 221, 223; not attached to lodges, 220; office-bearers and their installation, 222; oldest, 219, 220; petitions for, 222; quorum, 222; 'shutting,' 223; unchartered, 221
Scottish Crusaders, 40
Scottish lodges: central altar in, 245; Craft Installation ceremony late in coming, 192
Scottish Rite, Ancient and Accepted, 24
Scottish Royal Arch, 219-225; apron, Plate XXVI; beating the Candidate, 223; Candidates' qualifications, 223; ceremonial introduced from England, 220; chair degrees, 199; Christian ritual, 30; 'Encampments,' 205; jewel, 265; part of Fellow Craft Degree, 225; pedestal in old print, Plate XXI; prerequisite degrees, 224; Principals' Installations as separate degrees, 224; ritual, 223, 224; robes and their colours, 222, 252; Templar encampments, 221
Scribe Ezra, his precedence, 123, 177
Scroll, Biblical words on, 29
Scroll, Kirkwall Kilwinning, 49, 241, Plate VII
Scrolls, Dead Sea, 146
Sea Captains' Lodge, 207
Seal: early lodge, 158; First Grand Principal's, Plate XVI; Great, 81; including five-pointed star, 244; Premier Grand Lodge, 39; prescribed in Charter of Compact, 274
Secret, Royal, 36
'Secrets, true,' 26
Seditious meetings, law against, 83
Seller, John, 103
Septuagint, 144
Sequence degrees, 189, 201-207, 210, 211
Serendib Chapter, Ceylon, 206
Serious and Impartial Enquiry, 45
Serpent eating its own tail, 197, 228, 230, 266
Seven as a 'mystic' number, 246
Seven stars, 246, 251
Shakespeare quoted, 107, 173, 181
Shamir legend, 270, 271
Shaphan in Biblical history, 154
Shepherd-Jones, G. S., quoted, 161, 232, 248, 263-265
Shew-bread, 197
Shield of David 240, 244
'Shutting the chapter,' 223
Sidonians, 190

Simpkinson, Ro:, 275
Sincerity Chapter, Bradford: breastplate and crowns, 270
Sincerity Chapter, Taunton, 67, 190, 251
Sincerity Chapter, Wigan, 121
Slade's effigy: inscription to Plate XXVII
Sligo Regiment, lodge held in, 255
Smith, Joseph, 90
Snake—*see* Serpent
Sojourner: Assistant, 104, 122; depicted on jewels, 259, 260, 268; Plate XXIV; duties, 108, 162-164; his Election, 108; his hat or cap, 253; as lecturer, 92; as Master of "Previous Lodge," 189
Sojourner, the word, 108, 126
Sojourners replaced by Craftsmen in Irish chapters, 212, 216; their report, 142, 143; three, 108
Solomon, Royal Arch of, 201
Solomon's Seal and a related legend, 240, 244
Solomon's Temple—*see* Temple
Solomon's Temple Spiritualized, 127
Somerset, early R.A. masonry, 120
Somerset Masters' Lodge, 130
"Songs of Degrees," 143
Spanish lodge in year 1728, 43
Spanish prison sentences on freemasons, 43
Spencer, Samuel, and his letters, 63, 64
Spencer, William, 103
Speth, G. W., quoted, 113
Spirit of Masonry, William Hutchinson's, 244
Sprig of cassia, 166
Square, circle, and triangle, 231, 229
Square, oblong, 229
Squaring the circle, 231
Star: five-pointed (*see* Pentalpha); morning, 244; seven-pointed, 243; six-pointed (*see* Hexalpha)
Stars, seven, 246, 251
Step degrees, 201-207, 210, 211
Steps: fifteen, 143; nine, 158
Steward's Lodge ('Antients'), 94
Stewards: ceremonial duties, 92
Stewartstown Lodge, 268
Stirling, R.A. worked at, 46, 47, 49
Stirling Kilwinning Lodge admits R.A. masons, 46, 47
Stirling Lodge brasses, 132
Stirling Rock Chapter 46, 219
Stolcius and geometrical figures, 231
Stole, priest's, 256
Stone: arch, 133; cape-stone or cope-stone, 133, 153; corner, symbolizing Christ, 29; cubic, 147, 231; double-cubical, 91, 136, 137, 164; foundation, of Temple, 29, 136, 137; "heavenly Corner," 228; the lifted, 44, 45; Philosopher's, its forms and many names, 228, 239; triangular 239
Stone-turning *motif*, 22, 25
Strathmore Chapter, Glamis, 219
Strictures on Freemasonry, 89
Suffolk, early R.A. masonry in, 120
Suleyman's (Solomon's) power over the Jinn, 240
Summonses, Plate X
Sun emblem, 229, 264
Sunday meetings, 41, 65, 84, 89, 90, 103, 197, 205; innkeeper fined for permitting, 84

Super-excellent,' and early uses of the term, 41, 49, 50, 132
Super Excellent Degree, 50, 87, 202, 205, 216, 217; in Ireland, 210, 211; and the veils ceremony, 196
Super Excellent Master Degree, 202; Scots, 221
Supreme Degree (1807), 98
Supreme Grand Chapter (1801), 83
Supreme Grand Chapter (the Grand Chapter of to-day): acknowledges registered chapters, 116; chapters to be attached to lodges, 116; Committee of General Purposes, 121; chaotic conditions following Union, 119, 120; constitution, 121-125; formed, 115, 116; Grand Lodge, reorganizes, 117; how Union came, 109, 110; meetings temporarily suspended, 120; petition for charter, 122; precedence of chapters, 122; prefixes and styles of address, 124; regulations (1823), 121; regulations (1956), 121-125; Sunday meetings banned, 84; suspension in the Craft and R.A., 123; sword, Plate XII
Supreme Grand R.A., Chapter of Ireland—see Ireland, Grand Chapter of
Supreme Grand Chapter of Scotland—see Scotland, Grand Chapter of
Surplices, Sojourners', 253
Sussex, Augustus Frederick, Duke of, Grand Master of R.A. Masons, 83, 111, 115, 116, 170, 171, 176, 230
Sussex, early R.A. masonry, 120
Sussex ritual, 171
Swalwell miniature pedestal, Plate XXIX
Swansea chapter warrant, 236
Swastika or fylfot, 234
Swift, Jonathan, 37, 38
Sword, 'Antients' Grand Lodge, now Sword of Grand Chapter, Plate XII
Sword, ceremonial use of, 24, 53
Sword and trowel: in early ceremonies, 40, 42; emblem, 141, Plate II; jewels, 261, 268, Plate XXIV; in Jewish history, 140; Order of the Templars, 140, 141
Symbolism: alchemic inspiration, 20, 226-230; arch, 132; Biblical, 226; crypt, 131; jewel of the Order, 263-265; teaching by, 226; Temple at Jerusalem, 143; veils, 140, 215; whence came it?, 226
Symbols and emblems—*see also names of symbols*, Circle, Square, Triangle, Tau, *etc.*: alchemic, common to freemasonry, 227-229; as banners, 247-249; Craft and R.A. mingled, 22; Christ, 239; death, 233; Almighty's power, efficiency, and truth, 232, 239; as ensigns, 250; eternity, 228, 230, 232, 251; gold, 230; immortality, 228, 230, 251; judgment, 269; life, 230, 233; light and excellence, 269; protection and completion, 228, 269; protection from fire, disease, etc., 230, 240; regeneration, 230; Sacred Word, 238; salvation, 229; Son of God, 239; sun, 230, 232

TABERNACLE, 136
Table catechism, 173, 174
Talisman, interlaced triangles, 240, 244
Talmud, Jewish, 248
'Tammy,' possibly for veils, 91

Tasker, R.A. Candidate, 51
Tau, 233-236; Egyptian nilometer, 235; triple, 233, 234, 235, 236, 237
Taylor, Charles, 272, 273, 275
Taylor, F. Sherwood: his *The Alchemists*, 227
Taylor, Thos., takes three degrees, 206
Templars, Order of the, 140, 141
Temple at Jerusalem: its chequered history, 138-142; dimensions, 143; Jinn legend, 240, 241; model of, 247; rebuilding, 126-130, 139-142; references, 228, 235, 248; repairing, 126, 145-147; Shamir legend, 270, 271; symbolisms, 143; steps, 143
Temple Chapter jewel, Plate XXII
Temple of Solomon, its frontispiece, Plate III
Templum Hierosolyma Eques, 236-237
Templum Hierosolymæ, 235, 236-237
Tetragrammaton, 152-155; Adonai, 153; Christian significance, 154, 155; *El, Elim*, 154; *Elohim*, 154; *Elyon*, 154; on foundation-stone, 137; Jews' need of, 152; Massoretic points, 153; its many meanings, 152; *Shaddai*, 154; within triangle, 238, 239, 241; as symbol and ornament, 155
Text Book of Freemasonry, The, 171
Thackray, Thomas, 103
Theca ubi res pretiosa deponitur, depository of sacred thing, 235
Thesaurus, treasure, 235
Third Degree—*see* Hiramic
Thistle Lodge, Dumfries, early Exaltations in, 49
Thorold, Mr, 110
Three as a 'mystic' number, 246
Three Crowned Stars Lodge, Prague, 260
Three Tuns Lodge, Portsmouth, 76
Thummin, Urim and, 269
Tiler, 108. *See also* Janitor
Toast, 'Antients,' 72
Toasts, the Wakefield, 159, 160
Torah's "five books," 146, 246
Torch, 158
T-over-H, 233; Christian meaning, 235; on early aprons, certificates, etc., 237; develops into triple tau, 233, 237; Dunckerley on, 236, 237; Initials of the Architect, 236; its meanings, 165; superimposed on H. AB., 236
Tracing-board, 72, 250, 251; Churchill Lodge, Plate XII; combined Craft and R.A., 251; eighteenth-century, 228; emblems on, 22, 132 251
Traditioner lodges and assimilation, 50, 55, 63, 86
Tranquility, Lodge of, 78
Treasurer, his precedence, 123, 177
Triangle, 238, 239 (*see also* Interlaced triangles); in alchemic illustration, 229; "all-seeing eye" within, 238; and circle interlaced, 231, 239; circle within, 238; or delta, 239; head or skull within, 238; as jewel emblem, 238, 261, Plate XXIX; its many meanings, 239; point within, 238; triple tine, 238, 239, 243; symbolism, 238, 239; Tetragrammaton within, 238, 239; triangle, Yod within, 232, 238
Triangular plate and pedestal, 158, Plate XXI
"Trible voice," 38, 39
Trine compass, 238, 239

INDEX

Trinity, symbols of, 231, 238, 239, 244
Trinity College, Dublin, M.S., 235
Triple Tau, 233–237, Plates VIII, XXII
Triple Tau, The, George S. Draffen's, 192, 219
Triple tine, 238, 239
Trowel—*see also* Sword and trowel: and the cross symbol, 141; *motif* in jewels, 141, Plate XXIV
Troy, swastika in, 234
Truth, Lodge of, Belfast, 255
Tubal Cain, 230
Tuckett, J. E. S., quoted, 19
Turban and mitre, 92, 168, 253, 254
Turk's Head Tavern, Chapter and Grand Chapter at, 70, 81, 272, 275
Turner, John, 275
Turner, Robert, 55
Twelve Brothers Lodge, 115
Tyler, 108. *See also* Janitor
Tyrian Lodge, 242

UNANIMITY CHAPTER, Bury, 78, 86
Unanimity Chapter, Penrith, 118
Unanimity Chapter, York, 103
Unanimity Lodge and Chapter, Wakefield, 190, 192, 256; 'the Arches,' 67; Jewels and breastplate, 88, 89, 261, 269, 270, Plate XXIV; ritual, 159, 160; toasts, 159, 160; 'virtual' ceremony, 189, 190. *See also* Wakefield
Union, Craft, 55; Act of (1813), 117; Articles of, 112; chaotic conditions and petitions delayed, etc., following, 115, 119, 120; how it came, 83, 109; lodges not entitled to work R.A. after, 117; place of R.A. in the discussions, 110. 111
Union Chapter, Dundee, 219, 220
Union French Lodge, 44
Union Lodge, Cape Town, 201
Union Lodge of York, 103
Union, Royal Arch, 115–119. *See also* Supreme Grand Chapter, 1817
Union Waterloo Chapter, 119, 196
United Grand Chapter—*see* Supreme Grand Chapter, 1817
United Grand Lodge—*see also* Union, Craft: formation, 109; recognizes R.A. and Grand Chapter, 113, 116
United States—*see* America
Unity Chapter (Leeds), 90
Unity, Chapter of (York), 103
Universality, Chapter of, 78
Urim and Thummin, 269

VAUGHAN, HON. EDWARD, 55
Vault—*see also* Crypt: Arched, 126, 130, 131; *motif*, 40; secret, in early French degrees, 24
Veils—*see* Passing the veils
"Verus Commodus," 41
Vestments, Sojourners', 253
Vibert, Lionel, quoted, 138, 142, 158
Vienna ironwork, "all-seeing eye" in, Plate IX
Vigilance Chapter (Darlington), 90, 91
'Virtual' ceremony—*see* Passing the chair
'Virtual' Masters, 67, 92
Virtue Lodge jewel, Plate XXVIII
Voltaire quoted, 226
V.S.L.—*see* Bible

WAITE, A. E., quoted, 130, 141

Wakefield—*see also* Unanimity Lodge and Chapter, Wakefield: Brother asks for *Ahimon Rezon*, 65; historical notes, 88; ritual, 159, 160; possible "P.Z. Degree," 180; T-over-H symbol, 237
Walford, Edward, translator of Philostorgius, 127
Walker Arnott, Dr George Arnott, 222
Wallace Heaton Collection, 259
Walton's *Compleat Angler*, 173
Wands, broken, thrown into grave, 217
Waples, William, quoted and referred to, 90, 91, 207, Plate XXIX
Warden's collar jewel, 268
Wardens, some American, automatically received 'P.M. Degree,' 194
Warrants and charters: 'Antients,' 99, 183; Cana Chapter, 87, Plate XVI; centenary, difficulty in obtaining, 117; chapters with two, 119; delayed following Union, 119, 120; dispensation pending issue of, 78; early, 78; 79, 117; Irish lodge and chapter, 209, 210; petitions for, 122, 215; Royal Arch worked under lodge warrant, 58; sale of, 120; Scottish chapters with English, 119; Swansea Chapter, 236
Washington Chapter, Connecticut, 194
Washington, George, initiated, 49
Water-clock, Plate XXIX
Watson, William, quoted, 42
Way, Samuel, 275
Webber, Bob, 41
Weekley, Ernest, on the word 'Chapter,' 105
Westcott, Dr W. Wynn, 271
Westminster Abbey, pentalpha in windows of, 244
Westminster, college at, 105
Westminster and Keystone Lodge, 242
Wexford Chapter, 217
Wheel symbol, 231
Wheeler, Francis: his funeral, 217, 218
Whitby lodge, old, 256
White, William, Grand Secretary, 239
Whitney, Geoffrey: his *Choice of Emblemes*, 141, Plate II
Whole Institutions of Free-Masons Opened, The, 38
Whytehead, T. B., quoted, 100, 101
Wice, Companion, presents a Cord of Amity, 160
Wickham, Dr, 118
Wigan Grand Lodge, 55, 121
Wigton banner, Plate XVI
Willett, Rev. Waring, 179
Wimber, L. C., his *Folk Lore in the English and Scottish Ballads*, 207
Windsor, college at, 105
Wisdom, symbol of, 230
Witham Lodge, 110
Wodrow, Alexr., 49
Wolseley, Viscount: Irish jewel, Plate XXXI
Wood, James, 86
Woodford, Rev. A. F. A., 21, 76
Woolen, James, 89, 90
'Word, the,' 23, 26, 27, 36, 38–40, 44, 128, 132, 148, 165, 172, 265
Wren, Sir Christopher: his chains in St Paul's dome, 134
'Wrestle' degrees, 221

"YAHOVAHI," made from *Adonai*, 153. *See also* Jehova
Yod within circle, or triangle, 232, 238
York Chapter, 72
York Company of Comedians, 51, 101
York 'congregation' of masons (year 926), 100
York Grand Chapter, 51, 69, 101, 102
York Grand Lodge, 51, 69, 101–103
York Lodge, 102–104; its meeting in crypt of York Minster, 102, Plate X
'York masons' and 'York rite,' 58, 100, 101
York: Punch Bowl Lodge, 51
'York Rite,' Paris, 136
York Royal Arch masonry, 45, 100–104
Yorkshire chapters, old, style of wearing sash, 256
Yorkshire, early R.A. masonry, 88–90, 120
Yorkshire ritual, 159, 160
Youghall, County Cork: procession and early exaltees, 45, 48
Young, Edward, quoted, 131

Z. CHAIRS, passing the, 179, 180
Zechariah the Prophet, 139, 142
Zerubbabel—*see also* Principals: as an historical figure, 139, 140, 142
Zetland Chapter, 103, 104
Zetland, Lawrence Dundas, Earl of, 103
Zimmer's *Myths and Symbols*, 244
Zodiac, signs of the, 229, 230, 250, 251